One Hundred Years of World Military Aircraft

One Hundred Years of World Military AIRCRAFT

Norman Polmar
and Dana Bell

Naval Institute Press
Annapolis, Maryland

Naval Institute Press
291 Wood Road
Annapolis, MD 21402

Library of Congress Cataloging-in-Publication Data

Polmar, Norman.

One hundred years of world military aircraft / Norman Polmar and Dana Bell.

    p.   cm.

  Includes bibliographical references.

  ISBN 1-59114-686-0 (alk. paper)

  1. Airplanes, Military. I. Bell, Dana. II. Title.

  UG1240.P65 2003

  623.7'46—dc22

                       2003018431

Printed in the United States of America on acid-free paper ∞

11 10 09 08 07 06 05 04   9 8 7 6 5 4 3 2

First printing

For the little ones: Jake, Mack, and Rachel

Contents

Preface

This volume lists and describes 100 "significant" military aircraft. In the years from Orville's Wright's first controlled flight at Kitty Hawk, North Carolina to the present, man has continually looked at the aircraft as a weapon of war. Thousands of different military aircraft have been designed and built (and hundreds of thousands of those have been manufactured). From that list of thousands, we have sought to identify the 100 "most significant" aircraft.

Such a list will immediately be challenged, as was this list when we reviewed it with friends and colleagues when it was being compiled.

The idea for such a selection of significant aircraft and hence this book was, in part, the result of a series of discussions by one of the authors with the late John W. R. Taylor, at the time the editor of *Jane's All the World's Aircraft*. Taylor published his selection of 100 in the book *Jane's 100 Significant Aircraft* (1969). Although Taylor later modified his list in conversations and correspondence with one of the authors, his original list consisted of 54 military aircraft and 46 civilian planes. Of the former, we have included 26 aircraft. However, even those numbers are misleading. Taylor listed Igor Sikorsky's *Grand*, a remarkable, four-engine civilian aircraft; we list his Il'ya Muromets, the military derivative of the *Grand*.

Taylor had asked in his foreword, "Hurricane or Spitfire?" He choose the latter. The choice for us was easy: We included both. The Hawker Hurricane was the world's first eight-gun fighter and the most numerous Royal Air Force fighter in the Battle of Britain (1940); the Supermarine

Spitfire was an outstanding combat aircraft and its public image made it *the* Allied fighter of World War II.

Taylor's subsequent revision to his published list adds the Boeing E-3 Sentry and the Lockheed SR-71 Blackbird, which we also include, while Taylor's addition of the Bell AH-1 Cobra is a helicopter that we have combined with the UH-1 Huey entry. Indeed, Taylor gave the Mil' Mi-24 Hind as an alternative to the AH-1, which he noted "sets entirely new standards of formidability for a helicopter." The Mi-24 is one of two Mil'-designed helicopters included in the present volume.

Thus the selection of aircraft was difficult—some might say convoluted. We have selected aircraft that were the "first" of their type, or the largest, or had the best performance, or, most often, aircraft that influenced political or military decisions (as the Lockheed U-2 spyplane) or public attitudes toward aviation (as the Savoia-Marchetti S.55).

Not only have we excluded strictly civilian aircraft, but also experimental and research aircraft, such as US X-aircraft and the Douglas D-558 series, the Hawker P.1127, the Junkers Ju 287, and Heinkel He 280. Similarly, we have not addressed lighter-than-air aircraft (blimps, Zeppelins, airships) nor unmanned aerial vehicles.

Some of our entries draw heavily on the column "Historic Aircraft" published in the Naval Institute's magazine *Naval History*. The efforts of Fred Schultz, editor-in-chief of the magazine, and Julie Olver, the managing editor, are greatly appreciated in that regard. Tom Cutler of the Naval Institute Press and Dawn Stitzel of the Naval Institute's photo archives were essential in making this book possible.

Finally, we wish to express our appreciation to several individuals who have assisted us in the compiling of this volume as well as having helped us with previous writing projects, upon which we have drawn for this book: Capt. Eric Brown, RN; Robert F. Dorr; Phil Edwards; Vice Adm. Donald Engen, USN; William Green; Dan Hagedorn; Peter B. Mersky; Vice Adm. Gerald E. Miller, USN; Gordon Swanborough; and John W. R. Taylor.

Glossary

AAF	Army Air Forces (US, 1941–47)
AEW	Airborne Early Warning
AFB	Air Force Base (US)
ASW	Anti-Submarine Warfare
AWACS	Airborne Warning And Control System
cal.	caliber
ceiling	*service* ceiling
ECM	Electronic Countermeasures
ELINT	Electronic Intelligence (collection)
gallon	US unless Imperial is indicated
hp	*maximum* horsepower
lbst	pounds static thrust
miles	*statute* miles
mm	millimeter
mph	miles per hour
NATO	North Atlantic Treaty Organization (1949–)
PR	Photographic Reconnaissance
RAF	Royal Air Force (Britain, 1918–)
recce	reconnaissance
RFC	Royal Flying Corps (Britain, 1912–18)
RNAS	Royal Naval Air Service (Britain, 1914–88)
SAC	Strategic Air Command (US, 1946–92)
SAR	Search And Rescue

shp	shaft horsepower
US	United States
USAF	US Air Force (1947–)
USMC	US Marine Corps
USN	US Navy
USSR	Union of Soviet Socialist Republics
VSTOL	Vertical/Short Takeoff and Landing
VTOL	Vertical Takeoff and Landing

One Hundred Years of World Military Aircraft

One

Before Conflict

From the time that the Wright Brothers made their first sustained flights in December 1903, there was considerable interest in the military potential of aircraft. Almost immediately both military officers and civilians expressed belief in the potential combat role for aircraft. In September 1908 aviation pioneer Orville Wright conducted demonstration flights for US Army and Navy officers with his Model A Flyer at Fort Myer, outside of Washington, D.C. Those flights led the Army Signal Corps to purchase Wright-built aircraft.

A year later, in August 1909, the US naval attaché in Paris, Comdr. F. L. Chapin, was directed to attend an aviation meet in Rheims. He was impressed by the men and machines he observed and submitted a proposal that the US Navy modify one of the new, 16,000-ton battleships of the *Connecticut* class to launch a Wright airplane; he also recommended that auxiliary ships be constructed with flight decks for aircraft operation.

That same year the brilliant French inventor Clément Ader described in his book *l'Aviation Militaire* how an aircraft-carrying ship should be constructed, and the procedures for aircraft to take off and to land back aboard.

Glenn Curtiss aroused the US Navy's interest in aviation. In 1908 the 30-year-old Curtiss designed, built, and flew his own airplane. He won

The United States led the world in the "acceptance" of military
aircraft. The US Army purchased a Wright Model A Flyer in
1909; in 1910–11 the US Navy sponsored the takeoff and landing of a Curtiss Pusher from warships. Here Eugene Ely takes off
from the cruiser *Pennsylvania* to the cheers of the crew and his
wife; earlier in the day he had landed aboard the ship. *US Navy*

nation-wide publicity in May 1910 when he flew the $142^{1}/_{2}$ miles from Albany to New York City in 2 hours, 50 minutes to capture the *New York World*'s $10,000 prize. Somewhat prematurely, the *World* claimed "The battles of the future will be fought in the air! The aeroplane will decide the destiny of nations."

The newspaper promptly set up a "bombing range" on Lake Keuka near Hammondsport, New York, arranging floats to simulate the 500-by-90-foot outline of a battleship. Curtiss flew over in his airplane and dropped 8-inch lengths of $1^{1}/_{2}$-inch-diameter lead pipe. Rear Adm. William W. Kimball, one of the observers, declared: "There are defects for war purposes: lack of ability to operate in average weather at sea; signalling its approach by noise of motor and propellers; impossibility of controlling its height and speed to predict approximate bombing ranges; difficulty of hitting from a height great enough to give a chance of getting within effective range."

The press interpreted the results differently: *The World* told of "an aeroplane costing a few thousand but able to destroy the battleship costing many millions." *The New York Times* acknowledged a new "menace to the armored fleets of war." The aircraft-versus-battleship controversy was fired before the Navy had its first flying machine; at the time the Army had only one Wright flying machine.

Another highly publicized bombing demonstration against "ships" came in September 1910, when the Harvard Aeronautical Society and Boston *Globe* sponsored an aviation meet at Atlantic, Massachusetts. Prizes were offered for distance flown, speed, altitude, duration, and the best record of dropping "bombs" against a "battleship model"—an outline of a battleship in the marshlands southeast of Boston, at Squantum. Contestants flew their rickety aeroplanes low over the battleship outline, dropping a total of 170 bombs.

British aviator Claude Grahame-White, flying a Farman biplane, won the $5,000 prize and the Harvard cup for "bomb throwing." Curtiss scored fourth in the bombing contest. The popular magazine *Aeronautics* wrote that the bombing event was "not only . . . one of the most interesting of the meet, but one which the Society deems most important from the standpoint of scientific investigation." Several US Army and Navy officers attended the meet, and President William Howard Taft made a brief appearance.

A more significant series of events occurred in November 1910 and January 1911, when the Navy sponsored Eugene Ely, a Curtiss pilot, in making history's first takeoff and landing aboard a warship with a Curtiss pusher aircraft.

The seeds were sown and in half a dozen countries military aviation had begun to sprout. The four aircraft described in this chapter are considered as the first genuine military aircraft.

Blériot Type XI

In July 1909, France's Louis Blériot distinguished himself by becoming the first man to fly an airplane across the English Channel.* His aircraft, the eleventh built at Blériot's factory, would become sire to a line of monoplanes built, licensed, and imitated around the world. An immediate favorite with sportsmen pilots, the Type XI also became the initial aircraft of many emerging air forces.

Later in 1909 the Blériot Type XI entered French military service and soon was being used to develop offensive capabilities with hand-held rifles, grenades, and small bombs, and mounted 37-mm cannon as well as machine guns. In 1910 the Type XI (along with several other Blériot designs) figured prominently in French military maneuvers.

In 1911 French aviator Roland Garros used a Type XI to demonstrate a mock bombing of enemy positions to the Mexican Army. Later that year the Mexican Army would perform history's first offensive aerial combat operation, lobbing homemade bombs from a Moisant copy of the Blériot XI during the Mexican Revolution. In October, Italian Blériot XIs carried out wartime reconnaissance missions of Turkish positions in Libya. The French sent four aircraft to Morocco for reconnaissance missions in early 1912, and the Turks used theirs against the Greeks in October. During the summer of 1913, the Romanians and Bulgarians used Blériot

*Although Blériot eventually dropped the accent mark from his name—becoming Louis Bleriot—his aircraft company would be called Blériot throughout its existence.

XIs against each other in the Second Balkan War, with the armed Romanian aircraft displaying a decided advantage over the unarmed Bulgarians.

With the beginning of World War I in August 1914, the French used their Type XIs for reconnaissance and light bombing missions, but newer, more powerful aircraft quickly eclipsed the aging Blériot. By early 1915 remaining Type XIs in French squadrons were withdrawn from combat and used as trainers.

The Blériot XI was a simple design, easily disassembled for ground transportation, and popular with its crews. The wood frame fuselage of rectangular cross section was diagonally braced for strength. The fuselage aft of the cockpit was generally left uncovered, with the forward portion sheathed in fabric, plywood, or aluminum sheet. (Some Italian-built Blériots placed transparent panels at either side of the cockpit in an effort to improve downward visibility.)

Crewmembers sat in an open cockpit, with the observer placed forward of the pilot in two-seat versions. In that position the observer's forward and downward view was severely limited by the shoulder-mounted monoplane wing, although a few Type XIs were produced with parasol wings to improve visibility. The wing itself was made of ash and poplar with fabric covering; Wright-style wing warping provided roll control. A single-piece rudder, with no vertical stabilizer, was attached behind the fuselage, and a horizontal stabilizer with a one-piece trailing elevator was mounted below the fuselage frame. (Civil Type XIs, including some pressed into military service, often had elevators at the tips of the horizontal stabilizer.) The Type XI was one of the first aircraft to use Blériot's now-familiar control system, using foot pedals to move the rudder and a single cloche-type control stick to warp the wings and move the elevators.

Several different rotary tractor engines were used in Type XIs, with 25- to 35-horsepower engines powering most trainers and 50- to 80-horsepower engines in operational variants.

The Blériot Type XI was the first aircraft flown by many of the world's embryonic air forces, and the first aircraft ever to enter combat. Although obsolete early in World War I, the tiny monoplane continued to serve as a trainer through the war's end. The rudder markings of this Type XI indicate that it served in the Imperial Russian Air Service. *Walter Wright Collection*

Blériot XI-2 Type Genie [Engineer] Reconnaissance Variant Characteristics

Design:	Blériot
Crew:	2 (pilot, observer)
Engines:	1 Gnome rotary radial piston; 70 hp
Weights:	
Empty:	705 lb
Maximum takeoff:	1,213 lb
Dimensions:	
Length:	27 ft, 3 in
Wingspan:	31 ft, 10 in
Wing area:	196.7 sq ft
Speeds:	
Maximum:	75 mph
Armament:	None

Curtiss Pusher

Although the Curtiss Pushers figured prominently in the development of the US Army's aviation program, the Pushers were far more influential in the establishment of US naval aviation. Curtiss Pushers were the first aircraft to take off from a ship, the first to land on a ship, the first to effectively take off and land on water, and the first to taxi to and be hoisted aboard a warship. Moreover, pontoon-equipped Pushers evolved into the world's first flying boats.

Glenn H. Curtiss was the driving force behind this innovation. Although the US Army had purchased its first airplane in 1909, the Navy had shown less interest in winged aircraft. Curtiss offered, without charge, to train a naval officer at one of his flight schools and arranged a series of experiments and demonstrations linking airplanes to warships.

On Sunday, November 13, 1910, sailors on board the cruiser *Birmingham* constructed a wooden platform 83 feet long and 24 feet wide over the ship's bow. The next morning a Curtiss Pusher was hoisted aboard. The aircraft was fitted with floats in the event it came down on the water. On November 14 the *Birmingham* steamed out into Hampton Roads, Virginia, followed by four torpedo boats. The *Birmingham* was to cruise in the Chesapeake Bay and head into the wind at about ten knots for the take off. The torpedo boats were stationed along the route the plane was to follow up the Elizabeth River to the Norfolk Navy Yard. Rainsqualls filled the sky. Waiting for the weather to clear, the *Birmingham* hove to and dropped anchor. Shortly after noon the weather cleared and the *Birmingham* and her consorts got under way. However, heavy rains forced the ships to again drop anchor before Ely could take off.

At about three o'clock the weather seemed to be clearing and the order was given to weigh anchor and go on with the flight. Eugene Ely, an exhibition pilot who worked for Curtiss, started up the plane's 50-horsepower engine. The plane's slipstream interfered with activities on the bridge and the ship was delayed in getting under way. The anchor came up slowly. Ely was impatient; he gave his mechanic the signal to release the plane and he raced the engine at full power. There were only 57 feet of deck in front of the plane as it started rolling down the inclined ramp at 3:16 P.M.

When the plane reached the end of the ramp it disappeared over the edge and glided down toward the water, 37 feet below the bow. Ely pulled back on the control stick. It was too late. The plane's wheels, floats, and propeller tips touched the water. Both blades of the propeller were damaged, but the wooden prop never stopped turning. Neither the speed nor control of the aircraft was affected. Slowly the airplane began to climb skyward. The sailors on the ship cheered and the *Birmingham*'s whistle announced the feat to nearby ships and small craft.

Once airborne Ely became lost because of the poor visibility, with his sight obscured by water that had splashed on his goggles. He landed as soon as he could, coming down at Willoughby Spit near Norfolk, 2¹/₂ miles from the *Birmingham*. The first flight of an airplane from a ship was history.

On January 18, 1911, he flew a second Pusher to the armored cruiser *Pennsylvania*, anchored in San Francisco Bay, California, and landed on a platform built onto the ship's stern just after 11 A.M. The aircraft was stopped by arresting gear (developed by another Curtiss pilot) as hooks beneath the aircraft snagged lines stretched across the deck and weighted with sandbags. Less than an hour later, Ely turned around, took off, and returned safely to shore. (Ely was killed in October 1911 when his aircraft crashed during a demonstration flight in Georgia.)

During this period Glenn Curtiss was developing a float system that would allow his aircraft to take off and land on water, which evolved into the world's first seaplane. At the time Curtiss referred to the type as a "hydroaeroplane" or "hydro." (Reportedly, Winston Churchill, First Lord of the Admiralty, disliked the term "hydroaeroplane" and called water-going aircraft simply "seaplanes.") On January 26, 1911, at San Diego, California, Curtiss took off and came down at sea using a complicated tandem float arrangement. This configuration was revised into a single, sled-shaped float by February. Later that month he reconfigured one of his Hydros as a tractor, taxied to the anchored *Pennsylvania*—then moored at San Diego—and was hoisted aboard by crane. In addition, that month another Hydro was fitted with wheels. Described as a "Triad," this was the world's first amphibian.

Navy officials were convinced, and on June 30, 1911, purchased a Triad, which was designated A-1 (changed to AH-1 in 1914). This was the first airplane procured by a navy. It was employed to train pilots, to develop naval aviation concepts, and to experiment with a variety of techniques—including airborne radio installations, night flights, and compressed-air catapult launches.

The A-1 flew 60 times before being withdrawn from service in October 1914. The US Navy purchased a total of 14 Curtiss Pushers. Curtiss Pushers had wood frame and fabric construction, with the pilot and passenger seated between the wings, just forward of the engine. Early Pushers mounted two elevators—one forward, and one aft—although the aircraft built for the US Navy were "headless" pushers, which had only the after elevator. Most Pushers carried ailerons, usually mounted on the outboard struts between the wings. As with most designs of the period, production aircraft often varied widely in fitting and details, with numerous modifications performed after delivery.

The Curtiss Pusher made history's first takeoff and landing from a ship. The 1910–11 trials were the harbinger of the development of aircraft carriers by several navies. This photo shows Eugene Ely taking off from the cruiser *Birmingham* in the Chesapeake Bay on November 14, 1910. *US Navy*

A-1 Characteristics

Design:	Curtiss
Crew:	Pilot + passenger
Engines:	1 Curtiss V-8 in-line piston; 75 hp
Weights:	
Empty:	925 lb
Maximum takeoff:	1,575 lb
Dimensions:	
Length:	28 ft, 7 $\frac{1}{8}$ in
Wingspan:	37 ft
Wing area	286 sq ft
Height:	8 ft, 10 in
Speeds:	
Maximum:	60 mph
Armament:	None

Curtiss Model H America

Although designed for peaceful uses, the Curtiss Model H sired the world's first great naval flying boats. When, in 1913, the *Daily Mail* of London offered a £10,000 prize for the first flight between North America and Great Britain, American Rodman Wanamaker commissioned Glenn L. Curtiss to build two aircraft capable of taking the prize. Only the year before Curtiss had designed the world's first practical flying boat. A greatly enlarged version of that aircraft became the Model H, and Wanamaker named the first of these *America*.

    The design team reflected the international nature of the competition, with the wings designed by Britons B. Douglas Thomas and John C. Porte. When flight tests began in June 1914, they revealed that the *America*'s bow tended to submerge when taxiing, and engineers designed the first sponsons to increase buoyancy in the forward fuselage. The sponsons became a standard feature in most of the world's larger flying boats over the next 30 years.

The trans-Atlantic flight, scheduled to begin on August 5, 1914, was cancelled by the outbreak of war in Europe. Porte returned home and persuaded the Admiralty to buy the two Model H aircraft for long-range patrol duties—a remarkable concept at a time when most of the world's air forces were equipped with small artillery spotters developed from prewar sport planes. Many reports have been generated to the effect that no US-designed aircraft saw combat in World War I, but the *America* boats—as the line was dubbed—served with distinction in the war.

Sixty-four of the H-boats—called H.4 "Small Americas" in Britain—were produced and armed with machine guns and bomb racks to operate with the Royal Naval Air Service. All but eight, which were built in Britain, were delivered by ship, leaving the *Daily Mail*'s prize to be claimed by a Vickers Vimy shortly after the war.

The Small Americas' pioneering anti-submarine patrols made significant contributions to the British war effort. The handful of H.4s assigned to Porte at the naval air station at Felixstowe were used in the development of the war's greatest flying boat designs. Larger Curtiss-built aircraft incorporated many of Porte's refinements and served the British and American navies as H-12s and H-16s (known in Britain as "Large Americas"). Those heavy flying boats claimed four U-boats sunk and two zeppelins destroyed in aerial combat. Porte would also create a new hull that would be fitted with the Curtiss-designed wings and tail to become the Felixstowe flying boats. Among those, the F.2A and F.3 saw extensive wartime use with British forces; the F.5 arrived too late for wartime service, but was produced at British and American factories and served both nations' militaries into the mid-1920s. Coming full circle, many F-5Ls were built by Curtiss, and, after the war, some were converted for civilian transportation, the original role for which the Model H was designed.

The H.4 Small America used a wooden hull with fabric-covered, wood biplane wings and tail surfaces. A unique control arrangement attached the ailerons to foot pedals, deflecting one or the other aileron downward to effect turns. (This was an attempt to avoid the Wright brothers' patent claims.) The control stick operated the elevators and the control wheel turned the rudder. Twin pusher Curtiss OX engines were fitted between the wings, with a third engine briefly added to the original *America*'s upper wing to help generate the power needed for the trans-Atlantic attempt. The

Designed in 1914 to fly the Atlantic, the Curtiss Model H
was at that time the world's largest flying boat. The design was
purchased by Britain for maritime patrol and anti-submarine
warfare. The Model H influenced flying boat development for
decades. Here the original *America* floats on Lake Keuka, New
York, near the Curtiss Hammondsport factory.
US National Archives

pilots and mechanic sat in an enclosed cockpit (although later H and F series designs had open cockpits).

Model H America Characteristics

Design:	Curtiss
Crew:	3 (2 pilots, mechanic)
Engines:	2 Curtiss OX pusher in-line piston; 90 hp each
Weights:	
Empty:	3,000 lb
Maximum takeoff:	5,000 lb
Dimensions:	
Length:	37 ft, 6 in
Wingspan:	74 ft
Height:	16 ft
Speed:	
Maximum:	65 mph
Range:	1,100 miles
Armament:	None

Wright Model A Flyer

The Wright Brothers' delivery of a Model A Flyer to the US Army on August 2, 1909, marked the first formal acceptance of an airplane by any military arm. Although the aircraft, given Army Signal Corp Serial No. 1, flew for only 18 months, it began a quest for control of the skies that continues to influence worldwide military planning to this day.

On December 23, 1907, the Signal Corps had requested proposals from aviation firms for a two-seat observation aircraft capable of carrying two people with a combined weight of 350 pounds for a distance of 125 miles at a speed of 40 miles per hour. Each airplane submitted for evaluation had to be capable of rapid assembly and disassembly, and be capable of being flown safely by Army personnel after a short period of instruction.

Of the 41 aircraft proposed, only the Wright Model A was delivered for Army evaluation. Orville Wright brought the aircraft by truck to Fort Myer, Virginia, just west of Washington, on August 20, 1908. He flew it before a small audience on September 3. Several flights followed over the next few days, with a record 70-minute flight on September 11. On September 17, the aircraft crashed when new—and larger—propellers struck the plane's bracing wires; Orville Wright was severely injured and his passenger, Army Lt. Thomas O. Selfridge, was killed.

Despite the accident, the Army's leadership was impressed with the Model A's performance and extended the Wrights additional time to deliver a new machine. The new, slightly modified aircraft was delivered on June 20, 1909. The trials resumed on July 27, when Orville Wright, with Lt. Frank P. Lahm as passenger, made a record flight of 1 hour, 12 minutes, 40 seconds, covering a distance of approximately 40 miles. The Army was satisfied with the aircraft's performance, and accepted it a week later, paying the Wrights $30,000.

The aircraft was moved to College Park, Maryland, where the Wrights instructed lieutenants Lahm and Frederic E. Humphreys in the art of flying. On October 17, 1909, Navy Lt. George Sweet was taken aloft, becoming the first US Navy officer to fly in an aircraft. The aircraft was involved in a low-level crash on November 5. No one was injured, but the Flyer remained grounded awaiting replacement parts from the Wright factory. In the interim, the Army chose to move flight training to the warmer climes of Texas, and—after a brief exhibition in Chicago—the Model A was delivered to Fort Sam Houston in February 1910. As Humphreys left the service, and Lahm was assigned to other duties, Lt. Benjamin D. Foulois took over as the Army's pilot. Not yet trained to fly, Foulois began a "correspondence course" with the Wrights, and successfully completed 61 flights between that March and September.

In August 1910, Foulois had added a tricycle landing gear to the Flyer, but this was soon replaced by Wright-designed wheels. In November, the aircraft was further modified to conform to the standards of the Wrights' new Model B, but flying was soon suspended until the new year. The Signal Corps No. 1 was available for a series of operational demonstrations in February and March 1911, but a new Wright B—loaned to the Army by publisher Robert F. Collier—performed most of these liaison and communications flights. The Wright A, even with modifications, was showing its age at a time when aviation was advancing rapidly, and on May 4, 1911, the War Department approved the aircraft's retirement and its transfer to the Smithsonian Institution in Washington.

The Wright Model A was a two-place, open biplane built of fabric-covered wood frame. The twin elevators were mounted in front and the twin rudders behind, with bank controlled by the Wright's patented wing-warping system. Pilot and passenger sat upright at the wing's leading edge, just ahead of the four-cylinder Wright engine that drove the twin, counter-rotating propellers through a chain drive. The original landing gear consisted of twin skids necessitated a launch rail, used in conjunction with a gravity-driven catapult.

Model A Flyer Characteristics

Design:	Wright
Crew:	Pilot + passenger
Engines:	1 Wright vertical four-cylinder in-line piston; 30–40 hp with chain drives turning twin propellers
Weights:	
Empty:	735 lb
Dimensions:	
Length:	28 ft, 11 in
Wingspan:	36 ft, 6 in
Height:	8 ft, 1 in
Speeds:	
Maximum:	44 mph
Armament:	None

This Wright Brothers Model A Flyer was the world's first aircraft to be purchased by a military organization. The aircraft, which would become "Signal Corps Number 1," is shown being prepared for a test flight at Fort Myer, Virginia, in July 1909. Orville Wright, in the dark suit, is walking toward the camera.
US National Archives

Two

World War I

On the eve of "the Great War," as it would be known until the conflict of 1939–45, aircraft carried out military missions in North Africa, the Balkans, and Mexico, mostly reconnaissance and scouting, and bombing enemy positions and transport. Those few actions had demonstrated beyond any doubt that the airplane had a role in combat.

When war erupted in Europe in August 1914 the belligerents were already procuring "combat" aircraft. The first months of the war, however, demonstrated how naïve military commanders were with respect to the numbers and importance of aircraft in combat. Soon the reconnaissance flights turned into counter-reconnaissance operations, as enemy observation balloons and reconnaissance aircraft became targets. The latter engagements led to the first air-to-air combat. Meanwhile, scouting planes dropped small, hand-held bombs and flechettes on enemy positions and troops on the march.

The rapid pace of technological development in wartime led to faster, better-armed, and otherwise more capable combat aircraft. At sea the aircraft found an important role in attacking enemy ships, at first with small bombs and then with aerial torpedoes. The latter proved devastating, as few ships had the underwater armor and compartmentation to resist the devastation caused by an underwater projectile. Subsequently, the German submarine campaign led to the employment of aircraft to scour the seas for signs of U-boats, opening another military role to aircraft.

Sikorsky's Il'ya Muromets was the world's first four-engine military aircraft based on Igor Sikorsky's innovative *Grand,* built only one year earlier. The aircraft featured unprecedented reliability as well as the ability to survive battle damage and still return safely to base, and to deliver a potent bomb load.
Air International

Naval aviation's role, expanding rapidly, included air strikes against ground targets. The Royal Navy employed aircraft, launched from shore bases, ships, and even towed sleds, to combat the dreaded German Zeppelins, used for both reconnaissance and bombing. Naval aircraft engaged Zeppelins in flight and bombed them in their berthing sheds ashore.

Two important factors in World War I military aviation were the rate of development of improved models and the numbers of aircraft produced. Here the European Allies far outpaced the United States. Indeed, the only US-developed military aircraft to see action in the war were the Curtiss *America*-series flying boats, produced in the United States and Britain. France, Britain, and Germany led in aircraft development, although, as will be noted in subsequent chapters, Imperial Russia produced some very advanced aircraft prior to the outbreak of the Russian Revolution. With respect to aircraft numbers, British designers and factories were able to far outpace the Central Powers in producing advanced aircraft in large numbers, firmly establishing the criteria for victory in the air.

The ten aircraft described in this chapter were important participants in World War I, although the Curtiss Jenny only saw combat with American markings in the campaign in Mexico in 1916. Although the Curtiss NC flying boats arrived on the scene too late for combat, they demonstrated the range/payload capabilities being developed for "maritime patrol aircraft," a term not coined for several more decades.

In many respects the most striking aircraft of the era was the Sikorsky Il'ya Muromets, the world's first four-engine military aircraft and only the second built, after Igor Sikorsky's *Grand* of 1913. The Il'ya Muromets, placed in series production for the Russian Army, provided to be a potent as well as imposing aircraft, and established Russian-Soviet aviation as a world leader that continues to this day.

Avro 504

The Avro 504, the most widely used trainer flown in Britain during World War I—and the most widely produced British aircraft of the war—served as the standard *ab initio* (primary) trainer for British flying services for more than 15 years. Several armed 504s also carried out pioneering combat missions in the war's early days, and a few were even called back into service to perform support duties at the beginning of World War II.

Although few 504s saw frontline service (there were never more than 13 in France at any given time), the 504's combat days were the stuff of legend. But the aircraft's combat debut was inauspicious—on August 22, 1914, a 504 was downed by German infantry fire, becoming the first British aircraft lost in World War I combat.

In October 1914 an Avro fitted with a flexible Lewis machine gun strafed a German troop train, then forced down a two-seat Albatross. On November 21, 1914, three Royal Naval Air Service 504s flew an audacious mission against the German airship sheds at Friedrichschafen. Armed with four 20-pound bombs each, the aircraft flew 125 miles to their target and caused extensive damage when a bomb hit on the hydrogen plant caused massive secondary explosions. Although one aircraft was lost, the other two returned safely to France. On March 24, 1915, a 504 joined in an attack on the German submarine depot near Antwerp: the planes destroyed two U-boats.

RNAS 504s based in Belgium also participated in attacks on individual Zeppelins. In the early morning hours of May 17, 1915, an aircraft intercepted the *LZ.38*. The British pilot was armed with two incendiary bombs and two hand grenades, but was unable to use them as the German airship climbed rapidly and escaped. That evening, however, a second 504 managed to drop four small bombs on the *LZ.39*; the airship, which suffered some fire damage to its tail, made a hard landing at Brussels.

Some early Avros also served in Egypt, flying reconnaissance missions, coastal patrols, and, occasionally, bombing raids. Most Avro 504s were used for pilot and gunnery training, remaining in service with the RAF until 1933. Seven civilian 504Ns were called to RAF service in 1940, towing wooden gliders for tests and calibration of ground-based radar.

Avro—the name an acronym for company founder Alliott Verdon Roe—designed the 504 in 1913 as a sport plane for civilian use. By the time of the first flight on September 18, 1913, the British War Office had ordered 12 aircraft. The Admiralty ordered seven more in 1914, with orders increasing slowly as World War I began. Initial variants included the 504, the original 80-hp-Gnome-powered version, with some used in early bombing raids; the 504A, the first major Royal Flying Corps production version, with a few used as bombers; the 504B, trainer ordered for the RNAS with many subsequent modifications (including one aircraft used for deck arresting gear experiments); the 504C, a single-seat RNAS anti-airship variant fitted with a Lewis machine gun and extra fuel (with some bomber conversions on an ad hoc basis); the 504D, an RFC version of the 504C; the 504E, a 100-hp-Gnome Monosoupape version for the RNAS with an extra fuel tank (with seven modified as light bombers); the single 504F with a Rolls-Royce Hawk engine; the 504G, 80-hp-Gnome-powered RNAS trainers, with practice bomb racks, synchronized Vickers guns, and a Scarff ring for a Lewis gun in the rear cockpit; and the 504H, a single modified 504C strengthened and tested as one of the first aircraft to be launched by catapult.

Several thousand Avro 504J and 504K aircraft were ordered by the services. The RFC's 504J trainer—known as the "Mono Avro" for its 100-hp Gnome Monosoupape engine—was light, powerful, and aerobatic. The 504K featured a new engine mount that allowed a variety of engines to be fitted. By the November 1918, some 3,000 J and K models were in British service, with most wartime production estimates somewhere in the range of 8,300. The 504K remained in production until January 1927, although the last deliveries were actually conversions.

Postwar versions included the 504L training seaplane, the 504M civil conversion, and the Lynx-powered 504N. About 600 504Ns were delivered (including some 80 converted 504Ks) when British production finally ended in 1933-some 20 years after the first Avro 504 flew.

The Avro 504 was used by many nations, with Australia, Belgium, Canada, and Japan producing the aircraft in their own factories. Due to confusion over conflicting aircraft production and modification figures, the final number of 504s built is unknown.

The Avro 504 saw combat with Britain's Royal Naval Air
Service and Royal Flying Corps early in World War I, and sur-
vived as a trainer in the Royal Air Force until 1933. The Navy
Avro 504B seen here intercepted but unsuccessfully attacked
the German Zeppelin *LZ.38* over Belgium on May 17, 1915.
Imperial War Museum

Avro 504K Characteristics

Design:	Avro
Crew:	Pilot + student
Engines:	1 110-hp Le Rhône or 130-hp Clerget or 100-hp Gnome Monosoupape rotary piston
Weights:	
Empty:	1,231 lb
Maximum takeoff:	1,829 lb
Dimensions:	
Length:	29 ft, 5 in
Wingspan:	36 ft
Wing area:	330 sq ft
Height:	10 ft, 5 in
Speeds:	
Maximum:	95 mph
Cruise:	85 mph
Ceiling:	Service: 16,000 ft
Range:	250 miles
Armament:	1 .303-cal. Lewis machine gun (flexible) on some aircraft modified as gunnery trainers

Curtiss JN-4 Jenny

The most prolific US training aircraft of World War I, the Curtiss Jenny is estimated to have trained 95 percent of all US and Canadian pilots who flew before the Armistice of November 1918. Not the best primary trainer of its day, the Jenny was advanced enough in 1914 to enter large-scale production, and soon so dominated the market that any thought of a replacement was postponed until after the war.

The more powerful Hispano-Suiza-powered variants also served as advanced trainers for bombing, gunnery, and reconnaissance before being withdrawn from service in 1927. Surplus Jennies, dumped on a civilian market below cost, were such popular barnstorming aircraft throughout North America that the early period of postwar aviation is often called the "Jenny Era."

Early Jennies also became the first US Army aircraft to see combat. On March 15, 1916, eight JN-3s of the 1st Aero Squadron arrived in Columbus, New Mexico, to take part in Gen. John J. Pershing's Punitive Expedition against outlawed Mexican revolutionary Francisco (Pancho) Villa. The first reconnaissance mission took place on the next day, and on March 19 the squadron began moving into Mexico. Two aircraft were soon lost to accidents, but the others began a series of flights delivering mail and dispatches to cavalry troops in forward locations. In the long-term, however, the JN-3s were not up to the rigors of the campaign—their engines did not have the power to cross many of the Mexican mountain ranges, and the harsh weather conditions took their toll on fabric and wood. With no replacements available, the repaired aircraft were restricted to liaison between forward positions and the American bases at Namiquipa and San Geronimo. Accidents and the hostile actions of Mexican nationals took their toll; by April 20, 1916, only two of the original eight JN-3s were still in commission, and these were condemned on that day. Those early Curtiss aircraft had provided valuable support of the field forces, while demonstrating the need for more-capable operational aircraft.

The development of the Jenny began in 1914 when the US Army—concerned over the poor safety record of its pusher-engine trainers—began searching for new tractor-powered replacements. Glenn Curtiss had developed his Model N, which was similar to several of his earlier trainers. However, Curtiss had also hired British designer B. Douglas Thomas—formerly an engineer with Avro and Sopwith—who developed the Curtiss Model J. The Army saw the best features of both the Model N and Model J, and Curtiss combined them into one aircraft. Eight aircraft were delivered to the Signal Corps as JN-2s, and the alliteration of

Sturdy and stable, the Curtiss Jenny was the most widely used US and Canadian trainer of World War I. This JN-4D, photographed in 1917, was marked with US Army field number 56 just below its Signal Corps No. SC 1638. After the war Jennys became known throughout the United States as the principal aircraft flown by "barnstormers." *US National Archives*

the designation led to the popular nickname "Jenny." (Despite conflicting reports, no aircraft were built with the simple "JN" or "JN-1" designations.) Although the date of the first JN-2 flight is not recorded, the first Army deliveries were made in April 1915.

Performance was substandard, and two aircraft were wrecked; Curtiss rebuilt the six survivors, which were then known as JN-3s. The Army also bought two new-production JN-3s from Curtiss; together with the rebuilt JN-2s these were the eight aircraft that initially participated in the Mexican Punitive Expedition.

The JN-3 was also produced in Canada for British service. A change in the control system led to those aircraft being designated JN-4, also called "Canucks"—although Canadian aircraft delivered to the United States were designated JN-4Can to avoid confusion with an American-developed aircraft with the same designation. The US-designed JN-4—similar to the JN-3—was developed for the Army observation role, and 701 were built. New tail surfaces, fuselage, wings, and ailerons led to the JN-4A, with 781 built. Five JN-4Bs were built with changes in dihedral, engine thrust line, and ailerons, and a single JN-4C flew with an experimental wing design.

The most widely produced Jenny was the JN-4D, with a total reported at 3,354 built by Curtiss and six other US firms. The need for more power led to the adoption of and American-built, 150-horsepower Hispano-Suiza engine in the JN-4H (the "H" designation was derived from the "Hisso"—Hispano-Suiza—power plant). The JN-4Hs were strengthened for other training duties, including gunnery, bombing, observation, and pursuit training. Improvements to the JN-4H design led to the production of 1,035 JN-6Hs, for a total Jenny production run estimated at 8,189 aircraft from both American and Canadian factories.

Following the Armistice, the Hisso variants were retained for postwar service. In 1923 the surviving JN-4Hs and JN-6Hs were rebuilt as "Standard Jennies" and redesignated "JNS." The last of these aircraft left Army National Guard service in 1927, a long service career for an aircraft of the 1914 era.

JN-4D Characteristics

Design:	Curtiss
Crew:	Pilot + student
Engines:	1 Curtiss OX-5 V-8 in-line piston; 90 hp
Weights:	
Empty:	1,580 lb
Maximum takeoff:	2,130 lb
Dimensions:	
Length:	27 ft, 4 in
Wingspan:	43 ft, 7 $^1/_8$ in
Wing area:	352.5 sq ft
Height:	9 ft, 10 $^5/_8$ ft
Speeds:	
Maximum:	75 mph
Ceiling:	11,000 ft
Range:	250 miles
Armament:	None

de Havilland D.H.4

The D.H.4 was first the effective purpose-built bomber to serve with the Royal Flying Corps. The aircraft fought with distinction in British squadrons until replaced by the D.H.9 near the end of the war. Produced in the United States as the DH-4 Liberty Plane (designated with the American hyphen rather than the British periods), it would be the only American-built *land* plane to see combat in Europe.

In 1915 the British Army's single-engine reconnaissance aircraft were badly outclassed by German and Austrian designs, particularly when Fokker monoplane fighters took control of the skies that summer. At the same time, Capt. Geoffrey de Havilland of the Aircraft Manufacturing Company (Airco) proposed a new single-engine reconnaissance and bombing biplane. The D.H.4 prototype first flew in August 1916; production was ordered, and

D.H.4s carried out their first combat mission on April 6, 1917. That mission was flown without escort as the D.H.4's speed, maneuverability, and ceiling allowed it to easily outmaneuver and outdistance pursuing German fighters.

Despite several flaws, including a tendency to nose over on landing, the dangerous positioning of the pilot between the engine and heavy fuel tank, and communications difficulties between the pilot and observer, the D.H.4 proved immensely popular with its air crews. Some D.H.4s were modified as fighters for anti-airship operations—one of these aircraft destroyed Zeppelin *L.70* on August 5, 1918. Other D.H.4s served with the Royal Naval Air Service on the Belgian coast, where their missions included reconnaissance, photography, artillery spotting, and anti-submarine patrols (including the destruction of U-boat *UB-12* on August 12, 1918.)

The D.H.4 served in the Royal Air Force until January 1920. The D.H.9 was scheduled to replace the D.H.4, but disappointing performance and critical engine problems kept the D.H.4 in production much longer than planned. By the war's end Airco and four subcontractors had delivered 1,449 D.H.4s, with 15 more aircraft produced in Belgium.

The first US DH-4s reached France in May 1918. They required numerous modifications, delaying the first operational mission until August 1. The Liberty Planes started their $3^1/2$ months of combat by serving as fighter escort for ground attack missions, and gave a good accounting of themselves on bombing and reconnaissance missions during the Allied offensive in September 1918. Two US Army lieutenants who died when their DH-4 was shot down resupplying the "Lost Battalion" were awarded posthumous Medals of Honor. Medals of Honor also went to two Marine pilots flying DH-4s when they were attacked by 12 enemy aircraft during a raid on October 14, 1918. Although both Marines were wounded, each succeeded in downing an enemy aircraft before retreating to friendly lines.

Postwar analysis cited the DH-4 as "a poor airplane for day bombardment," but American industry had been so wedded to the type that little funding remained to develop a successor. Accordingly, critical equipment was salvaged from surviving aircraft in Europe for use as parts to keep US planes flying. (The stripped airframes were then burned.)

The shrunken budgets after the war kept the DH-4 in service. Over the next decade, more than 60 major modification programs would continue the US DH-4's development, including steel-tube fuselages, new wing designs, dual controls for trainers, passenger compartments, single-seat mailplane revisions, superchargers, and a variety of engines. The DH-4 continued to serve the Marines until 1929 and the Army Air Corps until 1932. Most surviving DH-4s and DB-4Bs were employed for tactical training through the mid-1920s, and for support, developmental, and test-bed purposes through 1932. Some modified Marine Corps aircraft were used against Nicaraguan bandits in 1927.

In the autumn of 1916, British evaluators had found the D.H.4 to be light on the controls, comfortable to fly, and easy to land. The wood-frame fuselage had internal wire cross bracing in four bays behind aft cockpit, with plywood covering the forward fuselage and reinforcing beneath the tail.

The RFC aircraft had a single Vickers machine gun firing through the propeller arc, whereas RNAS aircraft had two; both services usually gave the observer twin Lewis guns mounted on a Scarff ring. The 460-pound bomb load was carried on external racks.

The difficulties of high-power engine design and production plagued all nations during World War I, and Britain was no exception. Although many different engines were produced for the D.H.4s, most frontline aircraft were powered by the excellent 375-horsepower Rolls-Royce Eagle VIII.

On April 6, 1917, when America entered World War I, neither the Army nor Navy had modern land-based combat aircraft. After studying Allied designs, US planners decided to build the DH-4 in American factories. The first British pattern aircraft arrived in the United States—sans engine—on July 27, 1917. It was rushed to the Army's Engineering Division at McCook Field, Ohio, for evaluation and modification to US standards. Plans were then passed to three American firms for production.

The McCook Field D.H.4 made its first flight with a Liberty engine prototype on October 29, 1917; a few weeks later the first D.H.9 was delivered to an RFC squadron. However, the United States was committed to the DH-4 and there was no time to restart the process.

As in Europe, America's high-powered aircraft engine design and production was in its infancy, and the much-vaunted Liberty engine experienced its share of problems, in-flight fires being among the most serious. Coupled with problems as the aircraft industry geared up for mass production, DH-4 deliveries never reached their potential or promise. Still, the United States

The first effective bombing aircraft in Britain's Royal Flying Corps was the de Havilland D.H.4, which was produced in the United States as the "Liberty Plane." This British-built D.H.4, with experimental camouflage, was photographed in 1918 at the British naval research station on the Isle of Grain. The aircraft has two machine guns mounted on the after cockpit.

Imperial War Museum

produced 4,846 of the de Havillands, three times the total of European factories. By the war's end US manufacturers had delivered 1,213 DH-4s to France; 196 of those were operational in 13 US Army squadrons, with others in four Navy and Marine squadrons.

The American firms introduced a number of wartime modifications, including a new fuel system in the DH-4A and revised undercarriage and seating (moving pilot and observer together, as in the D.H.9), and a plywood fuselage for the DH-4B.

DH-4 Liberty Characteristics

Design:	US Army
Crew:	2 (pilot, observer-gunner)
Engines:	1 Liberty V-1650 in-line piston; 400 hp
Weights:	
Empty:	2,732 lb
Maximum takeoff:	4,297 lb
Dimensions:	
Length:	29 ft, 11 in
Wingspan:	42 ft, 5 1/2 in
Wing area:	440 sq ft
Height:	9 ft, 8 in
Speeds:	
Maximum:	125 mph
Cruise:	113 mph
Ceiling:	19,500 ft
Range:	3-hour endurance
Armament:	2 .303-cal. Marlin machine guns (fixed); 2 .303-cal. Lewis machine guns (flexible); 322 lb of bombs

Fokker E. Series Eindeckers

From the summer of 1915 through early 1916, a relative handful of Fokker Eindeckers (monoplanes) ruled the skies over the Western Front. Before the arrival of the Eindeckers, air missions were not unlike cavalry missions:

if stealth and a quick escape failed to prevent contact with the enemy, survival depended on the skills of the individual pilots and the number of aircraft involved. But as the Fokkers began to take air superiority—long before the term was coined—even the best British and French pilots came to regard themselves as "Fokker fodder." In the hands of German pilots such as Max Immelmann and Oswald Bölcke, the Fokkers wrecked havoc on their lightly armed enemies.

The Eindecker was not a particularly capable aircraft. The original design, developed from the French Morane-Saulnier Type H, entered service with the German Army in 1913 as the A.I (long-span wings) and A.III (short-span wings) unarmed communications and training aircraft.

When French pilot Roland Garros was captured by the Germans in April 1915, his Morane-Saulnier Type L aircraft was found to carry deflector plates behind its propeller blades, allowing a machine gun to fire directly through the propeller arc with little risk of damage to the prop itself. Garros had used this arrangement to destroy three German aircraft in three weeks, a remarkable success rate for the times. Fokker engineers quickly improved on the concept, designing an interrupter gear to prevent the gun from firing as the propeller blades crossed the bullet's path, and fitted the mechanism to a Fokker A.III. By May, German authorities had placed initial orders for the aircraft, now designated "E.I" (for 1st Model Eindecker).

Fokker E.I operations began in June 1915, with the smaller E.II introduced in July, the E.III—the most capable aircraft of the series—arriving at the front in August, and the E.IV first flying in November. By January 1916 fears of the Eindecker's forward-firing machine gun had risen to the point that the Royal Flying Corps ordered each two-seat reconnaissance aircraft to be escorted by at least three "fighter" aircraft. That month the French introduced the Nieuport 11, and the British began deploying the Royal Aircraft Factory's F.E.2b; the Airco D.H.2 would follow in February. Those new aircraft still lacked the interrupter gear for their machine guns, with the British aircraft designed as pushers and the French Nieuports mounting their guns above the wing to fire above the propeller arc. However, all three aircraft relied on speed and maneuverability, traits the Fokker lacked. By March 1916 a British unit could report that "the once dreaded Fokker monoplane was completely outclassed and defeated, being, indeed, literally hounded out of the sky." The last

Fokker E.III Characteristics

Design:	Fokker
Crew:	Pilot
Engines:	1 Oberursel U.1 9-cylinder rotary piston; 100 hp
Weights:	
Empty:	920 lb
Maximum takeoff:	1,400 lb
Dimensions:	
Length:	23 ft, 11 $1/3$ in
Wingspan:	30 ft, 10 $1/3$ in
Wing area:	50.84 sq ft
Height:	9 ft, 1 $2/3$ in
Speeds:	
Maximum:	83 mph
Ceiling:	11,500 ft
Range:	2 $3/4$-hour endurance
Armament:	1 or 2 7.92-mm LMG.08 machine guns (fixed)

Fokker monoplanes were withdrawn from frontline service late in the summer of 1916. During its brief stay at the top of the "food chain," the Fokker Eindecker had established the concept of the offensive fighter aircraft. It had been used to develop the doctrines and tactics of fighter aviation, and had begun the quest for fighter dominance and air supremacy that continues to this day.

Eindecker fuselages had a welded steel-tube structure with aluminum sheet enclosing the engine and cockpit and fabric covering the after fuselage. Wings were wood and fabric, with Wright-style wing warping providing roll control. Rushed into production, the Fokkers never benefited from the luxury of a full-scale development program. Performance was generally considered poor by Eindecker pilots, who complained of the aircraft's slow speed, poor rate of climb, and lack of maneuverability. But the

The first true fighter aircraft was the Fokker Eindecker monoplane, which swept the skies of Allied opposition beginning in
the summer of 1915. The most successful aircraft of the family
was the E.III, seen here. It entered combat in August 1915 and
remained dominant in the skies until the spring of 1916.
US National Archives

Fokker's forward firing machine gun was an overwhelming advantage—one that would take the Allies time to counter.

It appears that total Eindecker production did not surpass 475 aircraft, of which approximately 260 were E.IIIs, and many of those aircraft were never completed. The number of aircraft available at any given time could be pitiful: at the end of 1915—when the Eindecker still reigned supreme— the German Army could report only 40 single-seat fighters in use on the Eastern and Western fronts.

Fokker D.VII

Germany's Fokker D.VII was the finest operational fighter of World War I. But despite the D.VII's many qualities, it arrived too late to change the course of the air war on the Western Front. Small production runs and shortages of fuel and experienced pilots meant that the new Fokker could only slow the inevitable Allied victory. It was, however, the only aircraft mentioned by name in the harsh terms of the 1919 Treaty of Versailles: Article IV demanded that all machines of the D.VII type be handed over to the Allies. (Of those turned over, 142 were brought to the United States after the war.)

The first D.VIIs began to reach German fighter units in April 1918. The new machines were generally reserved for the most experienced pilots, who took them into combat that same month. Although pilots noted that the British S.E.5a and French SPAD XII had superior climb and performance at altitude, the German fighter was more maneuverable, rugged, and capable of taking the stresses of combat flying and surviving damage from enemy fire. The D.VII was simply better than anything else then available.

By the late summer of 1918 a new version of the D.VII appeared. Powered by a 185-horsepower BMW engine that provided maximum power at an altitude of 18,000 feet, the new D.VII quickly bested every fighter that the Allies could produce. It easily outclimbed the S.E.5a, and so dominated the SPAD XIII that in September 1918 French pilots were ordered to avoid combat with the Fokkers. The D.VII achieved this with an engine fueled by a gasoline-benzine mixture, yet another sign of Germany's weakened industrial state.

By the end of the war the D.VII, particularly when powered with the

BMW engine, was the favorite of many surviving German aces, including Ernst Udet (62 victories), Rudolph Berthold (44 victories), Theo Osterkamp (32 victories), Josef Mai (30 victories), Kurt Wusthoff (27 victories), George von Hantelmann (25 victories), and Oliver Freiherr von Beaulieu-Marconnay (25 victories).

Development of the D.VII began in December 1917 when German officials demanded a new fighter capable of retaking control of the skies. The Fokker Dr.I Triplane, at that time the most capable German fighter, was outclassed by newer British and French fighters. German firms were invited to bring new fighter prototypes, all to be powered by the 160-horsepower Mercedes D III engine, to a competition scheduled for late January 1918. Fokker company designer Reinhold Platz, who had pioneered the thick cantilever wing design used on the Fokker Dr.I, developed the prototype, which was designated V.11. Anthony Fokker flew it in January, but found that it suffered from stability problems. At the competition later that month, Fokker learned that Manfred von Richthofen, the "Red Baron" himself, had also flown the V.11 and was dissatisfied with its handling.

Fokker explained that the aircraft had been damaged in a hard landing, and requested a weekend to make repairs. The "repairs" amounted to several major design revisions, including lengthening the after fuselage by 16 inches. When returned to the competition, the modified aircraft handily defeated the 30 other entries. Fokker was rewarded with an immediate order for 400 aircraft, which the German Army designated Fokker D.VII. Albatross factories in Germany and Austria-Hungary also received production orders for Fokker D.VIIs, including one aircraft built with a plywood fuselage (a hedge against possible steel shortages). The Fokker plant also designed and built 70 V.38s, two-seat variants of the D.VII. With no delivery orders from Germany authorities, the two-seaters were among the 220 D.VII-type aircraft (and 400 engines) that Fokker hid from the Inter-Allied Armistice Commission after the War. (All were smuggled to Holland, where the Dutch-born Fokker reestablished his company.)

Early D.VIIs had only a few developmental problems. Most notable were the lack of power from the Mercedes engines and a number of fires caused when engine heat ignited incendiary ammunition stored beneath the guns. Improved engine cooling vents and redesigned ammunition

An innovative structure and powerful engine made the Fokker
D.VII the single most effective fighter aircraft of World War I.
This example, complete with spare propeller and wheel lashed
to it, was flown by US pilots in America following the Armistice
of November 1917. *US National Archives*

solved the latter problem, but not before several fatal accidents. The new BMW engine took care of all power needs.

The Fokker D.VII had a fabric and plywood–covered steel tube fuselage, with metal cowling panels enclosing much of the engine. The wood wing structure was based on two box spars, with plywood leading edges and fabric covering overall. The cantilever design, secured with streamlined steel tube struts, eliminated the need for most drag-producing external bracing wires. Unlike the other German fighters in production, the D.VII featured a nose-mounted radiator, which helped to avoid the complicated cooling systems seen on the other water-cooled machines. There are no accurate records of total D.VII production; of the 2,000 ordered, approximately 1,000 are thought to have been delivered to the German and Austro-Hungarian air forces before the Armistice on November 11, 1918.

Fokker D.VIIF Characteristics

Design:	Fokker
Crew:	Pilot
Engines:	1 water-cooled, 6-cylinder BMW IIIa in-line piston; 185 hp
Weights:	
Empty	1,474 lb
Maximum takeoff:	2,112 lb
Dimensions:	
Length:	22 ft, 11 $\frac{1}{2}$ in
Wingspan:	29 ft, 3 $\frac{1}{2}$ in
Wing area:	221.4 sq ft
Height:	9 ft, 2 $\frac{1}{4}$ in
Speeds:	
Maximum:	125 mph
Ceiling:	22,900 ft
Range:	1 $\frac{1}{2}$-hour endurance
Armament:	2 7.92-mm Spandau machine guns (fixed)

Navy-Curtiss NC Flying Boats

The US Navy's Curtiss-built NC flying boats were developed for long-range anti-submarine operations against German U-boats. The NC-4 of this series was the first aircraft to fly across the Atlantic Ocean, albeit in stages. The NC aircraft were designed in 1917, intended from the outset for trans-Atlantic flight, to avoid taking up valuable shipping space to carry them to Europe, and to be ready to fly ASW patrols upon arrival at European bases.

The result was a Navy-designed, three-engine flying boat with rugged construction (to enable rough-water operation) and an endurance estimated at 15 to 20 hours. The Navy's detailed proposal for such an aircraft, incorporating a Navy-developed, two-step hull design, was converted to production plans by Curtiss, which initiated construction of the NC boats.

The NC-1, the first aircraft, made its first flight on October 4, 1918, a little more than a month before the Armistice ending World War I. Although designed for a crew of six, on November 25, 1918, the NC-1 took off with 51 persons on board to establish a new world record for passengers carried aloft.

Curtiss built the NC-1 through NC-4 at its facility in Garden City (Long Island), New York, and the Naval Aircraft Factory in Philadelphia built the NC-5 through NC-10. Although completed too late for war service, the Navy Department decided to demonstrate their trans-Atlantic capability, at a time that both American and British aviators sought to achieve the first flight across the Atlantic. The NC-1, NC-3, and NC-4 rendezvoused at Trepassy Bay, Newfoundland, and on May 16, 1919, took off on their ocean-crossing flight. The first leg of the effort was 1,400 miles to the Azores.

The NC-1 and NC-3 were both forced down at sea near the Azores. The NC-1 sank, her crew being rescued by a ship. The NC-3 managed to taxi the 200 miles to the Azores.

The NC-4, commanded by Lt. Comdr. Albert C. Read, reached the

Azores on May 17. The aircraft then proceeded to Lisbon, Portugal, arriving May 29, and reached Portsmouth, England, on May 31. Secretary of the Navy Josephus Daniels later wrote of the NC-4 flight, "It will rank with the laying of the Atlantic cable and other events which have marked a distinct and significant advance in the history of the mastery of the elements by man."

That aircraft subsequently was returned to the United States, disassembled, aboard the flying boat tender *Aroostook*. The aircraft was reassembled and made a multi-city publicity tour. (She was then handed over to the Smithsonian Institution, with the Congress legislating that she be placed on display in Washington, D.C. However, despite that legislation, the aircraft is "on loan" to the Naval Aviation Museum in Pensacola, Florida, where she is expected to remain.)

In the Navy redesignation scheme of 1922 the remaining NC boats were redesignated P2N indicating the second patrol aircraft design produced by the Navy.

The NC boats were distinguished by a very short hull (45 feet), using a Curtiss-developed laminated wood veneer construction. The tail assembly was held clear of the water by a lattice assembly, an arrangement that saved weight and provided a good field of fire for a machine gun mounted in the rear of the hull; another gun was mounted forward. Bombs were to be carried under the wing. The engines were mounted above the hull, between the wings.

The NC-1 initially flew with three Liberty engines installed as tractors. After initial NC-1 flight tests, the NC-2 was completed with two pairs of engines in tandem (two pusher and two tractor), with the pilots seated in a third nacelle between the engines. She first flew on April 12, 1919. The NC-3 and NC-4 flew with the three tractor-engine arrangement with a fourth engine mounted as a pusher in the center nacelle (with the pilots in the hull, as the NC-1).

The Navy-built NC-5 and NC-6 had a three-engine arrangement with the center engine installed as a pusher. The NC-7 through NC-10 had the NC-3 configuration.

The Navy-Curtiss NC-4 was the first aircraft to cross the
Atlantic Ocean, albeit in several stages. The NC flying boats were
developed for anti-submarine warfare, with the capability of "self-
deploying" across the ocean. The open cockpits and gun nose
position are evidence of the hardship of early flight. *US Navy*

NC-3 Characteristics

Design:	Navy-Curtiss
Crew:	6 (pilot, copilot, navigator/gunner, radio operator, 2 flight engineers)
Engines:	4 Liberty 12 in-line piston; 400 hp each
Weights:	
Empty:	15,874 lb
Loaded:	27,386 lb
Dimensions:	
Length:	68 ft, 3 in
Wingspan:	126 ft
Wing area:	2,380 sq ft
Height:	24 ft, 6 in
Speeds:	
Maximum:	85 mph
Ceiling:	4,500 ft
Range:	1,470 miles
Armament:	2 machine guns (2 flexible mounts) bombs

Nieuport Sesquiplanes

When France's Nieuport sesquiplane fighters became operational in January 1916 the German Fokker monoplane fighters had controlled the skies over the Western Front for the past six months. A sesquiplane was a biplane whose lower wing has a very narrow chord in comparison to the upper wing.

The nimble, powerful Nieuport and the British-designed F.E.2b and D.H.2 would quickly master the less-capable Fokkers. However, the two British designs were both pushers, and the day of the pusher was coming to an end. The sesquiplanes, however, brought new technical advantages that were soon imitated by allies and enemies alike and continued into the postwar years.

The diminutive, 80-horsepower Nieuport 11 was France's first modern fighter. Designated a Class B (light fighter) Biplane—or Type BB—by the

French Army, the aircraft was known as the *Bébé* ("baby") to its crews. Lacking an effective synchronization system to fire machine guns through the propeller arc, Nieuport designers mounted a Lewis machine gun above the upper wing to fire over the prop. By the autumn of 1916, as the larger and stronger Type 17 was entering service, French planners felt that they had developed enough of an advantage to organize independent fighter groups to hunt German aircraft over the front. The Nieuports also gave France its first great aces: Jean Marie Navarre, flying an all-red Nieuport 11, scored 12 confirmed victories (and at least 6 unconfirmed) in three months before being wounded in action; Georges Guynemer claimed an estimated 40 victories, most in a Nieuport 17, before transferring to Spads in June 1917; and Charles Nungesser made most of his 45 kills in a Nieuport 17 and a 24*bis*.

The Nieuports were also popular with other nations: Britain's Capt. Albert Ball recorded 49 combats over the Somme in his Nieuport 17 between August and October 1916; in those engagements he destroyed 10 aircraft, forced 20 more to land, and listed 1 probable. His final tally was 44 victories—some in an S.E.5—before he was lost in May 1917. The Royal Flying Corps No. 1 Squadron was equipped with Nieuport 17s in January 1917; by October the squadron's scoreboard claimed 200 aerial victories. Canadian William A. Bishop scored 40 victories in his Nieuport 17. That type was also preferred by many Belgian, Italian, and Russian aces. (The Italians referred to the design as the "mezzo-monoplane.")

The Germans were profoundly influenced by the sesquiplane's capabilities and encouraged Siemens, Albatros, Euler, Fokker, LVG, and Roland to develop similar designs. In the spring of 1917 the Albatros D.III sesquiplane began to reclaim the skies; newer and heavier Nieuports were developed, although none would have the advantages of the types 11 and 17.

The idea of a sesquiplane was reportedly suggested to Nieuport by the Swiss Franz Schneider several years before the war. Such a design offered strength superior to most contemporary monoplane designs, with less drag than conventional biplanes. When the Établissments Nieuport hired Gustave Delage as chief engineer in January 1914 he began work on a racer with the "wing-and-a-half" configuration. The first two Delage military sesquiplanes were the Nieuport types 10 and 12—both were two-seat tractors and neither was effective as a fighter.

The subsequent 80-horsepower Type 11, originally conceived as prewar

The Nieuport sesquiplanes—the first French fighters capable
of defeating German Fokker monoplanes—influenced aircraft
design by both the Allies and the Central Powers. This Nieuport
23 served with a French squadron at Lido, Italy, for the defense
of Venice. The Type 23 was similar to the Type 17 with changes
in the upper wing structure and machine gun synchronization.
Walter Wright Collection

racer, could be difficult, even dangerous, to fly, and it tended to break up in flight if the lower wing was overstressed. But it was light, fast, and extremely maneuverable—and popular with those who could handle it. The Type 16 was similar, but with a more-powerful, 110-horsepower engine, which made the aircraft extremely nose heavy. To handle the increased power, the larger Type 17 was introduced. Known to French ground troops as "Silver Hawks"—due to their aluminum-doped finish—the Type 17 was the most capable of the Nieuports. The 17*bis* introduced a 130-horsepower engine, more aerodynamic fuselage, and a synchronized Vickers machine gun (in addition to the Lewis gun). Additional Nieuport sesquiplane designs—types 21, 23, 24, 25, and 27—would attempt to extend the company's advantage, although they were quickly eclipsed by other Allied and German models. Still, Nungesser reportedly preferred the Type 24*bis* even into 1918, at a time when far more powerful British and French fighters were available.

Nieuport sesquiplane fighters were produced at several French, Dutch, Italian, Japanese, and Russian factories. Surviving records reveal neither the total numbers of aircraft built nor the first flight dates of each type.

Ni.17*bis* C1 Characteristics

Design:	Nieuport
Crew:	Pilot
Engines:	1 Clerget 9B or 9Z rotary piston; 130 hp
Weights:	
Empty:	825 lb
Maximum takeoff:	1,233 lb
Dimensions:	
Length:	19 ft, 6 in
Wingspan:	27 ft, 3 in
Wing area:	158 sq ft
Height	7 ft
Speeds:	115 mph
Ceiling:	18,000 ft
Range:	2-hour endurance
Armament:	1 Lewis machine gun (fixed); 1 Vickers machine gun (fixed); 8 Le Prieur anti-balloon rockets (mounted on wing struts)

Short 184

The Short 184 was the world's first aircraft designed specifically to launch aerial torpedoes against enemy warships. Although Italian and US naval officers had proposed dropping torpedoes from aircraft, the Royal Naval Air Service is believed to have been the first to accomplish that feat when, on July 28, 1914, civilian pilot Gordon Bell made a successful torpedo drop at Calshot flying a Short S.64 "folder" seaplane. The initial British trials used a 14-inch-diameter, 850-pound Whitehead torpedo. (At the time most "bombers" could carry only about 100 pounds of bombs.)

Subsequently the Royal Navy sponsored development of a torpedo-carrying floatplane, the Short Type 184 biplane—the world's first operational torpedo aircraft. (The designation "Short Type 184" was derived from the producing firm's name and the serial number allocated to the first aircraft. Later the aircraft was also known as the "225," which was the horsepower of its Sunbeam engine; subsequently more powerful engines were fitted to the aircraft.)

Two Short 184s were aboard the seaplane carrier *Ben-My-Chree* when she arrived in the Aegean in August 1915. The planes were initially used for reconnaissance work. On August 11 a Turkish ship was sighted on the north side of the Sea of Marmara; she was to be the victim of history's first airborne torpedo attack. Just before first light of August 12 the *Ben-My-Chree* hoisted out a Short 184 and a 14-inch torpedo was slung under the craft. Flight Comdr. C. H. Edmonds got the heavily loaded plane into the air after a relatively short run, climbed to 800 feet, and headed north.

He sighted his target, a 5,000-ton supply ship, and maneuvered into an attack position. He cut off his engine and glided in for the kill, releasing the torpedo from an altitude of 15 feet and approximately 300 yards from the ship. As he restarted his engine and began to climb, Commander Edmonds saw the torpedo strike the ship, which promptly began to settle in the water.

A victory for naval aviation? No one will ever know for certain as the British submarine E-14 claimed to have torpedoed the Turkish ship just before the seaplane arrived!

More aerial torpedo attacks with Short 184s followed.

A Short 184 was also the only aircraft that participated in the Battle of Jutland on May 31, 1916, the one occasion in which the British Grand Fleet engaged the German High Seas Fleet in World War I. As the British warships maneuvered in the North Sea, the seaplane carrier *Engadine* was ordered to fly off a seaplane to investigate a large amount of smoke seen in the distance. A Short 184 was soon in the air. Flight Lt. F. J. Rutland and his observer, Asst. Paymaster G. S. Trewin, flew toward the smoke and sighted several German light cruisers and destroyers. Rutland radioed three sighting reports to the *Engadine* and continued to shadow the German ships until a broken fuel line forced him to alight on the water. The pilot was able to repair the line and return to his ship. The force commander did not request additional reconnaissance, in part because of the delays in the information from the *Engadine* reaching the flagship.

That was the first occasion on which an aircraft communicated with warships during a fleet action.

After entering naval service in 1915, Short 184s were in action from British and French bases, throughout the Mediterranean and Aegean Seas, and the Red Sea. They were used for recce missions and as torpedo and bombing aircraft, and even carried out at least one night-bombing mission. It was also one of the most numerous aircraft flown by the Royal Navy with more than 900 produced by a number of firms. The Royal Flying Corps also flew it, and a small number were sold to Chile, Estonia, Greece, and Japan. (After the war a few were converted to civilian five-seaters.)

The Short 184 was a direct development of the Circuit of Britain Short S.68 seaplane of 1913, the principal change being a larger engine, an improved wing-folding arrangement (for shipboard stowage), and large, compartmented twin sprung floats. The fuselage was designed to enable easy access to the engine. The aircraft was given a distinctive silhouette by the large radiator mounted above the engine, although a late-production, 260-horsepower aircraft—known as "the Dover"—dispensed with this feature and was fitted with an automobile-type radiator behind the propeller. Most of the fuselage and the wings were fabric covered. Cylindrical air bags served as wingtip floats. In most aircraft the pilot sat in the forward cockpit and the observer-gunner in the second, with a Scarff ring mounting a Lewis gun.

There were several modifications to the aircraft. Several had wheels fitted to their floats for deck launches from ships, and one had the forward cockpit removed and a bomb bay fitted for nine 65-pound bombs, slung from their noses. Various propeller and engine configurations were provided during the aircraft's large production run.

The Short 184 was the first series-produced aircraft intended to launch torpedoes against enemy warships. The aircraft had an ungainly look, but proved effective in several actions and in the reconnaissance role. The torpedo was carried between the twin floats. The wingtip stabilizing floats and massive tail float are evident. *Imperial War Museum*

The aircraft's popularity and versatility was a harbinger of the Fairey Swordfish.

Short 184 Characteristics (*Data for Sunbeam 260-hp variant*)

Design:	Short Brothers
Crew:	2 (pilot, observer-gunner)
Engines:	1 Sunbeam piston; 225, 240 or 260 hp or 1 Sunbeam Maori III in-line piston; 275 hp or 1 Renault in-line piston; 240 hp
Weights:	
Empty:	3,703 lb
Loaded:	5,363 lb
Dimensions:	
Length:	40 ft, 7 1/2 in
Wingspan:	63 ft, 6 1/4 in
Wing area:	688 sq ft
Height:	13 ft, 6 inch
Speeds:	
Maximum:	84 mph at 6,500 ft
Ceiling:	9,000 ft
Range:	2 3/4-hour endurance
Armament:	1 .303-cal. Lewis machine gun (flexible), 1 14-inch torpedo or 520 lb of bombs

Sikorsky Il'ya Muromets

The Il'ya Muromets was the first four-engine bomber and, in many respects, the most effective bomber of World War I. Developed by aviation genius Igor Sikorsky, the aircraft was a direct development of his *Grand*, the world's first four-engine aircraft, which flew in 1913.

The first Il'ya Muromets flew in January 1914. With Europe arming for war, the Il'ya Muromets was immediately put into production. The first combat mission by an Il'ya Muromets took place on February 15, 1915, when one of the bombers crossed over the German lines to drop 600 pounds of bombs. Several more missions were flown during the next month, both reconnaissance and bombing, with some flights lasting up to four and a half hours.

This success was due not only to the plane's excellent flight characteristics, but also its survivability. Several times German fighters attacked the bombers, with some of the attackers being shot down by the bombers' machine guns. The Russian bombers were damaged by enemy fighters and ground fire, but losses were few. Only three of the large bombers were lost during the war: one to sabotage, one to a crash landing, and the third to enemy fighters, the last on September 25, 1916. That plane—an Il'ya Muromets XVI—shot down or damaged four of the attackers before expending all of its machine gun ammunition. It was then shot down with the loss of all four crewmen. (A few days later a German plane flew over the Russian airfield where the bomber was based, dropping a note with the location of the graves of the Russian fliers—a custom in that war.)

As an example of their ability to sustain damage, in June 1915, one Il'ya Muromets had both engines on one side stopped by hits from enemy fighters while over German territory. Although the captain of the plane was injured, he brought it safely back across the Russian lines. One of the attacking German planes was probably shot down in the engagement. The only major damage sustained from anti-aircraft guns came when the Il'ya Muromets X attacked a railroad station behind German lines. Gunfire severely wounded the pilot, hit the radiators of three of the four engines, severed several wing wires and damaged the wings. The pilot lost consciousness and the bomber went into a nosedive. The copilot, who was in the rear compartment releasing bombs at the time, raced forward and, pushing aside the wounded pilot, took the controls. While gradually losing all three damaged engines, the copilot was still able to fly the plane some 55 miles to land at a Russian base.

In December 1915—one year after the Squadron of Flying Ships had been established—the organization of the squadron was set at 30 heavy bombers and 20 light airplanes (presumably fighter and scout planes) with more than 1,300 officers and enlisted men to fly and maintain the planes, and to operate their base. The squadron operated on several fronts until the Russian Revolution erupted in the fall of 1917. During the political unrest one Il'ya Muromets was sabotaged by revolutionaries, with all four crewmen being killed.

A total of 79 Il'ya Muromets bombers were built and delivered through the end of 1917. About half that number saw action, with the others being used for training and tests, or being prepared for combat operations. Thus, some 40 planes carried out an estimated 440 bombing raids over enemy territory, dropping more than 2,000 bombs of all sizes on enemy targets. On all missions—bombing as well as reconnaissance—the planes carried a camera, providing the Russian Army with some 7,000 valuable aerial photographs.

By 1918 the Bolshevik forces, fighting a civil war on several fronts, controlled the few operational Il'ya Muromets bombers. About a dozen of the bombers supported Red Army operations during the Civil War. The large bombers were particularly effective on low-level missions, dispersing cavalry attacks as well as attacking fixed targets, such as supply depots and railroad stations. The Il'ya Muromets bombers dropped approximately ten tons of bombs on anti-Bolshevik forces during the Civil War (1917–22). The bombers were also used to spread propaganda leaflets, often at the same time they were dropping bombs. The success of these planes was discussed in a memorandum from a field commander dated October 24, 1920, which said, in part, "The Air Staff was quite right to entrust the Il'ya Muromets with both military and civil missions . . . . These aircraft have been flown successfully at all hours and in all weather. . . ."

In 1920 some of the remaining aircraft were pressed into service as civil transports on routes between Moscow and Kharkov, and Sarapul and Yekaterineburg (now Sverdlovsk), carrying mail, passengers, and important freight. The last recorded flight of an Il'ya Muromets was in 1923.

The Il'ya Muromets was designed by the 24-year-old Sikorsky, based on his four-engine *Grand,* a highly successful civilian transport built by the Baltic carriage works in St. Petersburg. The biplane bomber could operate with wheels or skids, and one aircraft was fitted with floats for operational missions with the Navy (all other aircraft were used by the Army).

The airplane generally carried up to 1,100 pounds of bombs although some documents cite a maximum bomb capacity of 1,764 pounds. A report from the US military attaché in Russia in 1915 reported an Il'ya Muromets carrying a 1,425-pound bomb, although the bombs carried during the war normally weighed from $4^1/_2$ to 900 pounds. Bombs were carried in racks under the fuselage and wings. They had a manual release mechanism until 1916, when an electrical release device was fitted. In the fall of 1917 one aircraft was fitted to carry naval mines, but no test flights were carried out.

Other features of the Sikorsky giant were a platform or "bridge" atop the relatively streamlined fuselage, a large pilots' cabin, passenger cabin, and a sleeping cabin with a berth. The cabin space—28 feet long, $5 \, ^1/_4$ feet wide, and $6^1/_2$ feet high—was heated and a toilet was provided. The airplane was fitted with "balconies" in front of and atop the fuselage, and there were provisions for mechanics to leave the cabin and climb out on the wings to service the motors while in flight. The engines incorporated special heating apparatus for starting up in the cold Russian weather.

The first bomber was assembled in late December 1913, and Sikorsky named it Il'ya Muromets for a legendary Russian hero of the tenth century. Test flights in January–March 1914 were successful. On February 11 the Il'ya Muromets took off with crew and passengers numbering 16, plus a dog, probably establishing an aviation record for the number of persons carried aloft. The second Il'ya Muromets was completed by April 1914. On June 18 one of the airplanes remained aloft for a record 6 hours, 33 minutes with seven persons on board.

Improvements, mostly in engines and defensive armament, continued to be made during the production run. Problems in the supply of engines led to a total of 11 different types of engines being used, not all of which were satisfactory. As a partial solution to this problem, the Baltic carriage works began to produce its own airplane engines, with the first ones being delivered late in 1916.

Total Il'ya Muromets production was 80 aircraft of several variants; of those, 32 were V-series aircraft (described below).

During production Sikorsky modified the aircraft to accommodate the added weight of a rear gunner, machine gun, and ammunition by increasing the size of the stabilizer and modifying the rudder arrangement. Up to

A four-engine Il'ya Muromets, the most advanced bomber at the beginning of World War I. This Type E is at Pskov in the summer of 1916. This type carried a crew of eight—two pilots, a flight engineer, and five gunners. Continuous improvements were made in the design during its brief production run with a variety of engines being fitted, even within the same model. *Courtesy J. W. R. Taylor*

eight defensive machine guns were thus mounted in some variants—two Vickers, three Lewis, and three Masden types. The Ye-2 subtype also had a 50-mm quick-firing cannon installed. (The first gun that was fitted in an I.M. bomber in 1914 had been a 37-mm Hotchkiss weapon.) These defensive guns destroyed a large number of attacking German fighters during the course of the war in exchange for the loss of only one Il'ya Muromets to enemy fighters.

Considering the strides made in aviation technology during the war years, the survival of the Il'ya Muromets bombers in an operational role for almost eight years was remarkable.

Il'ya Muromets V Characteristics

Design:	Sikorsky
Crew:	5 (pilot, engineer, 3 gunners)[*]
Engines:	4 Sunbeam in-line piston; 150 hp each (22 aircraft)
Weights:	
Empty:	6,944.5 lb
Loaded:	10,141 lb
Dimensions:	
Length:	57 ft, 5 in
Wingspan:	97 ft, 9 in
Wing area:	2,050 sq ft
Speeds:	
Maximum:	68 mph
Ceiling:	10,000 ft
Range:	4 to 5-hour endurance
Armament:	up to 8 machine guns (flexible) in some aircraft; 1 50-mm cannon (flexible); 1,120 lb of bombs

[*]Crews varied usually with additional gunners being carried.

Sopwith F.1 Camel

One of the most formidable fighters of World War I, the Sopwith Camel's claim of 1,294 enemy aircraft destroyed was a record unmatched by any aircraft of either side. Designed as a faster, more heavily armed successor to Sopwith's Pup and Triplane fighters, the Camel offered its British pilots a highly maneuverable gun platform, although it demanded constant attention. Popularly remembered as the aircraft that shot down the Red Baron, the Camel's contributions to Britain's aerial ascendancy far outweighed the oft-disputed claim of a single aerial victory.

When the Royal Naval Air Service introduced the Camel on the Western Front in the summer of 1917 its pilots found an aircraft with dangerous tendencies, capable of slipping into a spin without warning, with a nose that dropped quickly in right-hand turns, and rose just as quickly in left-hand turns. Moreover, the landing speed was high. Those pilots comfortable with the more stable S.E.5a, Sopwith Pups, Sopwith Triplanes, or Sopwith $1^1/_2$ Strutters were faced with the inherently unstable Camel.

But once mastered the Camel was a phenomenal fighting machine, extraordinarily maneuverable and powerful, even remaining capable against the best German fighters serving at the war's end more than a year later. Wing Comdr. Norman Macmillan later wrote of the Camel, "Here was a buzzing hornet, a wild thing, burning the air like raw spirit fires the throat."

In the Camel's first combat five British naval pilots attacked 16 German Gotha bombers on July 4, 1917, claiming one shot down in flames, and another driven down out of control. The Camel went on to also serve with distinction in the Royal Flying Corps, where 12 operational squadrons were equipped with the type by the end of 1917. Over France, two Camel squadrons shared six German aircraft destroyed on a single patrol on March 22, 1918. Two days later, Capt. J. L. Trollope claimed six victories on a single patrol. Capt. H. W. Woollett had a similar success on April 12.

Back in England, No. 44 Squadron employed the Camel as a night fighter. On the night of December 18–19, 1917, one of the squadron's

Camels forced down a German Gotha bomber—the first bomber defeated by a night fighter over Britain. Just over a month later, on January 28–29, 1918, a pair of No. 44 Squadron Camels shot down a second Gotha for the first direct nocturnal destruction of an enemy airplane. Other Camels were used as "trench fighters," mounting light bombs and downward-firing machine guns to support ground operations on the Western Front.

Camels also served at sea. On July 19, 1918, seven Camels from the British aircraft carrier *Furious,* each armed with two 50-pound bombs, launched against the German airship hangars at Tondern. Only two aircraft were able to drop their bombs, but they destroyed two zeppelin sheds and, stored within those sheds, the naval Zeppelins *L.54* and *L.60.* (Fearing future attacks, the Germans moved their airships to less vulnerable bases, thereafter using Tondern only as an emergency landing ground.) Other Camels were launched from towed lighters to counter German raiders over the North Sea. On August 11, 1918, one of these Camels destroyed the Zeppelin *L.53,* the last German airship to be shot down during the war.

Development of the Camel began in late 1916. British fighters were being eclipsed by newer German designs, leading the Sopwith firm to develop a high-performance aircraft that could quickly enter production. Working around a series of French and British rotary engines, the Sopwith F.1 (which, officially, was never called the Camel) had twin Vickers machine guns, synchronized to fire through the propeller arc. To speed production, the biplane's upper wing was designed without dihedral, with the lower wing dihedral doubled in compensation. The first flight was late in December 1916, with production deliveries beginning the following May. Final production figures are unknown, but delivery estimates suggest that approximately 5,600 Camels were completed (several hundred more than the approximately 5,200 S.E.5s and S.E.5As and just over 5,300 Bristol F.2B fighters).

By early 1919 the Camel was withdrawn from frontline service, and was replaced by the Sopwith Snipe, an aircraft that exceeded the Camel's virtues while eliminating most of its vices.

The Sopwith Camel was the most effective Allied fighter of World War I. The 2F.1 variant seen here was designed for Royal Navy shipboard use, particularly for anti-Zeppelin operations. Powered by a Bentley rotary engine, the 2F.1 was armed with a single fixed Vickers machine gun and an over-wing Lewis gun. *Flight International*

F.1 Camel Characteristics

Design:	Sopwith
Crew:	Pilot
Engines:	1 Clerget 9B 9-cylinder rotary piston; 130 hp
Weights:	
Empty:	929 lb
Maximum takeoff:	1,453 lb
Dimensions:	
Length:	18 ft, 9 in
Wingspan:	28 ft
Wing area:	231 sq ft
Height:	8 ft, 6 in
Speeds:	
Maximum:	117 mph
Ceiling:	19,000 ft
Range:	2 1/2-hour endurance
Armament:	2 .303-cal. Vickers machine guns (fixed); 4 25-lb bombs

Three

Between the Wars

Military aircraft development and production were greatly inhibited in the period between the world wars because of belief that the "Great War" had been—in the words of President Woodrow Wilson—"the war to end all wars" and the economic situation in several European countries that soon evolved into a world-wide depression. Most of Europe, financially depleted and rebuilding, had little effort to spare for military aircraft and the United States concentrated aviation resources on the development of commercial transport aircraft.

The vanquished Germany—forbidden military aircraft under the Treaty of Versailles—attempted to reinstitute aviation development on a clandestine basis in neutral Holland and (later) communist Russia (which became the Union of Soviet Socialist Republics in 1924). In the USSR, recovering from Revolution and Civil War, the spark of aviation development was rekindled. Despite many bureaucratic problems and resource limitations, a number of aircraft designers persevered and several outstanding aircraft emerged in this period; described below are the products of two highly innovative Russian designers, Nikolai N. Polikarpov and Andrei N. Tupolev. There were others.

Although Tupolev's design bureau produced a variety of designs for different types of aircraft (and small naval craft), he was particularly noted for

Aviation exploits between the world wars captured the imagination of the public around the world and led to popular and political support for aviation development. Among the most impressive flights were those of the Italian Air Force's Savoia-Marchetti S.55s to the New World, especially the formation of 24 S.55X aircraft led by Gen. Italo Balbo that flew from Italy to Chicago. Here the aircraft await takeoff from Orbetello Bay on the morning of July 1, 1933. *Crociera Aerea Del Decennale*

his large aircraft, which were primarily bombers. Further, after two decades of converting civilian-type aircraft to warplanes, Tupolev refined to a fine art the development of civil aircraft from military designs.

His design colleague L. L. Kerber wrote in *Stalin's Aviation Gulag* that Tupolev explained, "I think that this can be done by borrowing the wing, chassis, tail section, and sometimes even the cockpit and engine-propeller unit from a previous military airplane that has undergone severe operational testing, and by manufacturing a new fuselage." Tupolev successfully used the procedure to develop several passenger aircraft, and that methodology continued for Soviet civil aircraft design well into the jet era.

The bomber ruled in the period between the wars. Leading prophets of air power in the 1920s, principally Gen. Giulio Douhet of Italy, America's William (Billy) Mitchell, and Britain's Sir Hugh Trenchard, espoused victory through destroying enemy morale by the bombing of cities. These views were embraced by many national leaders who sought some alternative to the lengthy, bloody trench warfare that had characterized the Western Front in World War I, or the massive casualties suffered by the tsarist armies on Germany's Eastern Front.

The possibility of attacks on British cities by bombers dispatched by France and, after the rise of Adolf Hitler, by Germany, caused consternation in Britain. British Prime Minister Stanley Baldwin, speaking in the House of Commons in late 1932, declared: "In the next war you will find any town within reach of an airdrome can be bombed within the first five minutes of war to an extent inconceivable in the last war and the question is whose morale will be shattered quickest by preliminary bombing . . . . The bomber will always get through. . . ."

Thus, many nations sponsored the development of air forces with strong bomber components, especially Britain, the United States, and Germany. Accordingly, five of the eight aircraft described in this chapter are bombers.

In Britain the development of fighters was largely ignored by the Royal Air Force during the interwar period. That attitude in the United States led to the country entering World War II with its principal fighter, the P-40 Warhawk, being described by the head of Army aviation as little more than an advanced training plane. Germany, however, although stressing the development of high-speed bombers, did produce excellent single- and twin-engine fighter aircraft.

The effectiveness of German aircraft designs was demonstrated in the Spanish Civil War (1936–39), with German-designed transports, dive-bombers, and fighters all having major roles in the conflict. Similarly, the Japanese aviation industry produced several advanced aircraft, based in part on lesson from several campaigns against China in the 1930s. Soviet-supplied fighters and Japanese aircraft clashed in these conflicts, with Japan—especially the Japanese Navy—sponsoring the development of several advanced warplanes, most notably the G4M Betty long-range bomber and the A6M Zero or Zeke fighter.

By the late 1930s it was obvious to anyone who read newspapers or listened to news and commentary on the radio that another major war was in the offing. Aircraft would have a major role in any future conflict.

Curtiss O-52 Owl

In the US Army of the 1920s and 1930s observation aircraft were expected to be the eyes of the ground forces, reporting directly to ground commanders on enemy troop positions and spotting friendly artillery fire. The importance of observation aircraft to the US Army was reflected in the numbers ordered. A War Department study completed a few weeks before the attack on Pearl Harbor revealed that between 1930 and 1939, Army planners had ordered 784 observation aircraft compared to 14 photographic aircraft, 1,030 attack aircraft, 690 medium bombers, and 51 heavy bombers—clearly a procurement policy that favored close support aircraft.

However, as a class, observation aircraft were doomed to failure in modern warfare. Their lack of speed and maneuverability would have left them as easy prey for enemy fighters, and the new mobility of World War II ground combat would have required them to attempt reconnaissance deep beyond enemy lines to provide useful intelligence information.

The Curtiss O-52 Owl represented the end of 20 years of Army planning to refight World War I. As the German Blitzkrieg rolled through Europe, the US Army ordered 203 O-52s without even testing a prototype. The first aircraft flew in February 1941, and several Owls participated in

The Curtiss O-52 Owl was the last of the US Army's observation line—and was obsolete before it entered service. This February 1941 factory photograph shows a new O-52 with the rear decking lowered to increase the gunner's field of fire, the camera doors open beneath the fuselage, the pilot's access hatch propped up below the wing, and the MG ammunition door open in the nose. *Walter Wright Collection*

O-52 Characteristics

Design:	Curtiss
Crew:	3 (pilot, observer-gunner)
Engines:	1 Pratt & Whitney R-1340-51 radial piston; 600 hp
Weights:	
Loaded:	5,364 lb
Dimensions:	
Length:	26 ft, 4 $\frac{3}{4}$ in
Wingspan:	40 ft, 9 $\frac{1}{2}$ in
Wing area:	210.4 sq ft
Height:	9 ft, 11 $\frac{1}{2}$ in
Speeds:	
Maximum:	215 mph
Cruise:	169 mph
Ceiling:	23,200 ft
Range:	455 miles
Armament:	2 .30-cal MG (1 fixed, 1 flexible)

the Second Army maneuvers in Tennessee that June. The Owl's inability to operate from unprepared landing sites and limitations when flying near ground forces in the Tennessee mountains opened the door for a newer, lighter class of observation aircraft based on Piper Cubs and similar lightweight aircraft.

The Owl was a two-seat, high-wing, monoplane of stressed skin aluminum construction. The landing gear was retracted manually into the forward fuselage, using a technique proven on several Curtiss Navy designs, including the Navy's SBC Helldiver. The pilot and observer shared a long "greenhouse," with a fold-down rear turtledeck providing an exceptional field of fire for the rear machine gun. It was, in many ways, fortunate that the Owl found itself without a combat mission, as its performance fell short of the aircraft it was intended to replace. With a crew of three—allowing the observer to perform his duties while the gunner attempted to ward off enemy fighters—the earlier 239 North American O-47s serving in Army and National Guard observation squadrons could fly higher, faster, and farther.

Although the O-series aircraft had no offensive armament, they generally carried a single forward-firing light machine gun and a second rear-facing flexible weapon for defensive purposes. (Similar aircraft equipped with bomb racks and sights were assigned to attack aviation units, and carried A-series designations.)

At a program cost of $10.3 million, the O-52 represented a significant engineering failure in a completely failed mission concept.

Hawker Hart

When introduced in 1928, Britain's Hawker Hart light bomber was a phenomenon and an embarrassment. At a time when the newest British fighters posted top speeds near 175 miles per hour, the two-seat Hart reached 184 miles per hour. The Hart was subsequently developed for a number of roles, and in all of its variants was the most widely produced British aircraft of the interwar period.

In operational training, the Harts could not be caught by opposing interceptors until the Royal Air Force purchased the Hawker Demon, a fighter version of the Hart, and the Hawker Fury, a single-seat fighter developed with experience gained from the Hart's design. In June 1932 Harts took both first and third places in the Headquarters Race at the annual Hendon RAF Display.

RAF Harts also saw limited combat, flying bombing missions during tribal warfare on India's Northwest Frontier in May 1932. Nine export Harts were also flown by Sweden in support of Finland during the Winter War between Finland and the USSR in November 1939. The Swedish Harts flew reconnaissance, bombing missions, and night intruder attacks, and would be the only Harts to see combat in World War II.

Hawker's work on the Hart began with the goal of producing an aircraft with a maximum speed of only 160 miles per hour. The use of a new, light-

The world's fastest combat aircraft of the late 1920s, the Hawker Hart light bomber gave rise to a family of British aircraft that remained in production until 1937. With folding wings for shipboard storage, this carrier-based fleet spotter and reconnaissance version of the Hart was known as the Osprey. *Hawker Siddeley Aviation*

Hart I Bomber Characteristics

Design:	Hawker
Crew:	2 (pilot, observer-gunner)
Engines:	1 Rolls-Royce Kestrel IB V-12 in-line piston; 525 hp
Weights:	
Empty:	2,530 lb
Maximum takeoff:	4,554 lb
Dimensions:	
Length:	29 ft, 4 in
Wingspan:	37 ft, 3 in
Wing area:	348 sq ft
Height:	10 ft, 5 in
Speed:	
Maximum:	184 mph
Ceiling:	22,800 ft
Range:	430 miles
Armament:	1 .303-cal Vickers MG (fixed); 1 .303-cal Lewis MG (flexible); 2 250-lb bombs

weight steel wing spar, revision of the interplane struts and landing gear, a new fuel system, and the availability of lighter, more powerful engines led to a remarkably clean, speedy aircraft. The aircraft was flown by a pilot and observer-gunner, the latter with a machine gun on a Scarff ring.

Following the first flight in June 1928, Hart trials and evaluation were kept in the strictest secrecy for over a year. With no high-speed aircraft available to help pilots make the transition into the hot new bomber, the RAF purchased a number of unarmed, dual-control Hart Trainers. The total Hart bomber and trainer production was 992 aircraft.

The development of the Hart into a two-seat fighter resulted in the production of 303 Hawker Demons (64 of which were built for a Royal Australian Air Force order). Efforts to develop a Hart as a two-seat Fleet Spotter/Reconnaissance aircraft for aircraft carrier and float-equipped operation led to the Hawker Osprey, of which 133 were built. The RAF's need for a high-speed Army cooperation aircraft led to the development of the Hawker Audax (775 built). Development of the Hart and Audax for service in the Near East resulted in the Hawker Hardy, with 47 produced.

The Audax and Hardy were the only Hart descendants to see combat, flying against the Italians in East Africa in 1940 and against the Iraqis—who had purchased their own versions of the Audax—during the May 1941 Iraqi revolt. As the RAF began to rebuild in the mid-1930s, the Hart saw one further development—the Hawker Hind. Re-engined, with many detail and fitting changes, the Hind had the advantage of quick, inexpensive production. When the last of 527 Hinds rolled out in 1937, it was the last biplane bomber delivered to the RAF. In all, a between-war record 2,777 Hart and Hart variations had been produced.

Martin MB-2

The US Army's first standard heavy bomber, the Martin MB-2—also designated NBS-1—was used by the post-World War I Air Service to develop bombing tactics and strategy, and technical requirements. The aircraft will always be part of Air Force legend as the aircraft that sank the German battleship *Ostfriesland*.

The first Martin MB-2s—redesignated NBS-1 for Night Bomber, Short range—entered service with the 2d Bomb Group in 1921 and was available for the famous attacks on captured German warships that July. Brig. Gen. Billy Mitchell had in early 1920 declared that air attack—in conjunction with submarines to finish off the cripples—"will render surface craft incapable of operating to the same extent that they have heretofore, if it does not entirely drive them off the surface of the water." During a congressional hearing a few days later, Mitchell challenged the Navy to test his claim.

The Navy, already impressed by aircraft and pursuing a measured aviation program, had scheduled explosive tests against surrendered German warships. Officially, the tests were jointly run by the US Army and Navy to evaluate the effects of different explosives. The first target, a submarine, was dispatched by naval aircraft. On July 13, 1921, after Army SE-5s attacked the German destroyer *G-102* with machine guns and light bombs, 16 MB-2 raced in with 300-pound bombs. As the second run began, the destroyer sank. The cruiser *Frankfurt* was next, sinking 25 minutes after an attack with 600-pound bombs on July 18.

The climax of the bombing tests came on July 20–21 with air attacks on the *Ostfriesland,* a 22,800-ton German battleship completed in 1911. The *Ostfriesland* was considered the equal of any warship afloat although she had been damaged at the Battle of Jutland. This test began with Navy and Marine aircraft dropping 34 small bombs, six of which hit the battleship. Before a scheduled inspection of damage to the ship could be made, Army planes flew over to release a barrage of 600-pound bombs. Two bombs scored direct hits. After this attack the ship was inspected and no appreciable damage was found belowdecks.

On the morning of July 21 eight Army MB-2 bombers attacked the *Ostfriesland.* Each plane carried two 1,000-pound bombs, the largest aerial weapons in use at that time. The first bomb scored a direct hit. Five more bombs fell—three scoring direct hits—before the planes ceased their attack. An inspection party found the ship was still seaworthy and capable of absorbing more punishment.

That afternoon the Army bombers returned, each carrying a 2,000-pound bomb. This was the largest bomb yet carried by an aircraft. It had been developed in just four months at the specific request of General Mitchell. One bomb struck the battleship and glanced off; two more were near misses. Then one bomb scored a direct hit, fatally damaging the ship. She sank later in the day.

To the public, Mitchell appeared to have defeated both the battleship and the admirals. The Navy's protestations that evasive maneuvering and anti-aircraft fire could defend against attacks by high-altitude bombers would eventually be corroborated at the Battle of Midway (1942), when 26 B-17 Flying Fortress bombers failed to make a single hit on the Japanese fleet.

The September 5, 1923, bombing trials of the unfinished battleships *New Jersey* and *Virginia* were ordered to begin from 10,000 feet, but the MB-2 could not bomb from that altitude. By reworking six supercharged aircraft, the 2d Bomb Group proved up to the task, and both ships were sunk with 2,000-pound and 1,100-pound bombs.

The Martin MB-2 was the first US-developed bomber to enter production. Redesignated NBS-1 by the Army, 50 of the night bombers were built by Curtiss, including these two from the 2d Bomb Group seen during 1926 maneuvers. The MB-2 was used by Brig. Gen. William (Billy) Mitchell in his efforts to demonstrate the effectiveness of bombers against warships. *US Air Force*

MB-2 Characteristics

Design:	Martin
Crew:	4 (pilot, navigator-gunner, mechanic-gunner, radio operator-gunner)
Engines:	2 Liberty V-12 in-line piston; 420 hp each
Weights:	
Empty:	7,269 lb
Maximum takeoff:	12,064 lb
Dimensions:	
Length:	42 ft, 8 in
Wingspan:	74 ft, 2 in
Wing area:	1,121 sq ft
Height:	14 ft, 8 in
Speeds:	
Maximum:	101 mph
Cruise:	91 mph
Ceiling:	
Combat:	8,500 ft
Maximum:	10,000 ft
Range:	550 miles
Armament:	5 .30-cal Lewis MG (flexible; 2 in nose and dorsal positions; 1 beneath fuselage); 3,000 lb of bombs

Early in 1923, the Fairfield Depot (Ohio) began shipping night flying kits—landing lights, running lights, parachute flares—to modify 65 MB-2s. The new equipment was used at sunset on October 10, 1924, when nine aircraft of the 2d Bomb Group flew from Langley Field, Virginia, to Mitchel Field, New York, in a mass, cross-country night deployment. One aircraft arrived late, but all were available for missions the next morning.

Other MB-2s bombed ice jams on Platte River in Kansas in March 1924, saving railroad bridges down river from damage. Other tests in April 1926 evaluated bomber missions and fighter interception in a series of tactical problems. In 1926 the new Army Air Corps sought to declare MB-2/NBS-1 as limited standard—obsolete, but still useful for support—so that they would not be counted against the congressional limit of 1,800 planes for the Army.

Replacement Curtiss Condors and Keystone bombers began arriving in 1927, and the last MB-2s left service in 1928.

The MB-2 grew out of Martin's 1918 GMB (also called MB-1) bomber. Only ten GMBs were built. In the MB-2, the GMB's tail and wood fuselage were fitted with larger wings and revised landing gear, and a new fuel system and power plant installation. The wings hinged outboard of the engines for storage. Bombs were carried internally and on external racks.

The first MB-2 delivery was in 1920, although the date of the first flight was not recorded. As a night bomber, the MB-2 sacrificed speed and maneuverability for a larger bomb load. Twenty MB-2s were ordered from Martin in 1920, with 35 more—as NBS-1—from Lowe, Willard, and Fowler (LWF), 50 from Curtiss (20 with turbosuperchargers), and 25 from Aeromarine.

Pitcairn OP/YG-2

The first rotary-wing aircraft to be seriously evaluated by the world's air forces was the Pitcairn autogiro. It obtained lift with a horizontal propeller—or rotor—that drew energy from the air stream rather than the aircraft's engine. Although the engine could be connected to the rotor during takeoff or landing, in flight the engine was geared to a conventional propeller for forward motion. A ground speed of about 30 miles per hour was needed to create an airflow over the rotor blades to maintain flight. Thus, if wind conditions were right, the autogiro could take off and land vertically, but could not hover.

The US Navy, Marine Corps, and Army Air Corps evaluated the Pitcairn autogiro during the 1930s. The Navy acquired three XOP-1 autogiros in 1931. One was tested aboard the pioneer aircraft carrier *Langley* on September 23, 1931. The following June one of the autogiros was sent to Nicaragua for use by the Marine expeditionary force policing the guerrilla-infested mountain and jungle areas of that country. Assigned to Marine utility squadron VJ-6M, the autogiro operated without difficulty. However, it lacked the range for worthwhile work and could lift a payload of only 50 pounds beyond a pilot and passenger. Marine historian Robert Debs Heinl, Jr. referred to the autogiro as an "exasperating contraption" in recounting the experience in Nicaragua. It was rejected for further Marine service.

In 1935 the Navy had Pitcairn remove the wings from one autogiro, which, redesignated OP-2, flew with only the rotor for lift, a harbinger of the helicopter. The Marines also evaluated this wingless autogiro.

There was no serious effort by the Navy or Marine Corps to operate the novelty aircraft from carriers because of the normal short takeoff and landing characteristics of carrier aircraft and the severely limited performance of autogiros. However, the autogiro tests on the *Langley* and in Nicaragua were the portent of later amphibious warfare techniques employing helicopters.

The US Army acquired a Pitcairn autogiro designated YG-2 and a similar Kellett YG-1 in 1936 to determine the value of an autogiro for observation and artillery spotting. These aircraft were flown in competition and, subsequently the Army procured additional Kellett aircraft to serve as test-beds for rotary-wing development, but there was no large-scale procurement.

Britain's Royal Air Force acquired seven of the Pitcairn autogiros during World War II, of which three were lost at sea in 1942 while being shipped to England. Autogiros of other designs were flown by several countries in military and civilian roles, with Italy and Britain carrying out shipboard trials of autogiros in the 1930s.

The Pitcairn autogiros were based on the design of Juan de la Cierva, a Spaniard who successfully flew a rotary-wing aircraft near Madrid in 1923. That was the progenitor for some 500 autogiros built in Western countries in the 1930s and early 1940s. (The Soviets developed their own line of autogiros.)

The Pitcairn firm—established by Harold F. Pitcairn, founder of Eastern Airways (later Eastern Air Lines)—brought a Cierva autogiro to the United States in 1928. Combining Cierva licenses with their own designs, Pitcairn produced an autogiro with a standard aircraft fuselage and radial engine, with conventional tail surfaces. Stub wings were fitted, angled up

The Pitcairn OP-1 autogiro was evaluated by the US Navy and
Marine Corps in the 1930s, with the Army also flying one with the
designation YG-2. The Navy's trails included carrier operations
from the USS *Langley*, while the Marines flew one in counter-
guerrilla operations in Central America. The autogiro did not enter
service in significant numbers with any air force. *US Navy*

at their extremities. Above the open cockpit was a tripod-supported, three-blade rotor. The aircraft could carry a pilot and observer.

The autogiro lost favor when the practical helicopter appeared in the late 1930s, as those aircraft could hover and had considerably more flexibility.

OP-2 Characteristics

Design:	Pitcairn
Crew:	Pilot + 1 passenger
Engines:	1 Wright R-975-E radial piston; 420 hp
Weights:	
Loaded:	3,057 lb
Dimensions:	
Length:	23 ft, 1 in
Rotor diameter:	30 ft, 3 in
Speed:	
Maximum:	115 mph
Armament:	None

Polikarpov I-16

The bullet-shaped Polikarpov I-16 was probably the best-known Soviet fighter of the early part of World War II. It was a radical design for its time, and although obsolete by the start of the European War, it was an effective fighter until retired from frontline service late in 1942. The I-16 was highly maneuverable, rugged, and fast.

Production of the I-16 was ordered immediately after the prototype's flight trials and deliveries to Soviet Air Force squadrons began in the second half of 1934. It was clearly superior in performance to all foreign contemporaries. This was demonstrated when I-16s fought on the Republican side in the Spanish Civil War (1936–39). The Republicans called the I-16 *Mosca* (Fly) whereas their opponents, the Nationalists supported by Nazi Germany and Fascist Italy, called it *Rata* (Rat).

Initially the I-16 easily defeated Spanish and German fighters but had difficulties countering the highly maneuverable Italian Fiat C.R.32 in dog fights. Air combat in Spain also demonstrated the firepower limitations of the early I-16s, which had only two 7.62-mm ShKAS machine guns. Two additional 7.62-mm guns were added, as were 20-mm cannon in later models. Problems with the sliding canopy led to subsequent aircraft having an open cockpit. When the improved I-16 Type 10 fighters reached Spain in late 1937 they were confronted by the new Messerschmitt Bf 109B fighters. A total of 475 I-16 fighters were shipped to Spain during the war.

In 1937 the Soviets began supplying I-16s—with "volunteer" pilots—to Nationalist China in their conflict against the Japanese. The I-16 next saw combat over the Mongolian-Manchurian border as Soviet and Japanese forces fought a series of battles in 1938–39. The aircraft was widely used in the Soviet-Finnish conflict of 1939–40. When Germany attacked the Soviet Union in June 1941, the I-16 was the primary Soviet fighter, although it was outperformed by the Bf 109E and 109F. Nevertheless, the I-16 remained in first-line service until the end of 1942—a long career for a fighter that first flew a decade earlier.

The aircraft was conceived in 1932 while N. N. Polikarpov was interned by the NKVD, the state security organ. The prototype flew on December 31, 1933, but its performance was lackluster. However, fitting an imported American Cyclone engine greatly improved performance and cleared the aircraft for production. Through early 1940 just over 7,000 single-seat and 1,639 two-seat aircraft were built.

A low-wing monoplane, the I-16 had a radial engine with a large propeller spinner, a massive wing set well forward, and an open cockpit in the later variants. The main undercarriage fully retracted. The training variants had two cockpits, some with the rear cockpit having a plywood cover for blind flying. The term "Tip" (type) was used to indicate modifications.

The aircraft had a maximum speed of 326 miles per hour. Standard armament in later aircraft (Tip 27) was two 20-mm cannon and two 7.62-mm machine guns; small bombs or rockets could be carried under the wings of some aircraft. Drop tanks could be carried.

The Polikarpov I-16 performed admirably in several conflicts of the 1930s and against the Luftwaffe until the end of 1942. The fighter was easily identified by its "bullet" shape and large propeller spinner. Its long and successful career was unique for a fighter designed in 1932–33, testimony to the genius of N. N. Polikarpov, who designed the fighter while in prison! *Imperial War Museum*

I-16 Tip 24 Characteristics

Design:	Polikarpov
Crew:	Pilot
Engines:	1 Shvetsov M-63 radial piston; 930 hp
Weights:	
Empty:	3,252 lb
Loaded:	4,215 lb
Dimensions:	
Length:	20 ft, 1 $^1/_3$ in
Wingspan:	29 ft, 1 $^1/_2$ in
Wing area:	160 sq ft
Height:	7 ft, 9 $^3/_4$ in
Speed:	
Maximum:	304 mph at 15,750 ft
Range:	375 miles
Armament:	4 7.62-mm MG (fixed); 2 1,102-lb bombs

Savoia-Marchetti S.55

The Savoia-Marchetti S.55 was one of the most advanced—and radical—flying boats of the 1920s and 1930s. Designed as a torpedo plane, it achieved international fame for its trans-Atlantic flights.

Following its first flight in 1924 the Italian Air Force lost interest in the aircraft. By 1925 a civilian variant was flying a Brindisi-to-Constantinople (Istanbul) route. In 1926 the S.55 set 14 world records for speed, altitude, and distance. The Italian military quickly regained interest in the high-performance aircraft and in 1926 a contract was placed for 14 improved S.55A aircraft; more orders followed.

On February 13, 1927, more than three months before Charles Lindbergh's nonstop, solo flight across the North Atlantic, Italian lieutenant colonels Francesco de Pinedo and Carlo del Prete took off in an S.55 from Sesto Calende, Italy, and flew almost 30,000 miles around the Atlantic Ocean in 193 flying hours, making just over 50 stops—including Rio de Janeiro, Buenos Aires, and New York City. The historic goodwill tour took four months.

In 1930 the Italian air minister, Gen. Italo Balbo, commanded a flight of 12 S.55A aircraft from Rome to Rio de Janeiro, making the first mass flight across the South Atlantic. Three years later, in 1933, Balbo led a formation of 24 S.55X variants from Orbetello, Italy, to Chicago, flying over the Alps and via Iceland, Greenland, and Labrador, to attend the Century of Progress Exposition. The flight took just over 48 hours, with the aircraft maintaining a tight "Vee" formation during the entire flight. The planes returned to Italy via New York City. (Pilots still refer to a large formation of aircraft as a "Balbo.")

The S.55 had twin hulls, in which passengers could be carried, connected by a high wing. Two piston engines were mounted in tandem above the wing. The pilot and copilot sat side-by-side in an open cockpit faired into the thick center section of the high wing. The tail assembly, with two fins and three rudders, was mounted on lattice extensions of the single-step boat hulls. A torpedo or bombs could be carried in the military variants beneath the wing, between the twin hulls. The fuselage and wings were fabricated of wood. The water-cooled engines had adjustable-pitch pusher and tractor propellers. The early models had 400-horsepower engines—this was increased in later aircraft.

The S.55C and S.55P civil configurations the aircraft could carry 14 passengers. The enlarged civil S.66 had a similar configuration with three tractor-engines mounted above the wing and carried 18 passengers.

Although the S.55 never released a torpedo or bomb in anger, it attained international fame for its record flights. From an aeronautical viewpoint, the S.55 is remembered for its unique design. More than 200 S.55s were produced for civil and military use.

The Savoia-Marchetti S.55A shown here featured a most
unusual, catamaran hull design and combination pusher-puller
engines. However, the aircraft was an efficient flying machine.
Although designed as a torpedo bomber, it never released a
weapon in anger, but achieved international recognition for its
long-range "political" flights. *Fotographia Mari*

S.55X Characteristics

Design:	Savoia-Marchetti
Crew:	7 (pilot, copilot, 4 gunners, crewman)
Engines:	2 Isotta-Fraschini Asso radial piston; 800 hp each
Weights:	
Empty:	11,460 lb
Loaded	16,975 lb
Dimensions:	
Length:	54 ft, 2 in
Wingspan:	78 ft, 11 in
Wing area:	990 sq ft
Height:	16 ft, 5 in
Speed:	
Maximum:	146.5 mph
Ceiling:	13,776 ft
Range:	2,174 miles
Armament:	4 7.7-mm MG (single flexible mountings in the bow and stern of each hull); 1 torpedo or 4,400 lb of bombs

Tupolev ANT-6/TB-3

For most of the 1930s the world's most advanced heavy bomber was the Soviet ANT-6, designed by Andrei N. Tupolev. The ANT-6—given the military designation TB-3—was an extraordinary accomplishment for its time; at the time, the only aircraft to rival it was the Boeing B-17B Flying Fortress, which entered service in mid-1939. Moreover, although the American bomber could fly slightly higher and much faster, it still carried less than one-half the bomb load of the ANT-6.

The first production ANT-6 flew in January 1932, and Soviet leader Josef Stalin immediately ordered eight additional planes to be available for the May Day military parade. On May 1, 1932, nine of the large planes overflew Moscow's Red Square, followed by 70 twin-engine TB-1 bombers and 86 smaller aircraft—an impressive and inspiring flyover, demonstrating the Soviet leader's great interest in aviation.

Series production followed, reaching a peak in 1933–34, when 50 aircraft per month left two Moscow factories. (By that time the Soviet aviation industry was producing some 1,000 aircraft of all types per year, most of them military.) When production ended in late 1937 a total of 818 of the several models of the ANT-6 had been manufactured. This was a remarkable quantity for a four-engine aircraft in the between-war period. The ANT-6 formed the backbone of Soviet strategic aviation into World War II, flying against Japanese forces in Manchuria, against Finland, and against the Germans, including night attacks on Berlin. The ANT-6 was also employed in the transport and air assault roles. In 1935 an airborne brigade participated in the military maneuvers near Kiev, with 600 paratroopers being dropped by ANT-6 bombers to prepare a landing field for more troops and guns to be flown in. Later that same year an entire army rifle division of about 14,000 men, with their guns and some vehicles, was flown from Moscow to Vladivostok in a demonstration of the mobility provided by the large, bomber-type aircraft.

The most dramatic demonstration of the remarkable progress by the Red army and air force in airborne operations took place in Belorussia in August 1936 when foreign military observers were among the thousands who watched the mass airborne exercise. First ANT-6 aircraft arrived to drop 1,800 paratroopers who again floated down to seize a landing area. They were followed by more bombers that landed another 5,700 troops, with their field guns and equipment. Such an airborne operation was remarkable at the time and provided the impetus for several nations to develop airborne forces.

Some ANT-6 aircraft were allocated to Arctic operations, generally with the civil designation G-2. The most ambitious Arctic flight began in the summer of 1936. An icebreaker carried the expedition to Rudolph Island, the most northerly island in the world (82 degrees North). A vast landing field was carved out of the ice and five aircraft began operating from the ice base on March 21, 1937. Two months later, on May 21, scientists took off from the airfield in an ANT-6 for the North Pole. At 11 A.M. the plane landed some 12 miles from the North Pole. A second G-2 landed on May

25, the third on May 28, and the fourth on June 5. All four returned to the Soviet mainland on June 9.

The development of the ANT-6 began with a December 1925 requirement for an aircraft powered by engines with a total of 2,000 horsepower to lift more than two tons of bombs. Expanding his earlier ANT-4 design, Tupolev developed an all-metal monoplane, with a corrugated aluminum skin, and four engines fitted to the leading edges of the wing.

The prototype ANT-6 was assembled at the Fili works near Moscow and transported by road to Moscow's central aerodrome for flight tests. Passage of the aircraft required overhead power and telephone lines to be taken down. After additional work and preparations, the prototype—powered by four imported Curtiss Conqueror engines, each rated at 600 horsepower—was ready for flight tests on December 22. After the prototype's success, series production was undertaken at aircraft factories No. 22 (Fili) and No. 39 in Moscow. Those aircraft would differ from the prototype mainly in having indigenous M-17 engines with a nominal rating of 500 horsepower, but a maximum, short-duration rating of 730 horsepower. Later aircraft would have the more-powerful M-34 engine and could reach a speed of 276 miles per hour, carrying up to five tons of bombs for short distances. A large, fixed undercarriage was fitted, with the wheels being replaceable by skis for operations from snow-covered airfields and Arctic ice.

The ANT-6 had extensive instrumentation, permitting routine night flights, a necessity in the northern latitudes of the Soviet Union. The ANT-6's normal combat crew was nine. There was space for 12 troops and the aircraft could carry a small tanks (slung under the fuselage) in air assault operations. The G-2 commercial version could accommodate 30 paratroopers.

Improvements were made throughout the ANT-6 production run. More capable and more reliable engines were fitted, improved ShKAS machine guns allowed a reduction in the number of defensive weapons (and hence crewmen) from nine to six in the later models, and in the final (1936) series the corrugated aluminum skin was replaced by a smooth covering.

The ultimate refinement of the ANT-6 design was the four-engine ANT-41, developed under the direction of Viktor Bolkhovitinov at the Zhukovskiy Air Force Academy. Bolkhovitinov's aircraft, the DB-A, had four M-34RN liquid-cooled engines, each rated at 970 horsepower on takeoff. The aircraft had several advanced features, among them a monocoque fuselage with stressed-metal skin. Whereas most earlier large Soviet aircraft had a fuselage built up on frames, with monocoque construction the outer skin carries all or a major part of the stress. The landing gear was semiretractable, with the wheels being raised up into large "pants." The wingspan was $129\frac{1}{2}$ feet and fuselage length of 80 feet. The two prototypes flew in 1936, establishing load-to-altitude records. In its bomber role the aircraft was to carry 6,600 pounds of bombs a distance of 2,800 miles with a maximum takeoff weight of 48,281 pounds. The aircraft did not enter production.

In addition to defensive machine guns, the Soviets undertook *Zveno* fighter-carrying experiments with the ANT-6. The aircraft repeatedly took off carrying four fighters, two mounted above its wings and two suspended under its wings, all of which could be launched in flight. The ANT-6 could also carry a fifth fighter atop the fuselage, but the problems involved in loading that fighter made it operationally impractical.

A further "parasite" fighter concept was evaluated in 1934–35, with test pilot V. A. Stepanchenok *landing* a fighter by hooking onto a retractable hook-and-trapeze fitted to the underside of the ANT-6's fuselage. The fighter could then be carried by the bomber until hostile interceptors were encountered and then released to engage the enemy and return to base. In one *Zveno* series a *Vakhmistrov* (bouquet) of defending fighters was carried, two above the ANT-6 wings, two below, and a fifth on the trapeze, all dramatically released at the same time. When war came the concept was actually used with light bombers being carried by the ANT-6 aircraft. (Design was begun on a specialized aircraft-carrying mother plane, operating fighters without an undercarriage, but the project was never finished.)

The ANT-6 served in the red air force through World War II. Although outdated by the end of the war, the aircraft had achieved an enviable record in combat as well as in peacetime exercises.

The Tupolev ANT-6/TB-3 was the world's most advanced heavy bomber for much of the 1930s. The four-engine monoplane had impressive payload and range, a harbinger of Andrei N. Tupolev's turbojet bombers developed two decades later. The ANT-6 was also used as a transport and paratroop carrier. Here one functions in the latter role during an airborne exercise.

The nose of an ANT-6/TB-3 showing the aircraft's corrugated aluminum skin. This is an M-34R variant with 825-horsepower engines; note the laminated-wood propellers. The bomb aimer's position is visible below the red star; above is a gunner's position. The pilots sat side-by-side in an open cockpit just forward of the wing. The landing gear was fixed.

National Air and Space Museum

ANT-6/TB-3 M-34RN Characteristics

Design:	Tupolev
Crew:	6
Engines:	4 Mikulin M-34RN in-line piston; 820 hp each
Weights:	
Empty:	27,745 lb
Loaded:	41,616 lb
Dimensions:	
Length:	82 ft, 4 $\frac{1}{4}$ in
Wingspan:	137 ft, 1 $\frac{5}{8}$ in
Wing area:	2,524 sq ft
Height:	18 ft, 4 $\frac{1}{2}$ in
Speed:	
Maximum:	152 mph (at sea level)
Ceiling:	25,395 ft
Range:	1,200 miles with 4,400 lb of bombs
Armament:	4 7.62-mm ShKAS MG (flexible in nose, dorsal, tail, and lower rear fuselage positions); 4,410 lb of bombs

Vickers F.B.27 Vimy

Although the Vickers Vimy bomber—named for a battle site in France—arrived too late for service in World War I, it remained in Royal Air Force service for more than a decade, whereas its heavier and more expensive contemporaries were withdrawn from service in the early 1920s. Postwar economics dictated that the lighter Vimy would suffice for Britain's needs as a bomber, transport, ambulance, and (eventually) heavy bomber trainer. Vimys established Great Britain's long reach, claiming the *Daily Mail*'s pre-World War I prize as the first aircraft to fly between North America and the British Isles. They opened the air route between Britain and Australia, and explored airways to Britain's African possessions.

During World War I the British War Office initially saw little of interest in multi-engine bombers, considering them impractical, seeing little value in the bombing of German industrial targets, and, in some cases, questioning the morality of strategic bombing. The Royal Naval Air Service was of a different opinion, having ordered the twin-engine Handley Page O/100, a long-range bomber that began entering service in early 1917. Nor did the Germans share that opinion: on May 25, 1917, German twin-engine aircraft began a daylight bomber campaign against British industrial targets. The War Office, stung into action, ordered a variety of twin-engine prototypes, committing production funds to the Handley Page O/400 (an up-engined version of the O/100), the Handley Page V/1500 (a four-engine giant capable of carrying a 7,500-pound bomb load), the Airco D.H.10 Amiens (a de Havilland-designed medium bomber), and the Vickers Vimy.

Vickers engineers had already been working on preliminary designs for a heavy bomber when approached by the War Office in July 1917. Relying on its experience in steel-frame construction, the company was able to fly the first prototype at the end of November, only four months later. However, troubles and delays with powerplants slowed production. The Rolls-Royce Eagle was eventually selected for use on production aircraft (which would later be designated Vimy Mark IV). The first Eagle-powered Vimy was not delivered to France until October 1918, with the Armistice on November 11 probably saving Berlin from a retaliatory pounding from this aircraft and the few Handley Pages.

The RAF's Vimys, of which 244 were delivered through 1925, served as the primary British heavy bombers and bomber/transports in Great Britain and the Middle East into 1928, and as bomber crew trainers into the mid-1930s. No Vimy ever dropped a bomb in anger. As British doctrine of the 1920s endorsed strategic bombing, the Vimy was the only long-range bomber available with which to develop crews and tactics. The Vimy also led to the RAF's first purpose-designed troop carrier (the Vernon), and placed Vickers at the forefront of British heavy bomber and transport development for 20 years.

The Vimy was assured its place in history when, on June 14–15, 1919, Capt. John Alcock, Lt. Arthur Whitten-Brown, and their two mechanics flew a specially modified, Vickers-owned machine from Newfoundland to Ireland, making the first ever nonstop trans-Atlantic crossing by an aircraft.

The Vimy was an externally braced, three-bay biplane of steel tube and wood framework with plywood and fabric covering. The single pilot sat in an open cockpit, with a gunner/bomb-aimer in the nose and a second gunner aft of the wings. The bomb load, carried internally and on external wing racks, could include 2 230-pound and 18 112-pound bombs.

Vimy Mark IV Characteristics

Design:	Vickers
Crew:	3 (pilot, gunner/bomb-aimer, gunner)
Engines:	2 Rolls-Royce Eagle VIII in-line piston; 360 hp each
Weights:	
Empty:	7,101 lb
Maximum takeoff:	12,500 lb
Dimensions:	
Length:	43 ft, 6 $\frac{1}{2}$ in
Wingspan:	67 ft, 2 in
Wing area:	1,330 sq ft
Height:	15 ft, 3 in
Speeds:	
Maximum:	103 mph
Cruise:	95 mph
Ceiling:	10,500 ft
Range:	900 miles
Armament:	2 .303-cal. Lewis MG (flexible; in nose and amidships); 2,476 lb of bombs

The Vickers Vimy was Britain's standard bomber in the decade following World War I. Along with the de Havilland/Airco D.H.10 Amiens and Handley Page V/1500, the Vimy was developed for the strategic bombing of Germany had World War I continued. The first Vimy was delivered to the RAF units in France a month before the Armistice ending the conflict.

This Vickers Vimy was modified in 1919 for the first nonstop, trans-Atlantic aircraft crossing by RAF Capt. John Alcock, Lt. Arthur Whitten-Brown, and two mechanics on June 14–15, 1919. The aircraft was "nonstandard" and was owned by Vickers, not the RAF. *Imperial War Museum*

Four

World War II: The Axis

Both Germany and Japan entered World War II with excellent combat aircraft. The German Messerschmitt Bf 109 fighter, several high-speed light bombers, and the Ju 87 Stuka dive bomber were able to dominate the skies over Poland, Norway, Denmark, France, and the Netherlands in 1939–40. Similarly, in the Far East–Pacific areas the Japanese A6M Zero (Zeke) fighter, G4M Betty bomber, and D3A Val dive bomber swept aside all aerial opposition, and devastated Allied fleets, both at anchor (e.g., Pearl Harbor) as well as at sea.

However, those periods of air dominance were relatively short-lived, and by 1943 Allied aircraft were generally able to overcome all aerial opposition. In Germany, Adolf Hitler had envisioned a "short" war—one in which weapons that were not available by about 1942 would have no role in the conflict. Nevertheless, German designers and aircraft factories were able to produce some remarkable and outstanding designs during the war. Those included the outstanding Fw 190 fighter; the world's first operation turbojet aircraft, the Me 262; and the world's first—and only—operational rocket aircraft, the Me 163. When considered in the context of other German advanced weapon achievements—such as the V-1 and V-2 missile programs, Type XXI submarines and torpedoes—in the face of limited

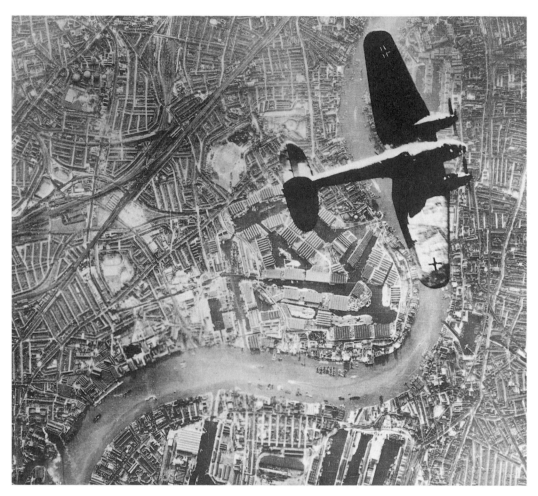

A Heinkel 111 bomber flies over the Thames River during the bombing of London in the summer 1940 air campaign known as the Battle of Britain. Neither Germany nor Japan developed a true strategic bombing force in World War II. However, German medium bombers devastated several European cities, whereas Japanese medium and light bombers inflicted savage ruin on several Chinese cities. *Imperial War Museum*

resources and Allied bombings, the accomplishments of the German aviation industry were impressive.

Similarly, Japan's limited industrial capacity coupled with the loss of oil from the Dutch East Indies from 1943 onward spelled the doom of Japanese military aviation. Although some new designs were introduced after the United States entered the war, few reached series production. Further, the loss of many experienced Japanese Navy pilots in the Guadalcanal-Solomons campaign of 1942–43 and an inadequate pilot training program meant that those aircraft that reached the war zone soon fell to the guns of outstanding American fighters, such as the F6F Hellcat and F4U Corsair. The final blow to the development and production of aircraft in Japan was the massive bombing assault by B-29 Superfortress bombers based in the Marianas from January 1945 (when Maj. Gen. Curtis LeMay took command of the XX Bomber Command) until the Japanese capitulation in mid-August.

In desperation, from October 1944 to the end of the war the Japanese employed thousands of aircraft and pilots—some with little flight training—in suicide attacks against the American warships and amphibious ships that were ravaging the Japanese empire. The Ohka (or "Baka"—Japanese for "fool") reflected the state of Japanese aviation at the end of the war.

Although German aircraft designs of World War II were far more numerous and innovative than those of Japan, several Japanese aircraft are noteworthy. In particular, the M6A1 Seiran floatplane represented the ultimate step in the development of submarine-launched aircraft, whereas the G4M Betty medium bomber and A6M Zero carrier-based fighter must be ranked among the best aircraft of their time.

Allied and Axis aircraft fought under many different circumstances. For example, radar and fighter direction in the Battle of Britain (1940) were critical to the success of the Hurricane and Spitfire fighters against the Bf 109 and the various types of bombers sent over England by the Luftwaffe. Similarly, in the Pacific, the element of surprise greatly contributed to the Japanese success at Pearl Harbor and in the attacks on Luzon a few hours later (1941). In the "Marianas Turkey Shoot" of the Marianas campaign (1944) the limited training of Japanese pilots and the overwhelming number of American F6F Hellcats were critical factors in the outcome of the battle.

Eric M. Brown, a British fighter pilot, test pilot, and author, has undertaken an extensive analysis of relative Allied and Axis aircraft performance in his book *Duels in the Sky*. Brown, who flew more different types of Allied and Axis aircraft than anyone else, and made more carrier landings than anyone in history, attempted to determine the "best" aircraft of the World War II era: "using my own experience test-flying the aircraft to assess how they would have faired against each other in single combat. . . . I will go one step further, pitting friend against friend. If we then compare these cases with actual ones, it should help us determine which was the greatest fighter of World War II."

He then undertook similar analysis for other categories of World War II combat aircraft. His conclusions, ranked in order are:

GREATEST SINGLE-SEAT FIGHTERS
1. Supermarine Spitfire and Focke-Wulf Fw 190
3. Grumman F6F Hellcat
4. North American P-51D Mustang
5. Mitsubishi A6M Zero (Zeke)
6. Hawker Tempest V
7. Kawanishi George 12

GREATEST NAVAL FIGHTERS
1. Grumman F6F Hellcat
2. Mitsubishi A6M Zero (Zeke)
3. Grumman F4F/FM Wildcat
4. Vought F4U Corsair
5. Hawker Sea Hurricane
6. Supermarine Seafire

MOST EFFECTIVE DIVE BOMBERS
1. Junkers Ju 87 Stuka
2. Douglas SBD Dauntless and Aichi D3A Val
4. Blackburn Skua
5. Curtiss SB2C Helldiver

TOP TORPEDO-BOMBERS
1. Fairey Swordfish
2. Grumman TBF/TBM Avenger
3. Nakajima B5N Kate
4. Nakajima B6N Jill

Aichi M6A1 *Seiran*

Beginning in World War I, several navies experimented with employing submarine-launched seaplanes, mainly for reconnaissance. The British, French, German, Japanese, and US navies undertook those efforts but only the Japanese employed such aircraft operationally during World War II.

Beginning in December 1941, Japanese submarines launched floatplanes for reconnaissance missions over areas including Madagascar, Australia, and the Solomon Islands. These aircraft were the Watanabe Type 96 (E9W1), a biplane that entered service in 1938, and the Yokosuka Type 0 (E14Y1), a monoplane that entered service in 1941, the latter given the Allied code name Glen. At the start of the war the Japanese Navy had 12 large I-series submarines that could each carry a single floatplane. More aircraft-carrying submarines were under construction, several of which became operational during the war.

In August 1942 the submarine *I-25* twice launched a Glen from a position off Cape Blanco, Oregon, on incendiary bombing raids of the United States. The Japanese hoped to ignite forest fires. Those were the only aircraft attacks against the continental United States; they inflicted no significant damage and no casualties.

In 1942 the Japanese Navy initiated the *I-400*-class special submarines or *Sen-Toku* (STo). The *I-400*s were the largest nonnuclear submarines ever constructed and each could carry three fully assembled floatplanes. The aircraft were prewarmed in the hangar through a system of circulating heavy lubricating oil while the submarine was submerged. The submarine then surfaced to launch aircraft, with crewmen unfolding the wings and tail surfaces. The three aircraft could be readied for flight and launched within 30 minutes of a submarine coming to the surface.

These submarines were developed specifically to launch aircraft to bomb Washington, D.C., and New York City. While the first units were under construction the changing course of the Pacific War caused the Japanese Navy's leadership to reassign the *I-400* submarines to strike the Panama Canal in an effort to slow the flow of US reinforcements to the Pacific.

The aircraft designed for these submarines was the Aichi M6A1 *Seiran* (Clear Mountain Haze). It was the first floatplane intended for strike missions. The plane became operational in early 1945 and was immediately assigned to two *I-400* class submarines as well as to smaller aircraft-carrying submarines to practice for an attack against the Panama Canal. The planes were finally embarked in the submarines, which departed Japan on July 26, 1945, for a six-plane bombing raid against US warships at Ulithi anchorage in the Caroline Islands. The attack, however, was canceled when Japan surrendered; the planes were destroyed and the submarines returned to Japan. Thus, the M6A1 never flew a combat mission.

The prototype Aichi-built floatplane was completed in November 1943. Seven additional prototypes were followed by 20 production aircraft with improved engines, the last two being trainers fitted with landing gear instead of floats; those two planes were designated M6A1-K *Nanzan* (Southern Mountain).

The M6A1 was a low-wing monoplane with a streamlined fuselage and an in-line (liquid-cooled) engine. Twin floats were cantilever mounted under the wings. The floats could be jettisoned after launch to improve performance. The wings folded backward against the fuselage and horizontal tail surfaces folded downward. With fluorescent paint applied to certain spots on the aircraft to aid assembly in darkness, a trained team of four men could have a plane ready for flight in just six minutes.

The plane could carry one 1,874-pound or two 551-pound bombs or an aerial torpedo under the fuselage. (In the planned attack against the Panama Canal both bombs and torpedoes were to be used.) The plane had a crew of two, with the second crewman firing a flexible 13-mm machine gun from the rear cockpit.

The plane was not assigned an Allied code name because its existence was unknown until after the war.

The Aichi M6A1 *Seiran* marked the end of a line of submarine-launched aircraft that were developed by several countries. The *Seiran* was a large, long-range bomber intended to strike American cities and, subsequently, the Panama Canal. It never flew a combat mission. This is the only survivor of 28 produced, now in the collection of the National Air and Space Museum in Washington, D.C. *Eric Long/National Air and Space Museum*

M6A1 Characteristics

Design:	Aichi
Crew:	2 (pilot, gunner)
Engines:	1 Aichi AE1 Atsuta 30 or 31 in-line piston; 1,400 hp
Weights:	
Empty:	7,277 lb
Loaded:	8,907 lb
Dimensions:	
Length:	38 ft, 2 $\frac{1}{4}$ in
Wingspan:	40 ft, 2 $\frac{3}{4}$ in
Wing area:	290.6 sq ft
Height:	15 ft, $\frac{1}{2}$ in
Speeds:	
Maximum:	295 mph at 17,060 ft
Cruise:	184 mph at 9,845 ft
Ceiling:	32,480 ft
Range:	740 miles
Armament:	1 13-mm machine gun (flexible); 2 551-lb bombs or 1,874-lb bomb or 1 aerial torpedo

Flettner Fl 282 *Kolibi*

The Flettner 282 was part of the massive German helicopter program of World War II and the diminutive aircraft, called *Kolibi* (Hummingbird), was the world's first helicopter to become operational with any military service. The Fl 282 was an advanced version of Anton Flettner's earlier Fl 265, with the later helicopter designed specifically for the anti-submarine role.

The German Navy had sufficient confidence in the Flettner design to order 30 prototypes and 15 preproduction aircraft in spring 1940—before the prototype had flown. After flight trials in 1940–41, which included

This Flettner Fl 282A *Kolibi* was part of the large German helicopter program, which produced a number of designs and a significant number of aircraft. The Fl 282 was developed specifically for anti-submarine warfare from ships. The German Navy
ordered 1,000 production helicopters following 30 prototypes.
The pilot sat forward, the observer sat behind the engine, facing
aft. *National Air and Space Museum*

Fl 282 Characteristics

Design:	Flettner
Crew:	2 (pilot, observer)
Engines:	1 BMW Bramo Sh. 14A piston; 140 hp
Weights:	
Empty:	1,410 lb
Loaded:	2,205 lb
Dimensions:	
Length:	21 ft, 6 $\frac{1}{4}$ in
Rotor diameter:	39 ft, 2 $\frac{7}{8}$ in
Height:	7 ft, 2 $\frac{5}{8}$ in
Speeds:	
Maximum:	93 mph
Cruise:	68 mph
Ceiling:	10,000 ft with 2 crew
Range:	186 miles with pilot; 106 miles with 2 crew
Armament:	None

operations from the cruiser *Köln* during heavy seas in the Baltic, the Fl 282 was ordered into mass production for the German Navy.

The Navy operated the single-seat Fl 282 *Kolibi* helicopters from ships in convoy escort operations in the Aegean and Mediterranean. The unarmed Fl 282 was used for anti-submarine reconnaissance. A production order for 1,000 Fl 282s was placed in 1944 for both the Navy and Air Force, but fewer than 30 preproduction aircraft were finished before the war ended. (The Air Force planned to use the Fl 282 for liaison duties.)

The Fl 282 featured the Flettner design of twin contra-rotating, inter-meshing rotors on two hubs mounted two feet apart, splayed outward 12 degrees and pitched forward 6 degrees. Longitudinal and lateral control were achieved by the unusual method of changing the pitch of both rotors in the corresponding plane; turns were produced by the differing torque of the two rotors.

The helicopter had a steel-tube frame with plywood covering. The later models had a glass-bubble cockpit that could accommodate a passenger, but at the cost of a significant amount of fuel. The reliability of the Fl 282 was demonstrated when one flew for 95 hours without the need for repairs or parts replacement.

The aircraft was designed with rapidly removable rotors, in part to facilitate possible stowage in canisters on submarines. (One Fl 282 was reported to have landed on the deck of a submarine.)

Three Fl 282s survived the war: two were taken to the United States and one to the USSR.

Focke-Wulf FW 190

The Focke-Wulf 190 was the finest single-engine Luftwaffe fighter of World War II. Introduced into combat in mid-1941, the Fw 190 was developed throughout the war, with changes in airframe, engine, and armament keeping the fighter competitive with the best in the Allied arsenals. Fw 190 variants were specialized for every altitude, from ground attack to the above 40,000 feet.

By the summer of 1941, Britain's Spitfire had finally attained superiority over the Luftwaffe's Bf 109. Although subsequent modifications to the Bf 109 generally increased weight and decreased performance, the Spitfire continued to evolve as an exceptional fighter. The deployment of the first group of Fw 190s that summer came as somewhat of a shock to the Royal Air Force—the new German fighter was superior to the then-current Spitfire Mk.V in every performance essential except rate of turn. It would take the up-engined Spitfire Mk.IX to reclaim a performance advantage over the Focke-Wulf, but the new Spitfires did not enter squadron service until July 1942. The balance shifted again in late 1943 with the introduction of the Fw 190D, and yet again with the Griffon-engined Spitfires of 1944.

The Fw 190's speed, ceiling, and maneuverability were a great advantage in fighter-versus-fighter combat, but its heavy armament made it a supreme bomber killer. Known as the "butcher bird" to its crews, the Fw 190 decimated unescorted Eighth Air Force bombers through 1943. It took the introduction of long-range P-51 Mustang escort fighter—both patrolling above the bombers and marauding over German fighter bases—to end the slaughter of American bombers.

The Focke-Wulfs also scored against RAF Bomber Command's night bombers. Guided by ground controllers and searchlights during their *Wilde Sau* (Wild Boar) missions, with some aircraft also equipped with rudimentary radar systems, the Fw 190s were quite successful through late 1943, when replaced by more capable two-seat, twin-engine night fighters. Although many early Fw 190s flew ground attack missions, Fw 190Gs were specially modified for that role. With additional armor and armament, the 190Gs were particularly capable against armored vehicles. In addition, a small number of "long-nosed" Fw 190s, powered by Junkers Jumo V-12 liquid-cooled engines, were developed as high-altitude interceptors. Early models were designated Fw 190D, although high-altitude models introduced after late 1943 were designated Ta 152, reflecting the name of series designer Kurt Tank.

The German Air Ministry first ordered the Focke-Wulf in the autumn of 1937, considering the design a second "iron in the fire" to supplement the Messerschmitt Bf 109. The prototype first flew on June 1, 1939, and was eminently successful, attaining 370 miles per hour in level flight. After correction of developmental problems, a series order for 100 Fw 190A-1 fighters was placed. By mid-1944 German records claimed production of 1,000 Fw 190s per month, with claims of 20,000 delivered by the end of the war. German production records, however, must be read with suspicion—thousands of early models, modified to later standards, were claimed as new production to satisfy Adolf Hitler's demands for increased production.

The Fw 190 was a relatively small, low-wing monoplane with a large radial engine; the wide undercarriage was fully retractable. The first production aircraft, the Fw 190A-1, had four 7.9-mm machine guns; later variants had two machine guns and two 20-mm cannon or four 20-mm cannon. Prototypes included one tank-killing model with seven 30-mm cannon (each fitted with a single round) and another with six 77-mm cannon (firing sabots containing a 45-mm armor-piercing round); another variant provided for upward-firing 30-mm guns triggered by a photoelectric

Germany's best single-engine fighter of World War II was the
Focke-Wulf Fw 190. Initially developed for the air superiority
role, the Fw 190 also flew ground-attack missions and served in
night fighter operations. This Fw 190 G-3 is one of the ground-
attack variants. *Courtesy Robert F. Dorr*

cell as the fighter passed under an Allied bomber. Several planes were also modified to carry wire-guided air-to-air missiles. A few two-seat trainer variants of the Fw 190 were conversions from single-seat aircraft.

Fw 190A-8 Characteristics	
Design:	Focke-Wulf
Crew:	Pilot
Engines:	1 BMW 801D-2 14 cylinder radial piston; 2,100 hp with methanol boost
Weights:	
Empty:	7,000 lb
Maximum takeoff:	10,800 lb
Dimensions:	
Length:	29 ft
Wingspan:	34 ft, 5 1/2 in
Wing area:	197 sq ft
Height:	13 ft
Speeds:	
Maximum:	408 mph
Cruise:	298 mph
Ceiling:	37,400 ft
Range:	500 miles
Armament:	2 13-mm MG 131 machine guns (fixed); 4 20-mm MG 151 cannon (fixed)

Heinkel He 111

The Heinkel He 111 was the most important German bomber of World War II. Never fully up to the many demands placed upon it, the He 111 was often employed simply because it was the most capable aircraft available. Early Luftwaffe reliance on the medium-capacity Heinkel—and lighter aircraft—delayed the search for a true heavy bomber, and when belated attempts to find a heavy bomber failed, He 111 production was further extended.

By World War II standards the He 111 was slow, lightly armed, and vulnerable to modern fighters, as proven during the Battle of Britain when He 111s fell easy victim to RAF Hurricanes and Spitfires.

Like many German warplanes designed in the 1930s, the He 111 was first revealed to the world in the civilian livery of Lufthansa, the German national airline. It was first publicly displayed on January 10, 1936, at Tempelhof Airport in Berlin as a ten-passenger transport that German publicists labeled "the fastest machine in civil aviation." The ostensibly civil aircraft were in fact the prototypes for high-speed medium bombers.

In 1937 He 111Bs were sent to Spain with the Condor Legion; their first combat mission was bombing Republican airfields at Alcala and Barajas on March 9, 1937. From the earliest days of the World War II the He 111 was employed in attacks against the French and British shipping. Subsequently, the aircraft served as the principal bomber in the Battle of Britain, where, as noted, it suffered grievous losses from British fighters.

Nevertheless, the He 111 continued to serve on many fronts. The He 111 was also used extensively on the Russian Front as a bomber and anti-shipping aircraft, with torpedo-carrying aircraft sinking numerous ships in the Russia-bound convoys, including ten Allied merchant ships in convoy PQ.18 in September 1942.

In September 1944 the aircraft became the first to launch a guided (or cruise) missile. Modified He 111s began launching FZG-76 (V-1) guided bombs against London from over the North Sea. (US B-17 Flying Fortresses had dropped unpowered GB-1 glide bombs against Cologne the previous May, although with little success.) By January 14, 1945, the He 111s had launched more than 1,200 missiles against London and other cities.

One of the more unusual variants was the He 111Z *Zwilling* (Twin)—essentially two aircraft connected by a stub wing with a fifth engine added. The *Zwilling*s were used to deliver supplies, to tow large gliders (such as the Me 321), and to transport saboteur parachutists.

Following World War II the He 111 remained in production in Spain. Powered by Rolls-Royce Merlins, the aircraft served into the 1960s before beginning new careers on the warbird air show circuit and in motion pictures.

The He 111 had a conventional, albeit streamlined, bomber design with a low wing mounting two in-line engines. The long, slim nose had a glazed bombardier's position. An early ventral "dustbin" gunner's position was soon

The Heinkel He 111 was the standard German bomber during most of World War II. This formation was photographed during a 1940 raid on England. British air defenses—radar, fighter direction, and Hurricane and Spitfire fighters—forced the Germans to adopt night bombing, and then totally defeated the Luftwaffe's bomber force. *German Railroads Information Office*

He 111H-6 Characteristics

Design:	Heinkel
Crew:	5 or 6 (pilot, bombardier-navigator, radio operator, 2 or 3 gunners)
Engines:	2 Junkers Jumo 211F-2 inverted V-12 in-line piston; 1,340 hp each
Weights:	
Empty:	14,400 lb
Maximum takeoff:	25,000 lb
Dimensions:	
Length:	54 ft, 5 ½ in
Wingspan:	74 ft, 1 ½ in
Wing area:	942 sq ft
Height:	13 ft, 9 in
Speed:	
Maximum:	258 mph (at 16,400 ft)
Ceiling:	
Cruise:	25,500 ft
Range:	1,740 miles
Armament:	6 7.9-mm MG15 machine guns (flexible in nose, waist, dorsal, and positions; remote control mount in rear fuselage); 1 20-mm MG FF cannon (flexible in forward in ventral gondola; 4,408 lb of bombs (internal) or 5,510 lb of bombs or 2 torpedoes (external)

later replaced by a streamlined gondola in production. The bombardier also fired a gun in the nose position. Early aircraft had a "stepped" cockpit; on the first He 111P, completed late in 1938, the pilot's position was faired into a smooth nose, a feature retained in all subsequent production. The aircraft's bomb bay comprised eight individual cells, four on each side of a gangway; each cell carried a 551-pound bomb in a "nose-up" position. The He 111P and 111H were the main variants used in the 1940 campaign, although a number of He 111F models still remained in service at that time.

In response to the He 111's vulnerability to fighter attack, early wartime modifications included machine guns being mounted to fire from side windows, another forward-firing gun fitted in the ventral gondola, and, in some aircraft, a remote-control machine gun fitted in the tail.

The Heinkel firm began development of the He 111 in early 1934 and finished the first prototype late that year. The prototype flew for the first time early in 1935, soon reaching a speed of 214 miles per hour—equal to that of many contemporary fighters. The speed of development can be seen with delivery of the first production bomber aircraft in late 1936. (Very few civil aircraft were flown and they were found unsuitable for airline use.) During 1942 production of the He 111 was to taper off in favor of the He 117 heavy bomber and the Ju 288 medium bomber; however, failure of both types necessitated continued manufacture of the He 111. When German production finally ended in the fall of 1944, after a run of nine years, Heinkel plants had produced more than 7,300 of these aircraft.

The aircraft was also flown by China, Spain, and Turkey.

Junkers Ju 52

The German Ju 52 trimotor transport was surpassed only by the US C-47 Skytrain/Dakota (DC-3) in popularity and importance among transport aircraft of World War II. Developed as a transport, the aircraft was also employed as a bomber with German and Nationalist forces in the Spanish Civil War. The aircraft's momentous role in that conflict occurred in late July 1936 when 20 German Ju 52s were used to ferry troops of Gen. Francisco Franco from Morocco to Spain, overflying Republican warships that would have intercepted the troops had they gone by sea. This marked the start of that tragic conflict.

When Germany went to war in September 1939 the Luftwaffe had 552 transport aircraft of which all but 5 were Ju 52s. The aircraft had vital roles in the German assaults on Norway, Denmark, Holland, and Crete, and operations on the Eastern Front as well as in North Africa.

When the German Sixth Army was surrounded by Soviet troops at Stalingrad in November 1942, Luftwaffe commander Hermann Göring, told

Adolf Hitler that cargo planes could supply the 280,000 German troops entire by air until they could be relieved. That meant 375 Ju 52 sorties per day, each carrying two tons, would have been required to provide that supply lift—assuming 100 percent availability and no losses. (The entire Luftwaffe transport force at the time contained some 750 Ju 52s scattered throughout Europe and North Africa.) Maintenance problems and weather conditions in the area reduced aircraft availability to about 35 percent. Moreover, Soviet fighters and anti-aircraft fire were fierce in the area.

The assigned airlift task was impossible. In the next two months the Luftwaffe's best efforts provided the troops in the Stalingrad pocket with an average of only about 80 tons per day. As the Soviet circle drew tighter, aircraft could no longer land to deliver supplies and carry out the wounded, and parachute drops and glider landings were substituted. (While airstrips were available the Luftwaffe had flown out 24,910 sick and wounded.) During 70 days of the airlift the Luftwaffe, using mainly Ju 52s, flew in 6,591 tons of supplies to the Sixth Army—an average of less than 100 tons per day.

On January 31, 1943, the German commander at Stalingrad surrendered. Stalingrad—the easternmost point German armies reached in the USSR—demonstrated that an army could not be supplied entirely by air. The operation had cost the Luftwaffe 488 aircraft destroyed, both cargo types and bombers pressed in supply service, of which 266 were Ju 52s.

During the war the Ju 52 served as a troop and paratroop transport, medical evacuation aircraft, cargo carrier, and glider tug. It was a trimotor, low-wing aircraft with a relatively large cargo compartment. The fuselage was made of corrugated duralumin skin. It had a fixed tail-sitting undercarriage. Some Ju 52s were fitted with twin floats.

When employed as an airliner the Ju 52 could carry 15 to 17 passengers; as a troop carrier it could accommodate 20 soldiers and their equipment.

The first Junkers-produced Ju 52 flew on October 13, 1930, as a single-engine transport. A succession of single- and then trimotor development aircraft followed, some fitted with skis and floats. The first definitive trimotor aircraft flew in April 1932 with production following for commercial use by several nations. The first military version was delivered in 1934, intended for use as a bomber with a four-man crew, up to four defensive machine guns, and a bomb load of 3,307 pounds. During 1934–35, 450 aircraft were

The Junkers Ju 52 trimotor aircraft was the workhorse of the
German transport forces. These aircraft, well liked for their
ease of handling and maintenance, flew on every German front.
Earlier, during the Spanish Civil War, Ju 52s had a major role in
the success of Spanish Gen. Francisco Franco's campaign
against the Republican government. *Imperial War Museum*

delivered to the Luftwaffe; production in Germany totaled 4,845 aircraft. (Engines in these aircraft varied; shown below is the standard for most war-built aircraft.)

An improved Ju 252 model was developed featuring smooth skin, a retractable undercarriage, a pressurized cabin, and more powerful engines. Capacity was 21 troops. Only three prototypes and a few production aircraft had been built when the war ended.

After the war Ju 52 production continued in Spain and France, where 170 and some 400 were built, respectively; the aircraft was in commercial operation in numerous countries after the war and was flown by the French Air Force in the Indochina War.

The aircraft was affectionately referred to by pilots and troops as "Auntie Ju" and "Iron Annie."

Ju 52/3 m Characteristics

Design:	Junkers
Crew:	2 to 5 (pilot, copilot, up to 3 gunners) + 20 troops
Engines:	3 BMW Hornet radial piston; 600 hp each
Weights:	
Empty:	14,354 lb
Loaded:	23,157 lb
Dimensions:	
Length:	62 ft
Wingspan:	95 ft, 11 $\frac{1}{2}$ in
Wing area:	1,189 $\frac{1}{2}$ sq ft
Height:	14 ft, 9 in
Speeds:	
Maximum:	168 mph
Cruise:	124 mph
Ceiling:	18,046 ft
Range:	568 miles with standard payload; 800+ miles with minimal payload
Armament:	Optional: 1 13-mm MG 131 machine gun (flexible; open cockpit dorsal position); 2 7.9-mm MG 15 machine guns (flexible; in windows)

Junkers Ju 87 *Stuka*

The backbone of German air support for the Blitzkrieg assaults against Poland, France, Holland, and the Soviet Union in World War II was the Ju 87 *Stuka*. The aircraft was an important factor in German ground victories and was also an effective anti-shipping aircraft. (*Stuka* was a derivation of *Sturzkampfflugzeug*, a term descriptive of all dive bombers.)

The first Ju 87s were delivered to Luftwaffe squadrons in the spring of 1937. Later that year Ju 87s began to arrive in Spain to support the Nationalist forces in the Spanish Civil War. Despite relatively poor performance, the Ju 87 was effective against both ground targets and shipping. Subsequently, the Ju 87 saw combat on every front that the Germans fought in World War II.

In the May 1940 assault on Holland and France, the Ju 87 devastated the city of Rotterdam. The plane was employed in the Battle of Britain beginning in July 1940, with some 280 Ju 87s available for strikes on Britain. But the Stuka was withdrawn on August 19 following heavy losses from RAF fighters. (For example, on August 17, of the 85 Ju 87s attacking targets in Britain, 26 were shot down and another 14 were damaged.) Subsequently, the aircraft was flown extensively in the Mediterranean theater and on the Eastern Front, again with great success.

Flying in the anti-shipping role, the Ju 87 was able to heavily damage two British aircraft carriers in the Mediterranean, and to sink and damage many others ships. (The only dive bombers to surpass the Ju 87's effectiveness in attacking warships were the US SBD Dauntless and the Japanese Val.)

Late in the war the Allied control of the air forced the employment of the Ju 87 as a night bomber. The Luftwaffe also planned to operate the aircraft from the never-finished German aircraft carrier *Graf Zeppelin*; those Ju 87T aircraft were fitted with folding wings and an arresting hook (the suffix "T" denoting their carrier role, *Träger*).

Initially intended to serve as "long-range artillery" to support the German Army, the Ju 87's bombing accuracy was less than 30 yards. However, the aircraft's effectiveness assumed control of the air and when that could not be guaranteed by German fighters, the slow, lightly armed Ju 87 was extremely vulnerable to interception. The Ju 87 was the product of the Junkers firm, pushed into service by Ernst Udet, who in 1931 had observed the dive-bombing technique being developed by the US Navy. Encouraged by Hermann Göring, Udet demonstrated dive-bombing in Germany. By the end of 1935 the Junkers firm had produced the prototype Ju 87, which was flight-tested late that same year. After its combat introduction in Spain, Göring ordered production accelerated and through September 1944 5,700 aircraft were produced. Italy, Romania, Hungary, and Bulgaria also flew the Ju 87 during the war.

The single-engine plane had inverted gull-shaped wings, an in-line water-cooled engine, and large fixed landing gear with "spats." Bombs were carried under the wings and fuselage, and the cockpit held a pilot and radio operator, the latter firing a machine gun to protect the rear of the plane when in a dive. In production aircraft an autopilot was fitted to take control if the pilot blacked out during a dive. The Germans found that when dive bombers pushed over into their dive they had a terrifying effect on troops; *Generaloberst* Udet, in 1939 appointed head of equipment for the Luftwaffe, conceived the idea of increasing the natural howling of the dive by attaching sirens to the undercarriage. The plane was considered easy to fly and very popular with its pilots and the troops they supported.

The Ju 87D-3 was experimentally fitted with twin pods on its wing, each for carrying two agents who were to be dropped behind enemy lines; despite extensive tests, this scheme was not adopted.

A higher-performance variant, the Ju 187, had a remote-controlled gun turret and retracting undercarriage and was under development when the war ended. The Ju 87 normally mounted two fixed, forward-firing 7.9-mm machine guns and a twin 7.9-mm machine gun on a flexible mount in the rear cockpit. The Ju 87D normally carried a single 2,205-pound general-purpose bomb or a 3,086-pound armor-piercing bomb. For short-range missions the Ju 87 could carry one 3,970-pound bomb or a variety of lesser weapons or two underwing pods with multiple machine guns or paired 20-mm cannon.

This Junkers Ju 87D-3 *Stuka* flying very low has an empty "bomb crutch" under the fuselage and empty wing racks. The dive bomber saw considerable action in the Spanish Civil War as well as in World War II. It was very vulnerable to effective fighter defenses. Still, Ju 87s were effective against warships—heavily damaging two British aircraft carriers—and against tanks. *National Air and Space Museum*

Ju 87D Characteristics

Design:	Junkers
Crew:	2 (pilot, gunner)
Engines:	1 Junkers Jumo 211J-1 in-line piston; 1,400 hp
Weights:	
Empty:	8,598 lb
Loaded:	12,880 lb
Maximum:	14,550 lb
Dimensions:	
Length:	37 ft, 8 $^3/_4$ in
Wingspan:	45 ft, 3 $^1/_3$ in
Wing area:	343.4 sq ft
Height:	12 ft, 9 $^1/_4$ in
Speeds:	
Maximum:	255 mph at 12,600 ft
Cruise:	115 mph
Ceiling:	23,900 ft
Range:	510 miles
Armament:	4 7.9-mm machine guns (2 fixed, 2 flexible) (see text for bomb load)

Junkers Ju 88

The Junkers Ju 88, a multi-purpose aircraft, was produced in greater numbers than any other German bomber of World War II. Designed as a *Schnell-bomber* (Fast bomber), the twin-engine medium bomber saw further development as a heavy day fighter, night fighter, crew trainer, anti-tank aircraft, photo-reconnaissance platform, and *Mistel* (Mistletoe) flying bomb.

Following a rapid development, the first Ju 88s entered Luftwaffe service in early 1939 and participated in virtually every German aerial campaign as high-speed bombers. Used extensively in unescorted Battle of Britain daylight raids, they suffered heavy losses to coordinated, ground-controlled, radar-guided British fighter defenses. The Junkers faired better at night and against shipping, over the Mediterranean, and on the Russian Front—anywhere that fighter defenses were less coordinated. Ju 88 bombers remained in service until 1945.

As *Zerstörer* ("destroyer") heavy day fighters, Ju 88s could carry a wide variety of heavy guns with little loss of speed. Effective against unescorted bomber formations, the day fighters were forced to withdraw from battle when escort fighters appeared to defend US bomber formations over Europe. Equipped for anti-tank missions, the Ju 88P variant was a failure, unwieldy in ground attack maneuvers and vulnerable to defending fighters.

As a night fighter the Ju 88 devastated the RAF's heavy bombers from 1942 through mid-1944. The Junker "fighters" had heavy armament (often including oblique, upward-firing cannon), long loiter, space for heavy radar installations, close crew coordination, and—as always—high speed. Marauding RAF Mosquito night fighters and intruders eventually challenged the Ju 88s over their home territory, and daylight attacks on night fighter bases scored heavily, but even as improved, purpose-built night fighters joined the Luftwaffe effort, Ju 88 night fighters remained effective through the war's end.

As *Mistel* flying bombs, an unmanned Ju 88 was loaded with high explosives and mated to a single-engine fighter by a trestle mounted above the bomber. The fighter pilot would take off and upon reaching a target, the Ju 88 would be released and radio-controlled to its target by the fighter pilot, who would then would return to base. The first of *Mistel* missions was flown on June 24, 1944, but the bomber was released prematurely when a Mosquito night fighter appeared on the scene. Subsequent anti-shipping missions were flown without significant effect, although several bridge-busting missions met with success.

A variation of the *Mistel* concept was the *Führungsmaschine*—a long-range reconnaissance Ju 88H carrying an Fw 190 escort fighter that could be launched if the recce aircraft were attacked. In theory, after engaging the enemy plane was defeated, the two German aircraft would return to base independently, but there is no record confirming operational use of this unusual combination.

Photo-reconnaissance Ju 88D variants had cameras fitted in the bomb bay and carried underwing fuel tanks.

Developed as a high-speed bomber, the Junkers Ju 88 was the most numerous German bomber of World War II. The aircraft proved to be highly flexible, being configured for various roles, including fighter, reconnaissance, and even carrying unmanned attack aircraft. This Ju 88D was one of several variants developed for photo-reconnaissance. *US National Archives*

The Junker's bomber was developed in response to a 1935 Air Ministry requirement. The prototype Ju 88V-1 first flew on December 21, 1936, just 11 months after design work had commenced. Additional prototypes and pre-production models followed, with changes being made in engines and wingspan as well as other features. Variant development continued into 1945. The total number of Ju 88s built is generally quoted as 14,676 production air-craft, plus prototypes. This number comprised about 9,000 bomber variants and about 6,000 nonbombers, but because many fighters were converted bombers, the final number of new airframes is certainly somewhat lower.

Ju 88A-4 Characteristics

Design:	Junkers
Crew:	4 (pilot, copilot-bombardier, radio operator-gunner, engineer-gunner)
Engines:	2 Junkers Jumo 211B-1 inverted V-12 in-line piston; 1,200-hp each
Weights:	
Empty:	21,737 lb
Maximum takeoff:	30,870 lb
Dimensions:	
Length:	47 ft, 2 3/4 in
Wingspan:	65 ft, 7 1/2 in
Wing area:	586.63 sq ft
Height:	15 ft, 11 in
Speeds:	
Maximum:	292 mph
Cruise:	230 mph
Ceiling:	26,900 ft
Range:	1,696 miles
Armament:	5 7.9-mm MG 15 or MG 81 machine guns (4 fixed in nose; 1 flexible)* 3,960 lb of bombs

* Armament varied; could include 13-mm MG 131 machine guns or 20-mm MG FF cannon.

Messerschmitt Bf 109

The Messerschmitt Bf 109 was one of the world's finest fighters at the beginning of World War II. In concept, the design was simple—a combination of the largest possible engine and the smallest, lightest possible airframe. But the increasing demands of combat brought an end to the Bf 109's advantages—more armor, more armament, and more fuel all degraded the Messerschmitt's fighter-versus-fighter performance at altitude while improving its capabilities against bombers.

Beginning in 1936, Bf 109B-1 and 109C models fought for the Nationalist (fascist) cause in the Spanish Civil War. The conflict established the fighter's outstanding reputation against an increasingly obsolescent opposition while "blooding the warriors" of the Luftwaffe's fledgling fighter arm. That combat experience led to the development of the improved Bf 109E (or Emil), which was tested in the last days of the war in Spain and became the Luftwaffe's principal fighter.

The Emil continued to dominate through the invasions of Poland (1939), the Low Countries, and France (1940). The Battle of Britain in the summer of 1940 marked the first defeat for the Bf 109, which was hampered by short range and poor tactical decisions. The German fighter suffered greatly from RAF Spitfire Mk.IIs and Hurricanes. Although at altitude the Bf 109E had a performance advantage over both British fighters, the British had ground radar, ground observers, ground controllers, and their fighters enough fuel to press attacks even after the Luftwaffe pilots were forced to turn back toward their bases in France. The improved Spitfire Mk.V cancelled the few performance advantages enjoyed by the Bf 109E.

In May 1941 the Messerschmitt Bf 109F (Friedrich) entered service. With more refined lines, a more powerful engine, and reduced armament, the Friedrich enjoyed a performance edge over the Spitfire Mk.V, but Germany was about to begin war against Soviet Russia, much to the detriment of its fighting forces in Western Europe and North Africa.

The Bf 109G (Gustav), which entered in combat June 1942, was the most widely produced variant. It was with this model that gross weight began to climb and performance began to drop, although top speed for the Bf 109G-10 was rated at 428 miles per hour at 24,250 feet. The Gustav was still being flown by some of the Luftwaffe's finest pilots and was used effectively on the Russian Front and over the Mediterranean. When defending against Allied bomber raids over Germany the Bf 109 enjoyed many of the same tactical advantages that had benefited the RAF's fighters in the Battle of Britain. The up-engined Bf 109K improved somewhat on the Gustav's performance, but to no avail. Hampered by dwindling fuel supplies, insufficient training for new pilots, and roving Allied fighters—both at altitude and at home bases—even the improved Bf 109s could not delay the inevitable defeat.

The prototype Bf 109, designed by Prof. Willie Messerschmitt for the Bayerische Flugzeugwerke AG, first flew in September 1935. (The company was renamed Messerschmitt AG in July 1938, and the new fighter was often popularly known as the Me 109, but the Bf designation remained standard in official German records throughout the war.)

Besides the major production variants, Bf 109s were built as two-seat trainers, photo-reconnaissance platforms, ground attack aircraft, and carrier fighters, the last designated Bf 109T for *Träger* (like the Ju 87, intended for the never-completed aircraft carrier *Graf Zeppelin*). There was also a *Zwilling* variant—the Bf 109Z—that mated two Friedrichs or Gustavs laterally through a common wing and horizontal tail. Those aircraft were intended as a fast bomber and high-altitude interceptor. The *Zwilling* never saw operational service. The standard production Bf 109s featured a variety of armament, power plant, and configuration improvements from the factory or through field modification kits.

Some later variants had a 30-mm cannon firing through the propeller spinner. Machine guns were fitted on top of the engine cowling and 20-mm cannon under the wings.

Production figures for the Bf 109 are generally cited at more than 33,000 aircraft between 1936 and the final days of the war—a record of more than 60 percent of all single-engine fighters built by Germany. As always with wartime German production figures, many later new Bf 109 airframes were actually rebuilds of earlier aircraft, but the total production was still remarkable.

After the war Czechoslovakia and Spain continued to build versions of the Bf 109 for their own use and for export. Among the countries flying the

A Messerschmitt Bf 109G-1 warms up in preparation for taking off from a muddy airfield in Russia. The 109 fought in Spain and was one of the world's best fighters at the start of World War II. Despite continuous efforts to upgrade the aircraft's performance, it was outfought by several British and US fighters. Still, the fighter served to the end of the war, with several specialized variants being produced.

Czech-built Bf 109s in the late 1940s was the new State of Israel. These aircraft were used in combat against Arab forces and on at least one occasion flew escort for Israeli B-17 Flying Fortress bombers attacking targets in Egypt—which were defended by Spitfires!

Bf 109G-6 Characteristics

Design:	Messerschmitt
Crew:	Pilot
Engines:	1 Daimler Benz DB 605A inverted V-12 in-line piston; 1,475 hp
Weights:	
Empty:	5,953 lb
Maximum takeoff:	6,945 lb
Dimensions:	
Length:	29 ft, 7 in
Wingspan:	32 ft, 6 $\frac{1}{2}$ in
Wing area:	172.75 sq ft
Height:	11 ft, 2 in
Speeds:	
Maximum:	387 mph
Cruise:	325 mph
Ceiling:	39,700 ft
Range:	615 miles
Armament:	2 13-mm MG 131 machine guns (fixed); 1 30-mm MK 108 cannon (fixed); 2 20-mm MG 151/20 cannon (fixed)

Messerschmitt Me 163 *Komet*

The Messerschmitt Me 163 was one of only two rocket-propelled aircraft ever to fly in combat (the other being the Japanese Ohka/Baka suicide aircraft). The swept-wing Me 163 is one of the few aircraft that have legitimately deserved the accolades "unique" and "sensational."

Intended to kill Allied bombers over the Third Reich, at full power the Me 163 had an endurance of only 230 *seconds*. With a maximum powered flight of 12 minutes through judicious adjustment of throttle, the Me 163 would climb above an Allied bomber formation, reaching 40,000 feet in four minutes, and then weave in and out of the formation both powered and gliding. To further enhance its effectiveness, the Me 163 was directed to intercepts by ground controllers employing radar.

The first Me 163B encounter with Allied aircraft occurred on July 28, 1944, and within a month 29 aircraft had been delivered to the Luftwaffe. The Allies countered the threat by routing bombers around bases of the short-range Me 163 and by using fighters to attack those bases to catch them on the ground. Because of fuel shortages, the lack of trained pilots, and the Allied bombing of Me 163 bases, only one Me 163 wing became operational before the war ended.

The small aircraft was built around a rocket engine designed by Helmuth Walter that burned hydrogen peroxide (known as *T-Stoff*) with a solution of hydrazine hydrate in methanol (*C-Stoff*) as a catalyst. The aircraft had a metal fuselage with a fabric-covered plywood wing. The wing was swept back 23.3 degrees. There was a tall tail fin and rudder but no horizontal tail surfaces. The Me 163 took off on a two-wheel trolley, which dropped away as the aircraft became airborne. A center skid was lowered for landing (the steerable tail wheel was retained in flight). Although the Me 163 handled beautifully in flight, remains of the highly volatile fuel and skid landing technique caused numerous accidents and pilot fatalities. The Me 163D project, in the flight test stage when the war ended, had a normal retractable undercarriage and a greater endurance.

Development of an aircraft around a rocket engine designed by the ingenious Walter began in the late 1930s. A rocket-propelled aircraft (DFS 194) was completed early in 1940. The airframes of two Me 163 prototypes were finished a year later with preliminary flight tests being flown in a glider mode. Powered flight testing began in August 1941 and the fourth powered test surpassed the existing world speed record of 469.22 miles per hour; in October 1941, after being towed aloft, a prototype reached 623.85 miles per hour in level flight. The first Me 163B fighter version flew in August 1943; this aircraft featured increased fuel and armament. Not until a year later did the Me 163B enter operational service, with several improved Me 163 fighter variants in development when the war ended, including a two-seat trainer that was tested in a glider mode. When production ceased in February 1945 a total of 279 Me 163s had been delivered; further production was impossible because of the lack of components.

The Japanese developed the Mitsubishi J8M *Shusui* (Sword Stroke), which was based on the Me 163. However, that aircraft was not used in combat.

British fighter pilot–author Eric Brown summed up the Me 163's place in history in his *Wings of the Luftwaffe:* "the *Komet* was of dubious operational effectiveness, and was probably more lethal to its pilots than to its enemies, and, on balance, its operational record hardly justified the tremendous research effort that carried it to service status. These is no gainsaying, however, that the Me 163 was a brilliant conception."

Me 163 Characteristics

Design:	Messerschmitt
Crew:	Pilot
Engines:	1 Walter HWK 509A rocket; 3,748 lbst
Weights:	
Empty:	4,206 lb
Maximum takeoff:	9,502 lb
Dimensions:	
Length:	19 ft, 2 $\frac{1}{3}$ in
Wingspan:	30 ft, 7 $\frac{1}{3}$ in
Wing area:	199 sq ft
Height:	9 ft, 2/3 in (on trolley)
Speeds:	593 mph at 10,000 feet 29,500 ft; 516 mph at sea level
Ceiling:	
Combat:	39,370 ft
Range:	12 minutes maximum radius;22 miles at 497 mph
Radar:	None
Armament:	2 30-mm Mk 108 cannon (fixed)

The Messerschmitt Me 163B *Komet* was the world's only rocket-propelled fighter to see combat. Despite its odd appearance and short endurance, once airborne the Me 163B was a deadly killer. But its landing procedure, volatile fuel, and vulnerability to Allied fighters when on the ground greatly reduced the aircraft's effectiveness. The wheels dropped off upon takeoff.

Messerschmitt Me 262 *Schwalbe* (Swallow)

The Me 262 was the world's first operational jet-propelled fighter. Eric Brown described the Me 262 as "the most formidable combat aircraft to evolve in World War II." The failure of the Me 262 to affect the aerial battle over Germany in 1944–45 was due primarily to the vacillation of the German leadership as well as to production delays. Nevertheless, the speed with which German industry and the Luftwaffe developed and placed the Me 262 into combat service is almost unprecedented for an aircraft of its complexity and advanced design.

Preproduction aircraft flew combat missions beginning in April 1944. They were able to intercept and shoot down the previously invulnerable Lockheed P-38 Lightning and de Havilland Mosquito reconnaissance aircraft. Despite some success against US bombers during raids over the Third Reich, the Me 262s were vulnerable to Allied fighter-bombers on the ground and during landing and takeoff, and lacked the numbers to provide an effective aerial defense.

Even when they did engage US daylight bombers over Germany, the results were often disappointing, in part because of poorly trained pilots as fuel shortages and Allied fighters prevented an effective Me 262 training program. For example, on April 10, 1945, almost 50 Me 262s shot down only ten US bombers in the Berlin area, the largest loss to jets in a single operation. In return, US fighters destroyed 20 Me 262s and damaged 13 others.

The Me 262 design stemmed from studies initiated by Willy Messerschmitt in the fall of 1938 for an aircraft to be powered by axial-flow turbojet engines. The first Me 262 flew with two piston engines on April 18, 1941; the first Me 262 flights with turbojet engines occurred on July 18, 1941. Delays were caused by disputes within the national leadership and Luftwaffe over the feasibility and role of the aircraft, technical problems, and Allied bombings.

Several prototypes were ordered and in June 1943 the Me 262 was released for series production. The 23 preproduction aircraft were completed by May 1944. Production rates of 500 aircraft per month were being planned with production planes being designated Me 262A *Schwalbe*. A total of 1,433 aircraft were produced (including prototypes),

The Messerschmitt Me 262A-1 shown here in 1945 was another indication of German innovation and expertise in aircraft design. Although it had several shortcomings, the Me 262 was the world's first operational jet fighter and the progenitor of all that followed. The earlier deployment of the Me 262 could have halted the Allied bombing of German-occupied Europe. *Imperial War Museum*

Me 262A Characteristics

Design:	Messerschmitt
Crew:	Pilot
Engines:	2 Junkers Jumo 109-004B-1 turbojets; 1,980 lbst each
Weights:	
Empty:	8,820 lb
Loaded:	14,938 lb
Dimensions:	
Length:	34 ft, 9 $\frac{1}{2}$ in
Wingspan:	41 ft
Wing area:	233.3 sq ft
Height:	12 ft, 6 $\frac{3}{4}$ in
Speeds:	
Maximum:	536 mph at 22,880 ft
Ceiling:	36,080 ft
Range:	525 miles at 19,680 ft; 650 miles at 29,560 ft
Armament:	4 30-mm cannon (fixed)

with between 100 and 200 participating in combat operations before the end of the war. Another 497 aircraft were reportedly destroyed by Allied bombers before delivery to the Luftwaffe.

The swept-wing Me 262 was powered by twin turbojet engines mounted under the wings providing speeds up to Mach 0.86. (Rocket boosters were also considered to further accelerate the Me 262's performance.) The low-mounted wings were moderately swept back, in other words, 18 degrees, 32 minutes, at the leading edge. Production aircraft were provided with a tricycle undercarriage. (The first four prototypes had retractable tail wheels.) The aircraft was relatively easy to fly. Adolf Hitler demanded that the aircraft be fitted with racks for two 551- or 1,102-pound bombs for service as a fighter-bomber. (Experiments were also conducted with the aircraft towing a 2,205-pound bomb!) The fighter-bomber variant was known as the *Sturmvogel* (Stormbird). A two-seat Me 262B trainer and a night fighter adaptation of that variant were also developed with the SN-2 Lichtenstein radar. An Me 262 single-seat aircraft successfully demonstrated night-fighting techniques when assisted by ground searchlights, scoring several kills against Mosquito night intruders. A long-range reconnaissance variant was also contemplated.

The single-seat fighter was heavily armed, with four 30-mm cannon fitted in the nose. In addition, later variants could carry up to 24 55-mm air-to-air rockets or air-to-air missiles. Several armament variations were evaluated, such as a long-barrel 50-mm cannon for attacking bomber formations. A planned Me 262D was to have been fitted with 12 50-mm rifled mortar barrels in the nose of the aircraft, pointing forward and upward; when lined up under a bomber, the mortar rounds would be fired in salvoes. A proposed Me 262E variant was to carry 48 of the 55-mm rockets.

Messerschmitt Me 321/323 *Gigant* (Giant)

One of the largest aircraft of World War II, the Me 321 was a cargo glider that demonstrated the agility and imagination of German aircraft design. Its development was personally supported by Adolf Hitler, who saw the giant glider being employed in the invasion of Britain that would follow the conquest of the Soviet Union. First flown in March 1941, the Me 321 was delivered to the Luftwaffe in May 1941. Originally, it could be towed into the air by only one aircraft—the four-engine Ju 90. Later, groups of 3 Me 110 twin-engine fighters were used to tow the glider, which was further assisted by rocket boosters. Eventually the five-engine "twin" He 111Z was developed as a tow plane.

The gliders were used in the Soviet campaign, although not at Stalingrad. Use of the Me 321 was limited, however, and it was succeeded by the powered variant, the Me 323. The official history *German Air Force Airlift Operations* by *Generalmajor* a.D. Fritz Morzik noted: "The troika tow [three Me 110s] demanded such a high degree of proficiency on the part of the tow plane pilots that it could never be used on a very large scale. . . . The preliminary preparations for a take-off were so complicated that it was utterly impossible to think of sending up several gliders at the same time. Only a few glider trains were ever employed in operations on the Russian front."

Through 1942 the Messerschmitt firm produced 200 gliders. Loads of 44,090 pounds could be carried although half that cargo or 130 troops

The Messerschmitt Me 323 was the powered version of the Me 321 *Gigant* glider. The Me 321/323 program was needed to support Germany's far-flung armies. While the aircraft had a large cargo capacity, with easy loading as shown here, it was not an easy plane to fly and was too vulnerable to Allied fighters.

was a more normal load. Large clamshell nose doors opened to facilitate loading troops and vehicles. The Me 321 was a high-wing aircraft with a structure of welded steel tubing and wood with a mixed covering primarily of fabric and wood. The fuselage was rectangular in cross section, with the cockpit atop the fuselage, faired into the leading edge of the wing. The basic Me 321 design had a large, multi-wheel bogey undercarriage to help distribute the aircraft's weight when on the ground. In the Me 321B this was replaced by two large wheels at the point of the wing braces attachment to the fuselage.

The Me 321B also had three gunners assigned with that aircraft and was armed with four 7.9-mm machine guns in openings in the nose and waist. In addition to the glider's machine guns, embarked troops could fire their guns through ports.

The subsequent Me 323 was a six-engine, powered version of the Me 321 *Gigant* cargo glider. The powered glider first flew in late 1941 and proved to be a highly successful if ungainly transport.

The Luftwaffe took delivery of 198 aircraft through early 1944, and it saw extensive service on the Eastern Front and in the Mediterranean area. The powered aircraft were armed with several machine guns and 20-mm cannons, both flexible and in turrets, providing a significant defensive armament. In late 1942–early 1943 these aircraft were used in large numbers to provide supplies to Gen. Erwin Rommel's *Afrika Korps* fighting the British and Americans in North Africa. The aircraft initially flew unescorted, but on April 22, 1943, British and South African fighters were able to shoot down 21 loaded Me 323s, flying across the Mediterranean, most carrying fuel desperately needed by Rommel's troops.

The powered version of this massive German aircraft was initially fitted with four engines, but in production six engines were mounted to provide the lumbering aircraft with a flight range of 685 miles with a maximum speed at sea level of 177 miles per hour. The Me 323D-1 variant, the first major production aircraft, was powered by six French Gnome/Rhône 14N radial engines, each rated at 1,140 horsepower.

To again quote General Morzik, the Me 323 "did not . . . come up to expectations. It was not very maneuverable and therefore was especially vulnerable to enemy attack. It could not be flown by instrument[s] alone, and it required a great deal of flying experience and skill on the part of the pilot to even take off and land."

The Me 323 had a maximum loaded weight of 94,815 pounds. The normal cargo load was 22,000 pounds or 130 troops. Experiments with the giant plane included carrying a 17.7-ton bomb, but as the weapon was being released the rear fuselage of the aircraft began to break up and the plane crashed. (The plane had been damaged a few days earlier in a strafing attack by US fighters.) Up to seven crewmen flew the plane, which had a defensive armament of two 20-mm cannons in wing turrets, plus several machine guns. The single Me 323E-2/WT aircraft evaluated a battery of no fewer than 11 cannons and 4 machine guns.

Me 321B Characteristics

Design:	Messerschmitt
Crew:	7 (pilot, copilot, crewman, 4 gunners)
Engines:	None
Weights:	
Empty:	26,460 lb
Loaded:	74,970 lb
Dimensions:	
Length:	92 ft, 4 1/4 in
Wingspan:	180 ft, 5 3/8 in
Wing area:	300 sq ft
Speed:	
Maximum:	99 mph safe towing speed
Cruise:	N/A
Ceiling:	N/A
Range:	N/A
Armament:	4 7.9-mm MG 15 machine guns (flexible)

Mitsubishi A6M Zero (Zeke)

The Zero was the most famous Japanese aircraft of World War II and, in the hands of experienced Japanese pilots, was a match for any other Pacific War fighter until the Grumman F6F Hellcat appeared in mid-1943. The P-38 Lightning and F4U Corsair had sufficient power to escape a Zero and make firing passes, but only the F6F could truly best it in a dogfight. The Zero was the world's first ship-based fighter that was superior to its land-based opponents since the Sopwith fighter series of World War I.

The Zero first entered combat over China on August 19, 1940, when 12 of the new fighters escorted 32 Navy bombers from Hankow on an attack against the temporary Chinese capital of Chungking. No Chinese interceptors were encountered. Nor was there any aerial interference with the succeeding Zero escort missions until September 13, when a flight of 13 Zeros encountered 30 Chinese fighters over Chungking. Twenty-seven Soviet-built I-15 and I-16 fighters flown by Chinese pilots were shot down without loss to the Zeros. Through September 1941, Zeroes shot down or destroyed on the ground 99 Chinese aircraft at a cost of only two Zeros lost to ground fire. On those missions the Zeros regularly made round-trip fights of 1,000 miles.

All six Japanese aircraft carriers of the Pearl Harbor striking force carried Zero fighters. The first attack group launched on December 7, 1941, consisted of 183 planes, including 43 Zero fighters, to gain control of the air over Oahu and strafe the island's airfields. One hour and 15 minutes later—while the first wave was still en route to Oahu—the second attack group was launched. This time there were 167 planes, including 35 Zero fighters to provide protection for this wave and to strafe the airfields on Oahu if there was no airborne opposition. Thus, 78 Zeros participated in the Pearl Harbor attack.

During the attack Zeros shot down a score of US fighters as well as four SBD dive bombers from the US carrier *Enterprise*. Of 29 Japanese aircraft lost in the attack, 9 were Zeroes.

Later that day (December 8 in the Far East), Zeros flew from Formosa to the northern Philippines, a round-trip of more than 1,000 miles, and engaged US aircraft in aerial combat. Zeros fought in all subsequent

The Mitsubishi A6M Zero was the outstanding fighter aircraft of the Pacific War prior to the appearance of the US Navy's F6F Hellcat in 1943. The Zero's speed, agility, and range were unrivaled when it entered combat over China in the summer of 1940. Although several improved variants were developed, from 1943 on the Zero could never recover its superior performance. Many ended the war as dive bombers and kamikazes. *Aireview*

carrier battles, and were used extensively from land bases, especially in the Solomons (1942–43) and the Philippines (1944–45). From October 1944 they were employed in the *kamikaze* (suicide) role, usually carrying two small bombs or a single 551-pound bomb. The aircraft remained in first-line naval service until the end of World War II.

Although given the Allied code name "Zeke" in 1942, the A6M became universally known by its Japanese designation, Mitsubishi Type "0," reflecting it have been accepted by the Navy in the Japanese year 2600 or "00." Early models were also (briefly) called Ben and Ray, whereas later variants were called Hap—in honor of Gen. H. H. Arnold, head of the US Army Air Forces—and subsequently Hamp (to spare the general's feelings).

Under chief engineer Jiro Horikoshi the Zero was designed in response to a Navy requirement for a long-range fighter to escort naval bombers. The Zero was a low-wing, all-metal monoplane, with a fully retractable main landing gear. It was carrier capable, with the outer 1 $1/2$ feet of each wing folding in most models to permit them to fit on carrier elevators. (In some models the wingtips were shortened.)

The standard models had two 7.7-mm machine guns in the fuselage and two 20-mm cannon in the wings. Some A6M3 models evaluated two 30-mm cannon and in later models there was one 7.7-mm and one 13.2-mm machine gun. Toward the end of the war the A6M5 night-fighter variant also had a fuselage-mounted, oblique-firing 20-mm cannon.

During its long production run there were numerous updates to the aircraft. The later A6M5 Model 52 production aircraft had a maximum speed of 351 miles per hour, could reach 19,700 feet in seven minutes, and had unequaled maneuverability.

The prototype A6M1 first flew on April 1, 1939; after minor teething problems were solved the aircraft met or exceeded all Navy requirements. Fifteen preproduction A6M2 variants were flown in combat over China from August 1940. Mass production followed with a total of 10,449 aircraft produced by the Mitsubishi and Nakajima plants. When the war ended the Navy had ordered a production run of 6,300 of the A6M8 variant, but none was completed.

In addition, Nakajima developed the A6M2-N Rufe, floatplane fighter variant, of which 327 were built. Others firms produced two-seat trainers based on the Zero, the A6M2-K and A6M5-K, with 515 being built.

In his biography of the Zero, *Eagles of Mitsubishi,* Horikoshi quoted a Japanese fighter pilot and engineer, Eiichi Iwaya: "If there is any respect left in foreigners' minds for the people of Japan, who lost everything in the war, it should be for those who produced and were able to [pilot] Zero fighters as they reigned over two oceans."

A6M2 Model 21 Characteristics

Design:	Mitsubishi
Crew:	Pilot
Engines:	1 Nakajima NK1C Sakae radial piston; 925 hp
Weights:	
Empty:	3,704 lb
Loaded:	5,313 lb
Dimensions:	
Length:	29 ft, 8 $^{11}/_{16}$ in
Wingspan:	39 ft, 4 $^{7}/_{16}$ in
Wing area:	241.5 sq ft
Height:	10 ft
Speeds:	
Maximum:	332.5 mph (at 14,930 ft)
Cruise:	207 mph
Ceiling:	32,810 feet
Range:	1,160 miles with drop tank
Armament:	2 7.7-mm machine guns (fixed); 2 20-mm cannon (fixed); 2 132-lb bombs or 1 551-lb bomb

Mitsubishi G4M Betty

The Mitsubishi G4M medium bomber was one of the best known Japanese aircraft of World War II. The performance of the twin-engine G4M Type 1 naval aircraft—given the Allied code name Betty—exceeded many contemporary four-engine bombers. One hundred eighty Bettys were in service at the time of the Pearl Harbor attack, reflecting the Japanese Navy's emphasis on land-based strike aircraft as well as carrier-based aircraft.

The Mitsubishi G4M—given the Allied code name Betty—
provided the Japanese Navy with an effective, long-range
bomber. However, like many Japanese aircraft it lacked armor
and self-sealing fuel tanks, making it highly vulnerable to
attack. This Betty was photographed as it was being shot down
by a US Navy aircraft near Truk in the Caroline Islands.
US National Archives

The G4M bombers first saw combat over China in the summer of 1941 as a deep-strike aircraft. Twenty-six of these planes joined with G3M Nell bombers to sink the British battleship *Prince of Wales* and battle cruiser *Repulse* on December 10, 1941. Betty bombers subsequently flew against land and naval targets during the Pacific War, and near the end of the war were modified to launch Ohka suicide aircraft.

The G4M was developed as the successor to the Mitsubishi G3M Nell twin-engine bomber. The G4M1 prototype flew in October 23, 1939, and the aircraft was put into production that same month, but as the G6M1 long-range escort fighter. That project, however, was quickly abandoned because of its degraded performance in the fighter role. The 30 units completed were subsequently employed as transports and trainers. Not until April 1941 was the bomber version placed in production.

The much-improved G4M2 prototype flew in November 1942. Total Betty production was 2,479 aircraft—more than any other Japanese bomber. These included 60 G4M3 variants with more armor, a fire extinguishing system, and more powerful engines. However, US bombing raids disrupted production of these advanced aircraft. Late-production aircraft also had a surface-search radar. (These were in addition to the 30 G6M1 aircraft.)

The mid-wing Betty had a rounded, cigar-shaped fuselage, with glazed nose and tail gun positions. Its appearance led to its Japanese nickname *Hamaki* (cigar). The aircraft had twin, radial engines. It was fitted with an internal bomb bay that could carry an aerial torpedo or up to 2,200 pounds of bombs. The excellent performance of the Betty was achieved at the expense of armor for the crew and fuel tanks, making the aircraft highly vulnerable to fighter attack.

The G4M2a variant, with two MK21 engines with methanol injection, could reach 272 miles per hour and was credited with a range of 2,260 miles. Defensive armament in the G4M2a consisted of four 20-mm cannons and one 7.7-mm machine gun, all in flexible mounts, with a crew of seven. The G4M3d, which came too late for operational service, had turbocharged engines.

In their final operational role, several Betty bombers were pressed into service carrying Japanese negotiators to negotiations with US officers after Japan's capitulation in August 1945. The aircraft were disarmed and painted white with green crosses. These planes are at Keise Shima, near Okinawa. The Japanese officials transferred there to US aircraft. *US Navy*

G4M1 Characteristics

Design:	Mitsubishi
Crew:	7 (pilot, copilot, radioman, 4 gunners)
Engines:	2 Mitsubishi Kasei MK4A radial piston; 1,530 hp each
Weights:	
Empty:	14,991 lb
Loaded:	20,944 lb
Dimensions:	
Length:	65 ft, 7 $^1/_2$ in
Wingspan:	82 ft, $^1/_4$ in
Wing area:	840.9 sq ft
Height:	19 ft, 8 $^1/_4$ in
Speeds:	
Maximum:	266 mph (at 13,780 ft)
Cruise:	196 mph (at 9,845 ft)
Ceiling:	approx. 29,000 ft
Range:	3,750 miles
Armament:	4 7.7-mm Type 92 machine guns (flexible in nose, dorsal, waist); 1 20-mm Type 99 Mod 1 cannon (tail turret) 1 torpedo (1,760 lb) or 2,200 lb of bombs

Yokosuka Naval Arsenal MXY7 *Ohka* (*Baka*)

The *Ohka* (Cherry Blossom) was a manned flying bomb, developed as a kamikaze weapon. It represented the ultimate Japanese suicide air effort during the latter stages of World War II in the Pacific. When the suicide air attacks began at the Battle of Leyte Gulf in October 1944, standard combat aircraft, especially older A6M Zero fighters, were employed in kamikaze attacks. The Ohka represented a specialized suicide aircraft, intended only for one-way missions against US warships and amphibious ships.

The Allied code name *Baka*—the Japanese word for "fool"—was considered by many Americans as more appropriate for this desperation weapon. Bomber-type aircraft ("mother" planes) were to take off with the Baka attached to their belly, fly to the vicinity of US warships, and release the suiciders to crash into ships. The G4M Betty was usually employed as the mother plane, with the kamikaze being released at about 27,000 feet at a speed of 200 miles per hour.

The first Baka attack took place on March 21, 1945, with 16 G4M2 Betty aircraft carrying Baka bombs flying from Japan against US warships off Okinawa. Despite an escort of 30 fighters, interception by US carrier-based fighters forced the bombers to jettison the Bakas (their pilots remained in the mother planes). All of the bombers were shot down. Another Baka attack on April 1 was also unproductive, although the Japanese claimed that a Baka damaged the battleship *West Virginia.* Evidence shows that the minor damage inflicted on the rehabilitated Pearl Harbor veteran was from another bomb-carrying suicide plane.

The first Bakas seen by US naval surface forces were the first to score a kill. On April 12 suicide aircraft were again attacking the US warships off Okinawa. The clear day brought out an estimated 185 kamikazes plus almost 200 conventional attackers against the US warships on radar picket duties off the embattled island. An A6M Zero smashed into the destroyer *Mannert L. Abele,* breaking the ship's keel and leaving her dead in the water. One minute later a Baka hit her and she sank in less than five minutes. Seventy-nine of her crew were dead or missing. The same day another Baka hit the destroyer *Stanly,* smashing through her bow before exploding on the other side of the ship. She was hurt, but kept moving and shooting. Within ten minutes a second Baka zoomed toward her, ripped the national ensign off the gaff, and hit the water 2,000 yards away. A Zero then dived on the ship, was hit by 40-mm gunfire, and broke apart over the ship, the fuselage and bomb falling 15 yards off.

The Bakas returned periodically to plague the US ships off Okinawa. However, their effectiveness was limited, in large part because of the vulnerability of the mother planes while en route to the attack area. Too often the Bakas were jettisoned or the bombers shot down far short of their targets; more dangerous were the single-engine fighters and

The Yokosuka MXY7 *Ohka*—given the US code name Baka or "fool"—was a dedicated suicide aircraft. Jet- or rocket-propelled, it was carried to the vicinity of US warships by a bomber aircraft and then released. For a variety of reasons, the Bakas were far less effective than conventional kamikaze aircraft. Hundreds were being readied to counter the planned US invasion of Japan when the war ended. *US Navy*

dive bombers pressed into the kamikazes and Army Air Force suicide efforts.

Design of the Baka is credited to Ens. Mitsuo Ohta, a Navy pilot who, with the help of the Aeronautical Research Institute of Tokyo University, drafted preliminary plans that were submitted to the Navy in August 1944. Unpowered prototypes were designed and constructed within a few weeks and flight trials began in October 1944 with powered trials in November. Large-scale production had already been ordered and 755 of the Ohka Model 11 bombs were delivered between September 1944 and March 1945.

The Ohka Model 22 was a smaller, turbojet-powered version, intended to be carried into combat by the Navy P1Y Frances medium bomber; this Baka had a smaller wingspan and a warhead of only 600 pounds of high explosive (compared to 2,646 pounds in the Model 11). Fifty of these Bakas were produced. The subsequent Model 33 was a "midsize" Baka intend to be carried by the G8N Rita four-engine bomber, having a warhead of 1,764 pounds. But the low priority given to the G8N led to cancellation of the Model 33 as well as the Model 43, which was to have been catapulted from surfaced submarines. A two-seat unarmed, powered training variant, designated Model 43 K-1 KAI *Wakazarura* (Young Cherry), was developed but only two were built. Thus, a total of 807 powered Bakas were produced.

The Baka was mostly fuselage, with stub wings, a glazed canopy over the cockpit, and a small twin-fin tail. The entire forward portion of the fuselage was taken up with the warhead. The Baka was carried aloft by a "mother" aircraft, usually a naval G4M2 Betty; the Baka pilot could enter the bomb while in flight. After release he would ignite the Baka's battery of three rockets, which provided a combined thrust of 1,764 pounds for 8 to 10 seconds, providing a terminal velocity of almost 600 mph. The weapon had an effective range of about 25 miles from the launching aircraft. (The Model 22 had a piston-powered turbojet in place of rockets in an effort to extend the aircraft's range.)

Ohka Model 11 Characteristics

Design: Yokosuka Naval Arsenal

Crew: Pilot

Engines: 3 Type 4 Mk 1 Mod 20 solid-propellant rockets;
                          588 lbst each

Weights:

  Empty: 970 lb

  Loaded: 4,718 lb

Dimensions:

  Length: 19 ft, 11 in

  Wingspan: 16 ft, 9 $\frac{1}{2}$ in

  Wing area: 64.6 sq ft

  Height: 3 ft, 9 $\frac{3}{4}$ in

Speed:

  Maximum: 403 mph

Range: approx. 25 miles

Armament: 2,646 lb warhead

Five

World War II: The Allies

The United States and Great Britain entered World War II with a broad variety of aircraft—most outdated in the face of advanced German and Japanese aircraft, with only a few of truly advanced design in service and advanced development. The concentration on bomber development in the 1930s had left both countries with predominately second-rate fighter aircraft and, in some instances, even bomber aircraft that were inferior to their rivals.

There were a few exceptions in Britain, mostly due to private developments. The British Hurricane and Spitfire, and soon the Mosquito, would stand as outstanding aircraft by any criteria. With continued improvements the "Spit" and "Mossie" would serve as first-line aircraft throughout the war and in the years beyond in other air forces. With respect to bombers, the high-speed and "strategic" aircraft sought in the 1930s produced few bombers that would survive daylight missions in the face of determined German air defenses, both fighters and anti-aircraft guns. But the British designers rapidly responded and several outstanding bombers did take to the skies, most spectacularly the Lancaster, in many respects the most capable bomber to see combat during the war except for the US B-29 Superfortress.

The Grumman F6F Hellcat was the best Allied carrier-based fighter of the war, flown by the US and British navies, and subsequently by several others. This F6F-3 Hellcat is about to take off from the US carrier *Yorktown* in the Pacific. By World War II many carrier aircraft were the equal or superior to their land-based counterparts. *US Navy*

Significantly, only one British carrier-based aircraft appears below, the Swordfish. To say that British carrier-based aircraft were second rate would be an overstatement. Indeed, the Royal Air Force largely controlled British carrier aviation during the 1920s and 1930s, and gave it scant attention and funding. British naval officer and historian Capt. S. W. Roskill wrote in his *White Ensign* that "the most astonishing thing about British naval aviation in the last war is not that it occasionally failed to meet the heavy demands made on it, but that the carriers and their aircrews accomplished so much with the inadequate types of aircraft which they had to use."

Only when British aircraft carriers began operating US-produced aircraft—the F4F/FM Wildcat, F6F Hellcat, F4U Corsair, and TBF/TBM Avenger—did those invaluable ships begin making a major contribution to the war at sea in the Atlantic, Arctic, and Pacific areas. The lone exception, in the opinion of the authors of this book, was the Fairey Swordfish. A biplane, slow and vulnerable, with open cockpits, that aircraft made remarkable contributions to the war.

The US efforts of the 1930s were less sterling than those of the British in preparing for modern war. When the Japanese brought the United States into the conflict with the carrier air attack on Pearl Harbor, the Army Air Forces was bomber oriented. The new B-17 Flying Fortress was an able long-range bomber and potent defensive firepower. Nevertheless, by the fall of 1943 it had been chased from the skies over Germany by Bf 109s and Fw 190s.

The AAF's lack of interest in fighter aircraft in the prewar years was rectified by arrival of the P-51 Mustang, an aircraft initiated for British service, which was capable of long-range bomber escort from British bases to Berlin and back. Other Army Air Forces fighter aircraft certainly ranked high in capabilities, especially the Lockheed P-38 Lightning and Republic P-47 Thunderbolt. But it was the P-51 that turned the tide of daylight air combat over the Third Reich by providing effective fighter escort for US heavy bombers as far as Berlin and back to bases in Britain.

The excellence of the North American Mustang was further demonstrated by being flown by other air forces after the war, its service in the Korean War, and it being the basis for the F-82 Twin Mustang. At the same time, the high-performance P-38 and P-47, which both served as admirably as attack aircraft as well as fighters, were quickly discarded from US service after the war. (The P-38 had also served extensively as a reconnaissance aircraft.) Although the prewar F4F Wildcat and later F6F Hellcat were also discarded by the US Navy after the war, their successors, the F7F Tigercat and F8F Bearcat were in first-line service for several years. However, when the Korean War began in June 1950 the F-51 Mustang and F4U Corsair were the piston-engine fighters that saw action, the latter as a carrier-based night fighter and attack aircraft. Indeed, the only US fighter ace in the Korean conflict who did not fly an F-86 Sabre was Lt. Guy P. Bordelon, flying an F4U-5N against piston-engine night intruders.

The US B-17 Flying Fortress carried the brunt of the daylight air offensive against Germany, suffering heavy losses that could be sustained only by the huge American aviation industry and the well-developed air crew training base. More effective as a heavy bomber in the early stages of the war was the B-24 Liberator, which was a more capable aircraft, albeit not as rugged. Further, the Liberator proved to be one of the most effective maritime patrol/anti-submarine aircraft of the war. (The basic Liberator design flew in maritime roles well after the war as the Navy's PB4Y-2 Privateer.)

But the ultimate bomber of World War II, eclipsing even the German Arado Ar 234 Blitz turbojet bomber and the Lancaster, was the American B-29 Superfortress. This large, advanced technology bomber was the most capable of the war in terms of range, payload, and survivability. Two of these aircraft gained immortality when, in August 1945, the *Enola Gay* and *Bockscar* dropped the only atomic bombs ever used against an enemy on Japanese cities. The B-29 survived after the war as a bomber—being used in combat in the Korean War—and as a reconnaissance, weather, and tanker aircraft. Further, copied meticulously by Andrei Tupolev, it served as the basis for the first Soviet atomic bomber (with some of the Soviet Tu-4s later being transferred to China).

Significantly, the US Navy and the Marine Corps retained complete control of their own naval air arms during the 1920s and 1930s, when Britain, Germany, and Italy scorned such an arrangement. The result was two outstanding late-1930s carrier aircraft, the F4F Wildcat and SBD Dauntless dive bomber. The former was able to defeat the Zero under certain conditions, whereas the latter probably sank more warship tonnage than any other aircraft in history.

Early in the war more capable combat aircraft joined Navy and Marine Corps squadrons, the F6F Hellcat and TBF/TBM Avenger on carrier flight decks, and the F4U Corsair ashore. The fighters could best the Zero (or any other enemy piston fighter) under virtually all combat conditions. The F4U, after being initially used only ashore by US forces, went aboard carriers in late 1944 and provided an excellent and long-lived carrier-based fighter/bomber.

"Maritime operations" implies seaplanes—flying boats and floatplanes. Almost all of the belligerents developed these aircraft. And, many aircraft, like the Swordfish, were convertible from wheels to floats. Two US aircraft, however, tend to receive high marks for effectiveness and longevity, the PBY Catalina flying boat and the SOC Seagull floatplane.

The only other Allied nation that was able to maintain a viable aircraft industry during the war was the USSR. Despite the massive relocation of most of the aircraft industry from the western portion of the country to the Ural mountains as German legions advanced, several design bureaus and manufacturing plants were able to produce large numbers of excellent designs and impressive numbers of aircraft. Further, some designers, including Tupolev, led their design teams while incarcerated by the NKVD (state security organ) on orders from Josef Stalin.

Avro Lancaster

The Lancaster was the ultimate British heavy bomber of World War II and the world's only aircraft capable of carrying the gigantic 22,000-pound Grand Slam bomb. It was employed exclusively against German ground and naval targets in Europe during the War, although it was planned to use Lancasters against Japan in the final stages of the Pacific War.

The bomber began wartime service with a minelaying mission in Heligoland Bight on March 3, 1942; its first night-bombing mission was flown against Essen on March 10–11. Subsequently the Lancaster was used primarily in night-bombing missions but flew daylight strikes on occasion, such as the low-level raid against the MAN diesel engine factory at Augsburg on April 17, 1942.

Lancasters sank the battleship *Tirpitz* at anchor in a Norwegian fjord on November 12, 1944, using 12,000-pound Tallboy bombs. Even heavier bombs were delivered by Lancasters against tunnels, dams, viaducts, and other difficult-to-reach targets in Europe. In 1942 the Lancaster became the dominant aircraft of the RAF Bomber Command: by January 1942 there were 256 Lancasters (of 882 bombers); by January 1943 the command had 652 Lancasters (of 1,093 bombers).

In terms of loss rate per bomb load delivered, the Lancaster was the most effective heavy bomber of the war. From 1941 to 1945 Lancasters flew 156,000 sorties over Germany, dropping 608,612 tons of bombs. The RAF planned to have 36 squadrons of improved Lancaster Mk.VI bombers assigned to the US Twentieth Air Force by mid-1946 for operations against Japan. Those planes would have been based on Okinawa.

Interestingly, in the spring of 1944, Maj. Gen. Leslie R. Groves, head of the US Manhattan (atomic bomb) project told Gen. H. H. Arnold, head of the Army Air Forces, that "there was a chance that we might not be able to fit the [atomic] bomb into the B-29 . . . [and] we would have to consider the use of a British plane, the Lancaster, which I was sure the Prime Minister would be glad to make available to us." In his autobiography, *Now It Can be Told,* Groves told how Arnold said that he would make every effort to ensure that the B-29 Superfortress could deliver the bomb— Arnold wanted an American plane to drop the bomb.

After World War II the Lancasters were used extensively as troop carriers to repatriate 75,000 prisoners of war. Several Lancasters were modified for a photo-reconnaissance role; the last Lancaster P.1 was retired in December 1953. The aircraft also succeeded the Liberator in RAF Coastal Command for Maritime Reconnaissance (MR) until October 1956, which was the last Lancaster in operational service. Some Lancaster MR aircraft were transferred to the French Navy.

Ironically, the Lancaster was developed as a result of the failure of its twin-engine predecessor, the Manchester. The original Avro Lancaster was a twin-engine Manchester airframe fitted with four Rolls-Royce Merlin engines. This aircraft first flew on January 9, 1941; the first production Lancaster flew in October 1941.

A massive-looking aircraft, the Lancaster was a mid-wing, four-engine

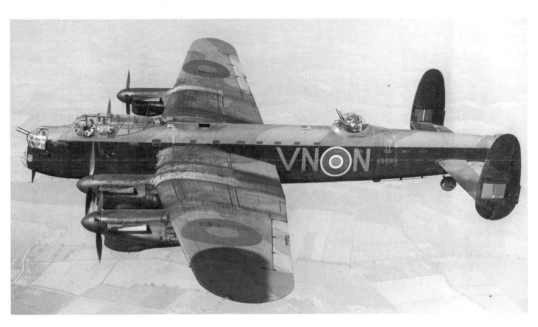

The Avro Lancaster was the most effective strategic bomber of the European conflict in terms of range, bomb tonnage, and survivability. This Lancaster Mk I reveals the massive appearance of the aircraft and the nose and dorsal power turrets; a two-gun turret was fitted in the ventral position and a four-gun turret in the tail.

Lancaster Mk.I Characteristics

Design:	Avro
Crew:	7 (pilot, bomb-aimer, fight engineer, radio operator-gunner, navigator, 2 gunners)
Engines:	4 Merlin 20 or 22 in-line piston; 1,460 hp each or 4 Merlin 24 in-line piston; 1,640 hp each
Weights:	
Empty:	36,900 lb
Loaded:	68,000 lb; 70,000 lb with 22,000-lb bomb
Dimensions:	
Length:	69 ft, 6 in
Wingspan:	102 ft
Wing area:	1,297 sq ft
Height:	20 ft
Speeds:	
Maximum:	287 mph (at 11,500 ft)
Cruise:	210 mph
Ceiling:	24,500 ft
Range:	1,660 miles with 14,000 lb of bombs; 1,000 miles with 1 22,000-lb Grand Slam bomb
Armament:	10 .303-cal. machine guns (twin nose, dorsal, ventral turrets; quad tail turret); 14,000 lb of bombs or 1 22,000-lb bomb

aircraft with characteristic nose, ventral, and tail gun turrets. The twin tail fins were set forward of the tail (the aircraft was originally fitted with triple fins). The main undercarriage of the tail-sitting landing gear was retractable. Most aircraft eventually were fitted with a radar protruding beneath the after fuselage (with the ventral two-gun turret removed). From the outset the Lancasters could carry a 4,000-pound bomb; this was increased until they could carry the heaviest payload of any wartime aircraft—one 12,000-pound Tallboy or one 22,000-pound Grand Slam in modified aircraft.

The Lancaster Mk.VI—planned for the strategic bombing of Japan—had more powerful Merlin engines and a heavier gun armament in a longer fuselage than previous aircraft. Those aircraft in production were renamed Lincoln. The Mk.VI prototype aircraft flew on June 9, 1944, but the first aircraft for service trials were not delivered until August 1945. Hence no Lancaster or Lincoln saw combat against Japan.

The Royal Navy operated three Lancaster Mk.Is in 1945–47, and 54 Lancasters were transferred to the French Navy in 1952. Those planes supplanted RAF Coastal Command maritime patrols in the Eastern Atlantic and Mediterranean for ten years.

Lancaster production run totaled 7,377 aircraft including 430 built in Canada. The last aircraft was delivered in February 1946.

Boeing B-17 Flying Fortress

The most famous Allied bomber of World War II, the B-17 was not the fastest bomber, nor did it have the largest bomb capacity, nor the longest range, nor was it produced in the greatest numbers. Rather, its fame came from an effective Army Air Forces public relations program and its wide use. From the combat viewpoint, the B-17 was able to sustain considerable damage and still fly and had a heavier defensive gun armament than any aircraft except for the US B-29 Superfortress.

The first combat mission to be flown by the Flying Fortress took place on July 8, 1941, when 20 B-17C aircraft flown by the Royal Air Force Bomber Command attacked the German port of Wilhelmshaven. The British were not impressed with the aircraft.

When the Japanese attacked Pearl Harbor, there were 12 B-17s at Hickam Field, adjacent to the US naval base and anchored battle fleet; six of the B-17s were being used for training and the six others were undergoing repair. Another 12 unarmed B-17s began landing at Hickam during the raid, flying in from California. Several of these B-17s were destroyed in the Japanese raid.

Of 35 B-17s in the Philippines when the war began, Japanese planes destroyed 16 on the ground at Clark Field near Manila on the first day of war. (The seventeenth plane at Clark Field, suffering generator troubles, was late getting off after a pre-attack warning and was still airborne when the other 16 had landed at Clark Field and were caught by Japanese bombers.) On December 10 the surviving B-17s began the first US offensive action of the war with attacks against Japanese shipping. By the end of the year the few remaining B-17s were withdrawn to Australia. Several new B-17E models were sent to Java in the desperate attempt to stop the Japanese assault on the Dutch East Indies. That effort also failed as the Japanese overran the Dutch East Indies.

Subsequently, the B-17 became one of the two Army Air Forces heavy bombers in the Southwest Pacific and European theaters (the other being the B-24 Liberator). The first AAF B-17E arrived in England on July 1, 1942, assigned to the Eighth Air Force; the first US B-17 bombing mission was against Rouen, France, on August 17. Eighth Air Force B-17s were deployed to North Africa from the fall of 1942 following the Allied landings in early November 1942.

B-17s continued to bomb German-held territory throughout the war. However, US daylight bomber raids against Germany halted in the fall of 1943 because of heavy losses; they were resumed in December 1943 because of the availability of P-51 Mustangs for long-range escort of the B-17s.

The peak AAF inventory for B-17s was 6,043 aircraft in September 1943. At that time there were 33 B-17 groups overseas (compared to $45\frac{1}{2}$ groups of B-24 Liberator bombers at the time). US B-17 Flying Fortresses dropped 640,036 tons of bombs on European targets during 1942–45 compared to 452,508 tons dropped by B-24s. Further, B-24s continued in service in the Pacific after the end of the war in Europe, whereas the B-17s were retired from frontline service.

Boeing engineers initiated design work on a four-engine bomber in June 1934. Known as Boeing Model 299, it embodied features of the Boeing 247 twin-engine, high-performance airliner and the firm's experimental XB-15 four-engine bomber. The first prototype Model 299—with the Boeing trade name Flying Fortress—flew on July 28, 1935. That aircraft flew 2,000 miles nonstop from Boeing's plant in Seattle, Washington, to

Wright Field in Ohio at the impressive speed of 252 miles per hour. The last of 13 Y1B-17 developmental aircraft was delivered in August 1937. The aircraft was ordered into production in 1938 as the B-17B. This would be the first model assigned to combat units.

The B-17 was a mid-wing aircraft with a tail wheel, easily recognized by its circular-section fuselage with a stepped cockpit, four engines, and large tail fin. Early models carried defensive .30-caliber machine guns in blisters; beginning with the B-17E a manually operated tail gun turret and power-operated dorsal and ventral turrets were introduced, all with twin .50-caliber machine guns, in addition to several hand-operated guns. The B-17G added a "chin" turret with twin .50-caliber guns giving that plane a total of 13 guns, justifying the term "flying fortress." Despite this defensive armament, losses to German fighters and, to a lesser extent, anti-aircraft fire were considerable, with some of the B-17 raids over Germany suffering losses of more than 15 percent.

A total of 12,726 aircraft were built by Boeing (6,981), Douglas (2,995), and Lockheed-Vega (2,750) before the war ended.

In 1941 the RAF received 20 B-17C aircraft under Lend-Lease. The British flew only a few combat missions with the B-17 and, as mentioned above, were not impressed with the performance in the frigid skies over Europe. The surviving aircraft were used for anti-submarine operations and a few were used in the Middle East in 1942.

About one-third of all B-17s built were lost in the European theater. After the war virtually all surviving B-17s were quickly scrapped. (When the Strategic Air Command was established in 1946 no B-17s were listed among its tactical aircraft.) The Navy acquired several B-17s toward the end of the war and, fitted with the AN/APS-20 radar, were designated PB-1W for use in developing airborne radar picket aircraft to provide early warning of Japanese air attacks against the fleet.

There were several B-17s converted to C-108 transports, with one converted from a B-17E used by Gen. Douglas MacArthur as his personal transport; it was named *Bataan*.

Heavily armed and ruggedly built, the Boeing B-17 Flying
Fortress was the principal US heavy bomber in European skies
from 1942 to 1945. Despite suffering devastating losses over
Germany, the Flying Fortress was respected by its crews and
considered a tough opponent by Luftwaffe fighter pilots. This is
a B-17F "Flying Fort." *US National Archives*

B-17G Characteristics

Design:	Boeing
Crew:	10 (pilot, copilot, bombardier, navigator, engineer-top gunner, radioman-gunner, belly gunner, 2 waist gunners, tail gunner)
Engines:	4 Wright R-1820-97 radial piston; 1,200 hp each
Weights:	
Empty:	36,135 lb
Maximum takeoff:	65,500 lb
Dimensions:	
Length:	74 ft, 4 in
Wingspan:	103 ft, 9 1/3 in
Wing area:	1,420 sq ft
Height:	19 ft, 2 in
Speeds:	
Maximum:	287 mph (at 25,000 ft)
Cruise:	150 mph
Ceilings:	
Maximum:	35,600 ft
Range:	2,000 miles with 6,000 lb of bombs
Radar:	None
Armament:	13 .50-cal. machine guns (twin nose, dorsal, ventral, tail turrets, single dorsal, waist positions); 9,600 lb of bombs

Boeing B-29 Superfortress

The B-29 Superfortress was the most effective bomber of any nation to see combat in World War II and the world's first nuclear-capable aircraft. With advanced crew comfort and protection, fully remote-control weapon systems, and an innovative design, the B-29 was in many respects the most advanced bomber aircraft of the war.

The first B-29 bombing mission was flown against Japanese-held Bangkok from airfields in India on June 5, 1944, using landing fields in China as staging bases. B-29s subsequently bombed the Japanese home islands from bases in China and, from October 1944 from bases in the Mariana Islands, the latter a 13-hour round-trip flight to Tokyo. Beginning in March 1945 with a low-level, night incendiary raid on Japan by 279 B-29s, the bombers were used primarily for firebombing raids on Japanese cities.

The largest B-29 raid of the war came on August 1, 1945, when 836 aircraft were launched from the Marianas with 784 reaching their targets in Japan. In addition to dropping almost 170,000 tons of conventional bombs during 14 months of war, B-29s dropped over 12,000 aerial mines in Japanese and Korean waters to stop coastal shipping.

On August 9, 1945, the B-29 *Enola Gay* dropped a Little Boy atomic bomb on the Japanese city of Hiroshima; three days later the B-29 *Bockscar* dropped a Fat Man atomic bomb on Nagasaki. B-29s were modified to carry an atomic bomb under the Silverplate program: In early August 1945 there were 18 Silverplate-modified B-29s assigned to the 509th Composite Group on Tinian in the Mariana Islands, the unit having been specially trained for atomic bomb attacks. Six of their crews were briefed to deliver nuclear weapons (the additional aircraft being employed in scientific and other support operations). Silverplate aircraft had their bomb bays modified to carry only atomic weapons and large, conventional bombs called "Pumpkins." All guns except for the tail mount were removed, and improved engines were provided.

When the war ended the AAF had 40 groups of B-29s, of which 23—with over 1,500 aircraft—were based in the Marianas and on Okinawa. B-29 reconnaissance variants—designated F-13—followed most bombing strikes to obtain bomb-damage assessment photos. The standard photo recce aircraft arrangement was six cameras plus racks for additional film units.

The B-29 *Dave's Dream* dropped an atomic bomb on target ships arrayed at Bikini atoll on June 30, 1946, in Operation Crossroads. (Bikini and the two Japanese strikes were the only air drops of nuclear weapons by B-29s.)

After the war additional B-29s were modified for nuclear weapons delivery under the Silverplate program. The number of B-29s fitted with a nuclear weapons capability has been estimated at:

September 1945	46 aircraft
January 1946	29 aircraft
December 1946	23 aircraft
March 1947	35 aircraft
April 1947	46 aircraft
June 1948	32 aircraft
December 1948	38 aircraft
January 1949	66 aircraft
January 1950	95 aircraft

Official sources differ on exact numbers and not all were fully operational (i.e., only 20 of these appeared on the AAF roster in April 1946). And, there were never fully trained crews available for all of these aircraft.

The B-29 remained the principal US strategic bomber for several years after World War II. It was also flown in special roles, such as reconnaissance, search-and-rescue, and tanker. At the time of the Berlin crisis of 1948–49 several of the 32 Silverplate modified B-29s were sent to Britain in the summer of 1949 although the weapons were retained in the United States (nuclear components were not stored in Britain until 1954).

On September 3, 1949, a US Air Force WB-29 weather reconnaissance aircraft—fitted to detect atmospheric radioactivity—detected the first signs of a Soviet nuclear test while flying from Japan to Alaska. (The USSR had detonated its first nuclear weapon on August 25, 1949.)

The Korean War erupted on June 27, 1950, when North Korean forces invaded South Korea, forcing the few US troops in the country into a headlong retreat. During the late afternoon of June 28 four B-29s from Okinawa began bombing targets of opportunity along Korean highways and railroad tracks. To quote the US Air Force official history, "it was a strange employment for the strategic bombers, but General [Douglas] MacArthur had called for a maximum show of force." In the coming three years of war there would be only 26 days that did not record B-29 missions over Korea.

RB-29 photo planes (as the F-13s were redesignated in 1948) were also used extensively in the Korean War. Several RB-29s were attacked by communist MiG-15 fighters during the conflict; some were damaged, but none shot down. However, at least two and possibly three B-29s were shot down by Soviet fighter aircraft over international waters while on reconnaissance missions in the early 1950s.

The last B-29 bomber was withdrawn from the Air Force in late 1954; specialized variants, especially KB-29 tankers, survived in USAF service until 1957. After World War II the Navy flew four B-29s (designated PB2B) in research projects. The Royal Air Force flew 88 nonnuclear-capable B-29s in the strategic bombing role from 1950 to 1958 with the name "Washington."

The B-29 was designed for the US Army Air Forces as a very-long-range strategic bomber. It was a four-engine, streamlined aircraft, the first with pressurized compartments for the flight crew. It was also the first US bomber built with an integral radar (initially the AN/APQ-13 Eagle ground-scanning system), which supplemented the Norden bombsight. With a maximum takeoff weight of 140,000 pounds the B-29 was the largest bomber of World War II. Up to 20,000 pounds of bombs were carried in two internal bomb bays. Defensive armament was 8 or 10 .50-caliber machine guns in four remote-control turrets, plus a tail turret mounting two machine guns and one 20-millimeter cannon. The aircraft initially used the AN/APQ-13 bombing radar in addition to the Norden bombsight.

The first XB-29 flew on September 21, 1942, with the first delivery to an AAF unit occurring in July 1943. Early B-29s were plagued by engine fires, maintenance problems, and technical difficulties; engine burnout problems continued throughout the war.

Total B-29 production was 3,628 aircraft by the Boeing, Bell, and Martin companies, with all but 230 delivered by August 1945; the last aircraft was delivered in June 1946 (another 200 B-29 and 5,000 B-29C models were cancelled at the end of the war). The B-50 Superfortress was an improved variant of the B-29 (originally B-29D), flown after World War II in the bomber and reconnaissance roles.

When three intact B-29s landed in Soviet Siberia late in World War II the aircraft were carefully copied and produced by the Soviet Union as the

The Boeing B-29 Superfortress was the most capable strategic bomber of the war era. This aircraft from the 468th Bomb Group is shown in February 1945 with bomb bay doors open; the AN/APQ-13 radome is between the bomb bays. This aircraft operated from China. B-29s also served in a number of specialized roles. *US Air Force*

Mechanics and armorers ready a B-29 Superfortress at a base in China. Missions flown from China were difficult to support because of logistics, the lack of base facilities, and other factors. Only when US forces captured the Marianas in the summer of 1944 could effective B-29 bases be established for the aerial bombardment of Japan. *US Air Force*

Tu-4, given the NATO code name Bull. Some of those aircraft were transferred to China. After being employed as bombers, some Tu-4s flew in the research role into the early 1990s. The Chinese aircraft included conversions to an Airborne Early Warning (AEW) configuration.

B-29 Characteristics

Design:	Boeing
Crew:	11 (pilot, copilot, bombardier, radar operator, navigator, engineer, radio operator, 4 gunners-observers)
Engines:	4 Wright R-3350-57 or -57A radial piston; 2,200 hp each
Weights:	
Empty:	71,500 lb
Combat:	101,082 lb
Maximum:	140,000 lb
Dimensions:	
Length:	99 ft
Wingspan:	141 ft, 3 in
Wing area:	1,736 sq ft
Height:	27 ft, 9 in
Speeds:	
Maximum:	399 mph (at 30,000 ft)
Cruise:	253 mph
Ceiling:	39,650 ft
Range:	1,975 miles with maximum bombload
Armament:	10 or 12 .50-cal. machine guns (2 remote-control dorsal, 2 remote-control ventral turrets and tail turret); 1 20-mm M2 cannon in early aircraft (tail position); 1 nuclear bomb (Little Boy, Fat Man, Mk 3, Mk 4, Mk 5, Mk 6) in Silverplate aircraft or 20,000 lb of conventional bombs or mines in non-Silverplate aircraft

Consolidated PBY Catalina

The PBY Catalina was the most successful flying boat ever developed by any nation. The "Cat" was employed during World War II in the patrol, bomber, anti-submarine, torpedo, search-and-rescue, and transport roles. It was also produced in larger numbers than any other flying boat.

The PBY design originated with the Consolidated P3Y, which had been ordered by the US Navy in October 1933. An exceptionally clean, all-metal monoplane, the XP3Y-1 first flew on March 28, 1935. The aircraft was sufficiently impressive for the Navy to broaden its specification to bombing as well as patrol (hence the PB designation). The rebuilt prototype, redesignated XPBY-1, flew nonstop from Norfolk, Virginia, to San Diego, California, via the Panama Canal, a record-setting distance of 3,443 miles. Production PBY-1s first entered Navy squadron service in October 1936.

PBYs first flew on wartime patrols with the Coastal Command of the Royal Air Force in September 1940. A Catalina from RAF No. 209 Squadron spotted the fleeing battleship *Bismarck* some 700 miles west of Brest, France, on May 26, 1941, after the German warship had successfully evaded searching British surface ships. That sighting led to her sinking by British naval forces.

By December 1941 the PBY was being flown by 23 of the US Navy's 25 patrol squadrons (one flew the PBO Hudson and one the PBM Mariner). Although not all PBY squadrons were at full 12-aircraft strength, numerous PBYs were also flown by shore commands and a few by the US Coast Guard.

The Navy had 51 PBYs based on Oahu at the time of the Japanese attack on Pearl Harbor. Three of those Catalinas were exercising with US submarines and another three were on patrol that Sunday morning. One of the latter detected and attacked a Japanese midget submarine near the harbor entrance just before the air attack. Another 12 PBYs were at Midway Island. When the Japanese attack was over, of 33 aircraft caught on Oahu, Japanese bombing and strafing destroyed 27 planes and damaged the other six.

The US Navy had 28 PBYs in the Philippines when war erupted there. From the start of the conflict they scouted out Japanese naval forces and made bombing and torpedo attacks against Japanese shipping. As US forces withdrew from the Philippines, the surviving PBYs flew from the Dutch East Indies, where the Dutch had 36 PBYs when the war began.

PBYs had an important role in the US carrier victory at the Battle of Midway, making the initial sighting of the approaching Japanese naval forces. They subsequently were assigned patrol and bombing missions in the Southwest Pacific, and served in all war areas as anti-submarine aircraft. Although "Cats" were active through the end of the war, during the winter of 1944–45 the last PBYs left frontline patrol bomber service in the Pacific, having been replaced by PBM Mariners. The last Cat in a US Navy squadron was the PBY-6A, retired in 1949.

A graceful aircraft, the PBY had a high wing mounted on a pylon with large, distinctive supporting struts atop the stepped boat fuselage. It had twin, wing-mounted radial engines. A high tail was fitted with horizontal control surfaces level with the main wing. Beginning with the PBY-4 of 1938, the Catalina had distinctive glazed "blisters" on both sides of the after fuselage. The PBY-5A and later A-suffix aircraft were amphibious with retracting wheels for land operation.

The PBY-5A had a maximum speed of 179 miles per hour and a cruising speed of 117 miles per hour with a maximum range of 2,545 miles. In the bombing role a PBY could carry four 1,000-pound or smaller bombs, or eight depth charges, or two aerial torpedoes under its wings. The bombardier usually had a Norden bomb sight for level-bombing attacks.

The standard defensive PBY armament consisted of one .30-caliber machine gun in the nose, another in the ventral or tunnel position, and two .50-caliber guns in waist hatches or side blisters. In later models a twin .30-caliber power mount was fitted in the nose.

PBYs were fitted with radar to search for surface ships and submarines, and the PBY was the first aircraft equipped with Magnetic Anomaly Detection (MAD) gear for the detection of submerged submarines. These aircraft were soon dubbed "Madcats." PBYs were flown by the Dutch and various British Commonwealth air forces and navies as well as the US Army Air Forces and Navy during World War II. The Soviets purchased three PBYs and their plans, and borrowed 18 Consolidated technicians to help produce several hundred planes (designated GST) at Taganrog. Another 138 American-built PBNs and 48 PBYs went to the Soviet Union under Lend-Lease.

After the war many countries flew PBYs in both military and civil markings.

More Catalinas were produced than any other flying boat in history: US Catalina production totaled 3,062 aircraft through 1945, including the 155 PBN Nomad variants built by the Naval Aircraft Factory in Philadelphia; 290 PB2B Catalinas built by Boeing; and 230 Catalinas built by Vickers in Canada (PBV and OA-10, the latter the US Army designation). Vickers built additional Catalinas for British and Canadian service. The Army Air Force flew the OA-10 as Search-And-Rescue (SAR) aircraft. All SAR versions were called "Dumbo," referring to Walt Disney's flying elephant cartoon character.

Many PBYs continue to fly throughout the world although they have long since discarded their guns, bombs, rockets, and torpedoes.

PBY-5 Characteristics

Design:	Consolidated
Crew:	8 (pilot, copilot, copilot-bombardier, 2 radio operators, 3 machinists-gunners)
Engines:	2 Pratt & Whitney R-1830-92 radial piston; 1,200 hp each
Weights:	
Empty:	17,526 lb
Loaded:	34,000 lb
Dimensions:	
Length:	63 ft, 10 in
Wingspan:	104 ft
Wing area:	1,400 sq ft
Height:	18 ft, 6 in
Speeds:	
Maximum:	189 mph (at 7,000 ft)
Cruise:	115 ft
Ceiling:	18,100 ft
Range:	3,000 miles
Armament:	2 .30-cal. machine guns (flexible in nose, tunnel positions); 2 .50-cal. machine guns (flexible in waist blisters); 4 1,000-lb bombs or 2 torpedoes

Designed by I. M. (Mac) Laddon, the Consolidated PBY Catalina was the most successful military flying boat of the World War II era. This PBY-6A was the ultimate Catalina configuration; note the tall tail, the AN/APS-3 radome forward of the wing, and the twin .30-caliber nose turret (single .50-caliber guns were in the waist blisters). *US Navy*

Consolidated B-24 Liberator and PB4Y-2 Privateer

The B-24 Liberator heavy bomber was one of the most effective aircraft of World War II and was produced in larger numbers than any other US military aircraft in history. Although flown primarily as a long-range bomber, B-24 variants flew effectively as anti-submarine, reconnaissance, and cargo aircraft.

Entering US service in 1941, in its bomber role the B-24 was flown by the US Army Air Forces in every combat theater. Shortly before the Japanese attack on Pearl Harbor two B-24s were modified to fly (peacetime) photo-reconnaissance flights over Japanese bases in the Caroline and Marshall islands; one of those planes was destroyed at Hickam Field, adjacent to Pearl Harbor, on December 7, 1941.

The first American B-24s to be used as bombers were dispatched to Java where, on January 16, 1942, five Liberators bombed Japanese airfields and shipping in an effort to halt Japanese advances in the Dutch East Indies.

The B-24 first gained public attention for the dramatic low-level bombing attack by 12 B-24D aircraft against the Ploesti oil refineries in Romania on June 12, 1942. That was the first of several B-24 attacks flown from North Africa, a 2,400-mile round-trip against this vital source of petroleum for Germany. Neither the B-24 raids nor strikes by B-25 Mitchell medium bombers and P-38 Lightning fighter-bombers were able to completely close the Ploesti facilities, although bomb damage at times seriously reduced their production.

Although the B-17 Flying Fortress received more publicity during the war, B-24s based in England also participated in the strategic bombing of Europe and—operated by the US AAF and Navy and the RAF Coastal Command—were highly effective in anti-submarine operations in the Atlantic. Flying anti-submarine patrols of up to 20 hours' duration, the Liberators were the most effective land-based aircraft flown in that role. Fitted with additional fuel tanks and radar, and carrying depth charges and, subsequently, Mk 24 Fido homing torpedoes, the B-24s (called simply Liberators in British and Canadian service) sank several U-boats.

The US Navy received 977 B-24s (designated PB4Y-1) in addition to the specialized PB4Y-2 Privateer variants built specifically for the Navy long-range anti-submarine and reconnaissance missions. After the war some of the Navy PB4Y-1 aircraft were flown by the Coast Guard in the search-and-rescue role.

The B-24 was developed by Consolidated Aircraft in response to an AAF request in early 1939 for a new long-range bomber. Drawing heavily on Boeing's experience with the B-15 and B-17 bombers, as well as Consolidated's own P3Y flying boat (precursor of the PBY Catalina), the four-engine Consolidated XB-24 flew for the first time on December 29, 1939. By that time service test models were already on order for the AAF. As soon as the prototype flew, France ordered 60 of the four-engine bombers; the British took over that contract (with the designation LB-30), and when the United States entered the war 15 of those planes, nearly ready for delivery, went to the AAF.

The B-24 underwent almost continuous modification during production, with increases in bomb load and defensive gun armament. The B-24 was distinguished by its deep fuselage, which provided a commodious, two-door bomb bay, a high wing, and twin tail, making it much less attractive than the B-17. The B-24N had a single tail fin, but was not directly related to the Navy's PB4Y-2.

Production deliveries of the B-24 began in 1941 at Consolidated plants, with B-24 production also being undertaken by the Douglas Airplane Company and Ford Motor Company. The first Liberators provided to Britain were flown across the Atlantic in March 1941. Several were employed as unarmed transports to ferry pilots and other high-priority personnel across the Atlantic. Radar-equipped Liberator Mk.I ASW aircraft entered service with the RAF Coastal Command in September 1941; the plane's range and payload made it one of the best submarine-hunting aircraft to fly during the war. The RAF began using Liberators as bombers from June 1942 in the Middle East and then in the Indian Ocean area.

Between 1940 and the end of the war, 18,190 B-24s were produced. The AAF had a peak inventory of 6,043 planes in September 1944 (24 percent more than the peak B-17 force—a total of $45^{1}/_{2}$ bomber groups flew the B-24 compared to a maximum B-17 force of 33 groups). When the war in

Europe ended orders for 5,168 B-24N models were cancelled. The RAF took delivery of about 1,900 Liberator bomber and cargo models from US factories. One British LB-30 Liberator transport had its guns deleted and was modified—and later lengthened and fitted with a single tail fin—to become *Commando*, the personal transport of Prime Minister Churchill.

Major US variants included the C-87 and C-109 cargo aircraft, F-7 photo-reconnaissance model, and AT-22/TB-24 trainer. One B-24D was modified to an XB-41 "destroyer," intended to fly as a gunship escort for other B-24s in flights over German-held Europe, but that modification proved impractical. (Later B-24s had a standard armament of ten .50-caliber machine guns in four power turrets plus two flexible waist guns; the lower ball turret retracted for landing.)

The PB4Y-2 Privateer was designed specifically for Navy ASW operations (and is counted separately from the Liberators). Based on the B-24 design, it had a single tail fin, a seven-foot fuselage extension forward of the wing to carry additional electronic gear and operators, and other significant changes, especially the fitting of Pratt & Whitney R-1830-94 engines (without turbo-superchargers) for low-altitude operations. Consolidated began Privateer deliveries in March 1944 and continued through October 1945, with 740 PB4Y-2 Privateers being procured by the Navy, a few of which went to the Marine Corps. The Coast Guard flew several of these aircraft as the PB4Y-2G (later P4Y-2G) until 1960. Toward the end of the war in the Pacific some Navy Privateers were armed with the Bat television-guided, anti-ship missile.

A transport version of the Privateer was also produced, of which 33 went to the US Navy and Marine Corps as the RY and another 26 were supplied to the RAF as the Liberator IX. One of the latter was used by the Royal Canadian Air Force for ice-research flights until 1948.

As the Cold War heated up several Privateers were configured for the Electronic Intelligence (ELINT) role, to ferret out Soviet electronic signals by flying along the periphery of the Soviet empire. One of these unarmed PB4Y-2s on an ELINT flight off the coast of Latvia was attacked by Soviet fighters over the Baltic Sea on April 8, 1950. This was the first US spy plane known to be shot down by the Soviets. That plane had a crew of ten, none of whom survived, although there have been unsubstantiated reports of some being captured by the Soviets.

This Consolidated B-24D Liberator was a widely flown variant of this aircraft that served with distinction in many war theaters although it never achieved the "press" of the B-17 Flying Fortress. Many of these B-24D models had a .50-caliber MG mounted in the ventral "tunnel" position; later D aircraft had a retractable "belly" turret with two .50-caliber guns. *US Air Force*

Privateers from active and reserve Navy squadrons flew in the Korean War, mostly in the overland flare-dropping role to support Marine night air-attack missions. The Privateer served in Navy squadrons until June 1954, with a few individual aircraft remaining in service for several more years.

B-24D Characteristics

Design:	Consolidated
Crew:	10 (pilot, copilot, bombardier, navigator, flight engineer, 5 gunners)
Engines:	4 Pratt & Whitney R-1830-43 radial piston; 1,200 hp each
Weights:	
Empty:	32,605 lb
Loaded:	60,000 lb
Dimensions:	
Length:	66 ft, 4 in
Wingspan:	110 ft
Wing area:	1,048 sq ft
Height:	17 ft, 11 in
Speeds:	
Maximum:	303 mph (at 25,000 ft)
Cruise:	200 mph
Ceiling:	32,000 ft
Range:	2,850 miles
Armament:	9 .50-cal. machine guns (twin dorsal, tail ventral turrets; single flexible guns in nose and waist positions); 8,800 lb of bombs

A PB4Y-2 Privateer taking off. Based on the Liberator, the single-tail, lengthened Privateer was optimized for ASW operations. It was also used by the US Navy to launch anti-ship missiles. There were power turrets in the nose, two dorsal, and tail positions, each with two .50-caliber MG, plus waist guns. Low-level operations alleviated the need for a "belly" turret. *US Navy*

PB4Y-2 Characteristics

Design:	Consolidated
Crew:	11 (pilot, copilot, bombardier, navigator, radar operator, flight engineer, 5 gunners)
Engines:	4 Pratt & Whitney R-1830-94 radial piston; 1,350 hp each
Weights:	
Empty:	37,485 lb
Loaded:	65,000 lb
Dimensions:	
Length:	74 ft, 7 in
Wingspan:	110 ft
Wing area:	1,048 sq ft
Height:	30 ft, 1 in
Speeds:	
Maximum:	237 mph (at 13,750 ft)
Cruise:	140 mph
Ceiling:	20,700 ft
Range:	2,800 miles
Armament:	12 .50-cal. machine guns (twin in two dorsal, nose, tail turrets, and waist blisters); 8,800 lb of bombs

Curtiss SOC Seagull

By the end of World War I it was evident that aircraft could enhance the effectiveness of battleships by "spotting" the fall of their shells beyond the vision of men aboard the ships. Subsequently, aircraft were modified and built specifically for scouting and observation flights from large warships.

The US Navy's Curtiss SOC Seagull was probably the most effective of these ship-based scout-observation aircraft and was the only US biplane to see aerial combat in World War II. During the Japanese air attack on Pearl Harbor, a pair of SOC floatplanes from the heavy cruiser *Northampton* encountered an A6M Zero fighter, apparently damaged during the attack. The pair of SOCs engaged the Zero for some 20 minutes, finally shooting it down. (At the time of the raid the *Northampton* was part of the aircraft carrier *Enterprise* task force, approaching Pearl Harbor after flying off Marine fighters for Wake Island.)

This float-equipped biplane was the principal gunfire-spotting and scout plane carried by US battleships and cruisers until the end of World War II. It was in combat in virtually every engagement involving major surface ships, and also scouted in the South Pacific for PT-boat squadrons. Fitted with wheels and arresting hooks, in late 1941 several squadrons of SOCs began serving aboard escort carriers as scouting planes.

One destroyer operated a Seagull: In 1940 the USS *Noa* was fitted to carry a floatplane, and the XSOC-1 carried out successful operations from the ship in May 1940, including flying a stricken seaman from the ship to the naval hospital in Philadelphia. Immediately the Navy ordered six new destroyers of the *Fletcher* class to be fitted with catapults and to carry floatplanes, but after limited operations that project was cancelled.

The SOC design originated with the Curtiss XO3C-1 of 1932. First flown in March 1934, the open-cockpit prototype was modified to the XSOC-1 configuration, the March 1935 designation change reflecting the combination of scouting (S) and observation (O) roles in the same aircraft (with C indicating Curtiss). The first operational aircraft were assigned to the cruiser *Marblehead* in November 1935. Subsequently, each battleship was assigned three SOCs and each cruiser two or four of the aircraft; major fleet commanders also had their own SOCs aboard their flagships. Other SOCs served ashore, some with Naval Reserve and Marine aviation units.

A dozen SOC-3A variants—fitted with wheels—formed Anti-Submarine Squadron (VS) 201 aboard the pioneer escort carrier *Long Island* in 1941–42. At the time the *Long Island* also operated Marine fighter squadron VMF-211 flying seven F2A-3 Buffalo fighters. Subsequently, other escort or "jeep" carriers flew Seagull scouting squadrons, given the designation VGS for escort scouting squadron.

The Curtiss-designed SOC was a graceful aircraft with a large central float and small stabilizing floats fitted under the lower wing. The fuselage had a steel-tube structure with fabric covering. A pilot and observer-gunner were housed under a single glazed canopy. The wings folded back for ship-board stowage, reducing the plane's width to only $12^1/_2$ feet from its normal wingspan of 36 feet.

The floatplanes were launched from shipboard catapults and recovered by coming down at sea alongside the warship and being hoisted back aboard by crane. The aircraft could readily be fitted with a wheeled under-carriage for land-based operations; those fitted with arresting hooks for escort carrier operation were given the designation suffix A, for example, SOC-3A.

Curtiss production totaled 261 SOCs, and 44 identical SON-1 aircraft were built by the Naval Aircraft Factory in Philadelphia—a relatively large aircraft buy for the between-war period. (By law the Navy could build up to 10 percent of its aircraft during that period at the Philadelphia factory.) The Seagull buy included three SOC-4s produced specifically for the Coast Guard; those were transferred to the Navy in 1942. A single, improved XSO2C-1 prototype was built, but did not enter production.

With SOC/SON production ending in early 1938, the Navy began pro-ducing a replacement with the monoplane S03C. But when that aircraft encountered operational problems, the surviving SOCs were returned to first-line service.

The SOC was powered by an extremely rugged (and noisy) Pratt & Whitney R-1340 radial engine producing 550 horsepower. The SOC-1 had a maximum speed of 165 miles per hour with a range of 675 miles. Armament included one fixed, forward-firing .30-caliber Browning M-2 machine gun and a flexible .30-caliber gun of the same type (to be fired by the observer). Two 250-pound bombs or depth charges could be carried under the wings.

The SOC outlasted the two floatplanes procured to succeed it—the monoplane S03C Seamew and OS2U Kingfisher. The last SOC was retired in November 1946. Its ultimate replacement was the SC-1 Seahawk, another Curtiss floatplane that entered service late in 1944. But the Seahawk's career was cut short by the decision to replace all floatplanes on cruisers and battleships with helicopters; by the end of 1949 all floatplanes were removed from warships with helicopters taking their place.

The graceful—and highly effective—Seagulls were gone.

The Curtiss SOC Seagull was a most effective scout-observation aircraft, outlasting several aircraft developed to replace it. This SOC from Observation Squadron 4 in prewar markings is about to be catapulted from the stern of the battleship *West Virginia*. Another dreadnought steams behind her. All US battleships and most cruisers carried two to four floatplanes until after World War II. *US Navy*

SOC-1 Characteristics (as floatplane)

Design:	Curtiss-Wright
Crew:	2 (pilot, observer-gunner)
Engines:	1 Pratt & Whitney R-1340-18 radial piston; 600 hp
Weights:	
Empty:	3,788 lb
Loaded:	5,437
Dimensions:	
Length:	31 ft, 5 in
Wingspan:	36 ft
Wing area:	342 sq ft
Height:	14 ft, 9 in
Speeds:	
Maximum:	165 mph (at 5,000 ft)
Cruise:	133 mph
Ceiling:	14,900 ft
Range:	675 miles
Armament:	2 .30-cal. machine guns (1 fixed, 1 flexible); 2 250-lb bombs or depth charges

Curtiss P-40 Warhawk

When the United States entered World War II in December 1941 the Curtiss P-40—eventually named the Warhawk in US service—was the most advanced fighter in service with the Army Air Forces. At the time it was considered obsolete and plans called for it to be quickly pushed aside by the P-38 Lightning, P-39 Airacobra, and P-47 Thunderbolt as those newer aircraft became available. In combat the P-40 was outclassed by its opponents, but the rugged, powerful, and heavily armed P-40 could be extremely effective when flown by skilled pilots and employing tactics that emphasized its advantages. With a desperate need for more fighters every-where, P-40 development and production continued into 1944. The P-40 was a valued asset with US, British Commonwealth, Soviet, and Chinese air forces through the end of the war.

Deliveries of early versions of the P-40 began in May 1940, with the Royal Air Force a principal customer. The RAF evaluation of the fighter (which the British named the Tomahawk) recognized the plane's deficiencies; several were passed to Army Cooperation (ground support) squadrons. Others were sent to the Middle East where they served well in the campaigns against early Italian and German aircraft.

In late 1941 the United States sent 99 P-40s to China to be flown by US "volunteers"—the group, which would soon be known as the "Flying Tigers," began combat missions against the Japanese three days after Pearl Harbor. All pilots of the American Volunteer Group (AVG) were US Army, Navy, and Marine Corps pilots on special leave.

At Pearl Harbor, 42 of the early P-40Bs and P-40Cs were destroyed in the Japanese attack. But several P-40s and earlier P-36s managed to become airborne. The Army pilots would destroy 11 Japanese aircraft (with 4 more probable kills) for a loss of 4 aircraft in air-to-air combat.

Newer versions of the P-40 were already in production. The P-40D and P-40E (called Kittyhawks in British service) featured new, more powerful engines and greatly improved armament (four and six .50-caliber machine guns, respectively). These fighters were rushed to the Philippines, where the danger of Japanese attack was considered greatest, and several squadrons were on hand when that attack finally came, several hours after Pearl Harbor was bombed. These and subsequent versions of the P-40 flew in the futile defense of the Dutch East Indies and in the China-Burma-India (CBI) Theater (where the AVG became part of the Fourteenth Air Force), Southwest Pacific Area, South Pacific, Central Pacific, Alaska, Middle East, Northwest Africa, and Italy before being taken out of US service in late 1944.

Normally the P-40s could carry only small bombs (see table). In India the AAF's 51st Fighter Group, after a series of experiments, modified P-40s to carry a 1,000-pound bomb. Those planes were informally referred to as "B-40" and were highly effective as dive bombers in the CBI theater.

The Curtiss XP-40, which first flew in October 1938, was a development of the firm's earlier radial-engine P-36. (The tenth production P-36A became

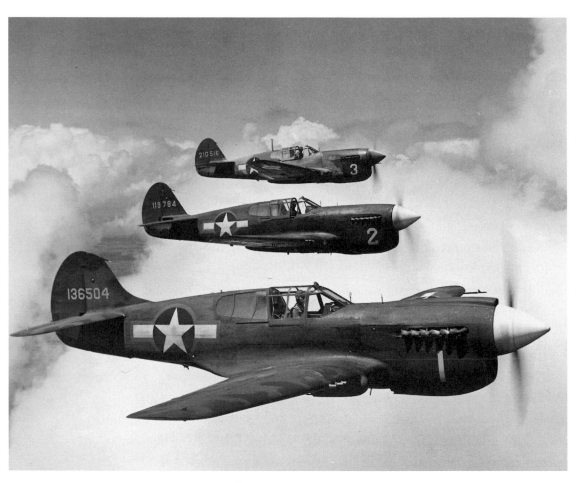

Although lagging well behind the capabilities of most
European and Japanese fighters at the beginning of World War
II, the Curtiss P-40 Warhawk remained in frontline service with
the US Army Air Forces until 1944. These Warhawks, used for
aircrew training at Randolph Field, Texas, in the summer of
1943, are a P-40E-1 (foreground), P-40F (center), and P-40L.
US National Archives

the XP-40 prototype.) A liquid-cooled V-12 Allison engine made the new P-40 the best American fighter of its day, but it was already outclassed by Europe's Spitfires and Bf 109s and the Japanese A6M Zero. The low-wing aircraft had a streamlined configuration for its day, with retractable landing gear.

A total of 13,738 P-40-type aircraft were built for US and export use between 1940 and 1944.

P-40N Characteristics

Design:	Curtiss
Crew:	Pilot
Engines:	1 Allison V-1710-81 V-12 in-line piston; 1,200 hp
Weights:	
Empty:	6,000 lb
Maximum takeoff:	7,740 lb
Dimensions:	
Length:	33 ft, 4 in
Wingspan:	37 ft, 3 1/2 in
Wing area:	236 sq ft
Height:	12 ft, 4 in
Speeds:	
Maximum:	350 mph
Cruise:	288 mph
Ceiling:	31,000 ft
Range:	360 miles; 750 miles with drop tank
Armament:	6 .50-cal. machine guns (fixed); 700 lb of bombs (normally 1 500-lb bomb, 2 100-lb bombs)

de Havilland Mosquito

In October 1938 pilot-aircraft designer Geoffrey de Havilland approached the British Air Ministry proposing a small twin-engine, long-range day bomber that would use speed rather than defensive armament to survive enemy defenses. At a time when doctrine expected defensive gunners to destroy enemy fighters, the entire thesis of an unarmed bomber was wildly radical; and, with aluminum alloy construction becoming more prevalent in the aircraft industry, de Havilland's intention to use molded plywood for the wings and fuselage seemed even more bizarre.

The proposal met with understandable resistance, but in December 1939 construction of the first prototype was authorized by the Air Ministry. The following March, before the first prototype had flown, de Havilland received a contract for 50 photo-reconnaissance and fighter aircraft. The name Mosquito was assigned and production of one of the war's finest aircraft began.

Early tests of the prototype, which first flew on November 25, 1940, revealed an aircraft with a then-phenomenal speed of 386 miles per hour—20 miles per hour faster than the Spitfire powered by the same Merlin 21 engine. As official interest increased, so did missions for the new aircraft, which would excel in nearly every role that it flew. The Mosquito became widely regarded as the most successful photo-reconnaissance aircraft of the war, the top Allied night fighter, an extremely capable strike and interdiction aircraft, and the spearhead of Bomber Command's night target-marking force. The only failure in the Mosquito's long list of missions was the role for which it was designed. Although the unarmed Mosquito day bombers could boast some spectacular successes (including several public attacks designed to embarrass Nazi officials), enemy fighter defenses soon determined the Mosquito's flight characteristics and daylight loss rates became unacceptably high. After a year of operations, the RAF's only two Mosquito day bomber squadrons were converted to the night-pathfinder role.

The German response to the Mosquito's mix bag of threats required a disproportionate amount of operational and industrial resources. Additional Luftwaffe squadrons were moved to defend Berlin after bombs from just three Mosquitos interrupted a radio address by Nazi party leaders on January 30, 1943. With nocturnal Mosquitos operating with relative impunity over the continent, Germany was forced to develop faster night fighters. Air base defenses required strengthening as Mosquito night intruders began striking German airfields across continental Europe.

The Mossie—as it was known to its crews—also had a profound influence on US planning, particularly in the areas of night fighting and photoreconnaissance. Unwilling to build the aircraft in US factories, US planners attempted to secure large numbers from Britain and Canada while developing domestic designs to match the de Havilland's performance. A comparable night fighter did not emerge from US plants, and improved reconnaissance aircraft were delayed until after the end of the war.

Although the Mosquito appeared in a wide variety of variants, it was best known for operations as a bomber, photo-reconnaissance platform, night fighter, and day/strike fighter.

Photoreconnaissance (PR)

Although the concept of the unarmed, high-speed reconnaissance aircraft had been proven with the Spitfire, the Mosquito could carry larger cameras both farther and faster—with the added advantage of a second crewman to navigate and keep watch for interceptors. The first operational Mosquito combat mission was a PR sortie flown in September 1941; although the cameras malfunctioned, the Mosquito's crew took some satisfaction in outrunning a trio of intercepting Bf 109 fighters.

Later PR Mosquito variants gained speed and altitude with the development of improved engines. A partially pressurized cockpit also bettered crew comfort and safety at higher altitudes. Even with the arrival of German jet-propelled interceptors in 1944, reconnaissance Mosquitos continued to be difficult targets to catch and destroy.

In 1943 a PR Mosquito flew 1,900 miles from Britain to Regensburg, Germany; Vienna, Austria; Budapest, Hungary; and Foggia, Italy, before landing in Catania, Sicily, after 6 hours, 30 minutes. The aircraft's average speed was 292 miles per hour.

Bomber

Although the PR Mosquitos were developed from the original bomber design, the first Mosquito bombers were in fact aircraft converted from PR airframes. The bomb bay (used for cameras and extra fuel on reconnaissance aircraft) was originally designed to carry four 250-pound bombs. It was soon found that the bomb load could be doubled by shortening the stabilizing fins on standard RAF 500-pounders. The load would be doubled again with a redesigned, bulged bomb bay capable of carrying a single 4,000-pound bomb (although that weapon would severely affect the aircraft's range, speed, and altitude).

Although high loss rates were suffered by Mosquito day bombers, the night bombers proved more difficult targets for interceptors. Aircraft could fly as part of the main bomber stream, adding their load to the tonnage of a major mission, or strike out individually on nuisance raids to divert the German night-fighter force.

Mosquitos carried out Bomber Command's last raid of the war, attacking Kiel on May 2, 1945.

Pathfinder

Fitted with electronic navigation aids, Mosquitos marked targets for the bomber force with flares and incendiary bombs. They could then loiter near the target, acting as master bombers to direct the course of the mission.

Night Fighter

The development of the unarmed Mosquito into night fighters required few physical changes. Four fixed 20-mm cannon were mounted in the bomb bay, forcing the relocation of the crew access hatch from beneath the floor boards to the fuselage side. The angled windscreen was replaced by a single flat panel, reducing glare for night operations. And, the bomb aimer's nose position was replaced by an early radar set and—on the early Mk.IIs—with four .303-caliber machine guns. As more sophisticated centimetric radars were developed, the Mosquito's nose was easily modified to carry them, although the machine guns were deleted.

The Mosquito combined speed, range, heavy armament, and the latest radar into the most capable Allied night fighter of the war.

Seated shoulder to shoulder, the pilot and radar operator were an effective team. It was the Mosquito that ruled the night skies over England, preventing German raids in 1944 from disrupting the Allied invasion buildup and later destroying hundreds of jet-powered V-1 flying bombs. And, Mosquitos could operate over German targets, hunting the Luftwaffe's own night-fighter force and protecting Bomber Command's heavy bomber force.

Day/Strike Fighter

Mosquito day fighters developed out of the basic night-fighter design, retaining the Mk.II's machine guns and cannon, adding racks for two bombs in the after section of the bomb bay, and eventually adding bomb racks and/or rocket rails under the outer wing panels. The FB.VI (see below) could carry two 2,500-pound bombs internally or two 500-pound bombs on its wings or eight rockets, which were highly effective against shipping and surfaced submarines.

As the Luftwaffe began ranging out over the Bay of Biscay to hunt Allied anti-submarine aircraft, the Mosquito was the one fighter capable of providing protective cover. Other Mosquito day fighters performed a variety of specialized missions across Europe, including attacks on power stations and the famous raid on the German prison at Amiens, France, in February 1944. In an attempt to free captured members of the French Resistance, 18 Mosquitos breached the prison walls; many of the prisoners were killed in the attack, but about 250 others managed to escape (although many were later recaptured).

Anti-Shipping

The combination of range and heavy armament made the Mosquito an ideal anti-shipping platform, and a wing of Mosquitos operating out of Scotland wreaked havoc on German shipping and surfaced U-boats in the North Sea. (Mosquitos claimed ten confirmed U-boat kills during the war.) On 30 aircraft, designated FB.XVIII, the four 20-mm cannons were replaced with a single 57-mm anti-tank gun—a remarkably effective anti-shipping weapon. Although additional Mossies were

The de Havilland Mosquito was one of the most successful aircraft of the war, flying in a variety of roles and using its speed to escape from pursuers. This Mosquito B.XVI shown here was a high-altitude aircraft that could carry a 4,000-pound "blockbuster" bomb in its enlarged bomb bay. Despite the enlarged fuselage and drop tanks, this was one of the fastest variants of the "wooden wonder." *Charles E. Brown/Imperial War Museum*

Mosquito FB.VI Characteristics

Design:	de Havilland
Crew:	2 (pilot, observer-navigator)
Engines:	2 Rolls-Royce Merlin 21 or 23 V-12 in-line piston; 1,460 hp each or 2 Rolls-Royce Merlin 25 V-12 in-line piston; 1,635 hp each
Weights:	
Empty:	13,727 lb
Maximum takeoff:	20,804 lb
Dimensions:	
Length:	41 ft, 2 in
Wingspan:	54 ft, 2 in
Wing area:	450 sq ft
Height:	15 ft, 3 in
Speeds:	
Maximum:	358 mph
Cruise:	220 mph
Ceiling:	37,000 ft
Range:	1,120 miles
Armament:	4 20-mm cannon (fixed); 4 .303-cal. machine guns (fixed); 2 500-lb bombs (see text) or 8 60-lb rockets

slated for the modification, the increasing effectiveness of the wing-mounted rockets soon made the heavy gun superfluous.

Highball/Carrier Operation

On April 1, 1943, No. 618 Squadron was formed within the RAF Coastal Command specifically to employ Mosquito Mk.IV bombers carrying spherical "bouncing" bombs known by the code name Highball. A number of targets were considered for the Mosquito/Highball project, including attacks against the German battleship *Tirpitz*.

The definitive Highball bomb weighed 1,280 pounds, including 600 pounds of the explosive torpex. It was detonated by a hydrostatic fuse upon reaching a preset depth. Each Mosquito could carry two Highball bombs. Released with a back-spin motion, upon striking the water the bombs would skip along the surface, passing over protective anti-torpedo nets and booms to strike an anchored (or slowly moving) ship. After hitting the ship the spinning bomb would adhere to the ship's side while it travelled downward to detonate under the keel.

However, the *Tirpitz* attack was carried out by Lancasters with Tallboy bombs, and No. 618 Squadron—with 29 modified Mk.VI aircraft and 3 camera-fitted Mosquito PR.XVI aircraft—was qualified for aircraft carrier operations. The aircraft were fitted with arresting hooks and their fuselages strengthened to withstand the shock of deck landings, among other changes. The squadron was shipped to Australia on board two escort carriers in late 1944, but languished at Narromine in New South Wales until the end of the war, never having been in combat from either carriers or land bases.

Douglas C-47 Skytrain/Dakota

The Douglas DC-3 airliner revolutionized the air transport industry; its military counterparts—the C-47 and C-53—did the same for military airlift. The official US Army Air Forces history of World War II observed, "A steady and proven aircraft, the C-47 earned for itself a reputation hardly eclipsed even by the more glamorous combat planes." When asked to cite the weapons that most helped win the war, General of the Army Dwight D. Eisenhower listed the bazooka, the jeep, the atomic bomb, and the C-47 aircraft.

The C-53 entered Army Air Forces service in October 1941 and the first C-47 was completed a month later. Both aircraft arrived as the United States was developing new doctrine for strategic and tactical airlift. For strategic airlift the Army's Air Transport Command (ATC, established as Ferry Command in May 1941) developed a worldwide air cargo network relying heavily on the C-47 and other aircraft to move critical supplies and personnel from the United States to the combat theaters. ATC was soon to be responsible for the dangerous and difficult India-China airlift over the Himalayas—the famous "Hump" route.

For tactical airlift the C-47 became the principal aircraft for the new troop carrier groups beginning in July 1942. They towed gliders, air dropped supplies, transported paratroops, and moved materiél between bases in every theater of operations. Developing new techniques through the early Allied parachute assaults in North Africa, Sicily, and Italy, troop carrier C-47s proved critical in the June 1944 invasion of Normandy with 1,200 C-47s inserting 13,000 US paratroopers and glider troops of the 82d and 101st Airborne Divisions behind German lines prior to the landings, while Dakotas and other transports inserted the British 6th Airborne Division. C-47s were also critical in the assaults on Dutch bridges in Operation Market-Garden, the Rhine crossing, and several Pacific and China-Burma-India air drops.

After the war, C-47s remained in service with the new US Air Force, participating in the Berlin Airlift (1948) and the Korean War (1950–53). C-47s added electronic reconnaissance, search-and-rescue (SAR), VIP-staff missions, and navigation training to their airlift duties.

The US Navy launched six ski-equipped Skytrains from the aircraft carrier *Philippine Sea* to land on the Antarctic ice in support of Rear Adm. Richard E. Byrd's 1947 expedition to the South Pole. (The planes could not land back aboard the carrier.)

During the Vietnam War C-47s were converted into AC-47 gunships, known as "Spooky" or "Puff the Magic Dragon." These aircraft were fitted with 40-mm cannon and other rapid-fire guns as well as searchlights for night operations. Called in by ground or air controllers, they put a high volume of fire on suspected concentrations of Viet Cong troops.

The C-47 was flown by several air forces until late in the twentieth century. Israel flew Dakotas for special operations until 2001, and South African Dakotas—upgraded with turboprop engines—continue to be used for close-in maritime patrol. And, the C-47 is still found in civilian service around the world—an aircraft noted for its rugged reliability.

Although officially called the Skytrain in US service and Dakota in British service, its nickname for millions of men and women who piloted them and flew in them was "Gooney Bird." In the 1930s US Army cargo aircraft were assigned to depots and individual tactical units for resupply and staff transport. In 1937 two C-33s (derived from the civil DC-2) assigned to the Hawaiian Air Depot were nicknamed the "Goon" by depot personnel—an apparent reference to a character in the Popeye cartoons. The nickname evolved into "Gooney Bird" and was applied to all military versions of the DC-2 and DC-3 for the next five decades. Officially, the

The versatile Douglas C-47 Skytrain (known to the British as the Dakota) was the primary US transport aircraft of World War II. The "Gooney Bird" remained in US service for various specialized missions through the early 1970s and much longer in other military services. This pair of Skytrains from the Army's Troop Carrier Command are a C-47B (foreground) and a C-47A.

US National Archives

C-47A (RAF Dakota Mk.III) Characteristics

Design:	Douglas
Crew:	3 (pilot, copilot, engineer) + 21 troops
Engines:	2 Pratt & Whitney R-1830-92 radial piston; 1,200 hp each
Weights:	
Empty:	16,865 lb
Maximum takeoff:	31,000 lb
Dimensions:	
Length:	64 ft, 6 in
Wingspan:	95 ft
Wing area:	987 sq ft
Height:	16 ft, 11 in
Speeds:	
Maximum:	230 mph (at 8,800 ft)
Cruise:	185 mph
Ceiling:	24,000 ft
Range:	1,600 miles
Armament:	None

AAF's C-53 personnel transport was known as the Skytrooper, and the C-47 cargo aircraft—with strengthened floor and enlarged cargo door—was named the Skytrain. US Navy Skytroopers and Skytrains flew under the designation R4D until adoption of the joint US military designation system in October 1962. Upgraded aircraft were designated C-117.

The C-47 is a twin-engine, low-wing aircraft, a "tail dragger" with main wheels that partially retract into the engine nacelles and a fixed tail-wheel. Several US Army C-47s were fitted with twin floats, each of which contained retractable wheels. This configuration complicated cargo handling and was not pursued. Engines were removed from another C-47 that was flown as a glider under the designation XCG-17.

Douglas factories produced 9,980 C-47s, C-53s, and C-117 aircraft, nearly one-half of the US military transport aircraft acquired from 1940 to

1945. Of those, 458 were delivered to the Navy as R4Ds, and approximately 2,000 went to Britain as Dakotas. Approximately 200 additional civil DC-3s were also impressed into military service during the war. Military DC-3 variants were produced under license in the USSR and Japan.

Douglas SBD Dauntless

The Douglas SBD Dauntless was the most effective dive bomber of World War II in terms of warship tonnage sunk. US Navy SBD scout dive bombers destroyed four Japanese aircraft carriers on June 4, 1942, at the Battle of Midway. Scores of other Japanese warships and merchant ships, as well as a few submarines, were sunk by SBDs.

Deliveries of the SBD-1 Dauntless to the Marine Corps started in late 1940; the improved SBD-2 began entering Navy carrier squadrons the following year. In December 1941 four of the US Navy's seven aircraft carriers each embarked two SBD squadrons of 18 planes, and two Marine land-based squadrons flew SBDs.

The SBD's baptism of fire began during the Pearl Harbor attack, when SBDs from the carrier *Enterprise* attempted to land on Ford Island (in the center of Pearl Harbor) during the Japanese raid. Several were shot down by overanxious anti-aircraft gunners at Pearl Harbor and probably two were lost to Japanese fighters. But SBDs may have shot down two of their antagonists in the aerial melees that day.

SBDs were used in the early air strikes on Japanese islands in the Pacific, the first flown from the *Enterprise* with 36 SBDs striking Kwajalein on February 1, 1942. At the battle of Coral Sea in May 1942 the SBDs and TBD Devastator torpedo planes sank the Japanese light carrier *Shoho*, while dive bombers damaged a large carrier (preventing the latter ship from participating in the subsequent Battle of Midway). Comdr. Robert E. Dixon, leading SBDs of Scouting Squadron 2 from the carrier *Lexington*, radioed back to his carrier, "Scratch one flattop!" as the *Shoho* began to sink, probably coining the term. At the Battle of Midway the following month, carrier-based SBDs alone sank four large carriers—the *Akagi*, *Kaga*, *Hiryu*, and *Soryu*—and a heavy cruiser. These were four of the six Japanese carriers that had struck Pearl Harbor.

In the Atlantic SBDs flew from US carriers to support the North African invasion in November 1942, and in both oceans they flew from fleet carriers and escort carriers in the anti-submarine role. The SBD served as the Navy's principal bomber aircraft until mid-1944, being embarked in all large carriers as well as escort or "jeep" carriers. The fleet introduction of the replacement SB2C Helldiver—on order before the war began—was delayed by teething problems. The SB2C did replace SBDs on the larger carriers in 1944–45, but never achieved the popularity of the older plane. The TBM Avenger replaced the SBD on escort carriers.

The Marine air arm reached a peak of 20 land-based squadrons flying the SBD; Navy land-based units also flew the Dauntless. Through 1944 the Navy and Marine Corps took delivery of 4,923 SBDs, more than half of which were the SBD-5 variant. The US Army Air Forces procured 953 similar aircraft as the A-24. Although the AAF flew them in combat in New Guinea, their losses were heavy and dive bombing never gained popularity with the Army.

World War II ended on September 2, 1945, and by the end of that month the last SBD was retired from frontline US Navy-Marine squadrons. However, SBDs remained in the training and utility roles for a few more years.

During the war nine SBD-5s were transferred to the Royal Air Force and Royal Navy for evaluation, but no procurement followed; however, New Zealand pilots did fly SBDs in combat in the Pacific War. The Free French Air Force began flying the A-24B in 1943 and the French Navy received SBDs for carrier training in late 1944. Beginning on April 2, 1947, SBDs were used to strike communist targets in Indochina. Flying from the *Dixmude*, an American-built escort carrier, these were the first combat strikes ever flown from a French aircraft carrier.

The SBD was the product of two brilliant aircraft designers, Jack Northrop and Ed Heinemann. Their XBT-1 flew for the first time in 1935 and production was quickly initiated for the Navy. Numerous changes were made for their XBT-2 model and in flight tests that aircraft reached the then-impressive speed of 265.5 miles per hour. The XBT-2 designation was changed to SBD—for Scout Bombing, Douglas—and production by the Douglas Aircraft Company began in April 1939.

The SBD was a low-wing monoplane with a distinctive canopy housing

The Douglas SBD Dauntless was one of the most successful
dive bombers of the war. Although scheduled for replacement
by the SB2C Helldiver when the war began, the SBD survived
on US carriers until 1944 as an effective "ship killer." It was
also effective against Japanese submarines; this SBD is carrying
a depth charge. *US Navy*

SBD-5 Characteristics

Design:	Douglas
Crew:	2 (pilot, radioman-gunner)
Engines:	1 Wright R-1820-60 radial piston; 1,200 hp
Weights:	
Empty:	6,675 lb
Loaded:	10,855 lb
Dimensions:	
Length:	33 ft
Wingspan:	41 ft, 6 $\frac{1}{4}$ in
Wing area:	325 sq ft
Height:	12 ft, 11 in
Speeds:	
Maximum:	245 mph (at 15,800 ft)
Cruise:	144 mph
Ceiling:	24,300 ft
Range:	1,100 miles
Armament:	2 .50-cal. machine guns (fixed); 2 .30-cal. machine guns (flexible); 1 1,600-lb bomb

the pilot and radioman-gunner. It had large dive brakes and used a swinging "crutch" beneath the fuselage to release the bomb clear of the propeller. Unlike most contemporary carrier planes, the SBD's wings did not fold for shipboard storage—the last first-line US carrier plane not to have folding wings until the appearance a decade later of the Heinemann-designed A4D Skyhawk. The SBD was the first carrier aircraft to have an autopilot, which was invaluable for long bombing and scouting missions.

The SBD-5, the principal production variant, had a maximum speed of 252 miles per hour. Normal range was 1,100 miles in a strike role and 1,565 miles when used as a scout. The SBD bomb load—all external—was one 1,600-pound bomb under the fuselage and two small bombs or (in later aircraft) fuel tanks under the wings; a 1,000-pound bomb was usually carried. One or two .50-caliber machine guns were fixed in the engine cowling to fire forward and the radioman-gunner had an aft-firing .30-caliber gun, changed to a twin mount and then to .50s in later models.

Pilots considered the SBD a reliable and rugged aircraft. But it was a relatively slow aircraft and had a slow rate of climb. Still, it was a highly effective dive bomber.

Fairey Swordfish

One of the most important and effective combat aircraft of World War II was an outdated, open-cockpit, biplane—the Fairey Swordfish. The Swordfish, which first flew in 1934, was the principal British carrier aircraft when World War II began in September 1939. Although the US and Japanese air forces had all monoplanes in their first-line carrier squadrons, the Royal Navy flew the antiquated Swordfish from carriers as a torpedo, dive-bombing, anti-submarine, and reconnaissance aircraft. The Swordfish not only performed admirably in combat, but outlasted its intended replacement, the Fairey Albacore.

At the outbreak of World War II in Europe in September 1939 the Fleet Air Arm had 13 squadrons flying the Swordfish, most of them based on the six fleet carriers, with some Swordfish fitted with twin floats to operate from catapult-equipped cruisers and battleships.

The Swordfish units saw little combat until the German invasion of Norway in the spring of 1940. A torpedo attack on German ships failed, but a Swordfish launched from HMS *Warspite* performed useful gunnery spotting and sank the *U-64*, the first German submarine sunk by an aircraft in the war.

Flown by the Royal Air Force and the Royal Navy, Swordfish operated ashore in France, covering the retreat of the British Expeditionary Force, and conducted minelaying and anti-submarine missions in European waters. Malta-based aircraft flew anti-shipping strikes against Italian convoys to North Africa, and, in October 1940, carrier-based Swordfish attacked French ships at Mers-el-Kebir and Dakar in North Africa.

The aircraft became world famous on the night of November 11–12, 1940, when 20 Swordfish flying from the carrier *Illustrious* made a daring night attack against the Italian battle fleet anchored in the port of Taranto. The first few aircraft over the target dropped bombs and flares—none of

The Fairey Swordfish was outdated when World War II began.
Still, it performed admirably as a dive bomber, torpedo plane,
anti-submarine aircraft, and in the reconnaissance role. The
"stringbag" was the last open-cockpit aircraft to fly from aircraft
carriers, including "jeep" carriers escorting Arctic convoys to
Russia. *Imperial War Museum*

the aircraft had radar—and the attack began. Three battleships were heavily damaged (two of which were repaired), and a cruiser and destroyer were also hit. Two aircraft were lost, with one two-man crew killed and the other captured.

In May 1941, flying in difficult wind and weather conditions, Swordfish from the carrier *Ark Royal* attacked the German battleship *Bismarck* in the Atlantic. A torpedo hit on the ship's rudder so damaged her that British surface ships were able to close in and sink the German giant.

Although intended to fly from fleet carriers, Swordfish also operated extensively from escort or "jeep" carriers in the Atlantic and in the arduous conditions of the Arctic. These planes were employed primarily for anti-submarine warfare, and performed successfully in that role as well.

The ability of the Swordfish to carry a variety of weapons and serve in numerous roles led to its nickname "stringbag," after the shopping bag used by British women. But the term also came to refer to its mass of external bracing wires.

The precursor of the Swordfish, the Fairey PV, was designed by Marcel Lobelle as a private venture to meet an order from the Greek Navy, which wanted a Torpedo-Spotter-Reconnaissance (TSR) aircraft. The prototype PV made its first flight on March 21, 1933. After modifications and replacement of its engine, the aircraft was designated TSR.I and flew in that form in July 1933.

Fairey then produced a modified aircraft, the TSR.II, with wings swept back slightly (to correct the center of gravity) and with a lengthened fuselage. The wings could be folded back for shipboard stowage. Either an aerial torpedo or 1,500 pounds of bombs were carried (the latter load consisting of up to three 500-pounders). The later Swordfish II could carry eight 60-pound anti-shipping rockets in place of bombs.

As a torpedo bomber it carried a pilot and gunner; as a spotting and reconnaissance aircraft an observer was added. The crew flew in a open cockpit, exposed to the elements.

The TSR.II flew on April 17, 1934, and a year later Fairey received a production order. The Swordfish entered service in 1936, when monoplane carrier aircraft were already in service.

The Swordfish was easy to fly and easy to land on a carrier deck. It could make remarkably short turns and could dive vertically with little speed buildup during the dive. These characteristics often enabled a Swordfish to escape pursuing fighters.

Originally a fabric-covered aircraft, later production Swordfish had metal-skinned undersides and launching rails for rockets (the metal needed to keep the rocket blast from burning away fabric). Also, beginning in 1941 many aircraft were fitted with radar for detecting surface targets.

Production totaled 2,391 aircraft built by the Fairey and Blackburn firms, the last delivered in December 1944. The Swordfish remained in Navy squadrons only until mid-May 1945, a few days after the war ended in Europe. The last recorded Navy operational flight was in June 1945.

Swordfish Characteristics

Design:	Fairey
Crew:	2 (pilot, radioman-gunner) in torpedo role; 3 (pilot, observer, radioman-gunner) in reconnaissance role
Engines:	1 Bristol Pegasus IIIM.3 radial piston; 690 hp, or 1 Bristol Pegasus XXX radial piston; 750 hp
Weights:	
Empty:	5,200 lb
Loaded:	8,330 lb
Dimensions:	
Length:	36 ft, 4 in
wingspan:	45 ft, 6 in
Wing area:	607 sq ft
Height:	12 ft, 10 in
Speeds:	
Maximum:	139 mph (at 4,750 ft)
Cruise:	104 mph (at 5,000 ft)
Ceiling:	15,000 ft
Range:	400 miles
Armament:	1 .303-cal. Browning machine guns (fixed); 1 .303-cal. Lewis or Vickers machine guns (flexible); 1 torpedo or 1,500 lb of bombs

Grumman F4F Wildcat

Although inferior in performance to its prime antagonist, the Mitsibushi A6M Zero, the Grumman F4F Wildcat proved to be an excellent aircraft. Moreover, in the Atlantic theater the Wildcat, in both the F4F and FM variants, was an effective U-boat fighter.

The Grumman F4F Wildcat was the principal US Navy fighter when the United States entered World War II. In December 1941 seven of the eight US Navy's carrier-based fighter squadrons and three of the Marine Corps's four fighter squadrons flew the F4F. (The other Navy and Marine fighter squadrons flew the F2A Buffalo).

The first combat for Wildcats came during the ill-fated American defense of Wake atoll in December 1941. The fighters were effective in attacking Japanese ships as well as intercepting Japanese bombers. But of 12 F4Fs on Wake on the first day of the war, eight were destroyed on the ground in the first Japanese bombing raid. The four others, eventually shot down or bombed, destroyed several Japanese twin-engine bombers and were credited with sinking a Japanese destroyer and damaging two cruisers and two transports with small bombs and strafing.

The Wildcat made major contributions to the American victories at Coral Sea, Midway, Guadalcanal, and the Solomons, as well as in the Battle of the Atlantic. In 1942 the F4F kill-to-loss ratio for air combat was 5.9 to 1 and for the whole war the Wildcat ratio was 6.9 to 1. The US Navy's first fighter ace, Edward (Butch) O'Hare, scored his first five victories flying an F4F on February 20, 1942. Including O'Hare, 26 US Navy pilots became fighter aces flying Wildcats; 48 Marine pilots became aces in Wildcats.

Beginning in 1943 the Wildcat was replaced on larger US carriers by the F6F Hellcat. The Wildcat continued in US and British naval service until the end of the war with the General Motors–built FM variant flown from most US and British escort or "jeep" carriers. In the Atlantic, US and British escort carriers employed FM Wildcats as well as TBM Avengers against German submarines.

Development of the XF4F-1 began at Grumman Corporation in 1935 as a biplane fighter, but the prototype was not completed. Instead the Navy ordered the XF4F-2 monoplane fighter in July 1936. The first flight occurred on

September 2, 1937, but the prototype lost to the Brewster F2A Buffalo in Navy competition. Subsequently, the F4F design was modified and a more powerful engine to produce the XF4F-3, which first flew on February 12, 1939. The potential of the aircraft was immediately evident and series production began. Export orders were placed by France, Greece, and Britain, all delivered to the Royal Navy after the fall of France in June 1940. The Royal Navy called the aircraft the Martlet until March 1944, when the name Wildcat was adopted.

The F4F had a short, stubby fuselage with short, square-tip wings. The F4F-4 and later aircraft had folding wings for carrier stowage. There were camera-equipped variants, including 20 unarmed F4F-7s with a range of over 3,500 miles, and one aircraft (designated F4F-3S) was evaluated with twin floats in 1943. Other Wildcats tested the feasibility of being towed to increase their ferry range with twin-engine A-20 Havoc and four-engine B-17 Flying Fortress bombers used as the tow planes.

During the war General Motors/Eastern Aircraft produced 5,280 FM variants of the Wildcat compared to 1,971 F4Fs manufactured by Grumman, the latter including prototypes that reached the XF4F-8 model. The F4F-4 and similar FM-2 had a maximum speed of 318 miles per hour and a combat range of 770 miles. It was armed with six .50-caliber machine guns; the FM-2 had only four guns (to save weight) plus wing racks for two 250-pound bombs or six 5-inch rockets for attacking submarines. All Wildcats were single-seat aircraft.

British fighter pilot and writer Eric M. Brown summed up his evaluation of the Wildcat in *Wings of the Navy:*

> I would still assess the Wildcat as the outstanding naval fighter of the early years of [World War II]. Its ruggedness meant that it had a much lower attrition rate on carrier operations than, say, the Sea Hurricane or the Seafire, and although it had neither the performance nor the aesthetic appeal of the latter, it was the perfect compromise solution designed specifically for the naval environment, to such a degree indeed that it was easier to takeoff or land on an aircraft carrier than a runway. . . . With its excellent patrol range—I actually flew one sortie of four-and-a-half hours in this fighter—and fine ditching characteristics, for which I can vouch as a matter of personal experience, this Grumman fighter was, for my money, one of the finest shipboard aeroplanes ever created.

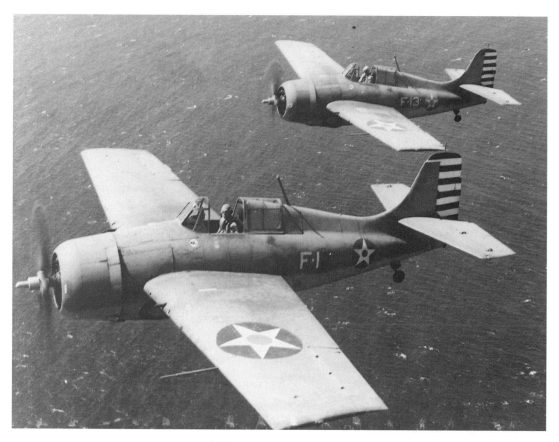

The Grumman F4F Wildcat was the principal US Navy carrier-based fighter at the start of World War II. The agile and rugged fighter served throughout the war, most being built by General Motors as the FM Wildcat. These F4F-3 aircraft, in early 1942 markings, are flown by Lt. Comdr. John S. Thach (F-1) and Lt. Edward (Butch) O'Hare (F-13). *US Navy*

F4F-4 Characteristics

Design:	Grumman
Crew:	Pilot
Engines:	1 Pratt & Whitney R-1830-86 radial piston; 1,200 hp
Weights:	
Empty:	5,785 lb
Loaded:	7,952 lb
Dimensions:	
Length:	28 ft, 9 in
Wingspan:	38 ft
Wing area:	260 sq ft
Height:	11 ft, 10 in
Speeds:	
Maximum:	318 mph (at 19,400 ft)
Cruise:	155 mph
Ceiling:	34,900 ft
Range:	770 miles
Armament:	6 .50-cal. machine guns (fixed);[*] 2 100-lb bombs[**]

[*] FM-2 had four guns.

[**] FM-2 could carry two 250-lb bombs or six 5-inch HVAR air-to-surface rockets.

Grumman F6F Hellcat

The Grumman F6F Hellcat was the world's most effective carrier fighter of the piston-era. The F6F was one of two US Navy carrier-based fighters that could defeat the Japanese A6M Zero fighter under virtually all conditions, the other being the Vought F4U Corsair.

Deliveries of the Hellcat to Fighter Squadron (VF) 9 aboard the USS *Essex* began in January 1943. The first action for the aircraft occurred during a strike on Marcus Island by aircraft from the carriers *Essex* and *Yorktown* on August 31, 1943. By the end of the war all US large (CV) and light (CVL) carriers had the F6F in their fighter squadrons, as did several escort carriers (CVE) as well as British aircraft carriers. (The British initially called the aircraft Gannet, but soon adopted the name Hellcat.)

Hellcats from British carriers and US CVEs flew against German aircraft in 1943–45. For example, Hellcats from the British escort carrier *Emperor* in Norwegian waters clashed with German planes on May 8, 1944. The Hellcats shot down two Bf 109s and one Fw 190. Lt. Blyth Ritchie downed the Fw 190 despite the German plane's superior speed (a margin of about 30 miles per hour). This is believed to be the only occasion on which a Hellcat fought an Fw 190.

In the Pacific the lighter and smaller Zero could outmaneuver the F6F, but the US fighter's superior speed, altitude, and dive capabilities ensured a sufficient margin of performance to put a Zero into the gunsight under almost any condition. And, a few-seconds burst from the six machine guns in the Hellcat's wings could destroy a Zero. The Hellcat itself was well armored with self-sealing fuel tanks, features denied to the Zero.

Japanese Navy pilot Masatake Okumiya and Zero-designer Jiro Horikoshi wrote in *Zero!*: "There is no doubt that the new Hellcat was superior in every respect to the Zero except in the factors of maneuverability and range," and "Of the many American fighter planes we encountered in the Pacific, the Hellcat was the only aircraft which could acquit itself with distinction in a fighter-vs.-fighter dogfight."

Even when compared with the faster P-51 Mustang and F4U Corsair, the F6F Hellcat was considered by the Japanese to be a more effective opponent. More than any other Allied fighter, the Hellcat would turn the tide against the Japanese with its ratio of aerial kills to losses exceeding 19 to 1. The F6F was credited with 4,947 of the 6,477 enemy aircraft destroyed in the air by US Navy carrier pilots.

US carriers flew more F6Fs than any other aircraft type during the war. Fighter strength in the *Essex*-class carriers by the end of the war was authorized at 73. To make space for the large number of fighters, the dive- and torpedo-bomber squadrons were reduced to 15 each. This reduction in bomber strength could be accepted because the F6F Hellcat could double as a dive bomber if required and there were few targets remaining for the torpedo planes.

During the winter of 1944–45 four of the *Essex*-class carriers also received Marine F4U fighter squadrons. Prior to the carrier *Wasp* taking aboard two Marine squadrons, VF-81 in that ship had 90 F6F Hellcats assigned, making it the largest carrier squadron in Navy history. (The *Wasp*'s SB2C Helldiver squadron had been sent ashore and her torpedo squadron had 15 TBM Avengers for an air group total of 105 aircraft.)

The single-seat F6F was flown in relatively small numbers by the Marine Corps, mostly the F6F-3N and -5N night-fighter variants operating from land bases. The Navy flew large numbers of the night-fighter variants. By 1945 the Navy had three aircraft carriers with night air groups; all carried Hellcats as their night fighters: 55 in the *Saratoga,* 16 in the *Enterprise,* and 16 in the *Independence.* Also, by early 1945 most of the *Essex*-class carriers had a four-plane F6F-5N night-fighter detachment.

As plans progressed for the invasion of the Japanese homeland in the fall of 1945 the Marine Corps formed four air groups that went aboard escort carriers. Each group consisted of 8 F6F-5N night Hellcats, 2 F6F-5P photo-reconnaissance Hellcats, 8 F4U Corsairs, and 12 TBM Avengers: a total of 30 aircraft. These CVE groups marked the largest use of Hellcats by the Marine Corps. (A total of eight escort carriers were scheduled to carry Marine air groups for the invasion, given the code name Olympic.)

Work on the F6F had begun in 1941 at Grumman, which took advantage of pilot experience with the Navy's first two monoplane fighters, the Grumman F4F Wildcat and Brewster F2A Buffalo, as well as air combat in Europe. The Navy ordered the first XF6F-1 in June 1941. That aircraft flew on June 26, 1942; the second prototype was modified and flew as the XF6F-3 one month later. The early flights were generally satisfactory and minor problems were quickly corrected. Large production orders for the F6F-3 had already been placed in May 1942 and deliveries to the fleet began early in 1943, possibly a record from the prototype to combat squadron acceptance. (Popular stories asserted that the F6F was based on secrets learned from a Zero that had crashed in the Aleutians on June 3, 1942, but that aircraft was not returned to the United States, repaired, and reassembled for flight until October 1942. The prototype F6F had flown several months earlier.)

Evolving from the F4F Wildcat, the F6F was larger and had cleaner lines, but retained the square wingtips and other appearance features of

A gaggle of Grumman F6F-5N Hellcats in formation shows the clean lines of this aircraft. The radome on the starboard wing identifies them as night fighters. The Hellcat was the mainstay of US Navy shipboard fighter squadrons from 1943 to 1945, and flew from British carriers during the same period, and from French carriers in the Indochina War. *US Navy*

F6F-5 Characteristics

Design:	Grumman
Crew:	Pilot
Engines:	1 Pratt & Whitney R-2800-10W radial piston; 2,000 hp
Weights:	
Empty:	9,238 lb
Loaded:	15,413 lb
Dimensions:	
Length:	33 ft, 7 in
Wingspan:	42 ft, 10 in
Wing area:	334 sq ft
Height:	13 ft, 1 in
Speeds:	
Maximum:	380 mph (at 23,400 ft)
Cruise:	168 mph
Ceiling:	37,300 ft
Range:	945 miles
Armament:	6 .50-cal. machine guns (fixed) *or* 2 20-mm cannon (fixed) and 4 .50-cal. machine guns (fixed) 2 1,000-lb bombs

the F4F/FM series. The night-fighter versions had wing-pod mounted AN/APS-4 and then AN/APS-6 radar. And, late in the war there were camera variants of the Hellcat.

Production of the F6F totaled 12,274 aircraft through November 1945, all from Grumman's Long Island plant. Of those, 1,182 went directly to the Royal Navy.

By the end of 1944 all of the fast carriers had the F6F-5 and F6F-5N variants of the Hellcat. These aircraft were slightly faster than the earlier F6F-3, had more armor, and could also carry two 1,000-pound bombs or six 5-inch air-to-ground rockets, although the bombs were rarely carried. (The F6F-5 could carry a Mk 13-3 torpedo, but that weapon was never carried in combat.) Gun armament consisted of six .50-caliber machine guns or two 20-mm cannon and four machine guns.

Despite the excellence of the F6F Hellcat and the large production run, the aircraft did not survive long in the peacetime US Navy. The F4U Corsair and the Grumman F8F Bearcat offered several performance advantages over the Hellcat.

Although the F6F was phased out of the fleet before the Korean War began in June 1950, several attacks were launched against targets in North Korea from US carriers using radio-controlled, explosive-laden F6F-5K aircraft; F6F-5D aircraft sometimes were used to control the drones. The French Navy also flew F6Fs in their Indochina war.

Although the F6F Hellcat served in first-line US Navy and Marine Corps squadrons for a relatively brief period, the aircraft rates as one of the most effective combat aircraft of World War II.

Hawker Hurricane

The Hurricane was the principal British fighter in the Battle of Britain, although in publicity it was overshadowed by the less numerous, albeit higher-performance, Spitfire.

The Hurricane entered Royal Air Force squadron service in December 1937 and by the outbreak of the European war in September 1939 almost 500 were being flown by 18 fighter squadrons. At the start of the Battle of Britain Hurricanes filled 29 of the 58 squadrons in RAF Fighter Command. (Nineteen squadrons flew the Spitfires.) In the savage air combat over England during the summer of 1940, only one pilot of Fighter Command was awarded the Victoria Cross: Flight Lt. John Brindley Nicholson in a Hurricane was leading two other Hurricanes against German Me 110 bombers when they were attacked from behind by Bf 109 fighters. Nicholson's aircraft was hit and burst into flames, and he was wounded. Still, he stayed with the aircraft long enough to continue his attack on the bomber before bailing out. He survived his wounds.

RAF Hurricanes flew throughout the war in Europe as well as in the Middle East and Far East, with the Royal Navy adopting the Sea Hurricane for carrier use. Some of the latter were converted Hurricane Mk.I aircraft

The Hawker Hurricane was the principal British fighter during the Battle of Britain in the summer of 1940. These Hurricane Mk.II fighters have four 20-mm cannon in place of the eight .303-caliber machine guns fitted in earlier aircraft. Although rugged and flexible, the Hurricane was soon outpaced by the Spitfire as Britain's principal single-engine fighter. *US Air Force*

Hurricane Mk.IIA Characteristics

Design:	Hawker
Crew:	Pilot
Engines:	1 Rolls-Royce Merlin XX in-line piston; 1,280 hp[*]
Weights:	
Empty:	5,150 lb
Loaded:	8,050 lb
Dimensions:	
Length:	32 ft
Wingspan:	40 ft
Wing area:	257 1/2 sq ft
Height:	13 ft, 1 in
Speeds:	
Maximum:	342 mph
Ceiling:	36,300 ft
Range:	470 miles clean; 950 miles with 2 44-gallon (Imperial) drop tanks
Armament:	8 .303-cal. machine guns (fixed) and 2 500-lb bombs or 8 3-inch rockets

[*] Some Mk.II aircraft were fitted with the Merlin 22 engine (1,460 hp).

further modified to "Hurricats" in 1941 for operation from merchant ships. Those planes were catapulted off when a German reconnaissance or anti-shipping aircraft was sighted; after intercepting the bomber (usually an Fw 200 Condor), the pilot would attempt to reach a shore base, if within range, or parachute into the sea in the hope that he would be picked up by the convoy he had protected.

The prototype Hurricane flew on November 6, 1935, the product of the Sydney Camm's design team at the Hawker firm. Production orders were soon placed and, including naval variants, Hurricane production in Britain and Canada totaled 14,533 aircraft. A number were provided to the Soviet Union, some modified as two-seat attack aircraft; some aircraft going to the USSR were flown by the French "Normandie" squadron that operated with Soviet forces.

The Hurricane was a single-place, low-wing aircraft with a large in-line Rolls-Royce Merlin engine, providing a top speed of 339 miles per hour in the Mk.IIB. It had retractable landing gear. Armament consisted of eight .303-caliber Browning machine guns, making it the world's first eight-gun fighter. In the ground attack role two 500-pound bombs or eight large rockets could be carried. Some Hurricane Mk.IIB and Mk.XII aircraft had 12 guns! Tank-busting variants had two 40-mm cannon or four 20-mm cannon.

Ilyushin Il-2/Il-10 *Shturmovik*

One of the most famous Soviet aircraft of World War II, this was a highly effective ground attack aircraft (*Shturmovik* means "attacker"). A reported 36,163 were produced—more than any other combat aircraft in history. Additional numbers of the improved Il-10 were also produced.

Sergei Ilyushin, a leading Soviet aircraft designer, in January 1938—ten months before war began in Europe—wrote a requirement for a heavily armored ground attack aircraft. He circulated the document to various officials, including Soviet ruler Josef Stalin. Although alienating some other aircraft designers, Ilyushin did obtain approval for his proposal, and agreed to have a prototype flying by November 1938. (A few days later he was seriously hurt in an air crash and continued his design work from a hospital bed.)

A major design problem was how to mount heavy armor without seriously degrading aircraft performance. This was achieved by making the armor integral with the airframe to help bear flight loads. About 1,540 pounds of armor was thus installed in the aircraft.

The first prototype flew on December 30, 1939, designated BSh-2, the letters indicating "armored attacker." In March 1941 a Stalin Prize Second Class was awarded to Ilyushin for the design, and a month later the designation was changed from BSh-2 to Il-2, a further personal honor for Ilyushin.

An Ilyushin Il-10 *Shturmovik*—the famed Soviet ground attack aircraft that was produced in greater numbers than any other aircraft design in history. The squared canopy is evident and the 20-mm cannon mounted in the right wing is visible just above the propeller hub.

An Il-2 *Shturmovik* is serviced between missions. This view shows the canopy configuration and the flexible 12.7-mm machine gun. Bombs, rockets, and forward-firing 20-mm and 37-mm cannon made the Il-2s highly effective ground attack and tank-busting aircraft.

Initial problems were overcome and the Il-2 entered squadron service in March 1941, shortly before Germany invaded the Soviet Union. The Il-2 soon established itself as an effective close air support, anti-tank, and "train busting" aircraft. The German troops attacked by Il-2s referred to them as the *schwarzer Tod* ("black death"). The Soviet Navy used the Il-2 extensively in the anti-shipping role in the Baltic and Black Sea areas. They attacked German ships with bombs, rockets, and, on occasion, torpedoes.

Stalin, on December 24, 1941, sent a telegram to the factories producing the aircraft that declared that the "Il-2 is need[ed] by Red Army as air or bread . . . I demand production of more Il-2s; this is my last warning!" Despite many design changes during the production run, and the relocation of much of Soviet industry from areas overrun by German troops, Il-2 production rates set record after record. Serving to the end of the war, the Il-2 suffered a low loss rate, especially after being modified to provide a second crewman, who fired a 12.7-mm machine gun to protect the aircraft from a rear attack by German fighters. The Il-2 fought in every region where Soviet troops were engaged.

A low-wing aircraft with an in-line engine, the Il-2 was a heavily armored and heavily armed aircraft. It had two wing-mounted 20-mm cannon and two 7.62-mm machine guns; the two-seat variants had an aft-firing gun. Four 220-pound bombs and eight 82-mm rockets could be carried under the wings. Later variants were fitted with high-velocity 20-mm cannon and then two 37-mm guns in place of the other 20-mm cannon.

Production of the Il-2 ended in November 1944. By that time the successor Il-10 Shturmovik based on the Il-2 was in production. That much-improved "attacker" saw limited combat at the end of the war. Production continued for several years, with about 2,000 being built. They served in the Soviet Air Forces into the mid-1950s. The North Koreans made limited use of them during the 1950–53 war.

Early in the Cold War the US code name "Bark" was assigned to both the Il-2 and Il-10 aircraft.

Il-2 Type 3 Characteristics

Design:	Ilyushin
Crew:	1 (pilot) or 2 (pilot, gunner)
Engines:	1 Mikulin AM-38F in-line piston; 1,720 hp
Weights:	
Empty:	9,976 lb
Loaded:	14,021 lb
Dimensions:	
Length:	38 ft, 2 $\frac{1}{2}$ in
Wingspan:	47 ft, 10 $\frac{3}{4}$ in
Wing area:	414.42 sq ft
Height:	13 ft, 8 in
Speeds:	
Maximum:	255 mph (at 4,920 ft)
Ceiling:	14,845 ft
Range:	475 miles
Armament:	2 7.62-mm machine guns (fixed); 2 23-mm cannon (fixed); 1 12.7-mm machine gun (flexible) in later aircraft; 2 551-lb bombs or 4 220-lb bombs or 8 RS-82 rockets

Lockheed P-38 Lightning

The P-38 Lightning was the only effective twin-engine, single-seat fighter of World War II although several nations attempted similar projects. The US Army's highest-performance and longest-range fighter when the United States entered the war, the Lightning was a radical design and expensive to produce. Although manufactured in smaller numbers than other major US fighters, the P-38 served in every theater of the war.

In Europe P-38s were used in the early efforts to escort B-17 Flying Fortress and B-24 Liberator bombers in an effort to make possible daylight bombing of German-held Europe. In the Pacific, the P-38's extreme range allowed the fighters to roam over distant Japanese bases, its speed and armament kept parity with the best enemy fighters, and its second engine improved its chances flying home safely after sustaining damage. Lightnings were used for the April 14, 1943 attack on Japanese fleet commander Adm. Isorouku Yamamoto over Bougainville in the Solomons. Sixteen P-38s flew 550 miles from Guadalcanal to destroy the G4M Betty bomber carrying Yamamoto, as well as a second Betty and three Zero fighters, all for the loss of one US plane. Top AAF aces Richard Bong and Thomas B. McGuire used P-38s to score all of their kills against Japanese aircraft. (Some sources cite the P-38 as having destroyed more Japanese aircraft than any other US fighter, but that accolade more likely belongs to the F6F Hellcat.) Still, it was appropriate that a P-38 was the first US aircraft to land in Japan after the Japanese capitulation in August 1945.

The Lightning was Lockheed Corporation's first venture into military aircraft. Flight testing of the XP-38 began on January 27, 1939, and production was initiated before the service-test models ordered in April 1939 had been completed. Production lagged and only 69 aircraft were in service on December 7, 1941. A total of 9,923 aircraft were delivered through August 1945. Those included a few hundred reconnaissance aircraft (designated F-4 and F-5) and several radar-equipped night-fighter (P-38M) variants. A handful of P-38J and P-38L models were modified as "droop snoots" with a bombardier position and Norden bombsight accommodated in a lengthened, glazed nose. Those aircraft led formations of Lightnings on bombing missions over Europe. Later bomb leaders used a radar (in place of the Norden) to permit bombing through cloud cover. Some P-38Fs were converted to two-seat trainers.

The Royal Air Force evaluated the P-38 but after taking delivery of three P-38E-type aircraft cancelled orders for almost 700 Lightnings.

The twin-engine Lightning had two fuselages and twin tails, with the bulletlike fuselage blister mounted on the wing between the engines. This arrangement alleviated the need to synchronize gun firing through propellers. The usual armament comprised four .50-caliber machine guns and one 20-mm or 23-mm cannon, with up to 3,200 pounds of bombs being carried externally in some models.

Unique among World War II fighters, the Lockheed P-38
Lightning was the only successful single-seat, twin-engine,
propeller-driven aircraft to serve with any nation's air force.
With its heavy armament and surprising maneuverability, the
Lightning could pour murderous fire into an enemy aircraft.
Depicted is a P-38F, photographed over the United States in
1942. *US National Archives*

P-38L Characteristics

Design:	Lockheed
Crew:	Pilot
Engines:	2 Allison V-1710-111/113 V-12 in-line piston; 1,475 hp each
Weights:	
Empty:	12,800 lb
Maximum takeoff:	21,600 lb
Dimensions:	
Length:	37 ft, 10 in
Wingspan:	52 ft
Wing area:	327.5 sq ft
Height:	9 ft, 10 in
Speeds:	
Maximum:	414 mph (at 25,000 ft)
Cruise:	290 mph
Ceiling:	44,000 ft
Range:	2,260 miles
Armament:	1 20-mm Hispano cannon (fixed); 4 .50-cal. machine guns (fixed); 2 1,600-lb bombs or 10 5-inch rockets

North American AT-6/T-6/SNJ Texan

More Allied pilots who flew in World War II and the decades immediately after trained in this North American aircraft than in any other. The aircraft originated with the North American Aviation NA-16, which first flew in 1935. After US Army evaluation it entered service as the basic trainer BT-1, and following several evolutions it flew as the definitive advanced trainer AT-6 in 1939 (that designation being assigned in 1940).

The US Navy ordered its first models in 1936 as the NJ-1; it was the first Navy aircraft to be built by North American. Given the popular name Texan, the aircraft was soon ordered in large numbers for both services, with the Navy shifting to the designation SNJ. The SN meant scout trainer, although the application of "scout" was meaningless. Those Navy aircraft with carrier arresting gear had the suffix letter C (e.g., SNJ-3C). In US aircraft one or two fixed .30-caliber, forward-firing machine guns and a flexible .30-caliber gun in the after cockpit could be provided for gunnery training. Racks for small practice bombs could also be fitted.

Meanwhile, numerous other countries were procuring variants of the aircraft, some of them armed. Japan purchased two early models and Germany acquired several French aircraft after the surrender of France in the spring of 1940. Thailand ordered six armed—and camouflaged— single-seat aircraft and six armed two-seat models. Those aircraft had machine guns, 20-mm cannon in the former, and could carry bombs. None reached Thailand. The US Army designated them P-64 and A-27, respectively, and the A-27s were diverted to the Philippines where US forces flew them at the start of the war. (Probably four were captured intact by the Japanese.)

The massive US military aircraft programs of World War II demanded thousands of training aircraft and the AT-6/SNJ was produced in prodigious numbers. More than 16,000 Texans were built in the United States and Canada. Just over 7,000 were flown by the Army Air Forces, the Navy procured 4,024 as SNJs, and about 5,000 Harvards were flown by Commonwealth air forces. (In Canada, the Noorduyn Company built another 1,500 aircraft under license, most going to the Royal Canadian Air Force as Harvards under the US Lend-Lease program.) Counting the early, pre-AT-6/SNJ aircraft and North American contracts for other countries, the count probably exceeds 21,000 aircraft.

Aircraft went to other nations during and after the war, with more than 30 nations using the aircraft. The British flew armed aircraft against the Mau Maus in Kenya and terrorists in Malaya, and the Egyptians and Syrians used them against Israeli forces (which also flew the T-6). During the Korean War a number of Texan variants were flown by the US Air Force carrying Army observers on sorties behind enemy lines to locate enemy forces. Those were known as "Mosquito missions" with the aircraft carrying smoke-rockets to indicate targets for air or artillery attack.

The aircraft remained in US military service as a first-line trainer into the late 1950s. Other nations kept them longer; the last known to be in military service were South Africa's Texans and Harvards, which were finally retired in 1996!

The Texan was an all-metal, low-wing monoplane that resembled a fighter-type aircraft, with a radial engine, clean lines, and the student and instructor sitting in tandem under a long, glazed canopy. The early models had a fixed landing gear, soon changed to a fully retractable main undercarriage. (Four Swedish NA-16-4M derivatives were fitted with tricycle gear as part of the development of the SAAB J21A fighter; other Swedish aircraft had skis.)

During the aircraft's production run of almost ten years there were several upgrades to the design. The AT-6C, of which 2,970 were built, and the SNJ-4 used low-alloy steel and plywood to save an estimated 1,246 pounds of aluminum alloy per aircraft. When the feared aluminum shortages did not occur the original materials were used in subsequent production.

In June 1948 the newly established US Air Force changed the Texan's designation from AT-6 to T-6, and the more than 2,000 aircraft remaining in Air Force service were redesignated. Most of those underwent an extensive modernization, the changes including a new cockpit layout, increased fuel capacity, improved propellers, repositioned radio aerial, steerable tail wheel, and P-51 Mustang-type main landing gear. Those upgraded aircraft were designated T-6G. There were a variety of G configurations. The aircraft used for the Mosquito missions in Korea were designated T-6F, and 59 additional aircraft that were modified for that liaison role by North American being called LT-6G. An updated and armed reconnaissance variant—the RLT-6G—was provided to Iran. (There was no T-6J model, despite numerous reports citing such aircraft.)

Navy models reached SNJ-7. An improved Navy SN2J of 1946 did not go into production.

Although no longer used as a military trainer, many Texans survive in the private sector. Periodically they are seen on television and in the movies standing in for Japanese A6M Zero fighters—the aircraft that thousands of pilots trained in the Texan to fight in World War II.

The North American AT-6 Texan probably produced more
pilots during World War II than any other trainer. Flown in
large numbers by US and British Commonwealth air forces, the
Texan (British Harvard) survived for decades after the war as a
training and combat aircraft. The US Navy had some fitted for
carrier operation. *US Air Force*

AT-6A Characteristics

Design:	North American
Crew:	Pilot + student
Engines:	1 Pratt & Whitney R-1340–49 radial piston; 600 hp
Weights:	
Empty:	3,900 lb
Loaded:	5,155 lb
Dimensions:	
Length:	29 ft
Wingspan:	42 ft
Wing area:	254 sq ft
Height:	11 ft, 9 in
Speeds:	
Maximum:	210 mph
Ceiling:	24,200 ft
Range:	630 miles
Armament:	optional: 1 or 2 .30-caliber machine guns (fixed); 1 .30-caliber machine gun (flexible); small practice bombs

North American B-25 Mitchell

The B-25 Mitchell was one of the best-known medium bombers of World War II. Named for aviation iconoclast William (Billy) Mitchell, the B-25's most famous action was the April 1942 raid against Japan led by Lt. Col. James (Jimmy) Doolittle from the aircraft carrier *Hornet*. Subsequently, the aircraft was flown on virtually every battlefront of the war, seeing action as a bomber, anti-shipping, and anti-submarine aircraft.

The US Army Air Forces flew three medium bombers during World War II—the North American B-25 Mitchell, the Martin B-26 Marauder, and the Douglas A-26 Indvader. Of the three aircraft, the B-25 was the slowest and had the lightest bomb load; like the Marauder, it left frontline service with the end of the war, although several hundred B-25s remained in USAF training and support duties until 1959. Still, the Mitchell's World War II combat record was without parallel, making it one of the most significant aircraft of the war.

The B-25 entered AAF service in 1941. Immediately following the Japanese attack on Pearl Harbor, Mitchells began defensive patrols along the US West Coast. Meanwhile, President Roosevelt asked his military commanders to plan a retaliation against Japan for Pearl Harbor. Four months later 16 B-25B bombers led by Doolittle carried out the first attack against the Japanese home islands. Launched from the aircraft carrier *Hornet*—no mean feat for a 13-ton, propeller-driven aircraft without the use of catapults—the B-25s bombed Tokyo, Kobe, Nagoya, and Yokohama on April 18, 1942. The attack inflicted little material damage but was a great morale boost for the United States. Fifteen of the bombers crashed in China on the night of April 18–19, with two crews (ten men) being captured by the Japanese. The other B-25 landed in Soviet Siberia. Its crew and the 13 from China eventually were returned to the United States.

(Prior to the Doolittle raid, on February 2, 1942, two B-25s were flown off of the carrier *Hornet* in the Atlantic to demonstrate the feasibility of such an operation; later, in November 1944, the Navy flight tested a Marine PBJ-1H fitted with an arresting hook for carrier operation.)

AAF B-25s were soon serving in China, the Middle East, Northwest Africa, Alaska, and the South Pacific, but it was in the Southwest Pacific that the Mitchell would be used to the greatest effect. Beginning in December 1942, Australian-based B-25Cs and B-25Ds were employed as "commerce destroyers" or "strafers," mounting up to eight nose-mounted .50-caliber machine guns. The first of these planes became operational as 16 Japanese ships moved toward Lae, New Guinea, on March 1, 1943. Flying low and working in concert with A-20 Havocs, B-17 Flying Fortresses, and Australian Beaufighters, the Mitchells strafed the enemy ships and "skipped" their bombs across the water's surface into Japanese ships. By March 4, all eight transports were sunk, as were four of the eight escorting destroyers. The Battle of the Bismarck Sea had destroyed the Japanese convoy and ushered in a new anti-shipping tactic for the AAF, which belatedly abandoned high-altitude attacks against ships.

The low-level B-25 attack was also developed for ground targets, particularly Japanese airfields. The heavy bombs favored by early AAF planners were replaced by large numbers of small, parachute-retarded fragmentation bombs (parafrags) that blanketed widely dispersed targets with devastating results, especially when coupled with the B-25's heavy battery of forward-firing machine guns.

North American began development of the B-25 in early 1938 and a company prototype aircraft flew in January 1939. In September 1939 a production contract was awarded. Thus, there was no XB-25 experimental prototype and the first flight of a B-25 occurred on August 19, 1940. Despite the B-25 production of 9,816 aircraft, during the war AAF squadrons reached a peak of only 2,656 aircraft (July 1944) because of the large numbers of B-25s flown by the US Marine Corps (with the designation PBJ-1) and by foreign air forces, especially Britain and the Soviet Union. B-25 production ended in August 1945 in favor of the A-26 Invader (which was redesignated B-26 in 1948).

The B-25 was a twin-engine, mid-wing aircraft with a distinctive twin-tail configuration. The aircraft was well liked by pilots (in contrast to the unpopular Martin B-26 Marauder). The standard B-25 models had a glazed nose, whereas the "gunship" version had a solid nose with several machine guns. Dorsal and tail guns and two flexible waist guns (fired by a single gunner) added another six .50-cal. machine guns, giving the B-25H solid-nose aircraft a total of 14 guns. Doolittle B-25B aircraft had painted broomsticks to simulate tail guns to deter attackers. Following the success of the Pacific strafer modifications, 405 B-25Gs and 1,000 B-25Hs were built with a 75-mm cannon firing through the nose. A hit with this heavy weapon could demolish most targets, but the weapon proved difficult to aim and slow to reload. The most widely produced variant, the B-25J, was built with either the glazed bombardier nose or an eight-gun nose configuration.

The B-25H could carry an aerial torpedo in place of bombs.

Although not the best-performing US medium bomber of World War II, the North American B-25 Mitchell established a war record unmatched by any other medium. This 340th Bomb Group B-25C was photographed during a raid against German positions in Yugoslavia in 1943. Note the dark patches on flak damage suffered during previous missions. *US Air Force*

B-25J Characteristics

Design:	North American
Crew:	6 (pilot, copilot, navigator or bombardier-navigator, engineer-turret gunner, radio operator-waist gunner, tail gunner)
Engines:	2 Wright R-2600-92 radial piston; 1,700 hp each
Weights:	
Empty:	19,480 lb
Maximum takeoff:	35,000 lb
Dimensions:	
Length:	52 ft, 11 in
Wingspan:	67 feet, 7 in
Wing area:	610 sq ft
Height:	16 ft, 4 in
Speeds:	
Maximum:	272 mph
Cruise:	230 mph
Ceiling:	24,000 ft
Range:	1,275 miles
Armament:	12 .50-cal. machine guns (8 in nose, twin dorsal and tail turrets, two in waist); 8 5-in rockets; 3,000 lb of bombs

North American P-51 Mustang

The most capable US land-based fighter of the war was the P-51 Mustang. But in the words of the official US Army Air Forces history, because of AAF reluctance to adopt the plane, the Mustang "came close to representing the costliest mistake made by the AAF in World War II."

By 1943 the US strategic bombing effort against Germany was failing because of the high loss rate during daylight missions. The first AAF P-51 fighter group was deployed to Britain in November 1943. Only the availability of the P-51 as a bomber escort aircraft from December 1943 permitted a resumption of daylight bombing. Its first long-range escort mission on December 13, 1943, was 490 miles from bases in England to Kiel and back, a fighter escort record at that time. The following March the P-51s accompanied the heavy bombers all the way to Berlin and back, a round-trip of 1,100 miles.

The Mustang also served in the Pacific theater. Based on Iwo Jima—midway between the US B-29 Superfortress bomber bases in the Marianas and Tokyo—the P-51s provided escort for those aircraft against far less effective Japanese air defenses.

The US Navy flight tested a P-51 with an arresting hook aboard the aircraft carrier *Shangri-La* in 1944, but no naval use followed. The liquid-cooled engine would require special facilities and the aircraft would have to be modified; the F6F Hellcat and F4U Corsair, already in service, and the future Grumman F8F Bearcat and Ryan FR Fireball were considered adequate for Navy requirements.

P-51s were retained in the US Air Force after the war, their designation changed to F-51 in 1948. Several active and reserve squadrons were in combat during the early part of the Korean War, as were some photo-reconnaissance planes with the designation RF-51.

The success of the P-51 led North American to produce the Twin Mustang as a very-long-range fighter. Two lengthened P-51H fuselages were joined by a short midwing section, providing a twin-engine, two-pilot fighter, usually with a large radar pod fitted under the midwing to provide a night-fighter capability. Six .50-caliber machine guns were fitted in the midwing. Their range was demonstrated on February 27–28, 1947, when a P-82B named *Betty Joe* flew 5,051 miles, from Oahu to New York, the longest nonstop flight in history by a piston engine fighter.

Designated P-82 (and later F-82), these fighters were flown primarily to the USAF Air Defense Command. In late 1948 there were 225 F-82s assigned to the command (of 273 produced). In 1949 three F-82 squadrons were sent to Japan and on June 27, 1950, three North Korean Yak-9s were shot down by F-82s, the first USAF kill of the conflict.

The Mustang was designed by North American for the British in 1940 as a substitute for the US P-40 Warhawk, which was considered unsuitable for European operations. The Mustang was a single-engine, low-wing fighter, much lighter than either the P-47 Thunderbolt or P-38 Lightning. It had a very clean airframe, differing from nearly all contemporary fighters in having square-cut wingtips and tail surfaces. The P-51 could be easily distinguished by the large under-fuselage radiator air intake for the liquid-cooled, in-line engine.

The first aircraft, with the North American designation NA-73, flew for the first time in October 1940 with an Allison engine. Production began in the second half of 1941 with orders for the Royal Air Force. Deliveries were delayed by the decision to provide the plane with the Rolls-Royce Merlin 61 engine. After trials with a pair of XP-51s the AAF belatedly began ordering the aircraft, initially called the Apache.

Production totaled 14,819 aircraft, of which 7,956 were the definitive P-51D variant, easily identified by having introduced the bubble canopy to the design. A single-seat photo version was designated F-6 and 500 aircraft carried the attack designation A-36, being fitted with dive brakes and wing racks for bombs. They were the first Mustangs to see combat, primarily in the 1943 invasion of Sicily.

Ten two-seat TP-51D trainers were built (with a single "bubble" canopy), one of which was modified for use by Gen. Dwight D. Eisenhower to inspect the Normandy beachheads in June 1944. However, when "Ike" did fly over the Normandy battlefield, on July 4, 1944, it was apparently in a P-51B that had a second seat crammed in. Piloted by Maj. Gen. Elwood R. (Pete) Quesada, the Allied commander flew some 50 miles beyond friendly lines, the low-flying P-51 was escorted by three others, their pilots scouring the skies for German aircraft. (Neither Ike nor Quesada wore parachutes in the crowded cockpit.)

The early aircraft, built to meet the short-range needs of the RAF, had a combat range of less than 400 miles; this was steadily increased, reaching 1,800 miles with the P-51H model, which had a top speed of 487 miles per hour; also, its ceiling was in excess of 40,000 feet, making it a truly high-altitude aircraft. The P-51 normally was armed with six .50-caliber machine guns and could carry 5-inch rockets or up to 2,000 pounds of bombs. Early British Mustangs had four 20-mm cannon in place of the machine guns.

The effectiveness of the North American P-51 Mustang as a
long-range escort fighter proved to be the most decisive factor
in the success of the US daylight strategic bombing campaign
over German-held Europe. This 361st Fighter Group P-51D
was over Britain in the summer of 1944. Later redesignated
F-51, the Mustang also served in the Korean War and was the
basis for the F-82 Twin Mustang. *US Air Force*

P-51D Characteristics

Design:	North American
Crew:	Pilot
Engines:	1 Rolls-Royce Merlin V-1650-7 in-line; 1,490 hp
Weights:	
Empty:	7,125 lb
Loaded:	11,600 lb
Dimensions:	
Length:	32 ft, 3 in
Wingspan:	37 ft
Wing area:	235.7 sq ft
Height:	12 ft, 2 in
Speeds:	
Maximum:	437 mph (at 25,000 ft)
Cruise:	362 mph
Ceiling:	41,900 ft
Range:	950 miles
Armament:	6 .50-cal. machine guns (fixed); 2 1,000-lb bombs or 10 5-inch HVAR rockets

Piper L-4 Grasshopper

The development of the Taylor Cub into the Piper Cub led to one of history's most successful civilian light aircraft. Subsequently, when the Piper Cub was introduced to the US Army in 1941 for artillery spotting and liaison with frontline troops, a new class of military aviation was born. Initially designated O-59 in the Army's observation series, the Cub became the L-4 when the new liaison series was created in April 1942. It became the most widely produced liaison aircraft of World War II, serving primarily with the US Army Ground Forces and as a civilian trainer at home, with the US Navy also flying a number of the aircraft.

The experiences of the German and other armies in the early days of World War II demonstrated to US military planners the extreme vulnerability of contemporary US observation aircraft (see Curtiss O-52 Owl entry in chapter 3). In June–July 1941 eight civil Cubs were evaluated by the Army for rough-field operation, durability, and troop support during field maneuvers. Nicknamed Grasshoppers—a name initially applied to the Cub, but soon used for all light liaison types—the light aircraft were a resounding success. Further field maneuvers in the fall of 1941 demonstrated the potential of these low-cost "puddle jumpers," and military orders quickly followed for several hundred Aeronca, Piper, and Taylor light planes.

The L-4 entered combat in November 1942 when the aircraft carrier *Ranger* carried three L-4 aircraft in addition to her naval aircraft for the North Africa invasion—Operation Torch. On November 9, as soon as an airfield was available ashore, the three Grasshoppers took off and were promptly fired on by a US cruiser. Two landed safely near a French fort; the third, hit by Army ground fire, made a "controlled crash" and the wounded pilot crawled away before the plane exploded.

Following this inauspicious start, other L-4s spotted artillery for US troops, evacuated wounded, laid telephone wires, and carried dispatches between various headquarters. They soon became an invaluable resource, both to ground commanders and foot soldiers. The aircraft could be hidden under trees and launched anywhere 500 feet of clear road or field was available. Other L-4s were launched from ships—plywood runways were built atop several LSTs (tank landing ships), allowing L-4s to be launched in immediate support of invasion forces in the Mediterranean.

Although normally unarmed, Pipers sometimes went aloft with the observer carrying an M1 Garand or other weapon for the odd shot at a German caught on the road. Several Pipers were jury-rigged with bazookas strapped to their wing struts, but their use brought mixed success.

Numerous Pipers were purchased by the US Navy for primary training (given the designations NE-1 and NE-2) and for air evacuation (designated HE-1 and, later, AE-1)

The L-4 was developed out of the Piper J-3 Cub, which first flew in late 1937. Not counting the four evaluation aircraft that the Army purchased from three light aircraft firms, Taylor built 1,936 O-57/L-2 Grasshoppers

With heavy observation aircraft unable to survive against modern air defenses, the US Army turned to light civil aircraft for artillery spotting (leaving tactical reconnaissance to specially equipped fighters). The best of these light aircraft was the Piper J-3 Cub, flown by the Army as the L-4 Grasshopper. This L-4B served in Italy with the 9th Field Artillery of the 3d Infantry Division. *US Air Force*

and the Army took over 41 from private users; Aeronca produced 1,435 O-58/L-3 aircraft and the Army took over 48 more from private users; and Piper built 5,549 O-59/L-4 Grasshoppers and another 117 were acquired from private users. In addition, the US Navy and Marine Corps acquired 350 Pipers, designated AE, HE, and NE, which were used for training and as aerial ambulances. Including the similar L-1 Vigilant and L-5 Sentinel aircraft of this type, the US military forces procured more than 12,500 of these aircraft during the war.

All of these Grasshoppers were single-engine, two-seat light aircraft with a high-wing configuration that made them excellent observation aircraft. Grasshoppers were built with small Continental engines, but Taylor, Aeronca, and Piper all developed glider variants by simply removing the engine and wheels, substituting a new nose and simplified cross-axle landing gear.

L-4J Characteristics

Design:	Piper
Crew:	Pilot + observer
Engines:	1 Continental O-170-3 4-cylinder in-line piston; 65 hp
Weights:	
Empty:	708 lb
Maximum takeoff:	1,220 lb
Dimensions:	
Length:	22 ft, 3 in
Wingspan:	35 ft, 2 $\frac{1}{2}$ in
Wing area:	179 sq ft
Height:	6 ft, 8 in
Speeds:	
Maximum:	85 mph
Cruise:	75 mph
Ceiling:	9,300 ft
Range:	190 miles
Armament:	None

Sikorsky R-4/HNS

Russian-born aircraft designer Igor Sikorsky's VS-316A is believed to have been the world's first helicopter designed specifically for military use and the first US rotary-wing aircraft to be produced in large numbers. A few of the helicopters were used by the US Army during World War II, primarily for rescue operations in Alaska, Burma, and other difficult terrain areas.

The first R-4 combat rescue occurred on April 25–26, 1944, when Army 2d Lt. Carter Harman lifted a downed observation plane pilot and the three injured British soldiers out of a Burmese jungle. Also in 1944 an R-4 flew an agent of the US Office of Strategic Services (OSS) into the Balkans on a clandestine mission, revealing another role for helicopters.

US Navy interest in helicopters during the war was under the aegis of the Coast Guard (which was then part of the Navy). The first shipboard trials began on May 7, 1943, with Army Col. Frank Gregory making 20 landings and takeoffs in an R-4 on the tanker *Bunker Hill* in Long Island Sound. The flights were made with the ship dead in the water and at speeds up to 15 knots, with winds up to 12 knots from various compass points. More than 50 observers—including Sikorsky—were on board for the trials.

In November 1943 the Coast Guard conducted extensive trials with the HNS-1 while the British evaluated an HNS-1 on board the merchant ship *Daghestan* in Long Island Sound. Subsequently, the US Coast Guard cutter *Governor Cobb* and the *Daghestan* operated HNS-1s in the mid-Atlantic while en route to Britain in convoy. However, those tests were severely limited by bad flying weather. Also, in November 1943 the Coast Guard established the first "naval" helicopter training base at Coast Guard Air Station Floyd Bennett Field, New York. A 60-by-40-foot articulated platform was installed at the air station to simulate the motion of a ship's deck at sea. British as well as US helicopter pilots trained there.

The single prototype XR-4 made its first flight on January 13, 1942, and was formally accepted by the Army on May 30, 1942. Three YR-4A and 27 YR-4B evaluation aircraft were ordered in 1943. The Army sent six to Burma and six to Alaska; another three went to the Navy/Coast Guard and seven went to the Royal Air Force, the remainder being used for evaluation

Sikorsky's R-4 (Navy HNS) was the first helicopter to be series produced by the Allies. In this demonstration flight a rescue is performed by an HNS-1 piloted by Coast Guard Comdr. Frank A. Erickson. During World War II the Coast Guard was part of the US Navy and was responsible for naval helicopter development. *US Air Force*

in the United States. The Navy designated their helicopters HNS-1, and the RAF assigned the name Hoverfly.

Subsequently, the Army ordered 100 more R-4B models, of which 22 went to the Navy and 45 to the RAF and Royal Navy. In all, 52 YR-4B/R-4B helicopters were transferred to Britain in 1943–45. As new helicopters were introduced, the surviving R-4 series became trainers; they remained in US military service until 1948.

The R-4/HNS was a refinement of Sikorsky's first successful rotary-wing aircraft, the VS-300, which made its first free flight on May 13, 1940. The R-4 had an enclosed cockpit with side-by-side seating for its pilot and single passenger. The main rotor had three articulated blades and a tail rotor provided stability. The helicopter could be fitted with wheels or floats, the latter being suitable for shipboard as well as water operations.

R-4B Characteristics

Design:	Igor Sikorsky
Crew:	Pilot + passenger
Engines:	1 Warner R-550-3 Super Scarab radial piston; 200 hp
Weights:	
Empty:	2,020 lb
Loaded:	2,535 lb
Dimensions:	
Length:	35 ft, 5 in
Rotor diameter:	38 ft
Height:	12 ft, 5 in
Speeds:	
Maximum:	75 mph
Ceiling:	8,000 ft
Range:	130 miles
Armament:	None

Supermarine Spitfire

The Supermarine Spitfire was the finest British fighter aircraft of World War II and is considered by many aviation historians to have been the best fighter of any nation in that conflict. Fast, acrobatic, and powerful, the Spitfire also pioneered the use of unarmed, lightweight fighter aircraft for long-range strategic and tactical reconnaissance. It was also one of history's few land-based fighters to be successfully modified for operations from aircraft carriers.

Entering Royal Air Force service in June 1938, the "Spit" looked the superior fighter aircraft, and before the war it was watched with expectation by the Luftwaffe pilots who would one day oppose it. On October 16, 1939, six weeks after the war began in Europe, Spitfires scored their first aerial victories, shooting down two unescorted He 111 bombers over the Firth of Forth in Scotland. Those were the first German aircraft to be shot down over Britain since 1918.

Britain had belatedly begun rearming in the 1930s and, despite those early victories in 1939, had far too few fighter aircraft with which to defend itself, let alone fight on the Continent. When the Battle of France began on May 10, 1940, all ten RAF fighter squadrons sent to confront the Germans flew Hurricanes. When reserves equivalent to two squadrons were sent, they too were Hurricanes, as were the six squadrons that followed soon after. Yet, such was the reputation of the Supermarine fighter that most Luftwaffe pilots downed during the battle for France would later claim to have been bested by a Spitfire.

The Spitfires, held in reserve for home defense, were finally committed to covering the British Expeditionary Force's withdrawal at Dunquirk, 14 days after the beginning of the German offensive. During the French campaign the British lost 453 fighters, but only 67 were Spitfires.

The hoarding of Spitfires had been critical. The Spitfire equipped only 19 squadrons of the RAF Fighter Command when the Battle of Britain began on July 10, 1940. (Hurricanes equipped 29 squadrons.) By the battle's end on October 31 the Hurricane had remained the dominant interceptor, with an average daily strength of 1,326 aircraft versus 957 Spitfires. Still, the Spitfire was the superior aircraft, and new engines and other refinements only increased its capabilities and reputation whereas the Hurricane had reached its design's performance limits. Spitfires would be the standard RAF air superiority fighter in every theater where British forces fought in World War II.

In 1942–43 two US fighter groups flew Spitfires pending the availability of American-built fighters. And, during the Normandy invasion on June 6, 1944, US Navy pilots flew land-based Spitfires to direct gunfire for naval ships.

Although retired from RAF service soon after World War II, Spitfires served in a large number of Third World air forces. British carrier-based Seafires served into the Korean War and also flew from French aircraft carriers.

The Spitfire and its Merlin engine had been developed by British aviation industry as private ventures, without government specification or sanction. The new fighter design was accepted by the Air Ministry in January 1935, and the prototype Spitfire flew on March 5, 1936. When production ended in October 1947, a total of 20,351 Spitfires and 2,408 navalized Seafires had been built. The Spitfire was the only Allied fighter being delivered at the beginning of the European war to still be in production when Japan surrendered in August 1945.

The Spitfire was a particularly clean design, with an in-line Rolls-Royce engine and distinctive elliptical wing and tail. Although less rugged and more vulnerable to enemy fire than the Hurricane, the Spitfire more than compensated for these limitations with its excellent acceleration and maneuverability.

The single-seat Spitfire was originally armed with eight .303-caliber machine guns, a configuration referred to as the "A" wing. Aircraft equipped with the "B" wing had two 20-mm cannon and four machine guns. Introduction of the "C" or "universal" wing allowed the Spitfire to be configured with either wing armament, or to carry four 20-mm cannon. Low altitude fighters usually had clipped, or squared, wingtips, whereas high-altitude fighters featured elongated, pointed wingtips. High-altitude variants also featured partially pressurized cockpits for pilot comfort and safety.

In the spring of 1943 the Rolls-Royce Griffon engine was adopted for the Spitfire, leading to a doubling of horsepower over the Mk.I with a commensurate speed increase of 35 percent.

The Spitfire's speed made it an excellent unarmed photo-reconnaissance aircraft. Beginning in 1941 Spitfires were produced with an arresting hook, folding wings, and other features for naval use, those being called Seafires. In addition, several Spitfires were experimentally fitted with floats.

Britain's most successful World War II fighter was the light,
speedy, and agile Supermarine Spitfire. The aircraft shown here
was delivered as a Mk.IA, then converted to a Mk.VB with a
new engine and two 20-mm cannons in the wings. Serving in
RAF No. 92 Squadron (East India Squadron), this aircraft was
shot down by an Me 109 on June 22, 1941. *US Air Force*

Spitfire Mk.Vb Characteristics

Design:	Supermarine
Engines:	1 Rolls-Royce Merlin 45, 46, 50, or 50A
	V-12 in-line piston; 1,440 hp
Weights:	
Empty:	5,065 lb
Maximum takeoff:	6,630 lb
Dimensions:	
Length:	29 ft, 11 in
Wingspan:	36 ft, 10 in (32 feet, 2 in for clipped-wing aircraft)
Wing area:	242 sq ft (231 sq ft for clipped-wing aircraft)
Height:	11 ft, 5 in
Speeds:	
Maximum:	369 mph
Ceiling:	37,000 ft
Range:	470 miles
Armament:	2 20-mm cannon (fixed); 4 .303-cal. machine guns (fixed)

Vickers Wellington

The Vickers Wellington had a pivotal role in the formation of Great Britain's bomber policy of the 1930s and formed the nucleus of the Royal Air Force Bomber Command's offensive force during the early years of World War II. The RAF accepted more Wellingtons than any other bomber in its history—a total of 11,460 aircraft.

At the beginning of World War II the twin-engine Wellingtons were operational in six Bomber Command squadrons. They were expected to enforce the RAF's belief that the bomber would always get through although, in the event, they proved that theory to be greatly flawed. Affectionately known as the "Wimpy" to its crews—a reference to the hamburger-eating character in American Popeye cartoons—Wellingtons mounted one of the first RAF wartime bomber raids on September 4,

1939, one day after war was declared. (The night before several Whitley bombers had flown over Germany dropping leaflets.)

As ten RAF Blenheims struck elements of the German fleet at Wilhelmshaven, 14 Wellingtons struck other warships at Brunsbüttel. No fighters intercepted the bombers, but flak was intense and a total of seven aircraft were lost—five Blenheims and two Wellingtons. (The only German ship damaged was hit by a Blenheim.) As was expected of all British bombers, unescorted formations of lightly armed Wellingtons were to fight their way through enemy defenses to destroy military targets (concurrently minimizing civilian losses), but improvements in German flak and air-defense fighter capabilities, coupled with the advent of ground-based radar, tipped the balance in favor of the defenses. Although the few early raids proved inconclusive, by December 1939 the dangers had become all too apparent: in two raids German defenses destroyed 21 of the 36 Wellingtons dispatched. The RAF Air Staff got the message and, with no long-range escort fighter available, abandoned daylight missions for a night-bombing campaign. When political restrictions on the bombing of Germany were lifted in late 1940, Wellingtons were in the vanguard of Bomber Command's attacks, dropping the first 4,000-pound blockbuster bombs in April 1941, providing well over half of the RAF force participating in the first 1,000-plane raid, in May 1942, and performing pioneering work in the RAF pathfinder force beginning in August 1942.

As four-engine bombers gradually took over the night-bombing campaign, more Wellingtons were shifted to Coastal Command's anti-submarine war, to torpedo and mine-laying roles, and to service with first-line units in secondary theaters. In 1942 Wimpies became the first RAF long-range bombers in the Far East. They also served in the training role until finally withdrawn from RAF service in 1953.

The Wellington was designed in response to a 1932 Air Ministry specification with the prototype flying on June 15, 1936. The extensively revised first production aircraft did not take to the air until December 1937. The Wellington had a fabric-covered, geodesic aluminum frame as first used in the Vickers Wellesley. Although stressed-aluminum construction quickly became the industry standard, the Wellington's framework proved

Britain's Vickers Wellington was the primary bomber of RAF Bomber Command until completely replaced by heavier, four-engine types in 1943. Usually referred to as the "Wimpy," the aircraft's fabric-covered geodesic structure could absorb tremendous punishment and continue flying. This Wellington Mk.II was photographed over Britain in 1940. *US Air Force*

extremely light and rugged, and often remained intact despite horrendous damage from enemy gunfire. The Wellington's designers often exceeded Air Ministry specifications, creating an aircraft of remarkable efficiency. The Mk.IC variant, introduced in 1940, featured improved electrical and hydraulic systems and, the addition in the after fuselage of two flexible guns for lateral defense. The Mk.IC became the most numerous variant, numbering more than 2,685 aircraft.

Wellington Mk.IC Characteristics

Design:	Vickers
Crew:	6 (pilot, navigator, engineer, bomb aimer, 2 gunners)
Engines:	2 Bristol Pegasus XVIII radial piston; 1,000 hp each
Weights:	
Empty:	19,002 lb
Maximum takeoff:	30,000 lb
Dimensions:	
Length:	64 ft, 7 in
Wingspan:	86 ft, 2 in
Wing area:	850 sq ft
Height:	17 ft, 5 in
Speeds:	
Maximum:	235 mph (at 15,500 ft)
Cruise:	180 mph
Ceiling:	18,000 ft
Range:	1,200 miles with 4,500 lb of bombs; 2,550 miles with 1,000 lb of bombs
Armament:	6 .303-cal. machine guns (twin nose and tail turrets, two single in flexible waist mounts); 6,000 lb of bombs

Vought F4U Corsair

The US Navy's F4U Corsair was the last US piston-engine fighter. It performed outstanding service in World War II and, as an attack aircraft, in the French Indochina War and the Korean War. It was the last piston fighter produced in the United States.

The F4U Corsair—developed as a carrier-based fighter—failed its initial carrier landing trials. Rejected by the Navy, it went to war as a land-based fighter with the Marine Corps. Yet, by the end of World War II Corsairs were found aboard most US and several British fleet carriers as well as on small escort carriers. US Navy and Marine pilots flew Corsairs in first-line Navy squadrons until 1955.

The Vought Corporation began development of the F4U in early 1938, designing the smallest possible airframe around the most powerful engine available: the Pratt & Whitney XR-2800 Double Wasp. To accommodate the 1,850-horsepower engine without overly long landing gear struts, the plane had an inverted gull wing with the main legs of the landing gear located at the wing knuckles. The wings folded upward for carrier stowage.

The prototype XF4U-1 first flew on May 29, 1940, and by the end of the year it had attained 404 miles per hour, faster than any US fighter then in the air. Production contracts, however, were delayed for more than a year. Deliveries of the F4U to Navy squadrons began in October 1942. Because of poor cockpit visibility and other problems the aircraft failed its initial carrier trials.

Most wartime-production Corsairs went to the Marine Corps for land use. The first US Corsairs to enter combat were Marine fighter squadron VMF-124, which arrived at Henderson Field on Guadalcanal in the Solomons in February 1943. Those F4U-1s had their first battle with Japanese aircraft on February 13, while escorting Navy PB4Y-1s (i.e., B-24 Liberators) on a bombing mission against Bougainville. The first US Navy squadron to fly the F4U in combat was fighter squadron VF-17, which arrived in the Solomons in September 1943.

The Corsair proved to be a highly effective long-range, land-based fighter and attack aircraft. Its great power enabled a Corsair pilot to choose the time and place he would fight, being able to break away from enemy fighters when an unfavorable situation developed.

Meanwhile, the British began flying the Corsair from carriers. The plane's first major carrier operation took place on April 3, 1944, in strikes from the carrier *Victorious* against the German battleship *Tirpitz*. Subsequently, a few US Navy squadrons flew the modified F4U-1A from carriers, followed aboard ship by small numbers of the radar-equipped F4U-2 night fighter and F4U-1P camera planes. The F4U-2 was the first single-seat radar-equipped night fighter to enter service with any country.

In response to the Japanese kamikaze attacks against US warships, in late December 1944 Marine F4U squadrons were assigned to US Navy fast carriers to rapidly increase their defensive fighter strength. Although initially there were many problems, the Corsair was aboard US carriers to stay. Marine and Navy F4Us flew from the larger carriers, whereas the Marines formed several air groups that included F4Us to fly from escort carriers to provide close air support and combat air patrol for amphibious landings.

In 1944, Charles Lindbergh, as a civilian technical specialist for United Aircraft, flew more than 50 combat missions with Marines in the Corsair. On one flight he took off with a 4,000-pound bomb load—one 2,000-pounder and two 1,000-pounders.

In World War II the F4U had an overall 11:1 kill-to-loss ratio over Japanese aircraft with an estimated 1,400 enemy planes of all types destroyed by F4Us in the Pacific. Twenty-three US Marine aces scored five or more aerial kills in Corsairs, whereas several other aces made some of theirs in the "bent-wing" fighter. In addition, 24 Navy fighter aces scored five or more kills in Corsairs.

More than 11,500 Corsairs had been completed when the war ended in August 1945. Vought produced most of them with identical aircraft being built by Brewster as the F3A-1 and by Goodyear as the FG-1. Production was continued after the war.

In the postwar era the Corsair was a mainstay of carrier fighter squadrons pending the arrival of jet aircraft. For example, the first US carrier to operate in the Mediterranean after the war was the *Franklin D. Roosevelt* (August–October 1946). On her decks was a 123-plane "battle group"—a fighter squadron with 33 F4U-4 Corsairs plus 4 F6F-5P and 4 F6F-5N Hellcats; a fighter-bomber squadron with 32 F4U-4B Corsairs; a bomber squadron with 24 SB2C-5 Helldivers; and a torpedo squadron with another 24 Helldivers and 2 TBM-3E Avengers.

When the Korean War erupted in June 1950, the only US carrier in the Far East was the *Valley Forge*. She embarked a typical air group of the period—two jet fighter squadrons with 30 F9F-2B Panthers, two fighter squadrons with 28 F4U-4B Corsairs, and an attack squadron with 14 AD-4 Skyraiders. The carrier-based Navy F4Us soon were complemented by Marine-piloted Corsairs operating from light and escort carriers in the close air support role.

During the war night-flying F4U-5N variants—flown by Marine and Navy pilots from shore bases—also shot down several North Korean aircraft. Lt. Guy P. Bordelon flying an F4U-5N was the Navy's only Korean War fighter ace. Assigned to the carrier *Princeton*, but operating from an airfield near Seoul, Bordelon shot down three Po-2 biplanes and two Yak-18 Max trainers used for night harassment over Allied lines.

Also during the Korean War, Marine pilots flying F4Us from the light carrier *Bataan* downed three Yaks and a Marine Corsair from the *Sicily* shot down a MiG-15. A Navy F4U from the *Valley Forge* shot down a Soviet Tu-2 approaching a carrier task force in the Yellow Sea.

When the Korean War ended in July 1953 the French were locked in conflict against the communist Viet Minh in Indochina. The following year the US Navy delivered 25 AU-1 (formerly F4U-7) models designed for low-level attack. Those planes had four 20-mm cannon and could carry four 1,000-pound bombs.

Corsairs also flew in the Suez conflict of 1956 from the French carriers *Arromanches* and *La Fayette*, the latter the former USS *Langley*. Both ships had F4U-7 squadrons that flew strikes against Egyptian positions. Several other nations also flew the Corsair. The Argentina Navy flew ex-US Navy F4U-5 and -5N variants from the light carrier *Independencia*.

Corsair production ended in the United States in January 1953. The Corsair thus was the last piston-engine fighter built in the United States. Production totaled 15,056 aircraft, including 2,486 that went directly to other countries. Corsairs also were transferred to other countries after US service.

The last Corsairs assigned to a first-line US squadron were F4U-5N night fighters with Composite Squadron (VC) 4, They served in that squadron until December 1955.

The Vought F4U Corsair was the last piston-engine fighter to be mass-produced by the United States. It achieved an outstanding record as a land- and carrier-based fighter and attack aircraft in World War II and the Korean War. The closest plane, piloted by Ira Kepford of Navy Fighter Squadron 17, has 16 Japanese flags indicating enemy planes shot down. *US Navy*

Eric M. Brown described the Corsair in his *Wings of the Navy*:

Chance Vought's F4U Corsair was not a comely aeroplane by any yardstick. It was an anathema to some pilots and shear ambrosia to others. There were those pilots that acclaimed it was the best single-seat fighter of any nation to emerge from [World War II]; there were pilots that pronounced it a vicious killer equally dispassionate towards killing its pilot as his opponent. Indeed, few fighters were capable of arousing within those that flew them such extremes of passion as was the Corsair.

F4U-4 Characteristics

Design:	Vought/United Aircraft
Crew:	Pilot
Engines:	1 Pratt & Whitney R-2800-18W radial piston; 2,100 hp
Weights:	
Empty:	9,205 lb
Loaded:	14,670 lb
Dimensions:	
Length:	33 ft, 8 in
Wingspan:	41 ft
Wing area:	314 sq ft
Height:	14 ft, 9 in
Speeds:	
Maximum:	446 mph (at 26,200 ft)
Cruise:	215 mph
Ceiling:	41,500 ft
Range:	1,000 miles
Armament:	6 .50-cal. machine guns (fixed);[*] 2 1,000-lb bombs[**] or 8 5-inch HVAR rockets

[*] F4U-5N and AU-1 had four 20-mm cannon in place of machine guns.
[**] AU-1 carried up to two 1,600-lb bombs and one 2,000-lb bomb and 10 5-inch HVAR rockets (maximum bomb capacity was 8,200 lb with runway takeoff).

Waco CG-4A Hadrian

Glider flight can be traced back through several centuries of experimentation, although many early efforts were tragic failures. Development and deployment of the combat glider began with the Germans, who used gliders and paratroopers to capture the Belgian bridges over the Albert Canal and fortress of Eben-Emael on May 10, 1940, opening the path for the German Army to rapidly defeat Belgium, the Netherlands, and France in May–June 1940.

The employment of airborne troops opened a new dimension in ground warfare. The ability to quickly place a unit of trained soldiers almost anywhere behind enemy lines was developed through parachute infantry, or "paratroopers," but that option required special—and time-consuming—parachute training of an elite force. During operational "drops" the paratroopers could be scattered over a wide area, losing critical time assembling as a fighting unit. Glider troops needed only to be trained for combat, and could be dropped in small units, even carrying small vehicles and light artillery in their unpowered aircraft. (Although the US Army required all paratroopers to be volunteers, glider-borne troops could, on occasion, be assigned to that duty.)

The US and British Armies recognized the potential of this new weapon, and the former responded with procurement of the Waco CG-4 Hadrian (originally known as the Haig), the most widely produced combat glider in history.

The CG-4 (Cargo-Glider 4) was first employed in Operation Husky, the Anglo-American invasion of Sicily in July 1943. Allied naval gunfire disrupted the glider/tow-plane formations, shooting down some aircraft, causing the premature release of some gliders, and scattering the survivors over a wide area. Still, acting in concert with paratroopers, the glider forces proved to be highly effective against German and Italian forces on the Mediterranean island.

Subsequent Allied glider operations in Burma, Normandy, Holland, and Germany increased in operational effectiveness. However, gliders were quickly discarded after the war. The advent of the troop-carrying helicopter provided considerably more flexibility in selecting landing sites, dispensed with the need for tow aircraft, and offered an aircraft that could withdraw to remove wounded or return with reinforcements (albeit, without the advantage of a silent entry).

Following the successes of German World War II glider operations, the US Army selected the Waco CG-4A Hadrian to insert troops behind enemy lines. Capable of carrying 15 troops or a small vehicle or howitzer, the Hadrian was history's most widely produced combat glider. This Commonwealth-built CG-4 was used for assault training at Lubbock Army Air Field, Texas. *Norman Taylor, courtesy Robert F. Dorr*

The XCG-4 first flew in 1942, and a total of 13,906 were delivered to US and British forces from 16 different manufacturers. (In comparison, only some 3,700 of the excellent British Airspeed Horsa glider were built, whereas the pioneering German DFS 230 and its replacement Gotha Go 242 saw respective production runs of 1,022 and 1,528 aircraft.)

The Hadrian was built of fabric-covered wood and metal frame. Noting the apparent fragility of the glider, one wag quipped that it might be safer to fly the somewhat more substantial crates in which the gliders were delivered. The glider's nose hinged upward to allow rapid exit for 15 troops, or loading and unloading of a jeep, small truck, or 75-mm howitzer. Although the CG-4 descended rapidly once released from its tow aircraft, its range when towed was limitless. One Hadrian delivered to the RAF was towed across the Atlantic by a C-47 (with the flight made in several stages).

Waco also developed a scaled-up version of the Hadrian, designated CG-13A, to carry 42 troops or four tons of cargo in its ultimate configuration. However, only 139 were built, including prototypes.

CG-4A Characteristics

Design:	Waco
Crew:	2 (pilot, copilot) + 15 troops
Engines:	None
Weights:	
Empty:	3,700 lb
Maximum takeoff:	7,500 lb
Dimensions:	
Length:	48 ft, 4 in
Wingspan:	83 ft, 8 in
Wing area:	852 sq ft
Height:	12 ft, 7 in
Speeds:	
Maximum:	120 mph towing speed
Stall:	44 mph
Ceiling:	N/A
Range:	N/A
Armament:	None

Westland Lysander

Designed for the British army cooperation role, the Westland Lysander was a contemporary of the failed American Curtiss O-52 Owl. But the Lysander, designed for extremely short takeoff and landing runs, successfully performed clandestine missions into German-occupied France through the end of 1944—a remarkable accomplishment for an aircraft savaged by the Luftwaffe in the spring of 1940.

Seven Lysander squadrons were sent into France early in World War II. During the "Phoney War" that followed the fall of Poland through May 1940, one Lysander actually shot down and destroyed an He 111 bomber. But the tide quickly turned against the lightly armed "Lizzie," as the Lysander was known to its crews.

When the Germans invaded France on May 10, 1940, the Lysanders, operating individually and without fighter cover, were savaged in the air and on the ground by German aircraft. In defending themselves, Lysander crews managed to claim six enemy aircraft destroyed (two Bf 109s, one Bf 110, two Hs 126s, and one Ju 87). The Lysanders dropped supplies to beleaguered Allied units and reconnoitered German forces. But of 174 Lysanders sent to France, 88 were lost in aerial combat with another 30 destroyed on the ground; 120 crewmen were killed.

The short field advantages designed into the Lysander brought a new mission. In August 1941, Lysander crews began training for night missions into occupied France. They landed in open fields and on abandoned runways to deliver special agents and supplies, and return with "passengers" whose missions had been completed. By the time France had been liberated in 1944, Lysanders had delivered 293 agents to France, and returned more than 500 persons safely to Britain, all for the loss of only two aircraft.

Lysanders also served in the Mediterranean area and in the Far East. On occasion they were used as light bombers. Again, their successes and failures depended on the level of enemy response. As other, more capable aircraft became available, the surviving Lysanders were used as target tugs, air-sea rescue, and other utility work. They were withdrawn from operational use in 1944.

The Westland Lysander suffered terrible losses to the
Luftwaffe in the May–June 1940 Battle of France. But blessed
with remarkable short field capabilities, the monoplane gained
new life in support of Allied spies and agents and Free French
forces in German-held Europe through 1944. This TT.IIIA carries the yellow and black underside stripes identifying British
target tow-tugs. *Royal Air Force*

The Lysander prototype first flew on June 15, 1936. When production ended in 1942, Westland had built 1,427 of the aircraft, with 225 more produced by National Steel Car in Canada.

The Lysander featured a high-aspect ratio wing—only two feet shorter than the Lockheed P-38 Lightning—with leading edge slats along most of the span. The fixed landing gear housed two forward-firing machine guns and could be fitted with external racks for small bombs, flares, or supply containers. A third bomb rack, which could mount an auxiliary fuel tank, could be mounted below the after fuselage. The crew sat under an elongated, greenhouse canopy.

Lysander Mk.II Characteristics

Design:	Westland
Crew:	2 (pilot, observer-gunner)
Engines:	1 Bristol Perseus XII 9-cylinder radial piston; 905 hp
Weights:	
Empty:	4,160 lb
Maximum takeoff:	6,015 lb
Dimensions:	
Length:	30 ft, 6 in
Wingspan:	50 ft
Wing area:	260 sq ft
Height:	14 ft, 6 in
Speeds:	
Maximum:	230 mph (at 10,000 ft)
Stall:	55 mph
Ceiling:	26,500 ft
Range:	600 miles
Armament:	2 .303-cal. machine guns (fixed); 1 .303-cal. machine guns (flexible); 16 20-lb bombs

Six

The Cold War

The end of World War II marked the beginning of another conflict—the Cold War. This 45-year period consisted of a series of confrontations and crises involving primarily the Soviet Union and the United States, and to a lesser degree the Soviet-led Warsaw Pact and the US-led North Atlantic Treaty Organization (NATO). Although there was no direct conflict between the United States and USSR—the so-called "super powers"—both sides contributed advisors and massive amounts of military equipment to surrogate forces that were engaged in combat.

During the Korean War (1950–53) the Soviets provided weapons to North Korea and to China for combat against the United States and its allies. In addition, Soviet pilots flew MiG-15 fighters in the skies over North Korea to give battle to American aircraft. The next open conflict between "east and west" was the Vietnam War (1962–75), in which the Soviet Union provided weapons, including their latest fighter aircraft and surface-to-air missiles, but no combat pilots—only advisors and ground-based air defense personnel. Other surrogate wars during the Cold War–era included the Arab-Israeli conflicts from 1967 onward, in which the United States supported Israel and the USSR supported Arab states, and the Soviet incursion into Afghanistan, with the United States providing

Much of the Cold War consisted of the threat of a nuclear confrontation between the United States and the Soviet Union. Most US and Soviet combat aircraft produced during that period—from "fighters" to strategic bombers—could carry nuclear weapons. The Douglas AD Skyraider was the world's first single-engine aircraft to carry a nuclear weapon. This A-1J Skyraider from Attack Squadron 176 is readied for takeoff from the US aircraft carrier *Intrepid*. *US Navy*

arms to the rebels. In all but the last US and Soviet aircraft flown by indigenous pilots and mercenaries fought in the skies above the ground conflict. Both the United States and USSR attempted to incorporate lessons from those aerial encounters into aircraft development. (The Soviets garnered less intelligence than the United States because of the much more successful Israeli pilots coupled with a Syrian pilot defecting to Israel with his MiG-21, and Israeli capture of other Soviet aircraft, equipment, and manuals.)

There were several direct air-to-air encounters between the United States and USSR during the Cold War. Those consisted of Soviet fighters downing US intelligence collection aircraft flying along the peripheries of the Soviet Union. (The Chinese also shot down several US reconnaissance aircraft.) The one acknowledged US overflight of the USSR that ended in a shootdown, the U-2 piloted by Francis Gary Powers, was downed by an SA-2 Guideline surface-to-air missile. There had been 23 previous overflights of the USSR by U-2s which, although detected, were beyond the capabilities of Soviet missiles and fighters.

That there was no direct conflict between the United States and Soviet Union was undoubtedly attributable to both sides having nuclear weapons (the USSR from the early 1950s). Both sides developed (and in the early years modified) aircraft to carry nuclear weapons. Of the 29 aircraft listed in this chapter, 18 were capable of carrying nuclear weapons. These included fighter-type aircraft, the F-86 Sabre, F-100 Super Sabre, and F4H Phantom as well as the HSS-1 Seabat anti-submarine helicopter.

Significantly, whereas virtually all previous "patrol" aircraft of various nations, whether land-based or flying boats, were "maritime patrol" or anti-submarine aircraft (e.g., the PBY Catalina and PB4Y-2 Privateer in chapter 5), the P6M Seamaster described below was a nuclear strike and mining aircraft. That aircraft had neither "patrol" nor ASW capabilities.

The aircraft developed by both the United States and Soviet Union during the Cold War were based largely on German aviation technology. After the war both countries picked through the ruins of Germany, acquiring scientists and engineers, plans, drawings, components, and aircraft. Of particular importance was German research and development in the fields of turbojet propulsion and swept-wing configurations.

Soviet industrial complex limitations and quality control problems plagued the development of advanced aircraft. Indeed, the best Soviet turbojet aircraft of the 1950s had British-developed engines. Still, the USSR produced several remarkable aircraft in the fighter and strategic bomber categories.

American (and British) aircraft were more rugged and, in some instances, unquestionably the world's best aircraft in their respective categories. These included the British Canberra as well as several US fighter aircraft and two US aircraft developed specifically as spy planes—the U-2 and the SR-71 Blackbird. The U-2 and SR-71 were produced in great secrecy under the aegis of the Central Intelligence Agency (CIA), with US Air Force collaboration, by Lockheed Corporation's "Skunk Works."

This chapter describes the "ultimate" iterations of two other specialized aircraft types that have become vital components of modern military aviation. The KC-135 Stratotanker reflects the use of tanker aircraft for in-flight refueling, needed because of the high consumption rate of modern aircraft engines, and the long ranges required for military operations. These aircraft had their beginnings in British and US experiments in in-flight refueling immediately after World War II (although there were earlier efforts by aviators in both nations).

The E-3 Sentry is an Airborne Warning And Control System (AWACS) aircraft, the descendent of the US Navy's efforts starting in 1944 to develop Airborne Early Warning (AEW) or radar-picket aircraft. They were developed primarily to detect Japanese suicide attacks against US warships and evolved through a long series of naval aircraft, among them the TBM-3W Avenger, PB-1W (converted B-17G Flying Fortress), AD-3W Skyraider, WF (E-1) Tracer, and W2F (E-2) Hawkeye. The last, a twin-engine aircraft, remains in service on US and French aircraft carriers and is flown from shore bases by several other air forces.

Finally, two remarkable cargo/transport aircraft are discussed in this chapter, the C-130 Hercules and the C-5 Galaxy. The former is remarkable as the turbine-era equivalent to the C-47 Skytrain/Dakota—an aircraft produced in large numbers, flown by many air forces, and employed in almost uncounted roles. (Like the C-47, the C-130 has been used as a warplane and has "operated" from an aircraft carrier.) The C-5 Galaxy is significant as the first "giant" airlifter of the jet age, predating the even larger Soviet giants produced by the Antonov design bureau.

As the Cold War progressed, fewer and fewer nonaligned nations were able to produce combat aircraft because of their complexity and cost. Two successful examples are, however, described in this chapter—the Israel Aircraft Industries's derivatives of the French Mirage III/Mirage 5 designs, and Sweden's SAAB 35 Draken. Both were excellent aircraft and represented difficult design and production achievements.

Avro Vulcan

The Vulcan was the last of the three British V-bombers and the last "heavy" bomber to be built by Great Britain. When the Vulcan was taken out of service in 1982 Britain's strategic deterrent role passed entirely to the Royal Navy's ballistic missile submarines.

The Vulcan operated in the nuclear strike role from 1957 to 1982. The delta-wing aircraft was also employed in a reconnaissance role.

The Falklands War was the only time that any of the V-bombers were used in combat. During that 1982 war three Vulcan B.2 aircraft flying from Ascension island, 3,800 miles to the northeast, attacked the airfield at Port Stanley. One aircraft carried 21 1,000-pound bombs, and two aircraft attacked radar installations with Shrike anti-radar missiles. All were single-plane strikes and each required several in-flight refuelings by Victor K.2 tanker aircraft (also flying from Ascension). Those Vulcan missions—despite the great skill with which they were carried out—inflicted minimal damage to their targets.

The Vulcan and the two earlier V-bombers—the Vickers Valiant and Handley Page Victor—had their origins in Air Ministry specification B.35/46, issued in early 1947, that called for a medium-range, subsonic bomber that could operate from available land bases to deliver a 10,000-pound bomb load almost anywhere in the world. At the time 10,000 pounds was considered the nominal weight of a nuclear weapon. (British did not have an operational atomic bomb until 1953.) The aircraft would not carry defensive weapons, but would rely on speed and electronic countermeasures to evade hostile fighter defenses.

Of six proposals from British aviation firms responding to B.35/46, the government selected two advanced-technology designs, the Handley Page Victor, which featured a crescent wing, and the Avro Vulcan, which had a delta wing. Those radical designs would take several years of development, including extensive small-scale aircraft testing. Accordingly, the Air Ministry asked Vickers, which had proposed a less radical design, to proceed with the Valiant.

The Valiant had a large wing with a mean sweep of 20 degrees, which was more sharply swept inboard than in the main outer plane. The horizontal tail surfaces rode high on the vertical tail to be well clear of the jet exhaust. The aircraft entered service in 1955 with a total of nine Valiant bomber squadrons being formed. (Later two were designated as refueling squadrons and one as a reconnaissance squadron.)

Subsequently, the Victor entered service in 1957 with a total of four Victor B.1 squadrons being formed. The improved B.2 variant entered service in 1961 with three squadrons flying that aircraft.

The first flight of the Vulcan prototype occurred on August 30, 1952. The B.1 variant entered service in 1957. A total of six squadrons flew the Vulcan B.1. The subsequent B.2, designed to carry stand-off nuclear missiles, entered service in 1960 with a total of nine squadrons flying the B.2. Thirty-three B.2 aircraft were converted to the B.2A configuration, carrying a single Blue Steel missile in a semi-recessed position. The B.2 was also intended to carry the US Skybolt strategic attack missile, which was cancelled in 1962. Some squadrons were permanently assigned to the conventional strike role, with the remainder giving up the Blue Steel capability by 1970. The aircraft could carry a single nuclear bomb or 21 1,000-pound conventional bombs.

The last Vulcan was withdrawn from the nuclear strike role on December 31, 1982, and the last Vulcan was withdrawn from service March 31, 1984. A total of 136 Vulcans were produced through 1965.

The Vulcan had a large delta wing with no horizontal control surfaces; there was a short fuselage protruding forward of the wing; an electronic sensor mounted on top of the tail fin gave the tail a squared-off appearance. The aircraft's four turbojet engines were buried within the wing roots. A fixed in-flight refueling probe extending from the nose was fitted in all aircraft from 1959.

An Avro Vulcan B.2 streaks low over the English countryside, showing the massive delta-wing configuration of this last of the British V-bombers. All three V-bombers had unusual designs for strategic aircraft. The engine intakes are visible in the wing roots. Vulcans carried out three conventional strike missions in the Falklands War of 1982. *Hawker Siddeley*

Aircraft with cameras fitted in the bomb bay for strategic reconnaissance were designated Vulcan SR.2.

Vulcan B.2 Characteristics

Design:	Avro
Crew:	5 (pilot, copilot, 2 navigators, electronics officer)
Engines:	4 Bristol Siddeley Olympus Mk.301 turbojet; 20,000 lbst each
Weights:	
Loaded:	200,000 lb
Dimensions:	
Length:	99 ft, 11 in
Wingspan:	111 ft
Wing area:	3,964 sq ft
Height:	27 ft, 2 in
Speeds:	
Maximum:	645 mph at 40,000 ft
Cruise:	600 mph
Ceiling:	60,000 ft
Range:	3,400 miles with low-level penetration to target; 4,600 miles with high-level penetration to target
Armament:	1 nuclear bomb Blue Danube, Yellow Sun, or WE177A/B or 21 1,000-lb bombs

Bell HU-1 Huey/Iroquois and AH-1 Cobra

The "Huey" series stands as the most widely used military helicopter in the Western world. The ubiquitous Huey is a light utility helicopter flown by almost 60 nations in the trooplift, medical evacuation, gunship, command, Electronic Intelligence (ELINT), search-and-rescue, and anti-submarine roles.

HU-1A deliveries to the US Army began in 1959 and an improved version, the UH-1E, entered service with the US Marine Corps in 1964. Hueys began arriving in Vietnam in 1963 and before the conflict ended more than 5,000 were flying the combat area. Both services used them as troop carriers, for medical evacuation, and—armed with a variety of rockets, grenade launchers, and machine guns—as gunships.

Subsequently the Huey was adopted by the US Air Force and Navy, as well as many other nations. The US Navy flew the UH-1B as ship-based gunships in the Mekong Delta area of Vietnam. A US Army Security Agency ELINT variants (EH-1) were employed to intercept, locate, and jam enemy communications (Project Quick Fix); the United States also flew HH-1 combat search-and-rescue, TH-1 instrument training, and VH-1 staff transport variants. An anti-submarine variant was produced in Italy by Agusta.

After the Vietnam War—often called the first "helicopter war"—the Huey was employed in crises and conflicts around the world by many nations. The Huey served in first-line US military service until the mid-1970s, when it was succeeded in the US Army by the H-60 Blackhawk series. However, specialized Hueys remain in US service into the twenty-first century, as well as in the military forces of numerous other countries.

The US military aircraft designation changes in 1962 made the HU-series into the UH-series. Although officially named Iroquois by the Army, following its custom of naming helicopters for American Indian tribes, by the late 1950s the designation HU-1 had led to the indelible name "HU-ey" being adopted for all models.

The Huey series began life as the Bell XH-40, designed in 1955 to fulfill a US Army requirement for a turbine-powered helicopter to be used for the frontline evacuation of casualties as well as general utility and training missions. The resulting helicopter had a single turbine engine turning a two-blade main rotor (which gave the Huey a distinct "blup-blup" sound). The fuselage is relatively wide with a tailboom mounting a stabilizing rotor. Twin skids provide a flexible landing gear.

The cabin can accommodate two crewmen and up to seven troops in the UH-1B and 13 troops in the longer-cabin UH-1H, introduced in 1967, which featured a 1,400-shaft-horsepower turboshaft engine vice 1,100 horsepower in the earlier models. The single-engine Huey configuration was succeeded by the twin-engine variants (beginning with the US Marine-Navy UH-1N variant).

The ubiquitous Bell Huey–series helicopters were produced in greater numbers than any other rotary-wing aircraft in the world. This US Marine Corps UH-1E shows the simple design; later Hueys had twin turboshaft engines and an enlarged cabin. Armed Hueys carried a variety of fixed and flexible machine guns plus grenade launchers and rockets. *US Marine Corps*

UH-1H Characteristics

Design:	Bell
Crew:	2 (pilot, copilot) + 13 troops or 6 stretchers + 1 attendant
Engines:	1 Avco Lycoming T53-L-13 turboshaft; 1,400 hp
Weights:	
Empty:	5,090 lb
Loaded:	9,500 lb
Dimensions:	
Length:	44 ft, 7 in
Fuselage length:	41 ft, 10 $\frac{3}{4}$ in
Rotor diameter:	48 ft
Height:	13 ft, 5 in
Speed:	
Maximum:	130 mph
Cruise:	126.5 mph
Ceiling:	12,700 ft
Range:	357 miles
Armament:	2 .50-cal. M213 or 7.62-mm M60D machine guns (single, flexible)

Normally two .50-caliber or two 7.76-mm machine guns were mounted in door positions. However, some Hueys were fitted as gunships with rotary-barrel guns and rockets. A variety of other weapons, including wire-guided, anti-tank missiles have been carried by Hueys.

The prototype XH-40 flew on October 22, 1956, and the first production variant, the HU-1A was delivered to the US Army in June 1959. More UH-1H variants were produced than other model. Beyond Bell production of 10,392 UH-1s in the United States, another 721 Hueys of various configurations were produced under license in Germany, Italy, and Japan—a total of 11,113 helicopters (not including the AH-1 gunships; see below).

An AH-1J Huey Cobra gunship flown by the Imperial Iranian Army prior to the fall of the Shah in 1979. The helicopter used the engine, transmission, rotor system, and other components of the Huey. The AH-1J/T/W variants had twin turboshaft engines. The chin turret holds a 20-mm M1973 rotary-barrel cannon; stub wings aft of the cockpit can accommodate rockets and anti-tank missiles. *Bell*

AH-1G Characteristics

Design:	Bell
Crew:	2 (pilot, gunner)
Engines:	1 Avco Lycoming T53-L-13 turboshaft; 1,400 hp
Weights:	
Empty:	6,073 lb
Loaded:	9,407 lb
Dimensions:	
Length:	52 ft, 11 $\frac{1}{2}$ in
Fuselage length:	44 ft, 7 in
Rotor diameter:	44 ft
Height:	13 ft, 6 $\frac{1}{2}$ in
Speeds:	
Maximum:	172 mph at sea level
Cruise:	
Ceiling:	11,400 ft
Range:	357 miles
Armament:	1 or 2 7.62-mm GAU-2B/A minigun multi-barrel guns or 1 or 2 40-mm M129 grenade launchers or 1 minigun and 1 grenade launcher various rocket pods on 4 attachment points

In 1962 the US Army for the first time officially endorsed the concept of a specialized helicopter gunship. The Huey's engine, transmission, and rotor system were adapted to a streamlined fuselage, evolving into the AH-1 gunship, in other words, numbered in the same series as the UH-1 Huey.

The AH-1—the world's first purpose-built gunship helicopter—was initially fitted with a turret-mounted multi-barrel minigun and grenade launcher combination, and rockets on four external attachment points. Later AH-1 variants could also carry anti-tank missiles. The two-man crew sits in tandem with the pilot above and behind the gunner, both protected by armor. Flown by the US Army (named Cobra) and Marine Corps (named SeaCobra and Super Cobra) as well as other nations, 2,216 AH-1 variants were produced by Bell in the United States and 88 by Fuji in Japan.

Boeing B-47 Stratojet

The B-47 represented the first true advance-design bomber of the Cold War era. The sleek, swept-wing B-47 was the first turbojet bomber to enter service with the US Strategic Air Command. It was considered a "medium bomber"—replacing the B-29 and B-50—and also flew in large numbers in specialized reconnaissance configurations.

The aircraft lacked the unrefueled range to reach the Soviet Union from bases in the United States. Accordingly, several permanent SAC bases were established in forward areas, such as Spain and Morocco, and a large number of piston-engine KC-97 tanker aircraft were procured to provide in-flight refueling. The first B-47 wing (45 aircraft) to deploy overseas was sent to England on a 90-day rotational training mission in June 1953.

During the late 1950s and early 1960s the B-47 provided the majority of SAC's manned bomber aircraft. The number of B-47s peaked in early 1957 with 28 medium bomb wings flying 1,260 aircraft. In addition, some 300 reconnaissance variants of the B-47 were flying missions around the world and 300 more B-47s were undergoing maintenance or used for training.

The aircraft's range was too limited for it to be used in the Chrome Dome airborne alert (which employed B-52 Stratofortress bombers).

In the early 1960s Secretary of Defense Robert S. McNamara accelerated the retirement of B-47s as part of his emphasis on ICBMs replacing manned bombers. The last B-47 bombers were withdrawn from SAC in February 1966. Some RB-47s remained in a reconnaissance role with SAC until December the following year. The last operational Stratojet was a WB-47, which was retired in November 1969. However, during the 1970s the US Navy took three B-47Es from storage and, with contractor flight crews, operated them as EB-47Es in support of missile and electronic warfare development programs.

B-47s set several endurance records with in-flight refuelings: In August 1954 a B-47 made a nonstop flight of 17,000 miles in 35 hours; in November 1954 B-47s made a nonstop flight from Davis-Monthan Air Force Base (Arizona) to England via North Africa, a flight of 21,000 miles in 47 hours, 35 minutes; and, on September 1, 1953, a modified KB-47B carried out the first US jet-to-jet aerial refueling of a B-47.

Designed by the Boeing Airplane Company, which had produced the famed B-17 and B-29 bombers, the B-47 was one of several designs considered by the AAF at the end of World War II for the initial generation of US jet-propelled bombers. After studying a number of configurations, Boeing engineers took advantage of German research into swept-back wings to produce the B-47 design.

The B-47 program remains the largest US bomber procurement since World War II. In both design and quantity the B-47 was a milestone in the development of strategic bombers and gave the United States a potent nuclear strike capability.

The aircraft was a relatively large, swept-wing aircraft, with six turbojet engines mounted in two twin and two single pods beneath the wings. The shoulder-mounted wings were swept back 35 degrees. The pilot and copilot sat in tandem in the narrow fuselage, with a bombardier-navigator in the nose, a total of 3 men compared to 10 for the B-17 and 11 for the B-29, both of which were smaller aircraft. Space and weight were instead allocated to fuel, with the B-47E carrying 14,610 gallons internally and 3,390 gallons in two wing drop tanks, totaling almost ten times the B-17 capacity and three times that of the B-29. The B-47 was fitted for in-flight refueling.

The internal bomb bay could accommodate two small or one large nuclear-thermonuclear weapon; the theoretical conventional bomb capacity was one 12,000-pound or six 2,000-pound or 18 1,000-pound conventional bombs.

The only defensive guns were fitted in a remote-control tail turret, initially twin .50-cal machine guns; twin 20-mm cannon were provided beginning with the B-47E (compared to about a dozen guns in the B-17 and B-29). The copilot's seat rotated to a rear-facing position to permit him to use the A-5 fire-control system for the tail guns. A vertical camera was fitted in the tail of all aircraft.

Thirty B-47s in the Ebb Tide program became DB-47Bs to carry the GAM-63 Rascal air-to-surface missile. That missile had a stormy history and was cancelled before entering service.

A program to have the B-47 operate as an unmanned bomb carrier was developed under the code name Brass Ring. As the MB-47 it would have to be air-refueled several times and manned until the last refueling. The crew

The Boeing B-47B Stratojet was a truly futuristic aircraft when it appeared in the early 1950s as the first US jet-propelled strategic bomber. The white underside was intended to reflect the flash of atomic detonations. The "chin"-mounted K-4A radar and remote-control tail guns are visible. Note the positioning of the six jet engines in twin and single pods under each wing. *US Air Force*

would then bail out over friendly territory and the MB-47 would continue on automatic control to its preset target. There were problems with the guidance system and as other ways of delivering H-bombs became available that program was cancelled on April 1, 1953.

The first flight of the XB-47 occurred on December 17, 1947. The B-47B entered service with SAC in October 1951. The definitive B-47E version made its first flight in 1953. B-47 production totaled 2,042 aircraft, including several hundred EB-47 electronic warfare and RB-47 reconnaissance variants. The last B-47E was delivered in February 1957. Production was undertaken by Douglas (274) and Lockheed (393) as well as by Boeing-Wichita. At one point the Air Force planned to procure over 2,700 aircraft.

B-47E Characteristics

Design:	Boeing
Crew:	3 (pilot, copilot-gunner, bombardier-navigator)
Engines:	6 General Electric J47-GE-25 turbojet; 7,200 lbst each
Weights:	
Empty:	79,074 lb
Maximum:	230,000 lb
Dimensions:	
Length:	107 ft, 1 in
Wingspan:	116 ft
Wing area:	1,428 sq ft
Height:	28 ft
Speeds:	
Maximum:	607 mph (at 16,300 ft)
Cruise:	500 mph
Ceiling:	39,300 ft
Range:	Radius of 2,378 miles
Armament:	2 20-mm M24A1 cannon (tail turret); 2 nuclear bombs or 18,000 lb of conventional bombs

Boeing B-52 Stratofortress

The B-52 Stratofortress is a large, subsonic, long-range bomber, that has been the backbone of the US strategic bomber fleet since the late 1950s. Designed originally for high-altitude nuclear deterrence, the mission of the B-52 expanded over the next five decades to include tactical strikes with conventional bombs and attacks with nuclear and conventional cruise missiles. For brief periods B-52s were also configured for the anti-shipping and mine-laying roles. Known as the Buff—for Big Ugly Fat F****r—the B-52 has served longer than any other US combat aircraft in history and is expected to remain in service for at least two more decades.

The first operational variant—the B-52B—entered service with the Strategic Air Command's 93d Bomb Wing in June 1955. Developed as a high-altitude strategic bomber, the B-52 participated in numerous Cold War deployments, exercises, and special missions to emphasize American preparedness and global reach.

As Soviet strategic forces increased in lethality and given the United States' lack of a satellite early warning capability, in 1958, the command began an "airborne alert" on a test basis, always keeping a few nuclear-armed B-52s in flight to reduce their vulnerability to attack while on the ground and to reduce flight time to targets. The SAC Commander-in-Chief, Gen. Thomas S. Power, told Congress that: "We in the Strategic Air Command have developed a system known as airborne alert, where we maintain airplanes in the air 24 hours a day, loaded with bombs, on station, ready to go to the target. . . . I feel strongly that we must get on with this airborne alert. . . . We must impress Mr. [Nikita] Khrushchev that we have it, and that he cannot strike this country with impunity."

From March 2 through June 30, 1959, the 92d Bombardment Wing kept five B-52 bombers continuously airborne in Operation Head Start II. Each B-52 crew flew a 24-hour sortie, being relieved aloft by another B-52. Relays of KC-135 tankers kept the airborne bombers fueled. The bombers carried nuclear weapons and target folders were on board. Airborne alert tests were continued into 1960, after which SAC instituted a permanent program with B-52s—a small number of bombers were kept aloft 24 hours per day, seven days per week, supported by continuous refuelings from KC-135 tankers.

On January 18, 1961, SAC headquarters announced that B-52 bombers were maintaining a continuous airborne alert—Operation Chrome Dome. This readiness condition continued until 1968, reaching a peak of 65 nuclear-armed bombers on airborne alert. (The failure of airborne alert bombers to respond to recall signals was the theme of the film *Dr. Strangelove* and the book and film *Fail-Safe*.)

The costs of keeping the B-52s airborne and maintaining other SAC bombers on 15-minute runway alert postures were considerable. An aircrew-to-aircraft ratio of 1.8 to 1 was established to help man the increases in alert status. During this period SAC aircraft were flying more than one million miles per year and burning 1.5 billion gallons of fuel, of which some 200 million gallons were being transferred in aerial refueling operations. Continuous bombing simulations were being conducted, worldwide, day and night. Transocean and even global flights were flown during exercises to demonstrate SAC bomber capabilities as well as for crew and staff training.

When, on October 22, 1962, President John F. Kennedy announced a blockade of Cuba to halt the further movement of Soviet nuclear weapons to that communist island, the Strategic Air Command had 639 B-52 Stratofortress heavy jet bombers compared to 880 B-47 Stratojet and 76 B-58 Hustler medium jet bombers. This was the peak B-52 strength with 22 SAC bomb wings operating the aircraft. (The USSR at the time had about 100 Tu-20 Bear and Mya-4 Bison heavy bombers that could reach the United States.)

The cancellation of the airborne alert followed accidents in which B-52s crashed while carrying four thermonuclear (hydrogen) bombs: On January 17, 1966, a B-52 and KC-135 tanker collided near Palomares, Spain, and on January 22, 1968, a B-52 crashed near Thule, Greenland.

The massive US involvement in the Vietnam War led to B-52s being used in tactical bombing operations. From 1965 to 1967, B-52D aircraft were given Big Belly modification, increasing their conventional bomb load to 108 500-pound bombs (84 internal, 24 external) or 42 750-pound bombs. Along with the B-52F—which was not included in the Big Belly program—the B-52D performed conventional bombing operations over South and then North Vietnam from 1965 to 1973. B-52Gs joined in the attacks during Operation Linebacker II against the North in 1972. Up to 120 B-52s flew simultaneous strikes. Despite heavy electric jamming support from Air Force and Navy aircraft, during an 11-day period 15 B-52s were shot down by SA-2 Guideline anti-aircraft missiles. Still, the Linebacker II strikes were credited with bringing North Vietnam back to the peace talks.

After the Vietnam War the Air Force continued to seek ways to expand the B-52 mission. These efforts included evaluation of the B-52 as an aerial minelayer and anti-shipping aircraft (with Harpoon missiles) to support a future war at sea.

The B-52Gs returned to conventional combat during Operation Desert Storm in 1991. On January 16, 1991, seven B-52Gs of the 2nd Bomb Wing took off from Barksdale Air Force Base, Louisiana, and flew $14^1/2$ hours, launched 35 conventional cruise missiles against Iraq from a position over Saudi Arabia, and returned directly to Barksdale. The $34^1/2$-hour flight, which required multiple aerial refuelings, was the longest combat mission in US aviation history. B-52Hs subsequently were used to launch weapons against Iraq in Operation Southern Watch (1991–2003), Operation Desert Strike (1996), Operation Desert Fox (1998); in Kosovo—Operation Allied Force (1999); and in Afghanistan—Operation Enduring Freedom (2001–2).

In 2003, the US Air Force still operates a force of 44 B-52Hs plus several specialized B-52s engaged in research and development projects. The bomber aircraft are expected to remain in service at least through the year 2024 with an engine update; other modifications could extend service life even longer.

The original July 1948 contract with the Boeing Airplane Company for two XB-52s called for a long-range, swept-wing, turboprop bomber design (analogous to the Soviet Tu-20 Bear). By the year's end the design had been revised around eight turbojet engines, mounted in pairs beneath the wings. The prototype YB-52 first flew on April 15, 1952, seven months before the first flight of the XB-52 on October 2, 1952. By the time the last B-52H was delivered on October 26, 1962, 744 B-52s of all models had been built. The B-52G was the most widely produced variant, with 193 leaving the Boeing production lines; 102 of the ultimate B-52H model were built.

The B-52 has a distinctive configuration with a blunt-nose fuselage and large, high-mounted swept-back wings. Eight turbofan engines (turbojet in models A through G) are paired in pods mounted on pylons projecting forward beneath the wing leading edges. Early aircraft had a tall tail fin; the G and H models introduced shorter fins for improved stability in high-speed, low-level flight. The earlier aircraft also had a tail-gunner position with four .50-caliber machine guns in a tail turret; in the G model the gunner was moved to the forward crew compartment. The B-52H was built with a single 20-mm ASG-21 multi-barrel cannon in the tail; the gun and gunner (in main crew compartment) were eliminated in 1991.

Weapons are carried in two large bomb bays with a capacity of 27,000 pounds of gravity nuclear bombs or, when modified for conventional bombs, over 40,000 pounds; weapons and decoys can also be carried on two wing pylons.

Two AGM-28 Hound Dog nuclear air-to-surface missiles could be carried under the wings of the B-52D and later aircraft; the Hound Dogs' J52 turbojet engines could be used for additional takeoff thrust to augment the B-52 engines. Four GAM-72 Quail (unarmed) decoy missiles were carried internally (each Quail was designed to imitate a B-52 on enemy radar). The B-52H was originally designed to carry four Skybolt air-to-surface strategic missiles (although the Skybolt program was cancelled in 1962). In 1972, the AGM-69A Short-Range Attack Missile (SRAM) became operational on B-52s. Subsequently, 98 B-52Gs were armed with the AGM-86B Air-Launched Cruise Missile (ALCM). The B-52H has been fitted with the rotary bomb bay launchers to carry free-fall nuclear weapons, SRAMs, and ALCMs. The development of a new generation of conventional standoff weapons through the 1980s and 1990s has allowed the B-52 to strike targets from outside the range of enemy defenses.

The B-52H can carry a payload consisting of these alternative loadouts:

20 ALCM missiles (nuclear/internal/external)

12 SRAM missiles (nuclear; external)

2 B53 bombs (nuclear; internal)

8 B61 bombs (nuclear; internal)

8 B83 bombs (nuclear; internal)

18 JDAM guided bombs (conventional; internal)

On May 21, 1956, a B-52B performed the first air drop of a US thermonuclear weapon, releasing a 3.4-megaton B15 hydrogen bomb over

The remarkable Boeing B-52 Stratofortress remains in front-line combat service with the US Air Force more than a half century after the YB-52 first took off. This B-52H, with white reflective paint protecting vulnerable sections from the energy of a nuclear flash, was photographed at Edwards Air Force Base, California, in the early 1960s. *US Air Force*

Bikini atoll. Through 1962 B-52s made a total of 30 nuclear weapons tests—58 percent of all US nuclear weapon air drops. Three B-52Bs also accomplished the first nonstop around-the-world flight on January 16–18, 1957. Refueled five times by KC-97 tankers, the B-52s flew 24,325 miles in 45 hours, 19 minutes. (All B-52s were fitted for in-flight refueling.)

B-52H Characteristics

Design:	Boeing
Crew:	5 (command pilot, pilot, electronic warfare officer, radar-navigator, navigator)
Engines:	8 Pratt & Whitney TF-33-P-3 turbofan; 17,000 lbst each
Weights:	
Empty:	195,000 lb
Maximum takeoff:	505,000 lb
Loaded:	566,000 lb after in-flight refueling
Dimensions:	
Length:	160 ft, 11 in
Wingspan:	185 ft
Wing area:	4,000 sq ft
Height:	40 ft, 8 in
Speeds:	
Maximum:	595 mph at altitude; 405 mph at sea level
Cruise:	521 mph
Ceiling:	55,000 ft
Range:	8,800 miles with maximum fuel; 6,380 miles with maximum weapons payload
Armament:	Removed; 60,000 lb of bombs or missiles (internal and external)

Boeing C-135 Stratolifter/KC-135 Stratotanker

With voracious appetites for fuel, few modern combat jets are able to deploy overseas or perform their missions without in-flight refueling. For more than 45 years the KC-135 Stratotanker has been the primary "flying gas station" of the US Air Force. With massive fuel tanks mounted in wings and below an open cargo deck, the aircraft has the capacity to provide cargo airlift at the same time that it refuels aircraft.

The Stratotanker design has been modified to provide specialized aircraft for electronic reconnaissance, aerial mapping, and flying command post functions, and well as acting as test beds for a wide variety of special weapons and systems.

The KC-135 began refueling the US strategic bomber force in June 1957, standing (and flying) alert with the Strategic Air Command. KC-135s have provided in-flight refueling for US military aircraft beginning with the Vietnam War and continuing to the present. Today the US Air Force operates 253 KC-135 tankers in active units and another 292 in National Guard and Reserve units.

Development of a jet-propelled replacement for SAC's propeller-driven KC-97 fleet began in 1954, concurrent with Boeing's design of the 707 airliner. Although the C-135 Stratolifter is superficially similar to the 707, it was a structurally discrete design given Boeing model number 717. (The name Stratotanker is used for the KC-135.) The aircraft has the large fuselage of a passenger-cargo aircraft with large, low-mounted swept wings. Four turbojet or turbofan engines are mounted in separate pods beneath the wings. A large access hatch on the forward left fuselage provides for the loading of up to 83,000 pounds of cargo or 37 passengers (in KC-135 variants).

Two re-engine programs have had a dramatic effect on KC-135 performance. Approximately 150 aircraft were provided with Pratt & Whitney TF33s and assigned to Air National Guard and Air Force Reserve squadrons as the KC-135E; the new engines improved fuel efficiency by 27 percent while reducing noise, air pollution, and maintenance costs. A second re-engine program installed the high-bypass F108 (CFM-56) engine on most of the remaining fleet, redesignated KC-135R. Two of the latter aircraft can perform the work of three KC-135As, saving almost 4 percent of the Air Force's annual fuel use while carrying greater payloads over longer distances.

A flying boom hinged beneath the tail is controlled by the boom operator who lays prone in the after fuselage; as the refueling aircraft moves into position behind the tanker, the boom operator "flies" the boom to connect the two aircraft and then control the pumping of several thousand pounds of fuel through the boom. Although the KC-135 can carry a drogue attached to its boom, this MA-3 coupling has to be attached on the ground, meaning that only one type of refueling system could be used on a mission. Although a separate drogue system has been fitted to a small number of KC-135R aircraft, most KC-135s still need the MA-3 coupling to refuel US Navy and foreign aircraft. (Helicopters must be refueled from their own dedicated tankers using the probe and drogue system.)

The KC-135 can carry approximately 200,000 pounds of fuel for transfer to other aircraft.

Boeing built 820 C-135 variants, of which 12 were tankers delivered to France; the remaining to the USAF. In addition to the 732 KC-135 tankers, these included (built or converted) EC-135 airborne command posts, RC-135 electronic reconnaissance aircraft, WC-135 weather reconnaissance aircraft, OC-135 "open skies" camera aircraft, EC-135N fitted for electronic instrumentation in support of the Apollo space program, and VC-135 executive (VIP) transports. The US Navy acquired two KC-135A aircraft in 1977 and 1978 for modification to stimulate hostile jamming aircraft in operations against US warships (designated NKC-135A).

Fifty years after work began on the KC-135, the US Air Force has begun to look for a KC-135 replacement. Although a number of KC-10 tankers have been acquired, the KC-135 remains the primary USAF tanker for the foreseeable future.

Most modern combat aircraft have voracious appetites for fuel, resulting in great value being placed on tanker aircraft like this Boeing KC-135E Stratotanker of the 146th Aerial Refueling Squadron, Ohio Air National Guard. It is "passing gas," via a drogue attachment on its refueling boom, to a US Navy F-14 Tomcat. *Courtesy Peter B. Mersky*

KC-135R Characteristics

Design:	Boeing
Crew:	4 (command pilot, pilot, navigator,[*] boom operator)
Engines:	4 General Electric/CFM F108 (CFM-56) turbofan; 21,634 lbst each
Weights:	
Empty:	119,231 lb
Maximum takeoff:	322,500 lb
Dimensions:	
Length:	136 ft, 3 in
Wingspan:	130 ft, 10 in
Wing area:	2,433 sq ft
Height:	41 ft, 8 in
Speeds:	
Maximum:	610 mph (at 30,000 ft)
Ceiling:	50,000 ft
Range:	1,500 miles with 150,000 lb transfer fuel; 11,000 miles ferry mission
Armament:	None

[*] Aircraft with advanced PACER CRAG navigation system do not have a navigator on board for most missions.

Convair B-36 Peacemaker

The B-36 was the largest combat aircraft ever built and was the mainstay of the US strategic bomber force during the early 1950s. Although never used in conventional conflict (as was its successor, the B-52 Stratofortress), the B-36 was considered by air power enthusiasts as an effective nuclear deterrent, although it appears to have been vulnerable to contemporary Soviet air-defense fighters. More significant but less recognized was the RB-36's role as a reconnaissance aircraft.

The B-36 was developed to bomb European targets from bases in the United States because in 1941 the US War Department believed that the United States would likely be drawn into the war and that all of Europe— including Britain—could be under Axis control. (Also developed under this transoceanic bomber program was the Northrop B-35 Flying Wing bomber, an early precursor to that firm's B-2 "stealth" bomber.) In the spring of 1943, when it appeared that the Chinese government might collapse under Japanese attack, the B-36 was considered for long-range operations in the Pacific in the event of problems in the B-29 Superfortress and B-32 Dominator heavy bomber programs. When the B-29 program achieved success the B-36 was continued, but with lesser priority.

The B-36 was the centerpiece for the 1948–49 debate between the Navy and Air Force on the relative effectiveness of land-based and carrier-based bombers. There was also controversy over the aircraft within the Air Force: Gen. George C. Kenney, the first commander of the Strategic Air Command, declared: "The B-36 is a night bomber. I would not use it in daytime," and suggested that the plane might be suitable for the Navy's anti-submarine mission. On December 12, 1946, he recommended the procurement of the B-36 only for test purposes, preferring to use the B-50 as a strategic bomber until jet-propelled bombers became available.

Kenney's successor as head of SAC, the outspoken and innovative Gen. Curtis LeMay, supported the B-36, claiming: "We can get a B-36 over a target and not have the enemy know it is there until the bombs hit." In an effort to overcome the vulnerability of the B-36, the Air Force developed the diminutive F-85 Goblin as a "parasite" fighter to be carried by the B-36, released when enemy fighters threatened, and subsequently taken back aboard the bombers. The XF-85 was flight-tested from a modified B-29, but never from a B-36. That scheme was quickly discarded (although SAC continued to operate its own land-based escort fighters until 1957). RF-84 Thunderflash reconnaissance aircraft also were evaluated in a "parasite" role with seven RB-36D bombers and 23 RF-84K aircraft being modified; after flight trials from December 1955 to February 1956 this scheme was also discarded.

Concern over B-36 survivability continued; a 1973 Air Force retrospective evaluation of strategic bombing noted: "The speed and operational radius of the B-36 left much to be desired, however. Because of its low speed, the B-36 was vulnerable to heavy attrition from fast, modern fighters. Relatively heavy losses, by comparison with World War II experience, could be tolerated within limits because of the destructive power of the A-bomb, but the unanswerable question was whether B-36 losses could be kept within tolerable limits."

Although the B-36 was relatively slow, it could fly an Arctic route to reach the Soviet Union from bases in the United States without in-flight refueling. Efforts to improve B-36 survivability by increasing the aircraft's ceiling led to the "featherweight" program of reducing weights.

Perhaps the most significant contribution of the B-36 was strategic reconnaissance. The potential of the B-36 for strategic reconnaissance was demonstrated as early as 1948 when a B-36 fitted with developmental cameras flying at 34,000 feet was able to provide photos in which golf balls could be discerned on a course near Fort Worth, Texas. Reportedly, on direct orders from General LeMay, four B-36Ds were taken from the Convair production for modification to camera aircraft, with additional fuel tanks fitted in their bomb bays.

The first mission flown by any B-36s beyond the continental United States began on January 16, 1951, when six of B-36D strategic bombers flew into the RAF base at Lakenheath, England. The modified camera planes participated in the flight. Reportedly, from Lakenheath three camera planes each flew a high-altitude reconnaissance mission over the Soviet base complex at Murmansk on the Kola Peninsula. The planes returned safely to Lakenheath, although two MiG fighters are said to have tried to reach them. The six B-36D aircraft flew back to their continental US base on January 20. (There is no official US confirmation of any B-36 overflights of the Soviet Union.)

The specialized RB-36 variant entered service with the Strategic Air Command in June 1951. Reportedly, there were two overflights of the Soviet base complex at Vladivostok by camera-equipped B-36D aircraft.

These overflights are said to have occurred during August–September 1953, when a flight of 23 B-36s temporarily operated from bases in Japan, Okinawa, and Guam. As part of this deployment—Operation Big Stick— the two B-36D photo missions were flown over Vladivostok from the US air base at Kadena, Japan. It is not clear from available records whether those were the same modified B-36Ds that may have earlier overflown Murmansk or were specialized RB-36D aircraft. Regardless, on both operations these camera-carrying aircraft were "hidden" among "straight" B-36s during the Far East deployment.

The B-36 force peaked in October 1955 with ten heavy bombardment wings—six with B-36s and four with RB-36s. Each wing had a nominal assignment of ten planes in each of three squadrons—a total of 209 B-36 and 133 RB-36 aircraft. When the last B-36J was retired in February 1959 SAC became an all-jet bomber force.

No B-36 ever dropped a conventional bomb in combat, although B-36s were used in six nuclear bomb drops in weapon tests.

The B-36 was propelled by six large piston-pusher engines, supplemented in the B-36D and later models by four turbojets in underwing pods to provide "burst" speed as the big bomber neared its target. The maximum bomb load was 72,000 pounds with a gross weight of 328,000 pounds, although the B-36D could carry two 42,000-pound Grand Slam bombs in the internal weapon bays. The B-36A aircraft were unarmed and were used mainly for training. The B-36B was the first model configured to carry nuclear bombs. Eighteen B-36B aircraft were modified to also carry two VB-13 Tarzon guided bombs; those aircraft had the AN/APG-24 bomb/nav radar.

The aircraft had the heaviest defensive armament every carried by an aircraft: Up to 16 20-mm cannon in twin turrets—the four side-by-side dorsal and two side-by-side ventral turrets were retractable (to reduce drag); additional two-gun turrets were mounted in the nose and tail, all directed by a central control system.

As Soviet air defenses, especially fighter aircraft, improved during the 1950s an effort was made to increase the altitude of the RB-36 through the featherweight program, in which most of the plane's guns and some other gear was removed to reduce weight. The featherweight aircraft could reach just over 45,000 feet, some 5,000 to 8,000 feet higher than a standard aircraft. The featherweight program reduced the number of guns until the modified B-36H (III) had only the tail turret with two guns. The crew of featherweight RB-36s was only 19 men.

The RB-36D had two of the four bomb-bays fitted with 14 cameras; the third bomb bay was provided with an additional fuel tank to increase endurance to 50 hours; and the fourth bay was fitted with electronic countermeasures gear. The RB-36D crew was increased to 22 men. (In June 1954 the RB-36s would be given a primary bombing mission; they retained a limited, secondary reconnaissance role.)

Maximum B-36 mission duration was almost 40 hours.

Many early B-36 models were updated; for example, 24 B-36B variants were upgraded to the B-36D configuration.

The first XB-36 did not fly until August 8, 1946, almost five years after the prototype was ordered. SAC received the first (unarmed) B-36A in June 1948; the first operational B-36B aircraft in November 1948; and the B-36D in August 1950. Those aircraft were not considered fully operational until 1951 and were not free of major mechanical problems until 1954. The ultimate B-36J entered service in 1953.

During World War II the Army Air Forces proposed a force of up to 3,740 B-36s. The AAF leadership in 1949 planned a B-36 force of four bomber groups—120 aircraft plus 39 spares aircraft—and two groups of the RB-36 long-range reconnaissance variant.

A total of 385 B-36 bombers were produced through 1954 plus one similar cargo aircraft (the XC-99, to have carried 400 fully equipped troops or 300 litter patients on 100,000 pounds of cargo). The YB-36G was a swept-wing, all-jet variant, which also carried the designation YB-60. Two aircraft were built (first flight in 1952).

The unarmed B-36A aircraft were later converted to the RB-36E bomber/reconnaissance configuration.

The Convair B-36 Peacemaker was large and graceful. But its effectiveness as a strategic bomber was often questioned, especially in view of Soviet deployment of the MiG-15 and later fighters that could reach the B-36's operating altitude. This RB-36D carried a payload of cameras and electronic countermeasures equipment. The six pusher-piston engines are supplemented by four turbojet engines in twin pods. *National Air and Space Museum*

B-36H (III) Characteristics

Design:	Convair/General Dynamics
Crew:	15 (pilot, copilot, engineer, navigator, bombardier, radar operator, radio operator, auxiliary crew member, 7 observers-gunners)
Engines:	6 Pratt & Whitney R-4360-53 radial piston; 3,800 hp each
	4 General Electric J47-GE-19 turbo jet; 5,010 lbst each
Weights:	
Empty:	164,522 lb
Combat:	248,900 lb
Maximum takeoff:	370,000 lb
Dimensions:	
Length:	162 ft, 1 in
Wingspan:	230 ft
Wing area:	4,772 sq ft
Height:	46 ft, 9 ½ in
Speeds:	
Maximum:	428 mph (at 38,400 ft)
Cruise:	250 mph
Ceiling:	45,100 ft
Range:	Combat radius: 3,640 miles
Armament:	2 20-mm M24A1 cannon (tail turret); 2 nuclear bombs or 86,000 lb of conventional bombs

Dassault Mirage III and Mirage 5

France's Dassault Mirage III and the export variant Mirage 5 are the most commercially successful fighters ever produced in Western Europe, with 1,410 aircraft sold to 20 air forces. Israel Aircraft Industries produced an additional 51 Nesher (Eagle) and 212 Kfir (Lion Cub) derivatives of the Mirage when France reneged on a sale of additional aircraft to Israel in 1973.

It was in Israeli hands that the delta-winged Mirage first captured international attention: Mirage IIIBs and IIICJs were used with great effect against air and ground targets in the 1967 Six-Day War. In air-to-air combat, Israeli Mirages destroyed 46 Arab fighters and 2 bombers for the loss of 4 of their own. The inexpensive yet capable fighter became desirable to a variety of customers—including several of Israel's enemies—and sales soared for Dassault.

The Mirage III and Mirage 5 were involved in several more conflicts: Pakistan against India in December 1971; Libya against Egypt, Israel, and Chad in different conflicts; Argentina, with former Israeli Neshers—renamed Daggers—against Great Britain in the 1982 Falklands Conflict; and Belgium for reconnaissance flights over Iraq in the Gulf War of 1991.

The Mirage was developed by France in the 1950s as a high-powered, lightweight fighter. It featured a delta-wing configuration with engine intakes in the "cheek" position alongside the cockpit with pronounced half-cones in the intake openings. Two cannon are mounted and external stores, including up to one thousand pounds of bombs or missiles, are carried on one fuselage attachment point and two wing pylons.

The prototype Mirage III first flew on November 17, 1956. The Mirage IIIA was a preproduction, developmental airframe, followed by the IIIB two-seat trainer, IIIC interceptor/ground attack aircraft, IIIR photo-reconnaissance aircraft, IIID two-seat trainer, and IIIE tactical strike fighter. The Mirage 5, developed as a tactical strike fighter for the export market, was built with less sophisticated and less expensive electronics and avionics systems.

By 1966, Israel had taken delivery of 76 Mirage IIIC aircraft and had ordered and paid France for an additional 50 aircraft. However, after the 1967 war Pres. Charles de Gaulle refused to deliver the 50 aircraft. They were subsequently sold to other nations and Israel initiated production of its Nesher and Kfir designs derived from the Mirage III. (Israel had also purchased a class of missile boats constructed in France that were withheld by the French government; they were stolen from the port of Cherbourg by the Israeli Navy.)

France's Dassault Mirage family has proven one of the most successful export fighters of the jet age while also being flown by the French Air Force in several roles. France produced several excellent aircraft during the Cold War, a contrast to their pre-World War II efforts. This delta-wing Mirage IIIE served in the Spanish Air Force. *Avions Marcel Dassault*

Mirage IIIE Characteristics

Design:	Dassault-Breguet
Crew:	Pilot
Engines:	1 SNECMA Atar 9C turbojet; 13,670 lbst
Weights:	
Empty:	15,540 lb
Maximum takeoff:	29,760 lb
Dimensions:	
Length:	49 ft, 3 $\frac{1}{2}$ in
Wingspan:	27 ft
Wing area:	375 sq ft
Height:	13 ft, 11 $\frac{1}{2}$ in
Speeds:	
Maximum:	1,460 mph
Cruise:	594 mph
Ceiling:	55,775 ft
Range:	745 miles
Armament:	2 30-mm DEFA 5-52 cannon (fixed); 3,000 lb of bombs or missiles

The Mirage III and V also served as testbeds for a number of technological advances, while several attempts were made to extend the type's service life. In the 1970s an engine upgrade and improved radar resulted in the Mirage 50, a fighter with improved takeoff and climb over its predecessors. The type never succeeded in production, although several earlier Venezuelan Mirage IIIEs and 5s were upgraded to Mirage 50 standards and redesignated Mirage 50M.

In the early 1980s Dassault developed the Mirage 3NG (*Novelle Generation*) with upgraded engine, modified delta wing with leading-edge root extensions, and a pair of fixed canards fitted above and behind the air intakes. The Mirage 3NG was never placed in production, although similar modifications were made to Brazilian Mirage IIIEs, which were given the designation Mirage IIIEX.

The aircraft were built cooperatively by Belgium and France, under license by Australia (as the Mirage IIIO strike fighters and interceptors) and Switzerland (as the Mirage IIIS interceptor), and, as noted above, under a hostile relationship by Israel. After service in the Israel Air Force, 13 ex-Israeli Kfir fighters were leased by the United States from June 1987 until September 1989; they were used for aggressor training by the US Marine Corps, designated F-21A and flown by training squadron VMFT-401.

Despite further attempts to upgrade the Mirage III and Mirage 5, the subsequent swept-wing Mirage F1 and twin-engine Mirage 2000 have replaced most of the earlier aircraft in worldwide service.

Douglas AD Skyraider

The Skyraider represented the ultimate in piston-engine attack aircraft and was probably the most versatile American-built aircraft. It saw extensive service with the US Air Force, Navy, and Marine Corps as well as Britain, France, Cambodia, and South Vietnam. The Skyraider was also the world's first single-engine aircraft to carry a nuclear weapon.

Although developed during World War II as a combination dive/torpedo-bomber, the Skyraider did not enter US Navy service until December 1946. The US Navy and Marine Corps flew the Skyraider extensively in the Korean War as a carrier-based attack aircraft, striking a broad array of ground targets with bombs, rockets, and torpedoes. After US Army Rangers had failed in efforts to capture the Hwachon reservoir dam, and B-29s using 6-ton guided bombs had failed to destroy the structure, Skyraiders from the carrier *Princeton* also failed to destroy the dam with dive-bombing attacks. On May 1, 1951, eight Skyraiders from that carrier armed with Mk 13 torpedoes set for surface running attacked and breached the dam. That strike remains the world's last aerial torpedo attack against a "surface target."

The Navy assigned the Skyraiders to the carrier-based nuclear strike role from 1952 to 1965. Nuclear attack training flights of up to 13 hours were flown by Skyraiders (without in-flight refueling).

The Royal Navy operated 36 of the AD-4W Airborne Early Warning (AEW) variant of the Skyraider from aircraft carriers and the French *Armée de l'Air* procured 100 ex-US Navy AD-4s for use in Algeria. A few of the latter subsequently were flown by the Cambodian Air Force. The US Navy and Air Force as well as the South Vietnamese Air Force employed Skyraiders extensively in the Vietnam conflict. In addition to the attack role, they were particularly useful in flying cover for helicopter rescue missions because of their slow speed and long endurance.

US Marine attack squadrons flew the Skyraider until 1958; attack and special-purpose variants were flown by the Navy until 1968, the last being the EA-1F electronics variant. The Air Force flew 150 A-1E Skyraiders from 1964 to 1972, with the surviving USAF aircraft being turned over to the South Vietnamese Air Force, where they were flown until 1975.

There were 28 possible configurations of the Skyraider, including attack, night/all-weather attack, AEW, Electronic Countermeasures (ECM), transport, medical evacuation, tanker, photographic, anti-submarine, target-tug, drone control, and nuclear strike. Skyraider pilot and author Rosario (Zip) Rausa wrote in *Skyraider: The Douglas A-1 "Flying Dump Truck"* that the aircraft's "most distinctive characteristic . . . was its straightforward, uncomplicated design. Its unadorned style gave it an aura of simplicity and strength."

The Skyraider was a low-wing, wide-fuselage aircraft with a large radial-piston engine; weapons were carried on fuselage and wing pylons. Designed from the outset for carrier operation, the plane's wings folded for carrier stowage.

The aircraft had a remarkable lift capacity with the AD-7 having an external payload of 8,000 pounds on 15 wing and fuselage stations in addition to four 20-mm cannon; in most aircraft the centerline position could carry 3,600 pounds and the two inboard wing positions could hold stores up to 3,000 pounds. In May 1953 a standard AD-4B flew at a gross weight of 26,739 pounds—a world record for a single-engine piston aircraft albeit not reflective of a combat loadout.

Various special-purpose aircraft carried multiple crewmen; the AD-5 was a two-place attack aircraft with side-by-side seating for the pilot and "assistant pilot" to facilitate night and long-range attack operations.

The plane was designed at Douglas under the direction of Ed Heinemann. The Skyraider began as the BTD Destroyer in response to a Navy request for a multi-mission carrier attack aircraft with an internal

A relatively simple design, the Douglas AD Skyraider series proved to be an outstanding land- and carrier-based attack aircraft. The Skyraider probably flew in more specialized variants than any other aircraft of the Cold War era. These are AD-5W "guppies" from Navy Airborne Early Warning Squadron 12 fitted with an AN/APS-20 air search radar. *US Navy*

AD-4B (A-1D) Characteristics

Design:	Douglas
Crew:	Pilot
Engines:	1 Wright R-3350-26WA radial piston; 3,150 hp
Weights:	
Empty:	11,783 lb
Maximum takeoff:	25,000 lb
Dimensions:	
Length:	59 ft, 3 in
Wingspan:	50 ft
Wing area:	400 sq ft
Height:	15 ft, 8 in
Speeds:	
Maximum:	417 mph at sea level; 320 mph at 15,200 ft
Cruise:	195.5 mph
Ceiling:	26,300 ft
Range:	1,450 miles with nuclear weapon and 2 300-gallon drop tanks; 645 miles with nuclear weapon
Armament:	4 20-mm M-3 cannon (fixed); 1 nuclear weapon (Mk 7 or Mk 8) or 6,200 lb of bombs and rockets (carrier operation) or 12,000 lb of bombs and rockets (land operation)

bomb bay. Heinemann sought a more efficient and simplified design, leading to the Navy accepting his XBT2D-1 design, originally called Destroyer II and than Dauntless II. The aircraft was changed to the AD-series and renamed Skyraider in 1946. Its nicknames were Able *Dog* and Flying Dumptruck, the latter reflecting its great load capacity, but most popularly Spad, after the popular World War I fighter.

The first flight of the XBT2D-1 took place on March 18, 1945. A total of 3,180 ADs were produced from 1945 to February 1957, with the AD-4 being the principal production model and the first to carry nuclear weapons (AD-4B variant). The suffix "B" indicated a nuclear capability with a single special weapon carried on a centerline bomb rack.

Surviving Skyraiders were redesignated in the A-1 series in October 1962.

Development of a follow-on A2D Skyshark—considered an enlarged Skyraider—with a T40 gas-turbine engine was begun in June 1945. The Navy choose a turboprop with contra-rotating propellers over a pure jet because of the limitations of existing turbojet engines for carrier operation. Excessive vibration and other problems with the T40 engine ultimately led to cancellation of the aircraft (and several other T40-powered programs). The prototype XA2D-1 flew on May 26, 1950.

Douglas A3D Skywarrior and B-66 Destroyer

The US Navy's A3D Skywarrior was developed as a carrier-based nuclear strike aircraft. It survived in operational service more than a decade after its planned successor—the A3J (A-5) Vigilante—was retired. Beyond serving aboard US carriers in the nuclear strike role from 1956 until 1971, the A3D operated in ELINT, photo-reconnaissance, and tanker roles. The US Air Force flew the much-modified B-66 Destroyer version in tactical strike, reconnaissance, and ECM roles.

The A3D-1 became operational in March 1956 with Heavy Attack Squadron (VAH) 1. The first operational deployment was from January 15 to July 22, 1957, in the Mediterranean with VAH-1 embarked in the USS *Forrestal*. The peak A3D strength was reached in 1961 with 11 operational squadrons with up to 12 aircraft per squadron.

A few Skywarriors carried out conventional bombing missions in the Vietnam War; however, numerous specialized aircraft were employed extensively in that conflict, both from shore bases and aircraft carriers. They carried out electric, photo-reconnaissance, and tanker missions. (Only the "straight" attack aircraft could carry bombs.) The tankers employed the probe-and-drogue system to refuel Navy and Marine Corps aircraft during the conflict.

ELINT variants flew from shore bases in the 1991 Gulf War.

The last operational Navy aircraft was an EA-3B (A3D-1Q) variant, retired in September 1991 (from 1987 until 1991 the aircraft were restricted to operations from land bases).

The A3D series was redesignated A-3 in 1962.

Development of the A3D began in late 1945 with a Navy requirement for a carrier aircraft with a gross takeoff weight of up to 100,000 pounds to carry 8,000 pounds of conventional bombs. Subsequently, the load was requirement increased to 10,000 pounds, the weight of an early atomic bomb. Douglas designer Ed Heinemann set a goal of 78,450 pounds for his design, which became the A3D, for which the Navy awarded a prototype contract on March 31, 1949. It would be able to operate from smaller Navy carriers of the *Essex* size and larger ships.

The A3D was the largest aircraft intended for regular operation from US aircraft carriers. The aircraft had shoulder-mounted wings swept-back 36 degrees, with twin turbojet engines in pods under the wings. The three-place cockpit was located relatively far forward, with most of the fuselage devoted to fuel and a large weapons bay. Twin 20-mm cannon were fitted in a remote-control tail turret. The wings and vertical tail folded for carrier stowage. The KA-3B tanker aircraft had a normal gross weight up to 78,000 pounds including 34,178 pounds of fuel, of which about two-thirds could be transferred to other aircraft. This was the world's heaviest aircraft to normally operate from carriers. Bomber aircraft could carry more than six tons of bombs including 12 500-pounders, 8 1,600-pounders, or 4 2,000-pounders.

The Navy briefly considered using the A3D for task force air defense—carrying air-to-air missiles and stationed as an aerial picket 90 to 200 miles out from the task force; the concept was not pursued.

First flight of the XA3D-1 occurred on October 28, 1952. The Navy took delivery of 282 Douglas-built Skywarriors through January 1961. These included 66 specialized aircraft that did not have a nuclear-strike capability—twenty-four for electronic surveillance (A3D-2Q/EA-3B), 30 for photo reconnaissance (A3D-2P/RA-3B), and 12 trainers (A3D-2T/TA-3B). Many "straight" attack aircraft were later modified to electronic, photo-reconnaissance, and tanker configurations.

In 1952 the US Air Force selected the not-yet-flown Navy A3D Skywarrior as a tactical bomber and day/night reconnaissance aircraft to succeed the B-26 Invader, which had entered AAF service in 1944. (The Invader entered service as the A-26, the wartime B-26 being the Martin Marauder. The Invader was redesignated B-26 in June 1948, as the Air

The Douglas A3D Skywarrior was the largest aircraft to regularly operate from aircraft carriers. The 70-ton "Whale" was developed as an all-weather, long-range nuclear strike aircraft. It also served in the carrier-based electronic warfare, reconnaissance, and tanker roles. The remote-control, 20-mm tail cannon are visible on this A3D-1 from Heavy Attack Squadron 3. *US Navy*

A3D-2 (A-3B) Characteristics

Design:	Douglas
Crew:	3 (pilot, bombardier-navigator, engineer)
Engines:	2 Pratt & Whitney J57-P10 turbojets; 10,500 lbst each
Weights:	
Empty:	37,077 lb
Loaded:	61,377 lb
Maximum takeoff:	73,000 lb (carrier operation); 78,000 lb (land operation)
Dimensions:	
Length:	74 ft, 8 1/2 in
Wingspan:	72 ft; 6 in
Wing area:	779 sq ft
Height:	22 ft, 9 1/2 in
Speeds:	
Maximum:	643 mph at sea level; 558 mph at 41,000 ft
Cruise:	528 mph at 35,000–43,400 ft
Ceiling:	43,400 ft
Range:	2,760 miles with 3,900 lb of bombs low-level attack; 2,656 miles with 6,100 lb of bombs high-level attack
Armament:	2 20-mm M-3 cannon (tail turret); 1 nuclear bomb (Mk 4, Mk 5, Mk 6, B7, B15, B18, B27, Mk 34 [Hotpoint], or B39) or 12,800 lb of bombs and/or mines

Force eschewed the use of the attack designation.) The B-66 was intended as an interim aircraft until the B-68 came into service, the latter plane being cancelled 1957.

The B-66 was to be an "off-the-shelf" procurement. However, the Air Force directed a major redesign of the wing and fuselage; proscribed new engines and ejection seats for the three-man crew; deleted various naval features, such as folding wings, strengthened undercarriage, and arresting hook; and provided a different radar and gun system. Thus, except for the general arrangement and external appearance, little of the naval aircraft remained in the B-66. The bomber variant could carry a single nuclear weapon or 15,000 pounds of conventional bombs or mines.

Further, of 294 aircraft produced by Douglas, only one-fourth were bomber aircraft; the remaining B-66s were built for specialized missions: RB-66A/B photo-reconnaissance aircraft, EB-66C electronic reconnaissance/ECM aircraft, and WB-66D weather reconnaissance aircraft. Two WB-66D variants were reconfigured to test laminar-flow control wings (changed to X-21A). Later, 13 of the bombers were converted to ECM aircraft (EB-66B/E) two others were modified for high-altitude parachute drops of Apollo and Gemini space capsules.

The RB-66A first flew on June 28, 1954, and the first B-66B on January 4, 1955. The bomber aircraft were deployed overseas primarily to bases in England. The specialized variants operated worldwide, and participated in the Vietnam War.

Through October 1957 a total of 294 B-66s were produced—72 bombers, 186 RB-66 variants, and 36 WB-66 variants. (The five prototypes were designated RB-66A; they were used exclusively for flight testing.)

Douglas A4D Skyhawk

The A4D Skyhawk was in many respects the most remarkable nuclear strike aircraft produced by any nation. Entering service in 1955 as a US carrier-based attack aircraft, the Skyhawk also served as a conventional strike, interdiction, and close air support aircraft in several air forces. Moreover, US and Israeli Skyhawk pilots were able to down MiG fighters.

The Skyhawk was flown by the US Navy and Marine Corps in the Vietnam War from both land bases and aircraft carriers, with 30 squadrons operating the aircraft in 1968. It was also employed by the Argentine Air Force against British forces in the 1982 Falklands campaign, by the Israeli Air force in several Middle East conflicts, and a few were flown by the Kuwaiti Air Force in the 1991 Gulf War. It continues to serve into the twenty-first century in several air forces and in the US Navy as a training aircraft.

The agility of the Skyhawk enabled a US Navy pilot, Lt. Comdr. Ted R. Swartz, to shoot down a MiG-17 over North Vietnam using Zuni air-to-ground rockets on May 1, 1967; an Israeli Skyhawk pilot, Col. Ezra (Beban) Dotan, shot down two Syrian MiG-17s over southern Lebanon on May 12, 1970, one with anti-tank rockets and the second with the aircraft's 30-mm cannon (which the Israelis fitted to the Skyhawk in place of the original 20-mm weapons).

Despite its versatility and effectiveness as a conventional strike aircraft, from the mid-1950s through the 1960s the US Navy considered the Skyhawk primarily a nuclear strike aircraft. Forward-deployed aircraft carriers, except those participating in the Vietnam War, usually had two, and sometime more, Skyhawks armed with nuclear weapons ready to launch in minutes, with their pilots briefed on Soviet or Chinese targets.

In 1950, soon after the Korean War began, the US Navy issued a requirement for an attack plane to deliver nuclear weapons and to perform nonnuclear interdiction missions, in the latter role a possible replacement for the piston-engine AD Skyraider. At that time the Navy was concerned with the increasing size, weight, complexity, maintenance requirements, and cost of aircraft as reflected by the new jet-propelled fighters and the A3D Skywarrior. Aircraft design genius Ed Heinemann attacked the trend.

In January 1952, Heinemann briefed Navy officials on his approach to designing an ultra-lightweight jet interceptor having a gross takeoff weight of about 8,000 pounds. Heinemann was asked if he could apply his methodology to an attack aircraft that, with a nuclear bomb, would gross no more than 12,000 pounds. Employing new concepts in both design and materials, his Douglas team set to work to meet the Navy's specifications, which included a speed of 500 miles per hour, a combat radius of at least 460 miles, and the ability to carry 1,000-pound bombs. These difficult requirements were met or bettered by Heinemann's design team. Nicknamed the "scooter" and "Heinemann's hot rod," the A4D-1 weighed in at 8,286 pounds empty, but could lift off at 11,700 pounds, including 3,000 pounds of weapons.

The single-engine, single-seat YA4D-1 first flew on June 22, 1954, two years and one day after the contract was signed, a very rapid response in jet aircraft development. With a span of 27 $\frac{1}{2}$ feet, the Skyhawk's delta wing was small enough that it did not fold for shipboard stowage, the first US carrier

The Douglas A4D Skyhawk was another exceptional carrier-based aircraft designed by Ed Heinemann. Developed to carry out daylight nuclear strikes, the A4D evolved into a flexible conventional attack aircraft. This later A-4F variant from the carrier *Bon Homme Richard* has a "hump" faired into the upper fuselage to accommodate avionics equipment. *US Navy*

plane not to have that feature since the SBD Dauntless (which had a span of 41½ feet). The Skyhawk had a fully retractable tricycle landing gear.

Fleet squadrons began receiving A4Ds in September 1956, providing the carrier striking forces with large numbers of aircraft capable of delivering a nuclear weapon. In an effort to hold down weight and complexity, the early A4D Skyhawks relied on highly trained pilots for navigation and bomb aiming. The Skyhawk had virtually no electronic or navigation equipment. For routine flights over land areas where electronic instruments were required a bomb-shaped electronics pod was carried. For the attack role there were three external bomb attachment points that could hold 3,000 pounds of bombs or fuel tanks. For self-defense and ground attack there were four 20-millimeter cannon in the plane's wing roots (subsequently reduced to two guns).

However, even before the first production A4D-1 was delivered the improved A4D-2 was being flown, signaling the beginning of a development program that would see a succession of single- and two-seat designs. Modifications would see the Skyhawk's gross weight increase marginally, but gave the aircraft a speed of 685 miles per hour at sea level (Mach 0.9), improved electronics, a navigation system, and the ability to lift a greater variety of ordnance, including Bullpup missiles, air-to-air missiles and rockets, "iron bombs" or nuclear weapons. A refueling probe was added to provide in-flight refueling from tanker aircraft or other Skyhawks carrying "buddy" fuel stores.

The A4D Skyhawk had a remarkable production run, with the last of 2,960 A-4s built for US and foreign use delivered by McDonnell Douglas in February 1979. Of those, 555 were two-seaters, including 293 TA-4J aircraft for the US Naval Air Training Command. Another 294 Skyhawks were built to foreign orders; ex-US aircraft were also transferred to other countries. This was one of the longest production runs of any combat aircraft in history with 21 variants being produced (the last being an A-4M).

In October 1962 the A4D series was redesignated A-4.

The Skyhawk served in US Navy and Marine combat squadrons until 1992. The two-seat TA-4J training variant serves with the Navy into the twenty-first century!

A4D-2 (A-4C) Characteristics

Design:	Douglas
Crew:	Pilot
Engines:	1 Wright J65-W-16 turbojet; 7,700 lbst
Weights:	
Empty:	8,777 lb
Loaded:	12,370 lb
Dimensions:	
Length:	39 ft, 5 in
Wingspan:	27 ft, 6 in
Wing area:	260 sq ft
Height:	15 ft
Speeds:	
Maximum:	675 mph at sea level; 608 mph at 35,000 ft
Cruise:	512 mph
Ceiling:	45,900 ft
Range:	Radius of 420 miles with 1 nuclear weapon; radius of 650 miles with 1 nuclear weapon and 2 150-gallon drop tanks
Armament:	2 20-mm cannon (fixed); 1 nuclear bomb (B7, B8, B12, B28, Mk 34 [Hotpoint], B43, B57, B61, B91 [TX-11 Elsie], or BOAR) or 6,000 lb of bombs, rockets, drop tanks

English Electric Canberra

The Canberra was Britain's first jet-propelled bomber and among the most versatile and longest-serving turbojet aircraft to be produced by any nation. Like its mission predecessor, the de Havilland Mosquito, the Canberra was highly maneuverable and relied on speed rather than defensive guns to escape enemy fighters; it also shared with the Mosquito simplicity of design and great adaptability to various roles.

Designed from the outset as a bomber, the Canberra B.2 variant entered service with the Royal Air Force's Bomber Command in May 1951; the first nuclear-capable Canberra, the B.(I)8 variant, entered service in May 1956.

The aircraft's superior performance led to the first known Western intelligence overflights of the Soviet Union. The initial reconnaissance mission by a British Canberra was flown in 1952 at the behest of the US government; the United States had no aircraft that could undertake such a photographic flight. The modified Canberra photographed the Soviet missile installation at Kapustan Yar, on the Volga River, below the city of Stalingrad (now Volgograd). That Canberra took off from a base in West Germany and landed in Iran. In July 1953 another Canberra flying a spy mission over Kapustan Yar was damaged by anti-aircraft gunfire but landed safely in Iran.

RAF Canberras were based in West Germany beginning in August 1954, in the Far East (Malaya) from February 1955, and in the Middle East from 1957. They first saw combat in 1955 with Canberra B.6 aircraft being used against terrorists in Malaya; the following year Canberra B.2 and B.6 aircraft flew 278 attack sorties against Egyptian targets in the Anglo-French intervention during the Suez conflict of October–November 1956.

RAF Canberra strength peaked in April 1955 with 390 aircraft, including 305 bomber and photo-reconnaissance aircraft, assigned to 23 squadrons in Britain and 4 in West Germany. The last RAF bomber aircraft was the B(I).8, which left service in January 1972. Four Canberra PR.9 and one T.4 continue to fly with RAF No. 39 Squadron into the twenty-first century. In the United States two WB-57F wide-wing aircraft were flown by NASA into the twenty-first century.

The first Canberra flew on May 13, 1949. The Canberra had a streamlined design with low-aspect-ratio wings with a rectangular center section and double-taper outer panels. Twin engine turbojet nacelles were embedded in the wings at mid-span. The wing design was intended to provide maximum endurance at the highest possible cruise altitude. An internal bomb bay was fitted; no defensive guns were installed.

The original design provided for a two-man crew to carry out high-altitude radar bombing missions during daylight. This was changed in the fifth prototype to the B.2 standard for visual bombing with a plastic nose and a third crewmember.

The B.6 had upgraded engines and increased fuel. The B.15/16 were intended for overseas operations in tropical areas; they could carry bombs, rocket pods, or Nord air-to-surface missiles on wing hardpoints and had a camera fitted in the nose. The B.6 and later bombers could accommodate one or (B.15/16) two nuclear bombs, the British Red Beard weapon or, in B(I).6/8 and B.15/16, US nuclear bombs. The standard conventional bomb load for the B(I) aircraft was three 1,000-pound bombs in the bomb bay and two 1,000-pound bombs under the wings.

The B(I) or Intruder aircraft returned to a two-man flight crew, with the pilot in a fighter-type, bubble offset to starboard and the navigator-bomb aimer in the fully enclosed nose. (The designation Intruder indicated an aircraft to penetrate heavily defended areas, primarily at night.)

A total of 878 aircraft of all types were produced in Britain; a further 48 B.20 variants were built in Australia. Some British-built bomber aircraft were produced specifically for India, New Zealand, and South Africa; several other countries subsequently flew former RAF aircraft. With the US production the total number of Canberras built was 1,329, more than any other Western jet-propelled bomber except for the Boeing B-47.

The US Air Force adopted the Canberra for the tactical strike, reconnaissance (including high-altitude "spy plane" configuration), and training roles. The first of two RAF Canberras flown to the Glenn L. Martin Company, in Baltimore, Maryland, to serve as development models arrived on February 21, 1951, having made the first unrefueled crossing of the Atlantic by a jet-propelled aircraft. Five days later the USAF awarded Martin a production contract; 403 B-57s of all types were produced by Martin, the last a B-57C delivered in May 1956. Production included 67 RB-57A and 20 RB-57D reconnaissance aircraft, and 68 B-57E target-tow aircraft.

The first flight of a B-57A occurred on July 20, 1953, with all eight B-57A aircraft relegated to tests and special projects. The RB-57A became operational in mid-1954 and the first Canberra "bomber" to enter USAF service was the B-57B, joining tactical bomb wings in late 1954. Bomber variants served in Vietnam until 1972 and then were turned over to the Air National Guard. Specialized B-57s remained in USAF service another few years. Subsequently, specialized B-57s were operated as research aircraft by

The English Electric Canberra was one of history's most versatile turbojet aircraft. Developed as a nuclear bomber, the Canberra relied on speed to evade pursuers. It served in many roles with the Royal Air Force and, as the B-57 Canberra, in the US Air Force as a bomber, photo-reconnaissance aircraft, and high-flying spy plane. This is a B.62 flown by the Argentine Air Force. *British Aircraft Corp.*

Canberra B(I).8 Characteristics

Design:	English Electric
Crew:	
B-series:	3 (pilot, navigator/plotter, observer/bomb aimer)
B(I)-series:	2 (pilot, navigator/bomb aimer)
Engines:	2 Rolls-Royce Avon 109 turbojet; 7,500 lbst each
Weights:	
Empty:	27,950 lb
Loaded:	43,000 lb
Maximum takeoff:	54,950 lb
Dimensions:	
Length:	65 feet, 6 in
Wingspan:	63 ft, 11 1/2 in
Wing area:	960 sq ft
Height:	15 ft, 7 in
Speeds:	
Maximum:	541 mph at 40,000 ft; 510 mph at sea level
Cruise:	
Ceiling:	48,000 ft
Range:	800 miles with 6,000 lb of bombs
Armament:	1 nuclear bomb (from 1958) US Mk 7 or Mk 43 or 6,000 lb of conventional bombs, rockets; 4 20-mm or 30-mm (in detachable fuselage pack) in B(I)-series aircraft

NASA, the National Science Foundation, and the National Center for Atmospheric Research.

The RB-57D and RB-57F were "wide-wing" photo aircraft for high-altitude flight: the standard B-57 wingspan was 64 feet; new wings had a span of 105 feet in the RB-57D and 122 1/2 feet in the RB-57F. The RB-57F could reach 68,500 feet and had a range of 4,250 miles. The RB-57D had a crew of only one, the RB-57F a more effective two-man crew.

Reaching an even higher altitude, on August 28, 1957, a B.2 aircraft fitted with a Napier Double Scorpion rocket in its bomb bay attained a record-setting altitude of 71,310 feet.

Several wide-wing B-57s were supplied by the United States to Taiwan for spy flights over China, with some of those being shot down by SA-2 Guideline missiles. Australian Canberras flew strikes against Viet Cong positions in South Vietnam from 1967 to 1971. India flew Canberras against Pakistan in their 1965 and 1971 conflicts, whereas Pakistan employed US B-57s against Indian targets. Argentine Canberras flew several ineffective strikes against British naval and ground forces in the 1982 war in the Falklands. Canberras continued to fly in several air forces as late as the 1990s.

Canberras were well liked by pilots, being easy to fly and highly maneuverable; ground crews found them easy to service and maintain.

General Dynamics F-111

The US F-111 was one of the most controversial aircraft of the Cold War era, marking an attempt by the United States to have one aircraft designed from the outset for multiple services and multiple missions. The F-111 was the first variable-geometry-wing ("swing-wing") aircraft to serve operationally with any air arm.

The aircraft began life with the designation TFX (for *tactical fighter experimental*) for the Air Force—but "fighter" in that context meant a tactical strike or attack aircraft, specifically intended to succeed the F-105 Thunderchief, a strike aircraft with minimal air-to-air capability.

The F-111 entered service in the strike role with the Tactical Air Command of the USAF in April 1968, and the modified FB-111 became operational as a limited strategic bomber in 1971. Forty-eight F-111A aircraft were used in bombing strikes against North Vietnam from a base in Thailand in 1968 and 1972–73; these were single-plane missions flown at night, demonstrating the night/low-level strike profile of the aircraft. Each F-111 could deliver the same bomb load as five F-4 Phantoms. The March–April 1968 combat deployment of six F-111As was aborted because of the loss of three aircraft to accidents and systems failure in the 55 missions that were flown.

Fifty-two F-111As returned to Thailand for missions against North Vietnam beginning in September 1972. On November 8, 1972, weather grounded all US combat aircraft except the F-111As, which flew 20 strikes over North Vietnam that day. Despite continued difficulties and accidents, the F-111s flew 3,000 missions before US air operations over North Vietnam halted in January 1973.

Sixteen F-111F aircraft and four EF-111A Raven ECM aircraft flew a strike against Libya from bases in England on April 15, 1986. Known as Operation El Dorado Canyon, the strike was in retaliation for Libyan-sponsored terrorist acts in West Germany.

Those aircraft flew the almost 15-hour, 5,800-mile round-trip with four outbound in-flight refuelings and two on the return flight, the mission profile being required because other NATO nations denied the use of their bases or territorial overflights for the attack. (A total of 30 US KC-10A and KC-135R tanker aircraft were required to support the strike mission.)

The F-111Fs carried Paveway II laser-guided 2,000-pound bombs and Snakeye 500-pound conventional bombs. The four EF-111s were supplemented by US Marine-piloted EA-6B Prowlers from the carrier *America*. The actual strike took only 12 minutes, and delivered 60 tons of bombs. One F-111 was lost, apparently to Libyan anti-aircraft fire. (US Navy carrier aircraft carried out simultaneous strikes against other targets in Libya).

Eighteen F-111E and 66 F-111F aircraft carried out strikes against Iraq in 1991 during the Gulf War, with 18 EF-111A aircraft also having a major role in that conflict. The F-111s used laser-guided bombs to destroy numerous Iraqi tanks in a technique known as "tank plinking." The last USAF F-111s were retired in 1996 and the last EF-111 in 1999, the latter replaced by Navy and Marine Corps EA-6B Prowler ECM aircraft.

During the Cold War F-111s were on nuclear quick reaction alert for sustained periods at two British air bases, Upper Heyford and Lakenheath.

The F-111 program was initiated by the Air Force to provide a successor the F-105 strike aircraft. The program—relabeled TFX—was redirected by Defense Secretary Robert McNamara in 1961 to provide a single aircraft design for tactical strike, close air support, fleet air defense, and battlefield interdiction. Following a review of proposals, the Air Force favored a design proposed by Boeing, but McNamara selected the General Dynamics proposal on November 24, 1962. The USAF F-111A first flew on December 21, 1964, followed by the first of seven Grumman-built US Navy F-111Bs on May 18, 1965. The Navy withdrew from the F-111 program in August 1968, contending that the aircraft was severely overweight and unsuitable for carrier operation.

Production of the F-111 tactical strike aircraft was initiated for the Air Force and 24 F-111C aircraft were produced for Australia. But a planned British procurement of 50 F-111K strike aircraft was cancelled in 1968. The F-111D, with new avionics systems, environmental control systems, and engines, first flew on May 15, 1970; the F-111E, which first flew on August 20, 1969, featured new air inlets to improve high-speed engine operation and improved stores systems; and the F-111F, a stripped-down version of the F-111D, began flight testing in October 1971. Subsequent upgrades of ECM and laser guidance systems made the F-111F the most capable aircraft in the Aardvark family.

A total of 563 F-111s of all variants was completed when production ended in 1976. Subsequently, 42 F-111A aircraft were converted to the EF-111A Raven ECM configuration with all weapons capability removed; the EF-111As were delivered in 1981–85.

In an effort to rationalize the truncated F-111 program, on December 10, 1965, Secretary McNamara announced the development of the FB-111 variant as a penetration strategic bomber. Two days earlier he had revealed that he was accelerating retirement of 345 B-52 Stratofortress and 80 B-58 Hustler strategic bombers.

The first of 75 FB-111A aircraft flew on July 31, 1967. The FB-111s were assigned to SAC from October 1969 (declared combat ready in October 1971) until June 1990 when the Air Force began modifying the 51 surviving aircraft for the tactical/theater strike role (redesignated F-111G).

The F-111 had shoulder-mounted, variable-geometry wings that swept from a fully extended position (16 degrees for landing, takeoff, and cruise, to a "tucked-in" position (72.5 degrees) for high-speed flight. There was

Born in a think tank, the General Dynamics F-111 evolved an effective strike and interdiction aircraft. History's first operational aircraft to use a variable-geometry or "swing" wing, the F-111 served ably with the US and Royal Australian air forces. Depicted here is the second F-111A produced, seen on a test flight with its wings swept back for high-speed flight.

General Dynamics

F-111A Characteristics

Design:	General Dynamics
Crew:	2 (pilot, weapon systems officer)
Engines:	2 Pratt & Whitney TF30-P-3 turbofan; 18,500 lbst each with afterburner
Weights:	
Empty:	46,172 lb
Maximum takeoff:	91,300 lb
Dimensions:	
Length:	75 ft, 6 ½ in
Wingspan:	63 ft extended (16 degrees); 32 ft swept back (72.5 degrees)
Wing area:	525 sq ft
Height:	17 ft
Speeds:	
Maximum:	1,451 mph
Cruise:	745 mph
Ceiling:	64,725 ft
Range:	2,655 miles with low-level target penetration
Armament:	1 20-mm M61A1 Vulcan rotary-barrel cannon (removable; fixed); 4 nuclear bombs (B43, B57, or B61) external or 2 nuclear bombs (B43, B57, or B61) internal or 24,000 lb of conventional weapons external

almost no gap between the wings and tail-planes at full sweep. The aircraft featured side-by-side seating for the two-man crew, based on Navy requirements (which also provided a wide nose to house a large radar antenna for the Navy's long-range intercept requirement).

The aircraft was designed to carry two nuclear weapons in an internal weapons bay; subsequently, wing pylons were added to carry nuclear or conventional weapons at subsonic speeds. Up to eight wing pylons could be fitted, four of which are retained when the wings were swept back.

Large weapons were usually carried on the four inboard pylons, which could each accommodate six 1,000-pound bombs—in other words, 24 bombs. Installing the Gatling gun displaced one of two internal positions for nuclear weapons.

The principal differences between the F-111A and FB-111A were the engines with the FB-111 having a higher gross weight, additional electronics, and 3½-foot extensions to both wingtips. There were six wing pylons; the outermost pylon on each wing was fixed so that it created the least drag at a 26-degree sweep angle; these pylons were used for fuel tanks and were jettisoned with the tanks when the latter were empty; weapons could not be carried on those pylons. The four other pylons could carry nuclear bombs, AGM-69 SRAM missiles, 24 conventional 750-pound bombs, cluster bombs, or 600-gallon drop tanks. Two nuclear bombs or SRAMs could be carried in the internal weapons bay.

The Royal Australian Air Force continues to fly F-111C and RF-111C variants, expecting to keep the type in service until 2020.

Lockheed P-80/T-33 Shooting Star

The P-80 Shooting Star was the first US jet-propelled combat aircraft and was flown in large numbers by the Air Force, Navy, and Marine Corps as well as several foreign air forces. Although it was evaluated aboard an aircraft carrier, the naval services flew the Shooting Star exclusively from shore bases.

The Allied air forces had lagged behind Germany in the development of jet-propelled aircraft during World War II. Development of the P-80 began in May 1943 as the Army Air Forces invited Lockheed to submit a proposal for a fighter built around the Halford H.1B turbojet engine developed in Britain. A Lockheed design team lead by Clarence L. (Kelly) Johnson—head of the famed "skunk works"—designed, built, and flew the XP-80A prototype in 178 days after being invited to submit a proposal. The first XP-80 aircraft flew on January 8, 1944, albeit suffering several problems. (The first US jet-propelled aircraft, the XP-59A Airacomet, had flown on October 1, 1942; but it served only as a development aircraft.)

Two additional XP-80A prototypes and 13 YP-80A service test aircraft were rapidly delivered. Only the first aircraft had the H-1 engine, produced as the Allis-Chalmers J36; subsequent P-80s had the General Electric I-40/J33 engine.

Two YP-80A aircraft reached a US base in Italy and two reached England shortly before the end of World War II in Europe (May 1945), but none saw action. But it was the first US jet aircraft to see combat in the Korean War (redesignated F-80 in 1948). On November 8, 1950, a US Air Force F-80 destroyed a MiG-15 in what is credited as the first kill in air combat between jet-propelled aircraft.

US Air Force F-80s were in aerial combat over the Korean peninsula until early 1953, being credited with shooting down 31 enemy aircraft while suffering 14 losses in aerial combat. RF-80 camera planes overflew North Korea and periodically penetrated into Manchuria as well as Soviet Siberia on reconnaissance flights to determine the aircraft buildup facing the allied forces in the Korean War.

Although replaced in US service by more-capable aircraft, the P-80 continued to serve in many roles and in many air forces. The two-seat TF-80C, redesignated T-33, was procured in large numbers by the USAF for the training role. Some still flew at the start of the twenty-first century in the air forces of Bolivia, Canada, and Japan in the specialized attack (AT-33) and electronic (CT-33) as well as training-utility roles.

The P-80 was the first US aircraft to exceed 500 miles per hour in level flight, was highly maneuverable, and gave promise of being an effective fighter. The engine—produced by Allison/General Motors and General Electric—was a production version of the I-40 turbojet. A streamlined, low-wing (laminar-flow) aircraft with the twin air intakes faired into the forward fuselage, the P-80 had a nosewheel undercarriage. A bubble canopy provided the pilot with excellent visibility.

US Navy interest in the P-80 led to three aircraft being transferred from the Army. One Navy P-80A was fitted with an arresting hook and underwent catapult and arresting trials at Naval Air Station Patuxent River, Maryland. Then, loaded by crane onto the large carrier *Franklin D. Roosevelt* at Norfolk, Virginia, the plane was taken to sea. On November 1, 1946, Marine Maj. Marion Carl made four deck-run takeoffs and two catapult launches; the takeoffs and five arrested landings were made without

The Lockheed P-80 Shooting Star was the first US jet-propelled aircraft to enter squadron service. As the F-80 it saw
combat at the start of the Korean War, but was soon outclassed
by the Soviet MiG-15 and US F-86 Sabre. It survived as a two-
place training aircraft (T-33) in many air forces for many years.
The US Navy and Marine Corps also flew the Shooting Star.
US Air Force

P-80A Characteristics

Design:	Lockheed
Crew:	Pilot
Engines:	1 Allison J33-A-9 turbojet; 3,850 lbst
	or 1 General Electric J33-GE-11 turbojet; 3,850 lbst
Weights:	
Empty:	7,920 lb
Loaded:	11,700 lb
Maximum takeoff:	14,000 lb
Dimensions:	
Length:	34 ft, 6 in
Wingspan:	38 ft, 10 $\frac{1}{2}$ in
Wing area:	237.6 sq ft
Height:	11 ft, 4 in
Speeds:	
Maximum:	558 mph at sea level
Cruise:	410 mph
Ceiling:	45,000 ft
Range:	780 miles
Armament:	6 .50-cal. machine guns (fixed); 2 1,000-lb bombs or 10 5-inch rockets

incident. Carl made additional landings and takeoffs aboard the *Roosevelt* on November 11.

In his *US Marine Corps Aviation, 1912–Present,* air intelligence officer-aviation historian Peter B. Mersky wrote: "There had been a growing problem in retaining young, eager Marine pilots who saw their fortunate Air Force counterparts getting racy new jet aircraft, while the Marines were forced to make do with outdated [F4U] Corsairs."

Thus, at the urging of the Marine Corps in 1948 the US Navy procured 50 single-seat P-80C aircraft, which became the TO-1, the T indicating a trainer and O being the designator for the main Lockheed plant at Burbank, California (later changed to TV). These aircraft were intended to transition Navy and Marine pilots to turbojet fighters, readying them for the forthcoming Navy carrier-based jets. Sixteen of the TO-1s, however, were assigned to Marine Fighter Squadron 311, a first-line fighter squadron based at Marine Corps Air Station El Toro, California.

In 1949 the Navy initiated the procurement of 698 two-seat TF-80C/T-33 variants of the Shooting Star, initially given the Navy designation TO-2 and then TV-2. These two-seat aircraft would bring Navy-Marine procurement to 751 Shooting Stars. None of was fitted for carrier operation.

Lockheed produced 5,819 F-80/T-33 aircraft; additional aircraft were built under license in Canada and Japan. The Shooting Star thus was built in greater numbers than any other Western turbojet aircraft except for the F-86 Sabre/FJ Fury. (The F4H/F-4 Phantom ranked No. 3 in numbers produced.)

The last US Air Force Shooting Stars were retired in 1987 after serving in the Air National Guard and in a variety of special-purpose roles.

Lockheed C-130 Hercules

In continuous production since 1954, the Lockheed Hercules has enjoyed the longest production run of any airplane in history. More than 60 nations have flown the aircraft in a variety of combat as well as transport and support roles. The "Herk" remains in high demand as new models offer increased range and payload with upgrades to avionic and navigation systems.

The roles in which this venerable aircraft has flown include aerial tanker; airborne command, control, and communications; strategic communications relay (for strategic missile submarines); AEW to counter drug-trafficking; medical evacuation; Arctic and Antarctic support; drone launch and control; electronic intelligence and reconnaissance; gunship; maritime patrol; aerial mapping platform; search-and-rescue; space and missile support operations; special (clandestine) operations; staff and VIP transport; systems test and evaluation; psychological warfare broadcast; and weather reconnaissance aircraft. It is currently flown by the US Air Force, Navy, Marine Corps, and Coast Guard.

Designed as a tactical transport to replace the C-119 Flying Boxcar (Navy R4Q), the first C-130A aircraft were delivered to the Tactical Air Command (TAC) in December 1956. Subsequently three C-130E wings were assigned to strategic airlift with the Military Air Transport Service (MATS) beginning in 1962 (although those aircraft were passed over to TAC in 1964 as heavier transports became available). MATS—later incorporated into Military Airlift Command (MAC)—continued to operate mapping, weather, and rescue versions of the Hercules.

The Lebanon crisis in July–August 1958 saw Europe-based C-130s delivering troops to the Middle East, whereas the Quemoy-Matsu crisis in August–October 1958 had Japan-based C-130s flying equipment to Taiwan in a face-off with China. In 1960, USAF C-130s participated in the UN airlift to the Congo. And 1965 saw the beginning of C-130 airlift operations within South Vietnam. The Hercules has participated in every subsequent US military action, humanitarian relief mission, or tactical airlift exercise.

In the Vietnam War the C-130s dropped 15,000-pound "daisy-cutter" bombs to clear jungle landing areas for helicopters. In 1966 two C-130s were rigged to drop eight-foot-diameter, 5,000-pound floating mines against North Vietnamese rail bridges. (Five of the mines were dropped from one aircraft without results; the second aircraft was apparently shot down by North Vietnamese anti-aircraft guns.) The most effective armed C-130s were the gunships, designated AC-130 "Spectre." Each Spectre orbited its ground targets in daylight or darkness, bringing 7.62-mm miniguns, 20-mm Vulcan cannon, 40-mm Bofors cannon, and (on later aircraft) 105-mm howitzers to bear on Viet Cong targets. Updated gunships remain in USAF service.

A USAF HC-130 configuration was developed with underwing probe-and-drogue aerial refueling pods to support rescue helicopters. The US Marine Corps procured a similar system with its KC-130 convertible cargo/tanker aircraft. The KC-130 can refuel both fixed-wing and rotary wing aircraft.

The US Navy and Air National Guard have operated ski-equipped LC-130s to provide support of Arctic and Antarctic research operations. In a demonstration of the aircraft's flexibility, a KC-130F carried out a series of carrier evaluation flights from the aircraft carrier Forrestal in October–November 1963. The Hercules made 26 touch-and-go landings and 21 full-stop landings. No carrier arresting gear was employed and the

Although several combat aircraft have remained in frontline service longer than the Lockheed C-130 Hercules, none has remained in production as long. New versions of the versatile airlifter continue in development after almost 50 years of service, with no indications of an end to production. This "Roman-nosed" C-130A was one of the first Hercules delivered to the US Air Force. *US National Archives*

C-130H Characteristics

Design:	Lockheed (now Lockheed Martin)
Crew:	5 (pilot, copilot, navigator, flight engineer and loadmaster) plus 92 troops
Engines:	4 Allison T56-A-15 turboprop; 4,591 shaft hp each
Weights:	
Empty:	75,661 lb
Maximum takeoff:	155,000 lb
Dimensions:	
Length:	97 ft, 9 in
Wingspan:	132 ft, 7 in
Wing area:	1,745 sq ft
Height:	38 ft, 3 in
Speeds:	
Maximum:	386 mph at 25,000 ft
Cruise:	355 mph
Ceiling:	42,900 ft
Range:	2,745 miles with 45,000 lb of cargo
Armament:	None

aircraft rollout was as little as 270 feet. After each of the full-stop landings the KC-130F took off with deck runs as short as 330 feet. In these trials, with Lt. James H. Flatley III, the primary pilot, the aircraft reached a maximum of 120,000 pounds, thus the Hercules was the largest aircraft ever flown aboard a carrier.

The latest "standard" cargo aircraft is the C-130J, which entered production in 1997. It provides major improvements over previous models including a "glass cockpit" and digital avionics that make the J-model easier and safer to operate in low-altitude maneuvers and introduces an all-weather airdrop capability. A new engine, with a six-blade propeller, enhances aircraft performance in terms of range, cruise altitude, rate of climb, speed, and airfield requirements, while halving the number of maintenance manhours required for each flight hour. A stretched version, the C-130J-30—now designated CC-130J by the USAF—offers a 15-foot longer fuselage, with an air refueling receptacle, and increased range. The CC-130Js are expected to provide long-range strategic as well as tactical airlift capabilities.

The C-130 was developed as a result of tactical airlift shortfalls during the Korean War. The first flight of a YC-130 occurred on August 23, 1954. The prototype proved capable of takeoff after a ground role of only 800 feet—and even shorter if external rocket assistance canisters (JATO) were installed. The aircraft, an immediate success with the US armed forces, was soon made available to foreign operators, with Australia receiving the first export C-130 in 1957.

Lockheed has produced more than 2,200 C-130s in more than 70 variations that have been delivered to more than 60 nations. With continuing advances in C-130 systems, the aircraft should remain in production for several more decades.

Lockheed C-5 Galaxy

Once the world's largest and heaviest operational military transport, the Lockheed C-5's size and capacity have been surpassed by more recent US and Russian designs. Now in its fourth decade of military service, the C-5 Galaxy has built an unequaled record combat airlift and humanitarian relief.

The first operational C-5A reached the USAF Military Airlift Command (MAC) in December 1969, with initial operational missions to South Vietnam beginning in August 1970. During the Yom Kippur War of 1973 USAF C-5s delivered arms and equipment to Israel. During operations Desert Shield and Desert Storm in 1990–91 C-5s airlifted almost a half-million passengers and more than 577,000 tons of cargo to the Persian Gulf region. This airlift included 15 air-transportable hospitals and the more than 5,000 medical personnel.

Subsequently, C-5s have flown worldwide in support of US military operations and in support of humanitarian efforts. And, in March 1989 C-5s transported nearly 1,000 tons pounds of equipment to Alaska in support of the oil spill cleanup.

The ability of the C-5 to carry M1 main battle tanks, large H-53

A Lockheed C-5 Galaxy takes off, revealing the aircraft's massive landing gear. The C-5 provides a worldwide lift capability for the heaviest weapons and vehicles in the US arsenal. Although worked hard and aging, the C-5s are expected to remain in service for the foreseeable future. *US Air Force*

A C-5 Galaxy loads a 60-ton scissors bridge vehicle; a C-5 can carry two M1 main battle tanks. In June 1989 the US Air Force claimed the world record for a parachute operation when a Galaxy successfully dropped 190,493 pounds of Army paratroopers and equipment consisting of four 21-ton Sheridan vehicles and 73 paratroopers. *Lockheed*

helicopters, or 60-ton scissors-bridge vehicles over great distances have made it an invaluable component of US strategic mobility. Even with the availability of the Lockheed C-141 StarLifter in 1964 and the Boeing (McDonnell Douglas) C-17 in 1995, the C-5 remains essential to US strategic airlift.

The US Air Force ordered the C-5A from Lockheed in October 1965, based in part on the requirement to support forward-deployment (afloat) forces being developed by the Department of Defense. The first C-5A flight occurred on June 30, 1968. The last of the initial orders for 81 C-5A aircraft were delivered in May 1973. A decade after production ended the USAF made the unusual decision to order 50 C-5B aircraft. The later aircraft had strengthened wings, updated avionics, and numerous system modifications to improve reliability and maintainability. The first C-5B was delivered in January 1986, and the last in April 1989.

The C-5 is a massive aircraft with a high, swept wing with four large turbofan engines mounted on underwing pylons. The aircraft has a tall T-tail. The fuselage has large front and rear cargo openings, with the doors opening for the full width and height of the cargo compartment. Full-width ramps deploy from both ends, easing the delivery of rolling equipment. The aircraft's landing gear also "kneels," lowering the parked aircraft to facilitate the loading of supplies at the heights of most truck beds.

The upper deck on C-5s accommodates 73 troops; for maximum personnel delivery, palletized seats can be mounted in the main cargo compartment for an additional 290 passengers. C-5 loads include alternatives of 2 M1 Abrams main battle tanks; 1 M1 Abrams and 2 M2 Bradley fighting vehicles; 4 M551 Sheridan light tanks and 1 tactical vehicle; 16 $^3/_4$-ton trucks, 10 LAV-25 light armored vehicles; or 4 Boeing AH-64D Apache attack helicopters.

Although C-5s are rarely used for airborne drops, the rear ramp can be opened in flight for the quick exit of 338 paratroopers, the parachute air-drop of 4 M551 Sheridan tanks, or a combination of those loads.

A C-5 was also used to drop a Minuteman ICBM by parachute on October 24, 1974; after being stabilized in descent, the Minuteman's solid-propellant missile was ignited at an altitude of about 8,000 feet.

C-5B Characteristics

Design:	Lockheed
Crew:	6 (pilot, co-pilot, 2 flight engineers, 2 loadmasters) + 73 troops (see text)
Engines:	4 General Electric TF39-GE-1C turbofan; 43,000 lbst each
Weights:	
Empty:	374,000 lb
Maximum takeoff:	769,000 lb
Dimensions:	
Length:	247 ft, 9 $\frac{1}{2}$ in
Wingspan:	222 ft, 8 $\frac{1}{2}$ in
Wing area:	6,200 sq ft
Height:	65 ft, 1 $\frac{1}{4}$ in
Speeds:	
Maximum:	571 mph at 25,000 ft
Cruise:	518 mph
Ceiling:	35,750 ft
Range:	3,435 miles with 261,000 lb cargo; 7,665 miles without cargo
Armament:	None

Lockheed U-2

The U-2 is world's best-known spy plane and was probably the first aircraft developed specifically for peacetime espionage operations. The U-2 is a US photo- and electronic-reconnaissance aircraft that was designed for overflights of the Soviet Union.

The aircraft was flown on 23 successful missions over the Soviet Union from July 1956 to May 1960. It was also flown extensively over other areas of interest to the United States, including Cuba, the Middle East, Indochina, and China, with China flights also made by Taiwanese pilots.

More than 800 U-2 flights were made over the Persian Gulf region in 1990–91. Improved U-2 variants continue in frontline US service into the twenty-first century, long outlasting its planned successor, the SR-71 Blackbird.

Work on the U-2 began in 1953 as a highly classified or "black" program sponsored by the CIA. Clarence (Kelly) Johnson, head of the Lockheed "skunk works," was the chief designer of the aircraft. His proposal for essentially a powered glider for very high altitude flight (about 70,000 feet) was rejected by the US Air Force, at the time responsible for all strategic aerial intelligence. The Air Force believed that multi-engine aircraft were needed for such operations.

However, the CIA undertook sponsorship of the aircraft and President Dwight D. Eisenhower personally approved the production of 30 U-2 aircraft. He supported the U-2 because of concern that Soviet strategic nuclear weapon developments could threaten the United States with a surprise nuclear attack—a nuclear Pearl Harbor attack.

The first U-2 flight occurred on August 1, 1955—made inadvertently during taxi trials of the aircraft. The first operational flight over the USSR occurred on July 4, 1956, with Moscow-area military installations the primary target. Although US officials hoped that the Soviets would not detect U-2 flights, all overflights were detected and most were tracked while over the USSR.

The flights over the Soviet Union were made by civilian pilots under contract to the CIA, although they were actually officers on loan from the Air Force. The U-2 squadrons were joint CIA–Air Force units known as Weather Reconnaissance Squadrons (Provisional). British pilots also trained to fly the U-2 and beginning on August 24, 1958, there were several British-piloted U-2 overflights. The 24th attempted overflight of the USSR occurred on May 1, 1960. That U-2, piloted by Francis Gary Powers, took off from at Peshawar, Pakistan. The plan was to cross the Soviet Union and land in Bödo, Norway, a 3,788-mile flight—of which 2,919 miles would be over the Soviet Union—to last some nine and a half hours. The U-2 was shot down by a Soviet SA-2 Guideline surface-to-air missile. Powers was able to parachute from the stricken aircraft and was captured and put on public trial for espionage. After being incarcerated, he was released in a "spy swap" on February 10, 1962.

American-piloted U-2 flights were made over numerous other countries and, during the Suez crisis of October 1956, over the eastern Mediterranean to monitor British and French military activities. Several U-2s were transferred to Taiwan for flights over China.

A Soviet-supplied SA-2 missile brought down a U-2 over China on September 8, 1962. That was the first of five Taiwanese-piloted U-2s to be lost over China. All were probably downed by SA-2 missiles. (The last flight over China was made in June 1974.)

From June 1957, U-2s were also operated by the Air Force in the strategic reconnaissance role, but none of these flights was over the USSR or China. The Air Force flew the U-2 missions over Cuba during the missile crisis of October 1962, when U-2 photographs revealed that the Soviets had clandestinely brought strategic missiles into Cuba. On October 27 a Soviet-manned SA-2 battery shot down a U-2 over Cuba. The pilot, Maj. Rudolf Anderson, Jr., was killed. (Prior to the missile crisis CIA-piloted U-2s flew periodic reconnaissance flights over Cuba.)

After those losses US-piloted U-2s were limited to missions along the periphery of hostile countries, or to overflights of areas where no advanced missiles were deployed. US-Taiwan U-2 losses totaled more than 40 aircraft shot down and lost in accidents.

Even with a maximum range of some 3,000 miles there were some areas of interest to the US intelligence community that could not be reached by U-2s flying from "safe" land bases. Accordingly, in mid-1963 the CIA initiated Project Whale Tale to adapt U-2s for carrier operation. There were several carrier landing and takeoff trails. The only operational carrier U-2 mission—Operation Seeker—occurred in May 1964 when the USS *Ranger* launched one or possibly two U-2G spy planes to monitor the French nuclear tests at Murora atoll in French Polynesia. The U-2G photographs indicated that the French would be ready for full-scale production of nuclear weapons within a year.

Kelly Johnson had designed the U-2 with stringent weight restrictions in an effort to gain additional altitude, the key to the aircraft's survivability.

The Lockheed U-2 spy plane was developed specifically to overfly the Soviet Union and search out nuclear delivery systems—long-range bombers and ballistic missiles. U-2s successfully overflew the USSR on 23 occasions, and have also brought back valuable intelligence from many other areas. This is an enlarged TR-1 (later U-2R) fitted with "slipper" pods in the wings for fuel and sensors. *Lockheed*

U-2 Characteristics*

Design:	Lockheed
Crew:	Pilot
Engines:	1 Pratt & Whitney J57-P-37 turbojet; 10,200 lbst
Weights:	
Loaded:	24,150 lb
Dimensions:	
Length:	49 ft, 8 ½ in
Wingspan:	80 ft, 2 in
Wing area:	565 sq ft
Height:	15 ft, 2 in
Speeds:	
Maximum:	430+ mph
Ceiling:	72,000 ft
Range:	2,950 miles
Armament:	None

* Original production model.

The early aircraft were unpainted, to save weight. The aircraft had only a bicycle landing gear, dispensing with wing-mounted wheels to save weight. The aircraft featured large wingspan, a single-engine, and fuselage-mounted fuel tanks (that were later supplemented by wing-mounted slipper tanks). The early U-2s had a maximum speed of 430 miles per hour; a more powerful engine provided 528 miles per hour in the later U-2C, and the current U-2R has a top speed of 510 miles per hour. Ceiling for the U-2 was originally some 60,000 feet, 85,000 feet for the U-2C, and 90,000 feet for the U-2R. The early U-2s had a range of 2,200 miles, extended to 3,000 miles in the U-2C, and 3,500 miles in the U-2R. A few U-2C aircraft were fitted for in-flight refueling to extend their range.

The aircraft was periodically upgraded, especially with improved engines and advanced sensors. The U-2B of the early 1960s had a camera fitted with a 944.7-mm lens that could take 4,000 paired photos of a strip of earth 125 miles by 2,174 miles.

Lockheed produced 55 in the original U-2 series from 1955 to 1969 (some of which were converted to two-place variants). In the late 1960s the Air Force and CIA together procured one enlarged, more-capable U-2R aircraft. However, in 1974 the CIA transferred its remaining U-2s to the Air Force.

The subsequent TR-1 Tactical Reconnaissance version was developed to provide surveillance over European battlefields; this aircraft was similar to the U-2R, From 1979 to 1989 the Air Force took delivery of 35 TR-1s and NASA received two similar Earth Resources ER-1 models. NASA also flew several earlier U-2s. (The TR-1s were redesignated U-2R in 1991.) Thus, a total of 104 U-2s were produced with 35 still flying for the USAF in 2003 as well as two ER-1s with NASA.

Lockheed A-12 Oxcart and SR-71 Blackbird

A strategic reconnaissance aircraft developed as the successor to the U-2 spy plane, the SR-71 retains the record as the world's fastest and highest-flying operational aircraft.

The SR-71 became operational in January 1966 with the US Air Force's 9th Strategic Reconnaissance Wing. In addition to flying from US bases, SR-71s regularly operated from Kadena Air base, Okinawa, and Mildenhall Royal Air Force base in Britain. They were first used over North Vietnam in 1968. The aircraft subsequently flew reconnaissance missions over Cuba, Libya, Nicaragua, the Falkland Islands, South Africa, the Middle East, and the Persian Gulf area. However, it was not used to overfly "denied areas," in other words, the Soviet Union and China, which had been declared off limits to US spy planes after the loss of the U-2 piloted by Francis Gary Powers.

The "final" SR-71 flights occurred in March 1990. The SR-71 was to be retired in a cost-cutting action, whereas its predecessor, the U-2, continued to fly strategic reconnaissance missions. An SR-71 continued to be flown by NASA in a research role.

In 1995 Congress provided funds to reactivate three SR-71 aircraft to provide a limited Mach 3 reconnaissance capability.

The first reactivated SR-71 flight took place on April 26, 1995. Two aircraft were reactivated, but were again "mothballed," the last flight being made on October 10, 1997.

SR-71s set numerous speed records. In September 1974, an SR-71 flew from New York to London in 1 hour, 54 minutes at an average speed of 1,894 miles per hour or Mach 2.8. In July 1976, an SR-71 set the absolute world speed record of 2,193 miles per hour or Mach 3.31 over a straight course; a closed-circuit record also was set at 2,092 miles per hour or Mach 3.17.

The SR-71 was derived from the A-12 Oxcart, designed by the Lockheed Skunk Works as successor to that firm's U-2 spy plane, both of those projects being under the aegis of the CIA (The A-12 could fly at Mach 3 and, after burning off much of its fuel, could cruise above 90,000 feet. The A-12 became operational in November 1965. The first—and only—operational flights of the A-12 were made in 1967 over North Vietnam under the code name Black Shield. Fifteen A-12s were built with two modified to the two-place M-12 configuration to carry reconnaissance drones.)

Whereas the U-2 had been designed for high altitude and had a relatively slow speed (Mach 0.7), the SR-71 was a Mach 3 aircraft intended to fly at 85,000 feet. Its cameras could sweep more than 100,000 square miles of the Earth each hour. Fabricated of titanium, the SR-71 has an unconventional design with a long, tapering fuselage of small cross-section blending into a delta wing with rounded wingtips. The forward part of the fuselage is flattened and has sharp chines along each side. A turbojet engine nacelle is blended into the middle of each wing and each nacelle supports a low tail fin, canted slightly inward. Skin temperatures on the fuselage rise considerably during high-altitude, high-speed flight and the fuselage stretches 11 inches. The immense amount of fuel needed for high-speed flight fills most of the fuselage and acts as a heat sink. Although unarmed, there were proposals to fit a pod under the aircraft for carrying a nuclear weapon. The aircraft is flown by a crew of two. It is fitted for in-flight refueling.

The initial contract with Lockheed called for four aircraft. Three were completed as YF-12A fighter prototypes. The fourth became the first

The Lockheed SR-71 Blackbird and its progenitor, the A-12 Oxcart, were the world's fastest aircraft to enter operational service. The Mach 3 spy planes, from the 1st Strategic Reconnaissance Squadron, have been retired from service because of their high operational costs and the effectiveness of satellite reconnaissance. Their predecessor, the U-2, continues in USAF service. *US Navy*

The SR-71 projects an ominous appearance from almost every angle, but especially from directly ahead. Developed in secret by the Lockheed Skunk Works under the aegis of the CIA, the aircraft was intended to succeed the U-2 in overflights of the USSR. However, overflights of the USSR were halted after a U-2 was shot down on May 1, 1960, while making the 24th overflight. *US Air Force*

SR-71A Characteristics

Design:	Lockheed
Crew:	2 (pilot, systems operator)
Engines:	2 Pratt & Whitney J58 (JT11D-20A) high-bypass turbojet; 32,500 lbst each with afterburner
Weights:	
Empty:	60,000 lb
Maximum takeoff:	170,000 lb
Dimensions:	
Length:	107 ft, 5 in
Wingspan:	55 ft, 7 in
Wing area:	1,800 sq ft
Height:	18 ft, 6 in
Speeds:	
Maximum:	1,980 mph at 78,740 ft (Mach 3)
Cruise:	
Ceiling:	85,000 ft+
Range:	Approximately 3,000 miles at Mach 3 at altitude
Armament:	None

SR-71, which flew for the first time on December 22, 1964. The plane was to have been designated RS-71 (for reconnaissance-strike) but President Lyndon Johnson inadvertently transposed the letters during his announcement of the plane's existence. (RS would have been a logical follow-on to the RS-70 Valkyrie.)

SR-71 production consisted of 3 YF-12A, 29 SR-71A, 2 SR-71B, and 1 SR-71C aircraft; the last, a trainer, was created from salvaged a YF-12A and functional mockup components. Just under 20 aircraft were in the inventory in 1990 when the SR-71 was retired, of which only 8 or 9 aircraft were operational at any one time because of the aircraft's high maintenance requirements. The Pentagon has announced the loss of eight SR-71s in accidents through 1970. Unlike the U-2s, none was lost to hostile fire. In his definitive *Lockheed SR-71: The Secret Missions Exposed*,

Paul Crickmore lists the operational loss of 5 A-12s, 1 MR-12 drone carrier, 13 SR-71s, and 1 YF-12A from 1963 to 1989.

The SR-71 tooling was destroyed after the production run, hence no more could be built. According to U-2/SR-71 designer Clarence (Kelly) Johnson, it was done on specific orders of then-Secretary of Defense Robert S. McNamara. Despite periodic reports of a follow-on high-Mach reconnaissance aircraft having been developed—sometimes known by the code name Aurora—no such aircraft has appeared.

Martin P6M Seamaster

The P6M Seamaster was a top-performing aircraft for its time—and the last flying boat developed for the US Navy. Designed by the Glenn L. Martin Company, the P6M was intended primarily for long-range minelaying and reconnaissance missions, with a secondary nuclear strike capability. In the minelaying role the Seamaster was to mine the approaches to Soviet submarine bases, denying them access to the sea and preventing submarines already at sea from returning for replenishment.

The P6M program began in July 1951 when the Navy requested 12 aircraft manufacturers to submit design proposals for a high-speed, mine-laying flying boat. Martin, which had built the highly successful PBM Mariner and P5M Marlin flying boats, won the design competition and the Navy proceeded with a development program. The Navy initially ordered two XP6M-1 test aircraft and six YP6M-1 flight demonstration aircraft.

The first XP6M-1 flew on July 14, 1955. That aircraft crashed into the Potomac River on December 7, 1955, because of a structural failure. The second XP6M-1 crashed near New Castle, Delaware, on November 9, 1956, because of control problems. After modifications were made to the six YP6M-1 aircraft there were no further accidents in the flight-test program.

The Navy had placed an order for 24 production P6M-2 aircraft on August 29, 1956. Engineering problems increased the costs of the aircraft and caused further delays in the program. Although the technical problems were solved, the costs and need to fund the Polaris submarine missile program led to the 24-plane contract being reduced to 18 aircraft on June 21, 1957, and then to only eight P6M-2 aircraft on November 24, 1958. At

The Martin P6M Seamaster was the last flying boat produced for the US Navy. The massive, four-turbojet aircraft was intended for aerial minelaying and reconnaissance, and like so many other Cold War aircraft, had a nuclear strike capability. Evident in this view are the T-tail, engines mounted above the wings, and wingtip floats (in the retracted position). *Martin*

that time the Navy announced a Seamaster patrol squadron would be formed with those eight units to explore the capabilities of the aircraft.

Four P6M-2 production aircraft were completed before full cancellation came on August 24, 1959. It was one of several Navy projects halted to help pay for the acceleration of the Polaris program. By the time of the cancellation four of the YP6M-1s had been partially disassembled and a fifth had been destroyed in static tests; all surviving aircraft were scrapped.

The 12 completed P6M aircraft had logged a total of 536 hours of flight time when the project was halted. Cancellation of the P6M marked the end of flying boat development by the US Navy. The development of military flying boats did continue in Japan and the Soviet Union.

A graceful-looking aircraft, the Seamaster's flying-boat hull had an extremely high length-to-beam ratio, and the wings were swept back 40 degrees. It had a high T-tail and fixed, wingtip stabilizing floats were fitted. The four turbojet engines were mounted in pairs within the shoulder-high wing.

A payload of up to 30,000 pounds of mines, bombs, or cameras and flash bombs was to be carried on a rotary bomb-bay door that formed part of the hull bottom. During trials the aircraft successfully released stores at a speed of 500 miles per hour. Two 20-mm cannon in a remote-control tail turret, beneath a gunfire control radome, comprised the aircraft's defensive armament.

The Seamaster was a large aircraft with the P6M-2 production models expected to weigh some 85,000 pounds empty and almost 190,000 pounds loaded for rough-water takeoffs. (The aircraft was designed for operation in six- to eight-foot waves.) The Seamaster was to remain in the water for as long as six to eight months, being maintained, refueled, and rearmed by seaplane tenders and by submarines. Weapons were loaded through the top of the fuselage, enabling the aircraft to be rearmed while in the water. Similarly, engines could be replaced while the plane was afloat. Clandestine refuelling of the aircraft in forward areas from submarines was proposed, with the fleet submarine *Guavina* being converted to a tanker configuration to evaluate at-sea refueling of flying boats.

The P6M was the last aircraft produced by Martin and the last military flying boat developed by the United States. About $445 million was spent on the program before it was cancelled, of which $85 million was recovered. Martin P5M (later P-5) Marlin flying boats remained in US Navy service until November 1967. The excellence of the land-based P3V (later P-3) Orion aircraft and the high cost of supporting seaplanes (including their specialized tenders) coupled with the lack of a follow-on flying boat meant the end of an important and, in many respects, one of the most colorful types of US naval aviation.

YP6M-1 Characteristics

Design:	Martin
Crew:	5 (pilot, copilot, navigator-minelayer, radio operator, gunner)
Engines:	4 Pratt & Whitney J75-P-2 turbojet; 15,800 lbst each
Weights:	
Empty:	84,685 lb
Combat:	147,609 lb
Maximum takeoff:	160,000 lb in rough water; 190,000 lb in sheltered water
Dimensions:	
Length:	134 ft, 4 in
Wingspan:	102 ft, 7 in
Wing area:	1,900 sq ft
Height:	37 ft
Speeds:	
Maximum:	685 mph at sea level
Range:	Radius: 673 miles for mining mission; 1,409 miles for high-altitude reconnaissance mission; 931 miles for strike mission
Ceiling:	43,900 ft
Armament:	2 20-mm cannon (tail turret); 1 nuclear bomb (Mk 28) or 30,000 lb conventional bombs and/or mines

McDonnell F4H Phantom

The Phantom was one of the most successful fighter-attack aircraft of the post-World War II era and was produced in larger numbers than any other US post-World War II aircraft except for the P-80/T-33 Shooting Star and

F-86 Sabre/FJ Fury. During the 1960s and 1970s the Phantom was the most numerous fighter aircraft in the US Air Force, Navy, and Marine Corps, and was flown by ten foreign nations; some air forces flew it into the twenty-first century.

Entering US Navy service in 1962 as a carrier-based fighter, the Phantom was forced on the US Air Force at the direction of President Kennedy's Secretary of Defense, Robert S. McNamara. The Phantom thus became the first shipboard fighter to be accepted in large numbers by a major land-based air force. The US Marine Corps and the Royal Navy also flew the Phantom from aircraft carriers.

The Phantom first saw combat in August 1964 when Navy Phantoms from the aircraft carrier *Constellation* escorted attack aircraft bombing targets in North Vietnam in the aftermath of the Tonkin Gulf incident. The first air-to-air encounter came on June 17, 1965, when two Phantoms from the *Midway* encountered four North Vietnamese MiG-17 fighters. The Phantoms used Sparrow missiles to down two of the more agile MiG-17s without loss.

After that Navy and Air Force Phantoms regularly engaged and defeated MiG-17s. On April 26, 1966, an Air Force Phantom used two Sidewinder missiles to destroy a MiG-21, probably the world's most maneuverable fighter. The kill demonstrated that in the hands of better trained pilots the Phantom could hold its own. All five US fighter aces of the Vietnam War (two Navy, three Air Force fliers—in two-man crews) scored their kills of MiG-type aircraft in Phantoms.

Overall the Phantom demonstrated a marked superiority over the MiG-21 and lesser aircraft encountered in Vietnam. Similarly, Phantoms in the hands of Israeli pilots easily defeated most Soviet-built fighters flown by Arab air forces.

US Phantoms were also used extensively in the strike role in the Vietnam War. Air Force Phantoms—both fighter and reconnaissance variants—could also carry nuclear weapons. (No US Navy or Marine Phantoms were wired for nuclear weapons.) The Air Force and Marine Corps also flew photo-reconnaissance variants of the Phantom.

The last active US Navy squadrons discarded their Phantoms in 1986; a year later it was retired from the Naval Reserve. The last Marine

Phantoms—RF-4B reconnaissance aircraft—were retired from active service in 1990, followed two years later by the last Phantoms being dropped by the reserves. The last US Air Force Phantoms in service were the F-4G Wild Weasel, which were used in the 1991 war in the Persian Gulf; they were retired in 1997.

McDonnell initially designed the Phantom as a single-place fighter-attack aircraft, at one point designated AH-1. During the plane's development the Navy's requirements changed to provide for a long-range, high-altitude interceptor, designated F4H. The four 20-mm cannon originally planned were deleted and sophisticated electronics and an all-missile armament were provided. A radar operator was seated behind the pilot to aid in operating the complex electronics system.

The Phantom is a twin-engine, swept-wing fighter with box-like "cheek" air intakes; the wings are swept back 45 degrees and fold for carrier stowage. The aircraft has a large nose radar housing and (in most models) a distinctive infrared sensor pod fitted directly beneath the radar. There is tandem seating for the two crewmen under a single canopy.

The first Phantom flew on May 27, 1958, and it soon became apparent that the aircraft was a "winner." Its principal competitor as the Navy's advanced fighter was the F8U-3 Crusader, the latest model in that successful fighter line. The F8U-3 was a single-engine, single-pilot, specialized interceptor compared to the two-engine, two-man F4H-1 multi-mission aircraft. Both were capable of level speeds in excess of Mach 2. Navy fighter-test pilot Don Engen wrote in *Wings and Warriors*: "The [evaluation] team agreed that, if possible, we would like to buy both airplanes; we felt we were in a win-win situation. If buying both was not possible, the F4H-1 offered the greatest growth potential because of its two engines, its space for two crew, its planned radar system, and its flexibility for carrying external stores. The F4H-1 would have less speed than the F8U-3 and the second-best flying qualities."

The Navy selected the Phantom over the Crusader for its standard carrier-based fighter in 1958. Subsequently, in 1962, Secretary McNamara directed the Air Force to procure the aircraft as the F-110 in place of additional F-105 Thunderchief production. (In October 1962 the US Department of Defense redesignated naval aircraft along the lines of the

The McDonnell F4H Phantom, developed for carrier operation, became one of the most successful land-based fighters
and reconnaissance aircraft of the Cold War era. This Phantom
from Fighter Squadron 114 on board the US carrier *Kitty
Hawk* was on a mission over North Vietnam; it was armed with
Sidewinder and Sparrow air-to-air missiles. *US Navy*

system used by the Air Force. Under this joint system the Navy F4H and the Air Force F-110 both became the F-4.)

The Phantom was the US Navy's first operational fighter built without guns, relying on an air-to-air armament of six Sparrow radar-homing missiles or four Sparrows and four Sidewinder infrared missiles for intercept missions. In the attack role a Phantom could carry a payload of almost six tons including such combinations as 11 1,000-pound bombs or 18 750-pounders or four Bullpup air-to-surface missiles. Four Sparrows could carried with any of these attack loads. (There are four semi-recessed Sparrow bays under the fuselage plus four underwing and one centerline pylons.) Maximum overload weight for the F-4B was 54,600 pounds with 13,320 pounds of weapons. Air Force aircraft could also carry Shrike and Falcon missiles.

Significantly, all US Air Force Phantoms—fighters as well as reconnaissance—could deliver a variety of nuclear weapons; however, no Navy or Marine Phantoms were wired for nuclear weapons. (Earlier carrier fighters—the F2H Banshee, F3H Demon, and FJ Fury—could carry nuclear weapons.) The subsequent Air Force F-4E had a 20-mm rotary-barrel Vulcan cannon, the only Phantom variant to have an internal gun. All F-4s had nine attachment points for bombs and missiles, and fuel tanks.

With a maximum speed of Mach 2.24 (F-4E variant), good maneuverability, and large payload, the Phantom was worthy of the numerous accolades heaped upon the plane during its 35-year career with the US armed forces. On November 22, 1961, a Navy F4H-1 Phantom reached a speed of 1,606.324 mph to establish a new world record. More records fell to the Phantom: sustained level flight at 66,443.8 feet; an altitude of 98,558.51 feet (Phantoms subsequently reached more than 100,000 feet); and streaking from Los Angeles to New York at an average speed of 869.7 mph while slowing for three in-flight refuelings.

US Phantom production from the McDonnell consisted of 1,244 aircraft for the Navy and Marine Corps, 2,870 for the US Air Force, and almost 1,000 for foreign users, with some US planes subsequently transferred to other nations. Another 124 Phantoms were manufactured in Japan. The 36 aircraft ordered for Iran were never delivered.

F-4E Characteristics

Design:	McDonnell
Crew:	2 (pilot, weapon systems operator)
Engines:	2 General Electric J79-GE-17 turbojet; 17,900 lbst each with afterburner
Weights:	
Empty:	30,328 lb
Maximum takeoff:	61,795 lb
Dimensions:	
Length:	63 ft
Wingspan:	38 ft, 5 in
Wing area:	530 sq ft
Height:	16 ft, 6 in
Speeds:	
Maximum:	1,220 mph at 40,000 ft
Cruise:	582 mph
Range:	825 miles with 4 AAMs, 1 B28 bomb, 2 370-gallon drop tanks with low-level target penetration; 575 miles with 4 AAMs, 1 600-gallon and 2 370-gallon drop tanks (combat air patrol); combat radius 413 miles
Ceiling:	58,750 ft
Armament:	1 20-mm M61A1 Vulcan multi-barrel cannon (fixed); 4 Sidewinder or Sparrow AAMs; 2 nuclear bombs (B28) or 4 nuclear bombs (B43, B57, or B61) or 16,000 lb of bombs and/or missiles

Mikoyan-Gurevich MiG-15 Fagot

The MiG-15 interceptor had a profound impact on US defense policies. It marked Soviet entry into the turbojet era with a high-performance aircraft that undertook history's first jet-versus-jet combat. And, the MiG-15—given

The Mikoyan-Gurevich MiG-15—NATO code name Fagot—had a profound impact on Western strategic planning. The aircraft was believed capable of intercepting strategic bombers attacking the USSR. Moreover, the massive commitment of MiG-15s in the Korean War, piloted by Soviets as well as North Koreans and Chinese, showed the extent to which the USSR would support client states. This is the two-seat MiG-15U Midget variant.

the Western code name Fagot—was produced in greater numbers than any other jet aircraft of any nation.

When Western intelligence learned of the MiG-15 in the late 1940s it became a factor in the debates over the US B-36 strategic bomber, which appeared to be vulnerable to the new Soviet fighter. As a result, the United States began to lighten B-36s (featherweight modifications) to increase their ceiling, and the US development of turbojet strategic bombers was accelerated.

But it was US fighters that first encountered the MiG-15, during the Korean War. In October 1950 US reconnaissance aircraft, some penetrating into Manchurian air space, sighted a large number of MiG-15s on Manchurian airfields, just across the Yalu River from North Korea. The first all-jet air battle in history was fought on November 8, 1950, when four MiG-15s crossed the Yalu to engage four F-80s. One of the Red planes was shot down. The following day MiGs intercepted an RB-29 reconnaissance aircraft over North Korea, shooting down the four-engine Superfortress. Allied air supremacy in the war was challenged.

The MiG-15s operated from bases across the Yalu in Chinese-controlled Manchuria, attempting to enter North Korean air space only when advantageous to them. The aircraft was easy to handle at low speeds, with superior climb, ceiling, and speed above 28,000 feet in comparison to Western fighters. Still, the US F-86 Sabre prevailed over the MiG-15. Those MiGs were flown by Chinese and by Soviet pilots. US pilots tended to be better trained and their tactics were superior. According to US records, the United States lost 121 fighters and 18 bombers in air-to-air combat against 792 MiG-15s shot down. Soviet accounts cite 1,200 US aircraft destroyed; Chinese accounts list only 85 kills.

Design of the MiG-15 was initiated in March 1946 as a single-seat fighter to intercept bombers at high altitude under clear weather conditions. In early 1947 Britain's Labour government sold 50 turbojet engines to the USSR. The Rolls-Royce Nene engine was mated to the MiG-15 airframe and the prototype took to the skies on December 30, 1947. Production was ordered the following March with the first deliveries in late 1948—a remarkably short development time for such an advanced aircraft.

MiG-15*bis* Characteristics

Design: Mikoyan-Gurevich

Crew: Pilot

Engines: 1 Klimov VK-1 turbojet; 5,952 lbst

Weights:

    Empty: 8,113 lb

    Loaded: 11,117 lb

    Maximum: 13,458 lb

Dimensions:

    Length: 33 ft, 1 ³/₄ in

    Wingspan: 33 ft, 1 in

    Wing area: 221.7 sq ft

    Height: 12 ft, 1 ³/₄ in

Speeds:

    Maximum: 591 mph at sea level; 598 mph at 9,840 ft

Ceiling: 50,840 ft

Range: 700 miles at 39,360 ft with 2 69-gallon drop tanks;
                     1,155 miles with 2 79-gallon drop tanks; 1,565 miles
                     with 2 158-gallon drop tanks

Armament: 2 23-mm NS-23 cannon (fixed); 1 37-mm
                     NS-37 cannon (fixed); 4 225 lb of bombs
                     or rocket pods

Beyond massive Soviet production, licensed manufacturing of MiG-15s took place in China, Czechoslovakia, and Poland with a total of more than 15,000 aircraft produced. More than 20 nations eventually flew the MiG-15. Two-place MiG-15UTI trainers (NATO Midget) were also produced in large numbers.

The MiG-15 had a barrel-like fuselage with mid-fuselage mounted wings swept back 35 degrees. The bubble canopy was placed well forward. By contemporary standards the MiG-15 was a very light aircraft. The aircraft had tricycle landing gear. Armament on most aircraft consisted of two 23-mm cannon and one 37-mm cannon.

The improved MiG-15*bis* had a heavy beam built into each wing to enable four two 225-pound bombs or four rocket pods to be mounted, in addition two wing-mounted drop tanks. In-flight refueling was tested with a Tu-4 Bull tanker and two modified MiG-15*bis* aircraft, but it did not become a standard procedure.

Mikoyan-Gurevich MiG-21 Fishbed

The MiG-21 was one of the most widely flown Soviet fighters of the Cold War era. Developed specifically for the air-superiority role, the MiG-21 had a revolutionary delta-wing design that provided Mach 2 speed and excellent handling characteristics, and allowed a significant payload.

The aircraft entered Soviet fighter squadrons in 1959 (NATO code name Fishbed). Subsequently, more than 50 nations have flown MiG-21s. During the 1960s and 1970s MiG-21s were flown in combat in the Vietnam War, Arab-Israeli conflicts, the Iran-Iraq conflict, India-Pakistan action, the Soviet invasion of Afghanistan, and the Gulf War of 1991.

Although 40 Soviet-piloted MiG-21s were sent to Cuba in 1962, none engaged US aircraft during the missile crisis. The first encounter between MiG-21s (flown by North Vietnamese pilots) and US aircraft occurred on April 26, 1966, when two MiG-21s attacked three US Air Force F-4 Phantoms escorting two RB-66 reconnaissance aircraft. One of the Phantom pilots fired two Sidewinder missiles at one of the MiGs, which was shot down.

Numerous encounters with MiG-21s followed. US Air Force, Navy, and Marine Corps pilots were generally victorious against MiG-21s, establishing a 5.5:1 kill-to-loss ratio to demonstrate the advantages of pilot training over aircraft performance. This truism was demonstrated in several Middle East Wars when, from 1967 onward, Israeli fighters almost always triumphed over MiG-21s flown by Arab pilots. Israel's second-ranking ace, Iftach Spector, shot down 13 MiG-21s and 2 MiG-17s while flying the Mirage and Phantom.

Israeli fighter pilots had become familiar with the MiG-21 in 1966 when, at the instigation of the Mossad, an Iraqi pilot defected, flying his MiG-21 to an Israeli airfield. (US intelligence was given access to that aircraft; subsequently, the US Air Force acquired about a dozen MiG-21s from "unknown" sources.)

The Mikoyan-Gurevich MiG-21—NATO code name
Fishbed—was probably the best-known Soviet aircraft of the
Cold War era. A rugged, simple, and potent aircraft, it saw
extensive combat in the Vietnam War as well as in several
Middle East crises and conflicts. This MiG-21F (Fishbed-C) is
a fighter-interceptor variant in Yugoslav livery. *US Navy*

This MiG-21*bis* (Fishbed-L) was a multi-role aircraft with air-to-air and ground attack capabilities. Note the small delta wing, a radical change from the swept-wing configuration of earlier MiG-designed turbojet aircraft. More than 50 nations flew the MiG-21 as the USSR and three other nations produced a prodigious number of the aircraft in numerous models.

India flew MiG-21s against Pakistan in their December 1971 conflict. Those aerial engagements included combat between MiG-21s and US-built F-104A Starfighters with at least four Pakistani aircraft shot down by the MiG-21s, which had superior performance. In the 1991 war in the Persian Gulf two USN F/A-18C Hornets shot down two MiG-21s, one with a Sidewinder missile and one with a Sparrow; subsequently, a USAF F-15C Eagle downed two MiG-21s with Sidewinders.

The Mikoyan-Gurevich design bureau produced the MiG-21 as a short-range interceptor in response to a 1953 requirement. The design incorporated the "tailed delta" configuration with a very thin wing developed by the Central Aerohydrodynamic Institute (TsAGI). The aircraft was intended for the air-defense role, to be directed to targets by ground controllers.

The MiG-21PF variant (1960) introduced air-intercept radar and the MiG-21S featured more powerful engines and blow-up flaps to produce a multi-role fighter. The MiG-21MF (Fishbed-J) flown from the early 1970s was one of several MiG-21s with an extensively re-engineered airframe, additional internal fuel, and a dorsal spine to house increased avionics. A twin-barrel 23-mm cannon and four pylons for missiles and bombs were provided plus a centerline point for a 23-mm cannon pod, fuel tank, or cameras.

MiG-21R reconnaissance and two-seat MiG-21U trainer (NATO Mongol) versions were also produced. Cannon were deleted in those aircraft although some trainers carried a single 12.7-mm machine gun for weapons training.

From the outset the MiG-21 demonstrated ease of handling, high performance, maintenance simplicity, and the ability to operate from relatively poor surfaces and short runways. Early MiG-21s suffered from short range, simple avionics, poor pilot visibility, and inadequate armament. The range problem was alleviated (but not eliminated) by adding two 108-gallon external fuel tanks. Avionics—including radars—were improved throughout the aircraft's career, and increased armament was provided. Thus, like many "lightweight" aircraft, the MiG-21 experienced lifetime growth as new variants took to the skies; engine improvements, however, generally kept pace to retain the aircraft's combat performance including Mach 2 speed at altitude.

The aircraft originally was armed with two 30-mm cannon, but one was removed to save weight. Two Atoll air-to-air missiles with infrared seekers (similar to the US Sidewinder) were normally carried in early aircraft. Later aircraft had four weapon pylons and could carry later missiles.

Soviet factories produced at least 8,000 MiG-21s through 1975 including several research variants. Additional aircraft were produced under license in China, India, and Poland, with a total of more than 13,500 reported to have been built by all manufacturers.

MiG-21s continue in service in several air forces. Some have been upgraded in the post-Cold War era by Israel Aircraft Industries.

MiG-21MF (Fishbed-J) Characteristics

Design:	Mikoyan-Gurevich
Crew:	Pilot
Engines:	1 Tumansky RD-11-300 turbojet; 14,550 lbst with afterburner
Weights:	
Empty:	18,078 lb
Loaded:	20,723 lb
Dimensions:	
Length:	44 ft, 2 in (plus probe)
Wingspan:	23 ft, 5 ½ in
Height:	14 ft, 9 in
Speeds:	
Maximum:	1,386 mph at 36,090 ft; 810 mph at sea level
Ceiling:	59,050 ft
Range:	700 miles with drop tanks
Armament:	2 30-mm Gsh-23 cannon (fixed); 4 Atoll AAMs or 2 16-tube rocket pods

North American F-86 Sabre and FJ Fury

The North American F-86 and FJ series was produced in larger numbers than any other Western aircraft of the Cold War era. The F-86 Sabre and FJ Fury series of the late 1940s might have been a forgotten footnote of aviation history but for the discovery of German reports on impact of swept-back wings on aircraft performance. With redesigned wings, the North American aircraft went on to set five world speed records, enter production in five countries, and serve with the military forces of dozens of nations before the last was retired (from the Venezuelan Air Force) in 1993.

The swept-wing F-86A Sabre entered service with the USAF in 1949. When Soviet-built MiG-15 (NATO Fagot) fighters were introduced in the Korean War the United States rushed F-86s into the aerial battle. All 38 USAF and the single US Marine Corps fighter aces of the Korean War achieved five or more kills in F-86s. (The one Navy ace of the war achieved his five kills in an F4U-5N Corsair operating from land bases.)

Although the MiG-15 had several performance advantages over the F-86, superior training and tactics gave US pilots the edge until the revised wings and upgraded engines of the F-86E and F-86F introduced a technological bonus. Final data on the air war have been difficult to tabulate, but by the Korean War's end the F-86 kill-to-loss ratio came out at about 10-to-1.

As F-86s proliferated among US allies they became involved in several regional conflicts. Of particular significance, they were flown by Pakistan in conflicts with India in 1965 and 1971. In the earlier conflict, on September 7, 1965, Pakistani Wing Comdr. Mohammed Mahmood Alam claimed five victories against Indian Air Force Hawker Hunters, four of them in less than one minute! Alam, who ended the conflict with 11 kills, became history's only jet "ace-in-a-day." In the later war, although out-classed by a new generation of advanced fighters, Pakistani-piloted Sabres accounted for a large portion of the 141 Indian aircraft downed.

The USAF operated the F-86 until 1960 and remained in the Air National Guard until 1965, the last model being the F-86L. Although most Sabres were employed in the fighter role by the Tactical Air Command (TAC) or Air Defense Command (ADC), several were produced for the tactical nuclear strike role. The 265 F-86F and 473 F-86H variants could each carry a single Mk 12 nuclear weapon (or conventional bombs).

The origins of the F-86 and FJ date to late 1944 when the US Navy ordered its initial jet-propelled aircraft, one being the North American XFJ-1 Fury, a straight-wing, carrier-based, turbojet fighter. The first flight of the XFJ-1 did not occur until September 11, 1946.

The US Army Air Forces ordered a land-based version of the Fury, designated XP-86, but before production began North American proposed a swept-wing configuration based on German aircraft research and development in World War II. First flown on October 1, 1947, the aircraft soon

The North American F-86 Sabre was the finest Western
fighter of the early 1950s and was flown by all US jet aces of
the Korean War. Flown by a well-trained pilot, it almost always
defeated the Soviet-built MiG-15 in that conflict. The Sabre
had the classic combination of small airframe and large engine
that had proven successful in many fighters since World War I.
Shown is the first XP-86, which made its maiden flight in
October 1947. *US Air Force*

F-86F Characteristics

Design:	North American
Crew:	Pilot
Engines:	1 General Electric J-47-GE-27 turbojet; 5,910 lbst
Weights:	
Empty:	10,950 lb
Maximum takeoff:	17,000 lb
Dimensions:	
Length:	37 ft, 6 in
Wingspan:	37 ft, 1 in
Wing area:	288 sq ft
Height:	14 ft, 8 in
Speeds:	
Maximum:	690 mph at 35,000 ft
Cruise:	
Ceiling:	45,000 ft
Range:	575 miles
Armament:	6 .50-cal. M-3 machine guns (fixed); 1 nuclear bomb (Mk 12) or 2,000 lb of bombs or rockets

became the first fighter to exceed the speed of sound—although a slight dive was required for this accomplishment. In September 1948 an F-86A set the first official Sabre world speed record of 570 miles per hour. (In June 1948 all Pursuit aircraft had been redesignated as Fighters.)

Mass production of the F-86 by North American followed. The firm built 5,893 aircraft for the USAF and another 460 aircraft for allied air forces. An additional 1,815 F-86s were built in Canada, 112 in Australia, 221 in Italy, and 300 in Japan—a total of 8,801 aircraft.

The Navy accepted 3 straight-wing XFJ-1 and 30 FJ-1 Furies, the first flight occurring on September 11, 1946. The swept-wing FJ-2 (similar to the F-86E) followed with that aircraft entering squadron service in January 1954 with a Marine squadron. The improved FJ-3 and FJ-4 succeeded the earlier Furies on the North American production line. The aircraft served in Navy and Marine fighter and attack squadrons, based ashore and on carriers. The 222 FJ-4B aircraft were nuclear capable; that plane could fire Bullpup conventional air-to-surface missiles or drop a Mk 7, Mk 12, or Mk 28 nuclear weapon. The Navy aircraft were configured with folding wings and four 20-mm cannon (the Air Force retained six .50-caliber machine guns in all F-86s until the F-86H introduced four 20-mm cannon).

Probably the only time that Furies saw combat was when the carrier *Lexington* launched FJ-4B aircraft with conventional ordnance during operations over Laos. This occurred during the *Lexington*'s February to March 1962 deployment to the western Pacific.

When North American F-86 production ended in December 1956 and the last of 1,112 Furies was delivered in May 1958, the total number built by all countries would come 9,913 aircraft.

North American F-100 Super Sabre

The North American F-100 Super Sabre was the world's first operational aircraft capable of supersonic speeds in level flight. Designed to be an interceptor, the aircraft evolved into the fighter-bomber role, serving with distinction in the early days of the Vietnam War. In the skies over North Vietnam the F-100 was used to develop the Wild Weasel anti-radar mission, hunting and destroying radars that guided SA-2 anti-aircraft missiles. The F-100 was also used to developed the "Misty FAC" or "fast FAC" forward air control mission of locating and marking targets for US artillery or other aircraft.

Although the F-100 began as a successor to the F-86 Sabre, the new aircraft never enjoyed the popularity nor success of the earlier aircraft.

The first production F-100A flew on October 29, 1953. That flight caused a sensation by setting a world speed record of 755.149 mph. F-100A squadron introduction took place in September 1954 although the aircraft did not become fully operational until September 1955. The delay was caused by accidents, structural failures, and performance problems.

In the fighter-bomber role the F-100 was configured to carry conventional bombs and nuclear weapons; one Mk 7, Mk 28, B43, B57, or B61

The first fighter aircraft of the US Air Force "Century" series, the North American F-100 Super Sabre was the first fighter capable of exceeding the sound barrier in level flight. This F-100C, with a fixed in-flight refueling probe near the root of the right wing, carries a variety of "iron bombs" on wing racks. *US Air Force*

could be carried, the nuclear store depending upon the aircraft variant. The F-100D and F-100F aircraft were flown extensively in the strike role in the Vietnam War. The F-100F was a two-seat aircraft (with dual controls); seven F-100F aircraft were configured for the Wild Weasel role. The latter were fitted with radar warning receivers to detect C-band and S-band radar signals; they were armed with the AGM-45 Shrike anti-radar missile.

F-100 losses over Vietnam were high, both to operational causes and enemy surface-to-air missiles. Almost all F-100s were gone from the active USAF inventory by the end of 1972. At that time the Air National Guard had 550 F-100s, operating those aircraft until 1979.

Six of the F-100A aircraft were clandestinely reconfigured for photo-reconnaissance; as RF-100As they made overflights of Soviet territory in Europe and the Far East. The Thunderbirds—the US Air Force aerial demonstration team—adopted the F-100 in 1956, thus becoming the first national flight team equipped with supersonic aircraft. Two F-100F aircraft made the first flight by jet fighters over the North Pole on August 7, 1959.

Denmark, France, Taiwan, and Turkey also flew F-100s.

Designed in the days before the area rule concept, the F-100 drew its speed from streamlining, 45-degree swept wings, and the pure power of an afterburning Pratt & Whitney J57 turbojet. It was a low-wing aircraft with weapons carried on wing and centerline stations. All models had 20-mm cannon and could carry 2.75-inch folding-fin, air-to-air rockets, and beginning with the F-100C, Sidewinder AAMs.

Fearing the destruction of major airfields in a nuclear war, the Air Force experimented with the Zero Length Launch (ZELL) rocket system—a massive solid rocket booster attached to the after fuselage that launched an aircraft with no takeoff run. The first F-100D Super Sabre to test this system flew successfully in 1958. Although the ZELL system was never deployed operationally, all late-production models of the F-100D and F-100F carried the rocket mounting lugs beneath their fuselages. Most aircraft were also fitted for probe-and-drogue aerial refueling.

The first of two F-100A prototypes flew on May 25, 1953.

North American produced 2,249 F-100s for the USAF and 45 for allies (with some ex-USAF aircraft later being transferred). The last F-100F was delivered in September 1959.

F-100D Characteristics

Design:	North American
Crew:	Pilot
Engines:	1 Pratt & Whitney J57-P-21A turbojet; 10,200 lbst
Weights:	
Empty:	20,638 lb
Maximum takeoff:	39,750 lb
Dimensions:	
Length:	48 ft, 5 in
Wingspan:	38 ft, 9 in
Wing area:	400.2 sq ft
Height:	16 ft, 2 $\frac{1}{2}$ in
Speeds:	
Maximum:	908.5 mph at 35,000 ft
Cruise:	587 mph
Ceiling:	47,700 ft
Range:	1,060 miles
Armament:	4 20-mm M-39E cannon (fixed); 1 nuclear weapon (Mk 28, B43, B57, or B61) or 7,040 lb of bombs or missiles

Saab 35 Draken

Sweden's remarkable Saab Draken (Dragon) was one of the most advanced combat aircraft designs of the 1950s. It was the first operational European-built aircraft to exceed the sound barrier in level flight, and later variants were capable of Mach 2. When the Draken's 20-year production run ended in 1975 the aircraft was still one of the world's most cost-efficient and capable fighters although it was in the air forces of only four nations.

Sweden's Saab Draken was the first operational European aircraft capable of exceeding Mach 1 in level flight. The remarkable double delta design, which first flew in 1955, is still in service. This J 35F interceptor carries two Rb 27 radar-guided, air-to-air beneath the fuselage (developed from the Hughes Falcon), and two Rb 28 infrared-guided missiles beneath the wings. *Saab*

No Draken ever saw combat. Still, the fighter has flown as an interceptor, trainer, photo-reconnaissance platform, and fighter-bomber for nearly four decades. Sweden, Finland, and Denmark have retired their Drakens, but the aircraft is still the primary fighter of Austria.

Design of a new Swedish all-weather, single-seat, supersonic fighter began in 1949 as project "1250." Saab engineers settled on a double delta wing shape, flight-testing a 70 percent scale version of the aircraft in 1952. With the fundamental soundness of the design established, the Saab Model 35—later named the Draken—was ordered into full scale development in late 1952. The prototype first flew on October 25, 1955, and exceeded Mach 1 in a climb without afterburner on January 26, 1956. Full-scale production was authorized that August, and the first Draken entered service with the Swedish Air Force in March 1960. The prototype J 35B exceeded Mach 2 in level flight on January 14, 1960.

As an interceptor, the Draken featured high speed and rate of climb, but a high rate of turn also made the aircraft a capable dogfighter. The final production version was the J 35F, which had advanced avionics and was equipped to carry US Falcon air-to-air missiles instead of shorter-range Sidewinder. The Draken was built around the Flygmotor RM6C, a license-built Rolls-Royce Avon 300.

In Swedish service designations identified the aircraft as J 35 (*Jakt* for fighter-interceptor), Sk 35 (*Skol* for trainer), or S 35 (S for reconnaissance).

Beyond the Drakens exported to Denmark and Austria, Finland assembled 12 under license (and later purchased a number of ex-Swedish aircraft). Swedish production ended in 1972, with the last Finnish-built aircraft delivered in 1974. A total of 604 aircraft were built, with many aircraft modification and upgrade programs instituted over the subsequent years. The aircraft modified for Denmark beginning in 1970 featured increased internal fuel capacity (requiring changes in the fuselage shape), an arresting hook, strengthened landing gear, new weapons pylons (with a completely new outer wing of slightly larger span), and an advanced stall warning alarm. During the 1980s, the aircraft received new weapons delivery and navigation systems with improved radar altimeter, head-up display, radar warning receiver, laser rangefinder, and radar jamming system.

J 35F Characteristics

Design:	Saab
Crew:	Pilot
Engines:	1 Flygmotor RM6C turbojet; 17,262 lbst with afterburner
Weights:	
Empty:	16,369 lb
Maximum takeoff:	27,998 lb
Dimensions:	
Length:	50 ft, 4 ½ in
Wingspan:	30 ft, 10 in
Wing area:	527.16 sq ft
Height:	12 ft, 9 in
Speeds:	
Maximum:	1,320 mph at 36,000 ft
Ceiling:	60,000 ft
Range:	2,020 miles
Armament:	1 30-mm Aden M/55 cannon (fixed); 2 RB 27 missiles or 2 RB 28 missiles or 2,205 lb of bombs or 12 135-mm Bofors rockets

Sikorsky HSS-1 Seabat, HUS Seahorse, and H-34 Choctaw

The H-34 series helicopter—originally the US Navy's HSS-1 and Marine Corps's HUS—was the workhorse of US Army and Marine helicopter operations in the Vietnam War and was widely used by the US Navy for anti-submarine warfare (ASW). The versatility and popularity of the Sikorsky-built helicopter was evident by more than two other dozen nations flying the aircraft, including the Soviet Union!

The US Navy's ASW carriers were generally assigned a 20-plane squadron of twin-engine S2F Tracker aircraft and a smaller squadron of HSS-1 Seabat helicopters. These HSS-1s were also used for search-and-rescue and to recover Project Mercury manned space capsules after they splashed down at sea. Beginning in 1954 the Navy took delivery of a reported 385 HSS-1 and HSS-1N helicopters; redesignated SH-34G and SH-34J, respectively, in 1962, the principal differences in the two versions were the automatic flight stabilization and night-flying capabilities of the -1N.

The US Marine Corps procured the helicopter as the HUS-1 (SH-34D) and HUS-1A (SH-34E), using the name Seahorse. The latter had external fuel tanks and floats (instead of wheels). The HUS-1 entered Marine service in February 1957.

In the official publication *Marines and Helicopters, 1962–1973,* Lt. Col. William R. Fails wrote,

> To Marines all over the world, the UH-34 became almost a legend in its own time. Ugly, rather crude . . . but thrifty and economical . . . it demanded the very best technique of the pilot to exploit its performance. . . . It was the workhorse of a number of international confrontations and of a major war.
>
> By its reliability, simplicity, and capability, it seems to have given a new slang word to the Marines. When its more sophisticated cousins were grounded periodically for technical problems at the height of the war in Vietnam, the Marine on the ground could always give a radio call for assistance and specify a helicopter that he knew would respond. . . . "Give me a HUS."

Although hundreds of HUS-1s served in Vietnam, they also flew from US helicopter carriers (LPH) in the 1960s and 1970s. Most LPHs carried a squadron 20 of HUS-1s plus perhaps four heavy-lift HR2S (CH-37) helicopters. The Marines bought 549 of the aircraft. One HUS-1 was used in June 1960 to test the feasibility of launch the Bullpup air-to-surface missile from a helicopter. That idea was not pursued.

The Army accepted its first H-34A in 1955 and the Choctaw became the Army's principal transport helicopter (in the 1962 redesignation it became the CH-34). The Army bought 437 CH-34s plus at least 26 transferred from the Marine Corps. A few aircraft were also flown by the Air Force. Seven HSS-1Z (later VH-34D) variants were given VIP accommodations and assigned to a joint Army-Marine Corps detachment flying the president and other government executives.

A German-built Sikorsky CH-34 in Israeli Air Force markings indicates the wide usage of this excellent helicopter. The IAF has made extensive use of helicopters for troop and cargo transport, including numerous commando raids into Arab countries. The H-34/HUS was also flown in large numbers by the US Army and Marine Corps in the Vietnam War. *Israeli Air Force*

A Sikorsky HSS-1 Seabat from Helicopter ASW Squadron 8 hovers while lowering a "dipping" active sonar. Helicopters have greatly extended the reach of warships for ASW, missile targeting and attack, as well as search-and-rescue. The rotors and tail section of this helicopter folded for shipboard storage. *US Navy*

During Soviet Premier Nikita Khrushchev's visit to the United States in September 1959, President Eisenhower took the Soviet leader on several flights in an H-34. Khrushchev's admiration of the aircraft led President Eisenhower to make him a gift of two!

Meanwhile, the Westland firm in England produced some 400 helicopters under license from Sikorsky. Called the Wessex, the principal difference between the HSS-1 and the Wessex HAS.1 was the British use of a gas-turbine engine in place of the piston engine. Although slightly less powerful, the British engine was considerably lighter than the piston unit and gave the Wessex a much improved performance. Despite the high fuel consumption, the gas turbine engine was suitable for helicopters because its smooth operation reduced the vibration present in all rotary-wing aircraft. Other advantages include simplified controls and the ability to be airborne only 45 seconds after a cold start (compared to an average of 15-minute warmings for the HSS-1 on a reasonably cold day). Finally, the adoption of the gas turbine Wessex HAS.1 simplified the aviation fuel problems in British carriers as the gas turbine burned the same fuel (essentially kerosene) as did the carrier-based turboprop and straight-jet aircraft.

The Wessex was flown by the Royal Navy, Royal Air Force, and Royal Marines; and in the VIP configuration it was used for the Queen's transport flight.

In France, Sud-Aviation built 180 airframes under license for the French Army and Navy and five for the Belgian Air Force.

The HSS-1 Seabat was developed in response to the Navy's 1952 requirement for a replacement for the Sikorsky HO4S/HRS (H-19) as a ship-based ASW helicopter. The older helicopter, which had first flown in 1949, was also used in large numbers by the Marine Corps, Army, Air Force, Coast Guard, and 36 other countries. The rapidity of helicopter development in the 1950s offered the promise of a more capable shipboard helicopter.

Evolving from the H-19 design, the later helicopter had a cockpit above and slightly forward of the cabin, with the radial engine mounted in the nose (providing easy access for maintenance). The tailboom was an extension of the fuselage, terminating in a vertical stabilizer with the four-blade tail rotor. The main rotor—56 feet in diameter—had four blades, which

H-34A Characteristics

Design:	Sikorsky
Crew:	3 (pilot, copilot, crewman) + 18 troops or 8 stretchers + 2 attendants
Engines:	1 Wright R-1820-84 radial piston; 1,525 hp
Weights:	
Empty:	7,675 lb
Loaded:	13,000 lb
Dimensions:	
Length:	Fuselage: 46 ft, 9 in
Rotor diameter:	56 ft
Height:	14 ft, 3 1/2 in
Speeds:	
Maximum:	122 mph
Cruise:	97 mph
Ceiling:	9,500 ft
Range:	210 miles
Armament:	door-mounted machine guns

folded for shipboard stowage, as did the tail pylon. (This reduced the helicopter's maximum length from 65 1/2 feet to 37 feet.) The aircraft was powered by a Wright R-1820 radial engine. All models had a fixed, three-wheel landing gear except for 40 Marine HUS-1A and six Coast Guard HUS-1G helicopters, which were fitted with pontoons.

The cabin seated 12 to 18 troops, depending upon the amount of equipment carried, or eight stretchers, or 5,000 pounds of cargo could be carried by sling. In the ASW role the HSS-1 was fitted with AN/AQS-4 dipping sonar and could carry two Mk 24, 43, or 44 homing torpedoes. Those helicopters had a crew of four—two pilots and two sonar operators.

The prototype XHSS-1 flew for the first time on March 8, 1954. The HSS-1 entered squadron service in August 1955.

With Sikorsky, Westland, and Sud-Aviation also producing the helicopter for other nations and civilian sales, the production total was just over 2,300 helicopters.

The last H-34 in US military service is believed to have been the UH-34D, which was in the Navy's inventory until March 1974. From 1955 into the 1970s the H-34 was the backbone of several nations' military operations, ashore and afloat. It's successor in US service was the HSS-2 Sea King (designated SH-3 in 1962). Although a different design than the HSS-1/H-34, the Navy retained the basic HSS designation. Like its predecessor, the Sea King was produced in large numbers and served in many roles with many nations.

Tupolev Tu-16 Badger

The Tu-16 bomber—given the NATO code name Badger—marked the Soviet entry into the field of turbojet-propelled strategic bombers. Initially flown a half-century ago, the Tu-16 remains in first-line Russian military service. In the 1950s the Tupolev bureau developed Tu-16 variants for the strategic (theater) bombing, anti-ship missile attack, reconnaissance, ECM, ELINT, tanker, and torpedo roles. Moreover, the Tu-16 was the precursor of the more-advanced Tupolev strategic bombers Tu-22 Blinder, Tu-22M Blackfire, and Tu-26 Backjack.

After World War II the Soviet aviation industry investigated jet engine propulsion, both domestic developments and German technology, for advanced aircraft. By 1948 engine designer A. A. Mikulin was developing the AM-3 turbojet with an expected thrust of some 15,000 pounds—an astonishing figure for the time.

Andrei Tupolev designed the Tu-16 around twin AM-3 engines, providing a "medium" bomber roughly equivalent to the Boeing B-47 Stratojet, propelled by six turbojets, each with 7,200 pounds static thrust. The Tu-16 entered service with Soviet Long-Range Aviation (*Aviatsiya Dalnovo Deistviya*) in 1954–55. Deliveries to the Soviet Navy began in the late 1950s. In 1959–60 the Soviet strategic air arm transferred most, if not all, of its missile-armed Tu-16 bombers to the Navy for the anti-ship role. (The only missile-armed bombers retained by strategic aviation at the time were the long-range Tu-20 Bears.)

The initial Tu-16s, called Badger-A in the West, carried a maximum weapons load of about 20,000 pounds of bombs in an internal bomb bay, a slightly greater capacity than the B-47. The subsequent Badger-B (Tu-16KS-1) was a maritime strike aircraft carrying two AS-1 Kennel missiles—with a range of about 100 miles—under its wings. The Badger-C (Tu-16K-10) carried two improved AS-2 Kipper or AS-5 Kelt anti-ship missiles, whereas the further improved Badger-G could carry three AS-5 Kelt or two AS-6 Kingfish missiles. The Badger-C and possibly other models could also carry bombs on wing-mounted pylons.

The Badger-D/K was employed in the maritime ELINT/electronic reconnaissance role, whereas the Badger-E (Tu-16R) was a photo-reconnaissance aircraft with cameras fitted in the bomb bay; the Badger-F combined those roles. The Badger-H/J (Tu-16PP) variants were ECM/strike escort aircraft that accompanied strike planes, and were fitted with powerful on-board radar jammers and chaff dispensers to jam and confuse defensive radars.

Numerous Badger-A aircraft were subsequently converted to tanker aircraft, designated Tu-16N. Fuel tanks were fitted in the bomb bay, with fuel delivered through a wingtip probe-and-drogue refueling method.

Strategic attack aircraft were assigned to strike missions against targets in Western Europe and the Far East, operating from bases in the USSR. Navy Tu-16s flew from Soviet bases as well as from Middle East airfields (Egypt, Libya, Syria) and from Cam Ranh Bay in Vietnam after the departure of US forces in the mid-1970s. Tu-16s have been transferred to China, Egypt, Indonesia, Iraq, and Libya.

Strategic aircraft were employed in bombing missions in Afghanistan during the 1980s, whereas Egyptian aircraft were used in bombing and missile attacks against Israel.

Tupolev's greatest challenge in designing the Tu-16 was the mounting of the massive Mikulin engines; they were too large to be fitted under the wings. Instead, drawing on photographs of the British Comet airliner (which had four small jet engines mounted in its wing roots),

A Tupolev Tu-16 Badger-E shows the clean lines and futuristic look of this long-serving bomber. The aircraft featured a swept-wing and tail configuration, and two massive turbojet engines buried in the wing roots. Unlike the contemporary US B-47 Stratojet, the Tu-16 retained multiple defensive gun positions and had twice the number of crewmen as the B-47. *US Navy*

The Soviet Union transferred Tu-16 Badgers to several nations and licensed production of the aircraft in China as the H-6 prior to the schism between the two countries in the early 1960s. This is the H-6 production line at Xian.
Liu Zhibin, courtesy J. W. R. Taylor

Tupolev's design team mounted the engines in the wing roots through the use of wing spars formed into circular ribbed frames. The long, streamlined fuselage has circular cross section; there is a tail gunner's position and turret and, depending upon the variant, numerous radomes and antennas protruding. A plexiglass "bombardier's nose" is fitted in all variants except the Badger-C/D, which have large nose radomes. The mid-mounted wings are swept back 37 degrees. All tail surfaces are swept at 42 degrees.

Most aircraft have two 23-mm cannon in remote-control dorsal, ventral, and tail turrets; bombers not having a large radome could mount a seventh cannon fixed on the starboard side of the nose (fired by the pilot).

The Tu-16T naval variant had a modified bomb bay that could accommodate four RAT-52 torpedoes or 12 AMD-500 mines or four AMD-1000 mines. The RAT-52 was a 17 $^3/_4$-inch, high-speed (rocket-propelled) anti-ship torpedo that could be released up to six miles from the target ship. (This aircraft fell within the NATO designation Badger-A.) Other Tu-16s have been employed as test beds for missiles as well as aircraft engines.

At the time of its first flight in early 1952 the Tu-16 was the world's largest swept-wing aircraft, some 15 tons heavier than the B-47. The aircraft provided to be "stable, highly responsive, and a forgiving aircraft," according to L. L. Kerber, a senior member of the design team, in his memoirs *Stalin's Aviation Gulag.* Josef Stalin ordered the aircraft into production without waiting for flight tests to be completed.

Approximately 2,000 Tu-16s were built in the Soviet Union through the mid-1960s. Following the transfer of aircraft to China in 1958, an estimated 120 additional Tu-16s were produced in China (designated H-6 for *Hongzhaji,* or bomber, No. 6).

The Tupolev bureau's design designation for the aircraft was Tu-88; the Tu-98 Backfin was a Badger airframe flown in 1955 in the research role; and the Tu-104 Camel was a civilian airliner derivation.

Badger-A Characteristics

Design:	Tupolev
Crew:	6 (pilot, copilot, navigator, weapons systems officer, radio operator, gunner)
Engines:	2 Mikulin RD-3M turbojet; 19,285 lbst each
Weights:	
Empty:	82,000 lb
Loaded:	165,350 lb
Dimensions:	
Length:	118 ft, 11 $\frac{1}{4}$ in
Wingspan:	108 ft, $\frac{1}{2}$ inch
Wing area:	1,772.3 sq ft
Height:	45 ft, 11 $\frac{1}{4}$ in
Speeds:	
Maximum:	616 mph
Cruise:	530 mph
Ceiling:	40,350 ft
Range:	1,955 miles
Armament:	up to 7 23-mm NR-23 cannon (3 twin turrets,1 fixed); 19,800 lb of bombs or 1 nuclear bomb

Tupolev Tu-20/Tu-95/Tu-142 Bear

The Soviet "Bear" has emerged as one of history's most-versatile and long-lived combat aircraft. It's accolades include being the fastest propeller-driven aircraft in history and the only swept-wing turboprop aircraft of any nation to achieve first-line status as a combat aircraft. And, by any criteria, it must be considered one of the most attractive aircraft to take to the skies.

Tu-95 is the Tupolev design bureau's designation, which is often used in the West to indicate military versions of the aircraft. The initial military designation was Tu-20; the Bear-F (NATO designation) and later production aircraft had the military designation Tu-142.

The aircraft was developed as a strategic bomber with the designation Tu-95M (NATO Bear-A) assigned to the first production aircraft. It entered service with Soviet Long-Range Aviation (*Aviatsiya Dalnovo Deistviya*) in early 1956. The Tu-95M normally carried up to 19,841 pounds of free-fall bombs or two large nuclear bombs internally. This could be increased to 28,660 pounds with a reduction in range.

In late 1955 a prototype was modified to the Tu-95SM-20 configuration to carry an experimental MiG-19S fighter recessed into the belly. The MiG-19S was launched without difficulty, and in trials the fighter tested guidance for the Kh-20 missile. The subsequent Tu-95K Bear-B carried the Kh-20 stand-off missile (NATO AS-3 Kangaroo), and Tu-95KM Bear-C carried the improved Kh-20M. Those missiles were intended for strategic attack.

The Navy's Tu-95RT Bear-D was configured for long-range maritime reconnaissance and for targeting anti-ship missiles, especially the ship/submarine-launched P-7 (SS-N-3 Shaddock) and P-350 (SS-N-12 Sandbox) anti-ship missiles; about 1967 this became the first Tu-95 variant to be flown by the Soviet Navy.

The few Tu-95MR Bear-E models were photo-reconnaissance aircraft rebuilt from Bear-A bombers. The Tu-95K-22 Bear-G aircraft were rebuilt B and C models armed with the conventional K-22 (NATO AS-4 Kitchen) anti-ship missile.

The Tu-142 was a redesigned and enlarged aircraft, with the Bear-F being a Navy anti-submarine aircraft and the Bear-J employed as a VLF communications relay aircraft for strategic missile submarines (a role similar to the US Navy's TACAMO program). The new airframe was also used for the Tu-142K Bear-H armed with the Kh-55 (AS-15 Kent) strategic cruise missile. (Some references call this aircraft, which first flew in September 1979, the Tu-95MS.)

Although Bear aircraft normally operated only from Soviet bases during the Cold War, beginning in April 1970 pairs of Bear-D aircraft took off from the Russian Kola Peninsula, flew around North Cape and down the Norwegian Sea and North Atlantic to land in Cuba; after a few days in Cuba the Bears returned to their home base. During these nonstop flights of more than 5,000 miles the Bears conducted surveillance operations

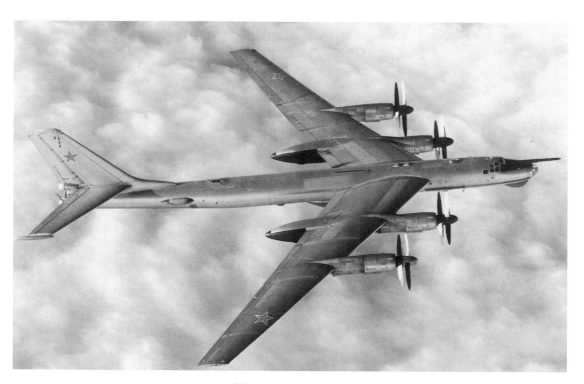

The Tupolev Tu-20 Bear was probably the most graceful air-craft of the Cold War. The massive, swept-wing, four-turboprop aircraft was also one of the longest-serving aircraft of the era. This is a Bear-D naval missile-targeting aircraft, with a large radome under the fuselage (not visible). Although one of the longest-range aircraft of its time, the Bear was fitted for in-flight refueling. *US Navy*

This photograph, taken from a film, shows a Bear-B launching a Kh-20 stand-off strategic missile (NATO AS-3 Kangaroo). The Bear-D featured a traditional bombardier's nose, whereas the missile-carrying Bears have large radomes built into the nose. Improved Bears continue to serve in the Russian Air Force and apparently a few remain in operation in the Russian Navy.

along the coast of North America, generally flying 200–250 miles off-shore.

In 1973 pairs of Bear-D aircraft began flying into Conakry, Guinea. On several occasions Bears in Cuba and Bears in Conakry appear to have carried out coordinated reconnaissance over the south and central Atlantic. From 1981 until the demise of the Soviet Union in 1991 the presence of Bears in Cuba was virtually continuous. (Bear-F anti-submarine aircraft joined the Bear-D flights to Cuba in 1983.)

By 1961 there were some 200 Bears assigned to LRA. When the START I agreement was signed in 1991 the LRA had 305 Bears in service. Variations of the Bear remain in service with both the Soviet Air Forces and Navy, and they are expected to remain in service until 2010–2015. Naval variants have also been transferred to Egypt and India for long-range maritime reconnaissance.

A prototype transport version of the Bear flew in late 1956 as the Tu-116. A modification flew in 1957 and entered production as the Tu-114D (*Dalnyi* or long range; NATO code name Cleat). That aircraft had a slightly greater fuselage diameter than the bomber but was otherwise similar, carrying up to 220 passengers. A Tu-114 carried Premier Nikita Khrushchev to the United States in 1959. In April 1960 a Tu-114D set a speed-with-load record at an average of over 545 miles per hour for a distance of 5,000 miles.

The Cleat evolved into a Soviet AWACS (Airborne Warning And Control System) aircraft, given the NATO code name Moss.

Designed by Andrei N. Tupolev in response to a 1949 requirement for an intercontinental bomber, the first of two prototypes flew on November 12, 1952; the first flight of a production aircraft occurred in late 1955. The Bear is a large, swept-wing aircraft with four turboprop engines turning contra-rotating, four-blade propellers. The plane's long range can be further extended through in-flight refueling with a fixed receiving probe installed in the nose of most aircraft from 1962. Defensive armament in production bombers consists of three 23-mm twin gun mounts (dorsal, ventral, and tail) with radar fire control; early aircraft had two additional 23-mm turrets. The Bear-D had the Big Bulge surface-search radar in a massive ventral radome and a Video Data Link (VDL), called Drambuie by Western intelligence services, for transmitting target data to missile-launching ships. The Bear-F carries an array of anti-submarine sensors and weapons. Bear-J aircraft has a large antenna housing atop the vertical fin with blade antennas above and below the fuselage; there is a shallow radome in the dorsal position, probably housing a satellite antenna as well as undernose and tail sensor mountings. The naval D/J variants carry no offensive weapons.

The enlarged Tu-142 aircraft have a fuselage plug 5 feet, 9 inches inserted ahead of the wing, an enlarged tail fin, enlarged inboard engine nacelles, a redesigned wing incorporating double-slotted flaps in place of the plain flaps previously used, slightly increased wing fuel tanks, improved crew rest and galley facilities, and upgraded avionics.

Tu-95M Bear-A Characteristics

Design:	Tupolev
Crew:	7 (pilot, copilot, bombardier-navigator, defensive systems operator, radio operator-gunner, flight engineer, gunner)
Engines:	4 Kuznetsov NK-12M turboprop; 15,000 hp each
Weights:	
Empty:	175,485 lb
Loaded:	401,234 lb
Dimensions:	
Length:	151 ft, 5 1/4 in
Wingspan:	164 ft, 2 in
Wing area:	3,054 sq ft
Height:	41 ft
Speeds:	
Maximum:	562 mph
Ceiling:	39,360 ft
Range:	8,200 miles with normal bomb load
Armament:	6 23-mm AM-23 cannon (twin turrets); 19,841 lb bombs

Tu-142K Bear-H Characteristics

Design:	Tupolev
Crew:	7
Engines:	4 Kuznetsov NK-12MP turboprop engine; 14,795 hp each
Weights:	
Empty:	
Loaded:	407,850 lb
Dimensions:	
Length:	162 ft, 5 in
Wingspan:	164 ft, 2 in
Wing area:	3,111 sq ft
Height:	43 ft, 7 in
Speeds:	
Maximum:	506 mph
Cruise:	
Ceiling:	39,360 ft
Range:	6,525 miles with normal bomb load; 4,040 miles with maximum bomb load
Armament:	2 23-mm GSh-23 cannon (tail turret); 6 to 16 AS-15 Kent (Kh-55) strategic missiles

Vought F7U Cutlass

The Vought F7U Cutlass was one of the most aerodynamically advanced aircraft of its time. A swept-wing, tailless fighter aircraft, its career as a US Navy carrier-based fighter was brief but significant.

Development of the Cutlass began in 1945 as Allied intelligence revealed German advances in high-performance, tailless aircraft. This intelligence led the US Navy to sponsor several advanced carrier-based fighters. Vought's recent fighter experience included the highly successful F4U Corsair, the radical F5U "flying pancake," and the F6U Pirate, one of the Navy's first turbojet aircraft and the first to be fitted with an afterburner.

The firm's advanced F7U design promised high speed and a rapid rate

A Vought F7U Cutlass piloted by Lt. Comdr. Edward (Whitey)
Feightner is catapulted off the carrier *Midway* during evaluation by the Naval Air Test Center (NATC) in Patuxent River,
Maryland. Although operational for only a brief period, the tailless F7U demonstrated the feasibility of the design. It flew as a
gun-fighter, missile-armed fighter, and nuclear-attack aircraft.
US Navy

of climb. The wing was swept 38 degrees, without horizontal tail surfaces, with fins and rudders located on the wings; pitch and roll control were combined in elevons on the wing. The outer wing panels folded upward for carrier stowage. The aircraft was initially powered by two Westinghouse J34-WE-22 turbojet engines with afterburners, each producing 3,000 pounds of thrust. On the flight deck the Cutlass sat at a nine-degree angle, increased to 15 degrees just before the wheels of the tricycle landing gear left the deck during a catapult takeoff.

The first XF7U-1 flew on September 29, 1948, but the plane was underpowered and the production of improved engines lagged. The plane's radical design also encountered previously unknown aerodynamic problems (which pioneered technology for later aircraft of more advanced design).

The definitive F7U-3 Cutlass first flew on December 20, 1951. This variant was powered by two improved Westinghouse J46-WE-8A turbojets rated at 4,600 pounds thrust that could push the plane past Mach 1. In afterburner the F7U-3 engines provided for single-engine flight for the large fighter, even in the critical period after a waveoff during a carrier approach. In air-to-air combat the F7U-3 also could outperform its contemporaries—the FJ-2 Fury and F9F-6 Cougar.

All F7Us were single-seat aircraft with a standard armament of four 20-mm cannon. The F7U-3 had provisions for underwing rocket pods and other stores, including a pair of 500- or 1,000-pound bombs. As most other early jet fighters, the Navy fitted the F7U-3 to carry a nuclear weapon, either the Mk 7, Mk 8, or Mk 12 "store" or "special weapon," as atomic bombs were euphemistically referred to. The F7U-3M missile-armed and F7U-3P photo-reconnaissance variants followed (the latter with guns deleted).

In March 1956, Attack Squadron 83 with F7U-3M aircraft—each fitted to carry four Sparrow I radar-guided missiles—deployed to the Mediterranean in the carrier Intrepid. This was the first overseas operation of a US Navy missile-armed squadron (predating F9F-8 Cougar/Sidewinder deployment by four months).

Unfortunately, the Cutlass still was underpowered and suffered from myriad mechanical problems, especially with its hydraulic system. Because of these difficulties the aircraft was not popular with pilots, who frequently referred to it as the "Gutlass," a play on the difficulty of keeping the aircraft in the air and in service. From mid-1952 to mid-1956 there were 78 mishaps and accidents involving the Cutlass, with more than a quarter of them fatal. The F7U was withdrawn from fleet squadrons in November 1957, only two years after delivery of the last aircraft.

Cutlass production totaled 307 aircraft: 3 XF7U-1 prototype aircraft, 14 F7U-1, 180 F7U-3, 98 F7U-3M, and 12 F7U-3P variants. Two of the F7U-1s were painted in Blue Angel colors and in 1952 flew with the team's F9F-5 Panthers as display aircraft. But the F7U's troublesome hydraulic controls led to its rejection as a Blue Angel formation aircraft and the plane's career with the "Blues" was very brief.

Although its service career was short and it never saw combat, the F7U Cutlass was an important addition to the Navy's arsenal, especially in the missile version. The F7U must be counted as a pioneer in the development of advanced post-World War II aircraft designs.

F7U-3 Characteristics

Design:	Vought
Crew:	Pilot
Engines:	2 Westinghouse J46-WE-8A turbojet; 4,600 lbst each
Weights:	
Empty:	18,210 lb
Loaded:	31,642 lb
Dimensions:	
Length:	44 ft, 3 in
Wingspan:	39 ft, 9 in
Wing area:	535 sq ft
Height:	14 ft, 7 in
Speeds:	
Maximum:	677 mph at sea level; 593 mph at 15,000 ft
Cruise:	517 mph
Ceiling:	36,100 ft
Range:	885 miles with 2 150-gallon drop tanks; 600 miles with Mk 12 nuclear bomb
Armament:[*]	4 20-mm cannon (fixed); 2 2,000-lb bombs or 1 nuclear bomb

[*] The F7U-3 did not carry air-to-air missiles; the F7U-3M carried 4 Sparrow I AAMs or 2 conventional bombs.

Seven

New Technology Aircraft

Several distinct generations of military aircraft were developed during
the 45 years of the Cold War. This chapter describes mostly third-
generation warplanes of post-World War II design, in general aircraft of
great complexity, requiring not only highly trained pilots and air crewmen,
but also skilled and well-trained mechanics to maintain them.

The economics of situation limited military aircraft design and development to a handful of nations—France, Great Britain, Germany, Japan, and
the Soviet Union (after 1991 the Russian Federation). Even mention of
those countries forces consideration of their many joint aircraft efforts (see
the Panavia Tornado, below), and the massive financial "industrial participation" (previously called "offsets") required by nations that purchase for-
eign-developed aircraft. This participation can include direct purchases of
components produced by the buying country, or nonaviation products, or
actual coproduction. Further, the high cost of modern aircraft has led to
extensive upgrading of older warplanes, both by the original producing
country and, in a few instances, by a third party. Probably the most successful nation in that regard is Israel, with Israel Aircraft Industries
upgrading such aircraft as the F-4 Phantom and MiG-21 Fishbed fighters.

A few relatively unsophisticated aircraft are still produced for military

Developed for Cold War nuclear-strike missions, the B-2A
"stealth" bomber has proven itself as a very-long-range conventional bomber in several conflicts. The high cost of modern
high-technology aircraft has severely limited production numbers with only 21 B-2A aircraft being produced although initial
plans called for several hundred. *Northrop Grumman*

purposes. A prime example is the British Aerospace Hawk (described below). It is a light-attack and training aircraft flown by a dozen nations including the United States. Similar to the Alpha Jet, F-5 Freedom Fighter, and M.B.326, the Hawk has the distinction of having been procured in large numbers by the US Navy as the McDonnell Douglas T-45 Goshawk. Extensively modified for US service, the T-45 is used as both a shore-based and carrier training aircraft.

Several "new" types of aircraft have appeared in this period. Those include the first operational Vertical/Short Takeoff and Landing (VSTOL) aircraft, the Hawker Siddeley Harrier (flown by the US Marine Corps as the AV-8) and the Yakovlev Yak-38 Forger. Interestingly, both aircraft were developed for shipboard use. The former continues in US and British service, whereas the Yak-38s have been retired and, with the demise of the Soviet Union, work on the follow-on Yak-41 was terminated.

Another "new" aircraft is the helicopter gunship. Although the extensive use of armed helicopters dates to French operations in Algeria in the 1950s, the Vietnam War led to development of specialized gunship helicopters. The Mil' Mi-24 Hind can be cited as the first truly purpose-designed gunship, as the earlier US AH-1 Cobra series was derived from the UH-1 Huey utility helicopter (which was also modified to several gunship configurations).

Finally, the new technology aircraft includes the first warplanes specifically designed to reduce the probability of detection by radar and infrared sensors—a technique known as signature reduction, but most often called "stealth." The F-117A Nighthawk stealth "fighter" was used briefly (in the face of nonexistent air defenses) in the US invasion of Panama in 1982. However, it was used to great effect in the Persian Gulf War (1991) and in Yugoslavia (1999), with one aircraft being shot down—apparently by a surface-to-air missile—in the latter conflict. It is significant that although called a "fighter," the F-117 is an attack aircraft. It can carry one B61 nuclear bomb or 5,000 pounds of conventional (laser-guided) bombs; it has no air-to-air capability.

The second stealth aircraft to fly is the B-2A Spirit, in some respects second-generation stealth technology. This aircraft is a long-range, strategic bomber, originally developed to penetrate Soviet air defenses in a nuclear conflict. However, it has demonstrated its effectiveness in long-range, conventional bombing missions, taking off and returning from the B-2 base in Missouri to strike targets in Yugoslavia (1999) and in Afghanistan (2002). Further, the aircraft has a large weapons capacity—20 B61 nuclear bombs or 80 500-pound conventional bombs.

Evidence of the high cost of stealth features—which include both design and materials—is found in only 59 F-117s and 21 B-2s having been procured.

All of the aircraft described below are in operational service, and a few remain in production.

British Aerospace Hawk

Training aircraft have been pressed into combat service since the earliest days of military aviation. In some instances hand-held weapons were the only modification needed for the new role, but most trainers have seen significant developments to improve their mission capabilities and chances of success. Currently the most successful of these advanced training/light combat aircraft is the British Aerospace (BAE) Systems Hawk. Of the many similar designs competing for a share of the world market, the Hawk has been without equal in performance as well as sales.

The Hawk has served the Royal Air Force in the advanced training and lead-in fighter training roles since 1976. In that period it has established a record for high performance, durability, efficiency, and economy—a record that British Aerospace has ably drawn upon to dominate the export market in this category with sales to 16 other nations. The largest order for the Hawk occurred in 1981 when the US Navy ordered a Hawk derivative as its standard fighter trainer. Developed for both land-based and carrier operation by McDonnell Douglas (now Lockheed Boeing) and British Aerospace as the T-45 Goshawk, the aircraft entered US service in 1994.

The Hawk's combat career has been limited. However, Abu Dhabi's Hawk 102s are known to have flown close air support missions for Coalition troops during the Gulf War of 1991.

The Hawk grew out of the Hawker Siddeley P.1182, which was selected as the RAF's new advanced trainer in 1971. (Hawker Siddeley was merged into British Aerospace in April 1977.) The prototype first flew on August 21, 1974, and the production Hawk T.1 entered service with the RAF in late 1976. The Hawk has been produced in several variants, testimony to the flexibility of the basic design:

Hawk T.Mk 1

> The original RAF advanced trainer with a total of 175 delivered. Three underwing racks can accommodate a variety of light weapons; alternatively, two wing racks can be fitted with a center-line 30-mm gun pod. The T.Mk 1 is used by the RAF Red Arrows aerial demonstration team. Between 1983 and 1986, 88 aircraft were upgraded for additional air defense duties with AIM-9 Sidewinder missiles, those aircraft being designated T.Mk 1A.

Hawk 50 Series

> The first export Hawk flew on May 17, 1976. An uprated engine, improved cockpit instrumentation, four external weapons stations, and increases in range and weapons load emphasized the Hawk 50's dual-purpose role as lightweight fighter and advanced trainer. Ninety Hawk 50s have been delivered.

Hawk 60 Series

> An advanced version of the Hawk 50 with a redesigned wing and more-robust landing gear, with further increases in power, range, and weapons load. A total of 120 Hawk 60s have been ordered.

Hawk 100 Series

> The Hawk 100 prototype first flew on October 1, 1987. The aircraft is suitable for lead-in fighter training for pilots, navigators,

and weapons systems operators. It has a nose-mounted forward-looking infrared (FLIR) and/or laser sensor for all-weather, day and night operations, a revised radar warning receiver (RWR), and uprated engine. A new wing employs combat maneuver flaps and provides seven underwing stations for a 6,600-pound weapons load, with additional wingtip racks for air-to-air Sidewinders. Orders for the Hawk 100 total 91 aircraft.

Hawk 200 Series

Developed at the same time as the Hawk 100 with extensive structural and systems commonality, the 200 Series is a single-seat, radar-equipped, lightweight, multi-role combat aircraft. It first flew on May 19, 1986. Hawk 200 orders total 64 aircraft.

Hawk LIFT

The Hawk Lead-In Fighter Trainer (LIFT) is an updated version of the Hawk 100 featuring enhanced avionics and systems for cost-effective training in the systems found in most frontline combat aircraft. Revised cockpit layouts include full-color, multi-function displays, instruments compatible with night-vision goggles, head-up display, hands-on-throttle-and-stick controls, "smart" weapons capability, inertial navigation/global positioning system for enhanced navigation and weapons accuracy, an on-board oxygen generation system, an uprated engine, and provision for a detachable, nose-mounted air-to-air refueling probe. Orders were pending for this variant when this volume went to press.

T-45 Goshawk

The US Navy's undergraduate jet training aircraft, the aircraft differs from the "basic" Hawk by having a strengthened landing gear, and the addition of an arresting hook and catapult launch fittings. The T-45A (with an analog cockpit) first flew on April 16, 1988,

The British Aerospace Hawk was developed as a trainer and lead-in fighter trainer in the 1970s. More recent Hawks have developed into single-seat, light attack combat aircraft. The aircraft has been procured by several air forces—including the US Navy's air arm—for a variety of roles. This is an early T.1 trainer in RAF service. *British Aerospace*

and the T-45C (with a digital cockpit) first flew in October 1997. The US Navy and Marines plan to order at least 268 T-45s in addition to two prototypes.

T-45A Characteristics

Design:	British Aerospace and McDonnell Douglas
Crew:	Pilot + student
Engines:	1 Rolls-Royce F405.RR-401 Adour Mk 851 turbofan; 5,845 lbst
Weights:	
Empty:	9,394 lb
Maximum takeoff:	13,000 lb
Dimensions:	
Length:	38 ft, 8 in
Wingspan:	30 ft, 9 in
Wing area:	179.6 sq ft
Height:	13 ft, 1 in
Speeds:	
Maximum:	620 mph
Ceiling:	52,500 ft
Range:	1,550 miles
Armament:	25-lb Mk 76 target bombs and 2.75-inch rockets

Boeing E-3 Sentry

The Boeing E-3 Sentry is one of the most important aircraft over any battlefield. Although unarmed, the Sentry is a "force multiplier" through tracking and identifying airborne targets and directing friendly aircraft to counter or avoid threats while performing their missions. This is an Airborne Warning And Control System (AWACS—pronounced "A-Wax") developed from the concept of Airborne Early Warning (AEW) aircraft, which the US Navy initiated in the latter stages of World War II.

The first E-3 became operational in March 1977. It immediately began to participate in US military exercises, replacing the earlier Constellation-type aircraft flown by the US Air Force and Navy in the land-based AEW role. (The USAF used the designation EC-121; the Navy used WV and, after October 1962, also EC-121.) Those aircraft had been used as a strategic warning barrier against potential Soviet air attacks against the United States; during the Vietnam War the USAF also used EC-121s as airborne command posts in early efforts to coordinate air operations.

The E-3 was first flown in a combat environment during the Persian Gulf War (Operation Desert Storm). From January 17 to March 1, 1991, E-3s flew around the clock, usually maintaining station over Saudi Arabia, with on-board controllers coordinating operations of aircraft from ten different nations, assisting in the air-to-air destruction of 38 of the 40 Iraqi aircraft kills, directing rescue efforts for downed pilots, and guiding fuel-starved aircraft to awaiting tankers.

Flying more than 400 missions that totaled more than 5,000 flight hours, the E-3 crews provided radar surveillance and control for more than 120,000 coalition sorties and recorded data for postmission analysis of the Iraqi conflict.

The E-3 has since been involved in every known USAF aerial combat operation as well as counterdrug operations. Following the terrorist attacks on the United States on September 11, 2001, US and British E-3s undertook extended airborne operations over the United States.

The USAF began the AWACS program in the early 1970s. Sixty-eight Boeing 707-320 commercial airframes were built to the E-3 configuration, each fitted with a pylon-mounted, AN/APY-1 or -2 radar, encased in a rotating radome, 30 feet in diameter and 6 feet thick. The radome is held 14 feet above the fuselage by two massive struts and rotates every 10 seconds.

The Sentry's radar has a range of more than 250 miles against low-flying targets and farther for aircraft at higher altitudes. An Identification-Friend-or-Foe (IFF) subsystem helps distinguish enemy from friendly aircraft. Provisions are made to eliminate the ground clutter that confuses most other airborne radar systems. Data can be sorted and acted upon by on-board controllers, or passed on to other command and control centers for action by appropriate authorities.

Although its airframe is 1950s technology, the Boeing E-3 Sentry's radar and computer systems are 1970s technology, with updates continuing into the twenty-first century. The 18 E-3s procured by the North Atlantic Treaty Organization posed a problem: NATO had never before owned its own aircraft and hence had never developed NATO aircraft markings. Accordingly, the star from the NATO flag was adopted. *Leo van Ginderen*

The USAF acquired 34 E-3 aircraft with 17 others going to NATO (the first aircraft owned by that organization rather than its individual member states), 7 to Great Britain, 5 to Saudi Arabia, and 4 to France. (One USAF E-3A was lost to a massive bird strike; the other 33 remain in service.) US and NATO E-3s fly with Pratt & Whitney TF-33 turbofans whereas other E-3s use more powerful CFM-56 turbofans.

Most AWACS upgrades relate to electronic systems, not engines. The Block 30/35 modification program, completed in 2001, included upgrades for passive detection and identification of air and surface-based emitters, addition of the Joint Tactical Information Distribution System (JTIDS) to provide secure, anti-jam communications, increased computer memory, and use of the Global Positioning System (GPS).

The E-3 can fly eight-hour missions with in-flight refueling and on-board crew rest areas allowing for extended missions.

E-3C Characteristics

Design:	Boeing
Crew:	17–23 (command pilot, pilot, navigator, engineer, 13–19 AWACS mission specialists)
Engines:	4 Pratt & Whitney TF-33 turbofan; 21,000 lbst each
Weights:	
Maximum takeoff:	347,000 lb
Dimensions:	
Length:	145 ft, 6 in
Wingspan:	130 ft, 10 in
Wing area:	3,010 sq ft
Height:	41 ft, 4 in
Speed:	
Maximum:	530 mph
Cruise:	360 mph
Ceiling:	30,000 ft+
Range:	5,750 miles
Armament:	None

Grumman F-14 Tomcat

Designed to intercept Soviet long-range strike aircraft, in several respects the F-14 remains the most-capable long-range, all-weather fighter aircraft in service with any air force. The aircraft's variable-geometry wing, large payload, and powerful engines enable it to operate in multiple roles.

The F-14 was the standard US Navy carrier-based fighter from 1975 into the late 1990s. It remains in service in limited numbers, serving with the F/A-18 Hornet as the Navy's carrier-based fighter and strike aircraft.

The F-14 first entered a combat area in late April 1975, when US Navy, Marine, and Air Force helicopters from the Seventh Fleet evacuated Americans from Saigon in Operation Frequent Wind. Fighter aircraft from offshore carriers, including the first two F-14 fleet squadrons—Fighter Squadrons (VF) 1 and 2 from the *Enterprise*—provided protective cover.

Subsequently, carriers operating F-14s participated in many Cold War crises and confrontations. They had several confrontations with Libyan aircraft as US warships operated in international waters claimed by Libyan dictator Muammar al-Qaddafi as territorial waters. On August 19, 1981, two Navy F-14s from the carrier *Nimitz* used Sidewinder missiles to shoot down two Libyan Su-22 Fitter fighters over the Mediterranean, about 70 miles off the Libyan coast. On January 4, 1989, two Libyan MiG-23 Flogger fighters were shot down with Sidewinder and Sparrow missiles fired by F-14s flying from the carrier *John F. Kennedy.*

Two years later carrier-based F-14s were in action in the Gulf War, but scored only one air-to-air kill. On February 6, 1991, an F-14A from the *Ranger* shot down an Iraqi Mi-8 Hip helicopter with a Sidewinder missile. (The two other Navy kills were made by F/A-18 Hornets.) The first use of the Tomcat in the air-to-ground role in combat occurred on September 5, 1995, when an F-14A from the carrier *Theodore Roosevelt* dropped two 2,000-pound bombs on Serb positions in Bosnia.

Following cancellation of the carrier-based variant of the multi-service TFX project (F-111B) in 1968, the Navy initiated the F-14 program to take advantage of the cancelled aircraft's AN/AWG-9 radar/fire control system and the Phoenix missile. The original AWG-9 radar could detect hostile aircraft at more than 100 miles and simultaneously track up to 24 targets;

the F-14D has the improved AN/APG-71 radar. The Phoenix air-to-air missile with a range in excess of 60 miles was intended for use against Soviet bombers. The F-14 evolved as a two-seat aircraft with variable-geometry wings that sweep back automatically as the aircraft maneuvers during flight; they extend for long-range flight and landings, sweeping back for high-speed flight (and carrier stowage). Normal sweep range is 20–68 degrees with a 75-degree "oversweep" position provided for shipboard hangar stowage; sweep speed is 7.5 degrees per second.

Up to 14,500 pounds of external stores can be carried by the F-14. The aircraft originally had four fuselage missile positions (4 Sparrow or 4 Phoenix) and two wing positions (4 Sidewinder, 2 Sparrow, or 2 Phoenix); alternatively fuel tanks or a reconnaissance pod could be carried with a reduced missile load. Subsequently, the F-14B/D variants have been fitted with racks for "iron bombs" and Laser-Guided Bombs (LGB); the F-14D also has pylon adapters for air-to-surface missiles HARM and Harpoon missiles.

With the demise of specialized photo-reconnaissance aircraft in the fleet, some F-14s in each carrier were fitted to additionally carry the TARPS (Tactical Air Reconnaissance Pod System). The TARPS package can be fitted to or removed from a standard aircraft in a few hours; it contains a KS-87 frame camera, KA-99 panoramic camera, and an AN/AAD-5 infrared line scanner.

During production—and after joining the fleet—F-14s were provided with upgraded engines and avionics; the F-14B and later variants have two F110-GE-400 turbofans rated at 27,000 lbst. And, beginning in 1996, all surviving F-14s were fitted with the AN/AAQ-14 Low Altitude Navigation and Targeting Infrared for Night (LANTIRN) targeting pod for aiming laser-guided munitions.

The first flight of an F-14A occurred on December 21, 1970. The first squadron to fly the Tomcat was VF-124, a transition squadron, beginning in January 1973. VF-1 and VF-2 were the first fleet squadrons to fly the aircraft. The F-14 originally was planned for Marine Corps use, but that service turned it down, in part because of the decision to procure instead the AV-8A Harrier VSTOL aircraft.

The final F-14 was delivered in May 1992; a total of 632 aircraft were produced. An additional 80 F-14A aircraft were built for Iran of which 79 were delivered in 1976–79, with one retained by Grumman after the Iranian revolution.

The Grumman F-14 Tomcat is the last in a long line of outstanding Grumman fighters. After almost 30 years in first-line
service, the swing-wing Tomcat remains a highly effective
fighter and, when upgraded, a strike aircraft. This F-14A from
Fighter Squadron 1 has its wings fully extended. All of the US
Navy's 11 operational aircraft carriers in 2003 had an F-14
squadron. *Robert L. Lawson*

An F-14 Tomcat shows its massive weapons load: four AIM-54A Phoenix missiles under the fuselage and two onwing pylons, with two Sidewinder missiles outboard of the latter; two large drop tanks are mounted below the engine nacelles. The aircraft is fitted with an internal 20-mm M61 Gatling gun. Air-to-ground guided missiles as well as bombs can be carried by the F-14D variant. *US Navy*

F-14A Characteristics

Design:	Grumman
Crew:	2 (pilot, radar intercept officer)
Engines:	2 Pratt & Whitney TF30-P-414A turbofans; 20,900 lbst each with afterburning

Weights:

Empty:	40,104 lb
Takeoff:	with 4 Sparrow/AMRAAM: 59,714 lb
Takeoff:	with 6 Phoenix AAMs: 70,764 lb
Loaded:	74,349 lb

Dimensions:

Length:	62 ft, 8 in
Wingspan:	64 ft, 1 ½ in (unswept); 38 ft, 2 ½ in (swept back)
Wing area:	565 sq ft
Height:	16 ft

Speeds:

Maximum:	1,544 mph at altitude; 912 mph at low level
Cruise:	633 mph
Ceiling:	50,000 ft+
Range:	Radius approximately 575 miles in strike role; 1,065 miles in intercept role; ferry 2,000 miles with 2 267-gallon drop tanks
Armament:	1 20-mm M61 Vulcan cannon (multi-barrel; fixed); 2 Phoenix + 3 Sparrow/AMRAAM + 2 Sidewinder AAMs + 2 267-gallon drop tanks; or 4 Phoenix + 2 Sparrow/AMRAAM + 2 Sidewinder AAMs + 2 267-gallon drop tanks; or 6 Phoenix + 2 Sidewinder AAMs + 2 267-gallon drop tanks; or 6 Sparrow/AMRAAM + 2 Sidewinder AAMs + 2 267-gallon drop tanks

Hawker Siddeley Harrier

The Harrier was the world's first Vertical/Short Takeoff and Landing (VSTOL) aircraft to enter series production and the first to be used in aerial combat. Its effectiveness was proven in the Falklands conflict of 1982, when Royal Navy Sea Harriers, operating from two small VSTOL carriers, inflicted major losses on Argentine aircraft. The US Marine Corps also flew Harriers in the Gulf War of 1991. Improved Harriers are currently in service with British, Italian, Spanish, and US military services.

The Harrier GR.1 (ground support-reconnaissance) entered service with the RAF in April 1969. Sea Harriers were delivered subsequently to the Royal Navy, which operated them from VSTOL carriers. At the time of the Falklands conflict the Harrier was in service with the RAF and the Sea Harrier was the only fixed-wing shipboard aircraft flown by the Royal Navy.

Both available British VSTOL carriers, the *Hermes* and *Invincible*, were deployed to the Falklands. When they went to sea the *Hermes* carried 12 Sea Harriers and 9 Sea King helicopters; the *Invincible* had 8 Sea Harriers and 11 Sea Kings—a total 20 fixed-wing aircraft and 20 helicopters constituted Britain's entire carrier-based air arm. Subsequently, additional Sea Harriers as well as RAF Harriers were delivered to the carriers.

Four RAF Harrier GR.3s made the 4,600-mile flight from Britain to Ascension Island, and then the nine-hour flight to the carriers with several in-flight refuelings from tanker aircraft. A British merchant ship carried another eight Sea Harriers and six RAF Harriers to the carriers. Another merchant ship brought four RAF aircraft to Port Stanley when that town was captured. Thus, a total of 28 Sea Harriers and 14 RAF Harriers participated in the conflict.

Those aircraft proved extremely effective against Argentine fixed-wing aircraft. Sea Harriers scored 16 kills and 1 probable kill with AIM-9L Sidewinder missiles; 4 kills and 2 probables were made with 30-millimeter cannon fire. The Sea Harriers flew 1,100 combat air patrols and 90 attack missions (including sinking an Argentine intelligence-collection trawler). The RAF Harriers flew 125 ground-attack and reconnaissance missions.

Six Sea Harriers were lost, two to enemy action—one to anti-aircraft gunfire and one to a Roland missile; four were operational losses (with four pilots lost). Three GR.3 aircraft were lost to enemy ground fire (their pilots survived). No Harriers were lost in air-to-air combat.

The US Marine Corps took deliveries of the Harrier beginning in 1971. Designated AV-8A Harrier, this was the first VSTOL aircraft to enter US military service. During the Gulf War of 1991, the Marines flew 86 improved AV-8B Harriers in the ground support role. They flew 3,380 combat missions without loss.

In 1957 the Hawker firm began development of an aircraft based on an advanced Bristol gas-turbine engine. This became the Hawker P.1127 development aircraft, which first flew in "free hover" in 1960. There was significant British, West German, and US military interest in the aircraft, with sea trials being flown from the British carrier *Ark Royal.*

The P.1127 prototypes evolved into the Kestrel, a VSTOL demonstration aircraft that flew in 1964. Extensive trials were carried out with a tripartite squadron—British, West German, US—as well as with the individual nations. Six Kestrels, evaluated by the United States as the XV-6A, were flown by Army, Navy, Air Force, and Marine pilots, from shore bases and ships.

After nine years of development the Harrier flew for the first time on August 31, 1966. Series production followed. While there have been several attempts to produce a supersonic Harrier-type aircraft, none has been pursued to fruition.

The Harrier is powered by a vectored-thrust turbofan engine (i.e., the exhaust is vented through rotating nozzles). The aircraft has large, semi-circular engine air intakes on each side of the forward fuselage; shoulder-mounted swept wings; tandem main wheels that retract into the fuselage; and outrigger landing gear that fold under each wing. The wings do not fold for carrier stowage.

The aircraft has no internal armament, but is fitted with under-fuselage pods for one or two single-barrel cannon (25-mm or 30-mm). In addition, bombs, missiles, rockets, and cannon pods are fitted to wing and fuselage attachment points.

Several two-seat variants were produced as advanced trainers (designated TAV-8 in US Marine Corps service). The aircraft is fitted for in-flight refueling.

The Hawker Siddeley Harrier was the world's first VSTOL aircraft to see combat, being flown by the Royal Air Force and Royal Navy in the Falklands conflict of 1982, and by the US Marine Corps in the Gulf War of 1991. The only other VSTOL combat aircraft to enter operational service was the now-discarded Soviet Yak-38 (NATO Forger). Shown here is an RAF Harrier GR.3 during a 1974 exercise in West Germany. *UK Ministry of Defence*

The Harrier remains in service with British, Italian, Spanish, Thai, and US services. Hawker Siddeley produced 14 P.1127s, 9 Kestrels, 261 Harriers, 98 Sea Harriers, and 115 AV-8A Harriers (the last for US service). McDonnell Douglas built 339 AV-8B aircraft, with some of the latter for Italy and Spain (with seven of the Spanish planes later being sold to Thailand). The AV-8A was equivalent to the British GR.Mk 50 and the AV-8B the British GR.Mk 7.

Harrier GR.3 Characteristics

Design:	Hawker/British Aerospace
Crew:	Pilot
Engines:	1 Rolls-Royce Bristol Pegasus 103 turbofan; 21,500 lbst
Weights:	
Empty:	13,535 lb
Loaded:	25,200 lb
Dimensions:	
Length:	46 ft, 10 in
Wingspan:	25 ft, 2 in
Wing area:	201 sq ft
Height:	11 ft, 11 in
Speeds:	
Maximum:	740 mph at sea level
Cruise:	
Ceiling:	51,200 ft
Range:	210 miles; 2,340 miles ferry with 2 330-gallon (Imperial) drop tanks
Armament:	2 30-mm cannon pods (removable); 5 1,000-lb bombs or 6 Matra multiple rocket launchers

Lockheed F-117A Nighthawk

The F-117 Nighthawk was the first low-observable or stealth aircraft to enter production and the first to see combat. Its ability to find targets in the dark, destroy them, and withdraw without being detected by defenses has provided the US Air Force an ability to strike with impunity, an ability currently unavailable to any other air force. Although designated a "fighter" by the USAF, the F-117 is a tactical strike aircraft with no air-to-air capability.

The F-117 entered combat on December 20, 1989, during Operation Just Cause, the US removal of Panamanian dictator Manuel Noriega. Two Nighthawks each dropped a 2,000-pound, laser-guided bomb beside the Rio Hato barracks in Panama, stunning troops there and allowing US troops to overrun the base with minimal casualties to either side. Still, few details of the F-117 were released to the public or news media until press conferences in April 1990.

Less than a year later, on January 17, 1991, ten F-117s helped to open Operation Desert Storm, the assault against Iraq following Saddam Hussein's invasion of Kuwait. The first laser-guided bomb struck an integrated air-defense operations center 65 miles from Baghdad. Moments later other laser-guided bombs slammed into Iraqi defense, communications, and command and control centers. Twelve F-117s in a second wave destroyed other high-priority targets—a total of 26 centers critical to Iraq's ability to mount a coordinated defense. No F-117 was fired on—most aircraft had departed the target areas before defenses had time to react.

Protected from radar and visual detection, the F-117s flew 40 percent of all Coalition air strikes against Iraqi targets in the first three nights of the conflict, although stealth fighters comprised less than 3 percent of the total air force. Because of the intense air defenses around Baghdad, F-117s were the only US aircraft to attack the central portions of the city. (US Navy ship-launched Tomahawk missiles were the only other Coalition weapons to strike targets in Baghdad.)

In total, F-117s flew approximately 1,300 sorties and scored 1,600 direct hits before flight operations ended on February 28, 1991. Forty-two F-117s were committed to Operation Desert Storm. They were based at King Khalid airbase at Khamis Mushait in Saudi Arabia, near the Red Sea, where they would be some distance from possible Iraqi attack.

The F-117 was again in combat in 1999 in support of NATO Operation Allied Force against the former Yugoslavia. Again, Nighthawks led the way, dropping bombs in the first air strike on March 24, 1999. F-117s continued to fly during the conflict, with the first Allied aircraft lost to enemy action occurring on the night of March 27–28 when an F-117 was shot down, apparently by an S-125 Neva (NATO SA-3 Goa) surface-to-air missile some 25 miles west of Belgrade. The pilot was rescued in the only combat loss to date of an F-117. (The only other Allied combat loss was a USAF F-16 Falcon.)

The USAF deployed 24 F-117A aircraft to Aviano air base in Italy, and Spangdahlem air base in Germany, in support of Operation Allied Force.

The development and existence of the Lockheed Stealth Fighter was kept secret for more than a decade. Rumors abounded in the aviation press, particularly when two of the aircraft crashed within the United States in the mid-1980s. The release of a plastic model kit of the "F-19 Stealth Fighter" in 1986 caused a congressional outcry over breached security. Finally, in November 1988 the Air Force admitted the existence of the aircraft and the designation F-117A, and released a poor-quality photograph. (Although the photo provided few details, it showed that the hobby kit bore no relationship to the actual aircraft—project security had remained intact.)

Development of the F-117 began in 1973 with Lockheed's "skunk works" response to a Department of Defense request. Two prototype stealth aircraft were produced under the project code name "Have Blue." The first of these flew in December 1977.

A production contract for the F-117A was awarded to Lockheed in 1978, and the first flight was made on June 18, 1981. The first F-117A unit, the 4450th Tactical Group, became operational in October 1983. A total of 59 aircraft were built, including 4 YF-117s; the last was delivered on July 12, 1990. Fifty-five aircraft remained in service in 2003—52 F-117s and 3 YF-117s.

The F-117A design employs flat, angled fuselage and wing panels to defect radar energy in a few, sharply defined directions. The aircraft also uses advanced surface materials and exhaust reduction features to attain stealth. The design presents several aerodynamic problems which are compensated for through the extensive use of computer-supported, quadruple redundant, fly-by-wire controls. The aircraft has two, nonafterburning engines that provide subsonic speeds. Weapons are carried in an internal weapons bay. The aircraft is fitted for in-flight refueling.

The Lockheed F-117A Nighthawk was the first "stealth" aircraft to enter operational service. Although designated as a fighter, the F-117A is a night-strike aircraft, carrying precision-guided missiles in an internal weapons bay. It has been in combat on several occasions, often with the first knowledge that the enemy has of its presence being missile detonations. *US Air Force*

The strange-looking F-117A Nighthawk gives the appearance
of a sinister, futuristic craft. The design represents first-
generation stealth technology, compared to the more-advanced
technology used in the Northrop B-2 bomber. The F-117s are
flown by the 37th Tactical Fighter Wing. *US Air Force*

F-117A Characteristics

Design:	Lockheed
Crew:	Pilot
Engines:	2 General Electric F-404 turbofan; 10,800 lbst each
Weights:	
Empty:	approximately 30,000 lb
Maximum takeoff:	52,500 lb
Dimensions:	
Length:	63 ft, 9 in
Wingspan:	43 ft, 4 in
Wing area:	1,070 sq ft
Height:	12 ft, 9 ½ in
Speeds:	
Maximum:	645 mph at sea level
Cruise:	625 mph at 35,000 ft
Ceiling:	45,000 ft
Range:	Classified
Armament:	1 nuclear bomb B61 or 5,000 lb of bombs

McDonnell F-15 Eagle and F-15E Strike Eagle

The F-15 Eagle is probably the world's most successful air superiority fighter. With a record of 104 enemy aircraft destroyed, no F-15 has ever been downed in air-to-air combat.

The F-15 was designed for the US Air Force, but its combat career began in the Israeli Air Force (IAF). Israel purchased its first 25 Eagles in large part because of its frustration over regular intrusions of Israeli air space by Syrian-piloted MiG-25s. Those overflights ended soon after the first F-15s were delivered in December 1976, although there were no encounters of the two aircraft in that period. Rather, the first IAF F-15 "kill" was the Israeli government: The first four F-15s arrived in Israel after sundown on Friday, December 10—during the Jewish sabbath. That act led the Orthodox parties to force the Labor Party from office.

Subsequently, Israeli F-15s-given the name *Baz* (Falcon) began their first combat patrols in 1978 while flying top cover for Israeli strikes into southern Lebanon. Their first air-to-air kills were five Syrian MiG-21s on July 27, 1979. When IAF F-15s downed two MiG-23s on November 30, 1985, the total Israeli F-15 aerial victory count had reached 57 Syrian aircraft. The Israelis also used six F-15s to fly escort for the eight bomb-carrying F-16 Falcons that bombed the Iraqi nuclear reactor near Baghdad on June 7, 1981. Pairs of the F-15s patrolled near three Iraqi fighter bases while the bombers struck. All 14 aircraft returned safely from Operation Babylon.

Demonstrating the aircraft's flexibility, eight Israeli F-15s were used to bomb the Palestine Liberation Organization (PLO) headquarters in Tunis on October 1, 1985. That mission required a round-trip flight of more than 2,500 miles.

Saudi Arabia was the second nation to use F-15s in combat, downing two Iranian F-4E Phantoms in June 1984. Saudi Eagles also claimed two Iraqi Mirage F.1 fighters during Operation Desert Storm in January 1991.

The US Air Force flew the F-15C Eagle and F-15E Strike Eagle during the Gulf War. By the end of the air campaign in late February 1991 the USAF had deployed 124 F-15Cs and 48 F-15Es to the area. US F-15C variants accounted for 33 of the 41 Iraqi aircraft shot down; in addition, a USAF F-15E downed an Iraqi helicopter in flight with a laser-guided bomb. Operating mainly at night, the F-15Es hunted Scud missile launchers and artillery with their night-optic systems and precision-guided munitions.

In the subsequent Balkan conflict, the USAF F-15Es were the only strike aircraft to attack ground targets around-the-clock, in all weather conditions, and F-15C variants added four more aerial victories—three of them MiG-29s—to their score.

The F-15, in both the fighter and F-15E strike variants, are in service with the USAF and five other air forces.

The origins of the F-15 can be traced to the mid-1960s Air Force FX program, which sought to develop a new, dedicated air superiority fighter.

The resulting design competition ended in December 1969 when a contract was awarded to McDonnell Douglas for the F-15. The prototype F-15A made its first flight on July 27, 1972, beginning what became an accident-free test and evaluation program. The first production aircraft, a two-seat TF-15A (later redesignated F-15B), was delivered to the Air Force in November 1974. The total F-15 production by McDonnell Douglas and—after 1997—by Boeing is more than 1,500 aircraft.

When introduced, the Eagle exhibited unprecedented maneuverability, acceleration, range, weapons, and avionics. The weapons and flight control systems were designed for ease of control, allowing each Eagle pilot to concentrate on the situation around the aircraft, not the instruments and controls inside the cockpit. The first operational fighter to enjoy greater engine thrust than its own weight, the Eagle easily accelerated in a climb, and used that capability to set several world's records. Thirty years after its introduction the F-15 began to lose its dogfighting edge against newer aircraft such as the MiG-29, Su-27, Su-35/37, Rafale, and EF-2000. Accordingly, the USAF has plans to replace the air-superiority F-15C with the Lockheed F/A-22 Raptor.

The US F-15A and two-seat F-15B variants have been shifted to the Air National Guard, with frontline USAF units flying the F-15C and two-seat F-15D. Those aircraft carry AIM-7 Sparrow missiles, AIM-120 Advanced Medium Range Air-to-Air Missiles (AMRAAMs), and AIM-9 Sidewinder missiles, in addition to an internally mounted 20-mm Gatling gun in the right wing root.

The F-15 pilot sits beneath a 360-degree canopy, well forward in the fuselage—with the prominent ramps for the engine air intakes behind him—for excellent visibility in every direction. The shallow fuselage of the F-15 houses side-by-side Pratt & Whitney turbofan engines. The large rectangular-cross-section, variable-geometry, horizontal-ramp intakes are mounted on either side of the fuselage. The engine burner cans are set in the after fuselage between extensions that support twin vertical tails above all-flying horizontal tails. The shoulder-mounted wing is a modified, cropped-delta shape featuring a leading-edge sweep of 45 degrees and high wing loading. For ferry purposes, the F-15C/D models carry low-drag, conformal fuel tanks under the wings.

No air superiority fighter has ever matched the McDonnell F-15 Eagle's combat record: after a quarter century of combat, no F-15 is known to have been shot down in aerial action despite the aircraft having achieved an impressive "kill" record in several conflicts. This F-15C was assigned to the 3rd Tactical Fighter Wing in Alaska in the mid-1990s. *Dana Bell*

The F-15E Strike Eagle is a two-seat, dual-role fighter for all-weather, air-to-air combat and deep interdiction missions. Known to its crews as the Beagle (for Bomb-Eagle) or Mud Hen, the F-15E can carry up to 23,000 pounds of weapons including such air-to-ground weapons as the Joint Direct Attack Munition (JDAM) and AGM-130, as well as the air-to-air missiles carried by air superiority F-15s. Two Low Altitude Navigation and Targeting Infrared for Night (LANTIRN) pods are carried by the F-15E.

The F-15A/B/D have been purchased by Israel, as has the improved, two-seat F-15I, a dual-role fighter similar to the F-15E. The F-15S was purchased by Saudi Arabia to join its fleet of F-15C/D aircraft. Boeing has produced derivatives of the F-15E for Greece (F-15H) and South Korea (F-15K). Under license, Mitsubishi produced 223 F-15J and two-seat F-15DJ air-superiority fighters for Japanese service.

F-15C Characteristics

Design:	McDonnell Douglas (Boeing)
Crew:	Pilot
Engines:	2 Pratt & Whitney F100-PW-220 or 229 turbofan; 23,450 lbst each with afterburner
Weights:	
Empty:	28,600 lb
Maximum takeoff:	68,000 lb
Dimensions:	
Length:	63 ft, 9 in
Wingspan:	42 ft, 9 in
Wing area:	608 sq ft
Height:	18 ft, 6 in
Speeds:	
Maximum:	1,875 mph
Cruise:	570 mph
Ceiling:	65,000 ft
Range:	3,450 miles
Armament:	1 20-mm M61A1 Vulcan cannon (rotary-barrel; fixed); 4 AIM-7 Sparrow + 4 AIM-9 Sidewinder AAM or 8 AIM-120 AMRAAM

Mil' Mi-24 Hind

The Mi-24 was the world's first helicopter to enter service designed for the gunship role. Although the US AH-1 Cobra series predated the Mi-24, the US helicopter was adapted from the UH-1 Huey (Iroquois). Moreover, the Soviet aircraft far outpaced it in terms of firepower.

Reportedly, the Mil' design bureau originally proposed a specialized gunship helicopter to the Ministry of Defense. The proposal was rejected and the Ministry demanded instead that troop-carrying capability be incorporated to avoid the costs of new gunship and troop-carrying helicopters. The result was the Mi-24 (given the NATO code name Hind). The Hind-A and Hind-B (actually developed in the reverse order) have limited gunship capabilities and appear to be primarily troop carriers; the Hind-C is similar but lacks some of their armament. These early variants had an empty weight of 10,360 pounds and a loaded weight of 18,250 pounds.

The Hind-D was extensively redesigned to emphasize the gunship role and the Hind-E is comparable in many respects to the US Army-Hughes AH-64 Apache, which flew several years later.

The Mi-24 entered Soviet service with the ground forces in 1972 and was subsequently flown extensively in combat in Afghanistan. The Soviets transferred Mi-24s to more than 30 countries; the Mi-25 was an export version of the Hind. Some export models of the Hind-F—with sensitive equipment removed—are designated Mi-35P; the Mi-35M has a reinforced airframe, enhanced avionics, and additional armament.

Iraqi Mi-25s have shot down at least one Iranian F-4 Phantom with an AT-6 Spiral missile. US Army-piloted Mi-24s in the United States are used in training exercises.

The Mi-24 incorporated extensive advanced helicopter technology, including a five-blade main rotor with titanium spars and fiberglass covering. An anti-torque rotor is mounted on the left side of the tail fin (early models had the tail rotor mounted on the right side). The semi-moncoque fuselage has stub wings with a marked anhedral of about 20 degrees to provide additional lift as well as hard points for weapons; the angle was intended to minimize rotor interaction problems. The tricycle landing gear is retractable. The twin turboshaft engines are mounted in a housing atop the fuselage. Significant armor is provided.

All variants have seating for 8 to 10 troops in addition to a three- or four-man crew, which is housed in a pressurized cockpit.

The armament of the Hind-A consists of a flexible 12.7-mm machine gun in the nose with six weapon stations on the wings for rocket pods or missiles or 92.5-gallon drop tanks. The Hind-B's wings have no anhedral and only four hard points (i.e., no wingtip positions). The Hind-C is similar but lacks a nose gun and wingtip weapon positions.

The transformed Hind-D has a four-barrel 12.7-mm Gatling gun in a turret fitted under the nose and six wing hard points for weapons; the outermost points have double rails for anti-tank missiles (as observed on some Hind-A aircraft). The Hind-D is fitted with radar (providing an all-weather capability), Low-Light-Level Television (LLLTV), and a laser rangefinder. The Hind-D was first observed in 1977. A variant of the Hind-D without a nose sensor pod is designated Hind-G by the US government.

The Hind-E can carry more advanced anti-tank missiles—the AT-6 Spiral vice AT-2 Swatter, while the Hind-F (Mi-24P, first seen in 1981) has further enhanced weapon capabilities with a twin-barrel 30-mm cannon in a fixed mount on the right side replacing the Gatling gun of the Hind-D/E. The internal troop space can be used for weapon reloads (with rearming done on the ground).

Other variants are the Mi-24R fitted for Nuclear-Biological-Chemical (NBC) detection on the battlefield; the Mi-24VM, featuring a night-vision compatible cockpit; the Mi-24K (Hind-G2) with a large camera installation and radios for artillery fire control; Mi-24BMT for battlefield minesweeping; and Mi-24PS with searchlight and sensors for the Ministry of Internal Affairs. Major missile countermeasures have been fitted to the Hind-E and later variants having the ASO-2 system that contains 32 flares and 192 decoys, with up to six launchers.

The first flight of an Mi-24 occurred in 1971 with production being initiated immediately. More than 2,500 have been produced, including some 250 A/B/C variants, about 350 D variants, and 1,000 E variants; production continues at a slow rate. The subsequent Mil'-produced helicopter gunship, the Mi-28 Havoc, which bears resemblance to the US AH-64, appears to be primarily an anti-helicopter aircraft.

An early Mil' Mi-24 (NATO Hind), the world's first purpose-designed gunship helicopter to enter operational service. Its fire-power consisted of a single machine gun and six wing stations for rockets (shown here) or missiles. Later Mi-24 variants have much heavier gun armament and carry advanced missiles. The Mi-24 is a combination gunship–troop carrier. *UK Ministry of Defence*

Mi-24P Hind-F Characteristics

Design:	Mil'
Crew:	3 (pilot, weapon systems officer, crewman) + 8 troops or 4 stretchers Engines: 2 Isotov TV2-117A turboshaft; approximately 2,200 hp each
Weights:	
Empty:	18,078 lb
Loaded:	24,691 lb
Maximum takeoff:	26,455 lb
Dimensions:	
Fuselage length:	57 ft, 5 in
Wingspan:	21 ft, 10 in
Rotor diameter:	12 ft, 9 1/2 in
Height:	13 ft
Speeds:	
Maximum:	208 mph
Cruise:	167.5 mph
Ceiling:	14,764 ft
Range:	280 miles on internal fuel; endurance 4 hours
Armament:	2 30-mm GSh-30-2 cannon (twin fixed mount); 1 7.62-mm AK-47 automatic rifle fitted in window (optional); 5,291 of rocket pods, anti-tank missiles, or bombs; up to 8 AT-6 Siral missiles can be carried

Mil' Mi-26 Halo

The Mil' design bureau's Mi-26 is the largest rotary-wing aircraft ever built. Known in the West by the code name Halo, the giant aircraft reflects the Russian penchant for heavy-lift helicopters, as demonstrated by the earlier Mi-6 Hook, Mi-12 Homer, and Mi-10 Harke, all record-setting aircraft.

In comparison to the 22-ton external lift capacity of the Mi-26, the most-capable Western helicopter is the Sikorsky H-53E series, operated by the US Navy as the MH-53 Sea Dragon and the Marine Corps as the CH-53E Super Stallion; those helicopters have an external lift of 16 tons.

The Mi-26 entered military service in late 1983. The Russian Army is reported to operate about 25 Mi-26s with others in use by various government agencies. In addition to the general cargo/troop configuration, the helicopter is known to fly in several specialized roles: the Mi-26MS is a medical evacuation aircraft with medical facilities on board; the Mi-26TZ is a fuel tanker, readily convertible to the cargo/troop role; and the Mi-26TM is the cargo variant. The Mi-26P in civil variant carries 63 passengers. Some 30 other nations also operate the Mi-26 in military and civilian various roles in addition to having been used by the United Nations in peacekeeping operations in Cambodia and Somalia.

Little information is available about Soviet military use of the Mi-26. After the 1986 nuclear catastrophe at Chernobyl Mi-26s were used to deliver heavy materials to the site. Protective screens were mounted in the cabin to protect the flight crew during those missions. Mi-26s worked in the area of intensive radiation for six months during which time no helicopter failures occurred.

An Mi-26 crashed in Chechnya in December 2001 when both engines suffered an in-flight failure. Another Mi-26 crashed in a minefield in Chechnya on August 19, 2002. It was carrying 147 soldiers and civilians, of whom 116 were killed and most of the others seriously injured, primarily by land mines. There was some evidence that Chechen rebels shot down the helicopter, less than 1,000 feet from the Khantala military base, near the capital city of Grozny, with a Strela anti-aircraft missile.

The first flight of an Mi-26 took place on December 14, 1977. It subsequently achieved numerous helicopter lift-to-altitude records. Some 300 have been built for domestic and foreign service. The aircraft remains in production.

Designed under the direction of Marat N. Tishchenko, work began on the helicopter in the early 1970s. It was the first design developed after Tishchenko succeeded Mikhail L. Mil' as head of the design bureau. The Mi-26 has a conventional appearance that belies its great size. It has an eight-blade main rotor and an anti-torque rotor on the right side of the tail boom. There are two doors on the left side of the multi-level fuselage with clamshell doors and ramp at the rear for loading vehicles and bulk cargo. There is an internal sling hoist for cargo.

The helicopter's cargo compartment is 39 feet, 4 inches long and 10 feet, 8 inches wide, with height varying from 9 feet, 8 inches to 10 feet, 4

With a long history of developing heavy-lift helicopters, the Mil' design produced the Mi-28 (NATO Halo), the world's largest helicopter with the heaviest payload—22 tons external lift. The Mi-28—in civilian (here Aeroflot) as well as military markings—has carried out a variety of military missions. It continues in slow-rate production.

Mi-26 Characteristics

Design:	Mil'
Crew:	5 (pilot, copilot, navigator, flight engineer, loadmaster) + 82 troops or 60 stretchers + 5 attendants
Engines:	2 Lotarev D-136 turboshaft; 11,400 shp each
Weights:	
Empty:	62,170 lb
Loaded:	109,125 lb
Maximum takeoff:	123,450 lb
Dimensions:	
Length:	131 ft, 4 in
Fuselage length:	110 ft, 8 in
Rotor diameter:	105 ft
Height:	26 ft, 5 $\frac{1}{4}$ in
Speeds:	
Maximum:	183 mph
Cruise:	158.5 mph
Ceiling:	14,760 ft
Range:	500 miles; 1,200 miles with 4 external fuel tanks
Armament:	None

inches; there is a fore-and-aft traversing crane within the cargo compartment. Maximum payload—internal or slung—is 44,090 pounds. Forty tip-up passenger seats are provided in the cargo configuration (with another four tip-up seats on the flight deck). A Doppler radar-driven map display is provided and three television cameras are fitted to enable the pilots to view the area around the helicopter. The two-level flight deck is air conditioned, with the pilot and copilot seated forward on the lower level, and the navigation and flight engineer seated above and behind them.

The design of the Mi-26 includes the requirement to operate in the field for two or three days at a time from forward bases without support personnel or special facilities.

Northrop B-2A Spirit

A second-generation stealth aircraft, the Northrop-developed B-2A is today's most effective bomber, having brought unprecedented capabilities to long-range bombing operations. The B-2 is believed to be only the second low-observable combat aircraft to reach operational status.

Employing a variety of advanced technologies, the B-2 can reach any conflict point in the world, launch a variety of precision-guided weapons at several targets, then turn for home, hopefully without being detected. The US Air Force estimates that a pair of unsupported B-2s could perform bombing missions that once required a mixed force of 75 conventional aircraft with less risk from enemy defenses.

The B-2 flew its first combat missions in Operation Allied Force on March 24, 1999, flying 30-hour missions from Whiteman Air Force Base (AFB), Missouri, to Kosovo and return. Able to deliver satellite-guided munitions in any weather conditions, the B-2 destroyed 33 percent of all Serbian targets struck during the first eight weeks of the conflict. During Operation Enduring Freedom in 2002, B-2s flew 44-hour missions from Whiteman Air Force Base to Afghanistan.

The need to review and/or restore special coatings after each mission meant that all missions were initially flown from the home base at Whiteman Air Force Base. Subsequently, the United States has established a second B-2 support facility on the British-owned island of Diego Garcia in the Indian Ocean.

The first USAF studies for the Advanced Technology Bomber (ATB) began in 1975 during research into what eventually became the Lockheed F-117 stealth fighter. Northrop lost to Lockheed for development of the F-117 stealth attack aircraft but continued efforts to develop a low-observable or stealth aircraft.

On August 22, 1980, Secretary of Defense Harold Brown announced that the United States was developing the ATB employing a new technology that "alters the military balance significantly." The disclosure came because of criticism of the Carter administration for not supporting advanced strategic weapons. The Northrop Corporation was awarded a production contract in 1981 for the firm's stealth bomber design. Northrop had designed and built flying wing bombers in the 1940s, the B-35 piston-engine and B-49 turbojet-powered aircraft. The flying wing configuration offered a number of attractive features for a large low-observable or stealth aircraft with a large payload.

The initial USAF plan was for 132 ATB aircraft including six test aircraft, of which five would subsequently be reconfigured to a combat capability. Because of major cost increases, in April 1990 Secretary of Defense Dick Cheney reduced the B-2 program to 75 aircraft; in January 1992 President George Bush announced that the total B-2 buy was limited to a total of 20 aircraft including flight test vehicles. Subsequently, a twenty-first aircraft was produced.

Hidden from the public—and foreign spies—for almost eight years, the B-2 prototype was unveiled in ceremonies at the Northrop factory at Palmdale, California, on November 22, 1988. The first flight was made on July 17, 1989, and the first production aircraft delivered to the USAF in December 1993, for service with the 509th Bomb Wing at Whiteman Air Force Base. (Its predecessor, the 509th Composite Group, had flown the B-29s that dropped atomic bombs on Japan in August 1945.)

The B-2 is a true flying-wing design, without fuselage or vertical tail structure. The wing leading edges are swept at approximately 40 degrees to the tips, which rake back toward the centerline. The trailing edge is a saw-tooth design to increase stability. The aircraft's shape and materials, combined with special coatings, help to reduce radar, infrared, and electromagnetic signatures. The four turbofan engines are buried deep within the wing, helping to reduce the acoustic signature. The aircraft has a high subsonic speed. The B-2 is fitted for in-flight refueling.

The characteristics of a flying wing design are evident in the B-2 having significantly less length and wingspan than the earlier B-36 Peacemaker, yet having greater payload and takeoff weights. Further, the B-36 was manned by crews of 15 to 22 men, compared to the two-man crew of a B-2.

A variety of conventional and nuclear weapons can be carried by the B-2 with a maximum weapons load of about 40,000 pounds. All weapons are accommodated internally in two weapons bays in the center of the aircraft with each bay having a rotary launcher and two bomb-rack assemblies. The B-2 can release B61 and B83 nuclear bombs and Mk-84 2,000-

B-2A Characteristics

Design:	Northrop
Crew:	2 (mission commander, pilot)
Engines:	4 General Electric F-118-GE-100 turbofan; 17,300 lbst each
Weights:	
Empty:	100,000–110,000 lb
Loaded:	336,500 lb
Maximum takeoff:	376,000 lb
Dimensions:	
Length:	69 ft
Wingspan:	172 ft
Wing area:	5,000 sq ft
Height:	17 ft
Speeds:	
Maximum:	630 mph at 40,000 ft; 570 mph at sea level
Cruise:	
Ceiling:	50,000 ft
Range:	6,600 miles
Armament:	20 B61 nuclear bombs or 16 B83 nuclear bombs or 80 Mk 82 500-lb bombs

pound conventional bombs from the rotary launchers, and Mk-82 1,000-pound bombs and other conventional weapons from the bomb racks. The B-2 can also carry the AGM-129 Advanced Cruise Missile with an estimated range of 1,500 miles. Sixteen satellite-guided Joint Direct Attack Munition (JDAM) missiles can be carried, as can an unspecified number of Joint Stand-off Weapon (JSOW), Joint Air-to-Surface Stand-off Missiles (JASSM), and the Wind Compensated Munitions Dispenser (WCMD). The B-2 has no defensive weapons.

The aircraft has two flat-plate antennas for the Hughes AN/APQ-181 multi-mode, phased-array radar.

Following the aircraft's combat debut over Kosovo there have been

A Northrop B-2A Spirit stealth bomber takes off during initial
flight trials in 1989. The B-2A employs second-generation
stealth technology—shaping, coatings, exhaust dampening, and
other features—in an effort to reduce its probability of detection.
It also incorporates advanced control features, enabling a two-
man crew to carry out intercontinental combat missions.
Northrop Grumman

efforts by the USAF and congressional supporters to reopen the B-2 production lines (now Northrop Grumman), but no funding has occurred.

Panavia Tornado

As the costs of developing new, frontline combat aircraft have become more prohibitive in recent decades, more nations have pooled their resources in collaborative efforts. The Panavia Tornado resulted from the most successful of these joint development/production programs, the Multi-Role Combat Aircraft (MRCA) program. The original program was intended to produce aircraft to perform close air support, interdiction, air superiority, interceptor, naval strike, and reconnaissance missions.

The Tornado participated in some of the most dangerous missions of Operation Desert Storm in 1991 and suffered the highest percentage of coalition aircraft losses. Racing across Iraqi air bases to release their JP-233 runway denial munitions, Tornados flown by several air forces completely closed eight Iraqi airfields in four days, and significantly damaged several others.

But this success came at a cost of six RAF, one Italian, and one Saudi Tornado destroyed by ground fire on their low- to medium-altitude strikes. Improvements were introduced during Desert Storm; accordingly, the Tornados that left Desert Storm were far more capable than those that began it. Those improvements included thermal imaging/laser designation pods, an advanced infrared reconnaissance system, ALARM anti-radar missiles, and reduced radar cross section through the use of stealth coatings.

Initial design studies leading to the MRCA began in 1968. The Panavia consortium was formed on March 26, 1969, to handle the contractual arrangements between member nations Britain, Germany, and Italy. The resulting design featured two advanced turbofans with a high thrust-to-weight ratio and good fuel economy, a fly-by-wire system, an advanced navigation/attack system (search, ground-mapping, and terrain-following radar), and a variable-geometry wing system. The participating nations were responsible for manufacturing different sections of the aircraft: Britain produced the nose and after fuselage, Italy built the wings, and Germany produced the center fuselage. Each nation assembled its own aircraft and tested its own prototypes. The first flights were in Germany on August 14, 1974, Britain on October 30, 1974, and Italy on December 5, 1975.

Early planning envisioned a procurement of more than 800 aircraft for the three participating nations. When the production of new airframes ended in 1999 a total of 985 Tornados had been built, including 4 British prototypes, 3 German, and 2 Italian. Thus, the multi-national effort could be considered a major aviation success.

The initial variant was the Tornado IDS (Interdictor/Strike), with minor differences introduced for each nation. The principal Tornado variants are:

GR.1.
The original RAF IDS version, designed for close air support, interdiction, and radar/defense suppression in all weather, day or night. Total production was: GR.1—192; GR.1(T) dual-control trainer—36; GR.1A tactical reconnaissance aircraft—14 new production and 16 converted GR.1s; GR.1B dedicated anti-shipping version equipped to launch Sea Eagle missiles and carry "buddy" in-flight refueling pods (conversions).

GR.4/4A.
Mid-life update of the GR 1/1A—142 conversions.

IDS.
290 built for the German Air Force and Navy and 90 built for the Italian Air Force.

IDS (Saudi).
Ninety-six built for the Royal Saudi Air Force.

ECR.
Electronic Combat Reconnaissance version with RB.199 Mk 105 engines for Germany (35 new production) and Italy (16 conversions).

F.2.
The initial Air Defense Variant (ADV) developed for the RAF featuring a longer nose housing a multi-mode Doppler radar and lengthened fuselage to carry four Sky Flash air-to-air missiles. Production run of 18 aircraft. First flight on October 27, 1979.

F.3.
F.2 airframe with an uprated engine. Of 176 built, 24 were delivered to Saudi Arabia, 24 leased from the RAF by Italy (pending arrival of the Eurofighter), and the balance assigned to RAF units.

The Tornado features a short, fat fuselage with a large, swept fin and rudder. Twin all-flying horizontal tailplanes are set in both sides of two horizontally paired Turbo-Union afterburning turbofan engines. The variable-geometry wings are mounted high on the fuselage, with a 25-degree sweep when fully extended. At higher speeds the wings sweep back to 67 degrees, with the intermediate sweep normally set at 45 degrees. The two-seat tandem cockpit is faired into the fuselage, restricting rear visibility. IDS versions of the Tornado are distinguished by a short, broad radome, while the noses on ADV Tornados are elongated and more streamlined.

Tornado GR.1 Interdictor/Strike Characteristics

Design:	Panavia
Crew:	2 (pilot, navigator)
Engines:	2 Turbo-Union RB199-34R Mk.103 turbofan; 16,800 lbst each with afterburner
Weights:	
Empty:	31,065 lb
Maximum takeoff:	61,620 lb
Dimensions:	
Length:	54 ft, 11 in
Wingspan:	45 ft, 8 in
Wing area:	286.3 sq ft
Height:	28 ft, 3 in
Speed:	1,453 mph
Ceiling:	50,000 ft+
Range:	2,420 miles
Armament:	2 27-mm Mauser BK27 cannon (fixed); 19,840 lb of bombs, missiles, and/or rockets

The Tornado series was developed as a joint venture by Britain, Germany, and Italy primarily because of the high cost of aircraft development. A true multi-role combat aircraft, the swing-wing Tornado is flown by Saudi Arabia as well as the sponsoring countries. This British GR.1B carries Sea Eagle missiles under the fuselage for the anti-shipping mission. *British Aerospace*

Bibliography

In compiling this book the authors have made extensive use of the Standard Aircraft Characteristics pamphlets issued by the US Air Force and Navy.

British Aircraft

Andrews, C. F., and E. B. Morgan. *Supermarine Aircraft since 1914*. London: Putnam, 1987.

Barnes, C. H. *Shorts Aircraft since 1900*. London: Putnam, 1989.

Jackson, A. J. *De Havilland Aircraft since 1909*. London: Putnam, 1987.

King, H. F. *Sopwith Aircraft 1912–1920*. London: Putnam, 1980.

Mason, Francis K. *The British Bomber since 1914*. London: Putnam, 1994.

———. *The British Fighter since 1912*. London: Putnam, 1992.

———. *Hawker Aircraft since 1920*. London: Putnam, 1991.

———. *The Hawker Hurricane*. Garden City, N.Y.: Doubleday, 1962,

Taylor, H. A. *Fairey Aircraft since 1915*. London: Putnam, 1988.

Thetford, Owen. *Aircraft of the Royal Air Force since 1918*. London: Putnam, 1979.

———. *British Naval Aircraft since 1912*. London: Putnam, 1982.

French Aircraft

Davilla, James J., and Arthur M. Soltan. *French Aircraft of the First World War*. Mountain View, Calif.: Flying Machines Press, 1997.

Huertas, Salvador Mafé. *Dassault Mirage: the Combat Log*. Atgeln, Pa.: Schiffer Military/Aviation History, 1996.

German Aircraft

Brown, Eric M. *Wings of the Luftwaffe: Flying German Aircraft of the Second World War.* London: Jane's, 1977.

Green, William. *Warplanes of the Third Reich.* Garden City, N.Y.: Doubleday, 1970.

Kens, Karlheinz, and Heinz J. Nowarra. *Die Deutschen Flugzeuge 1933–1945.* Munich: J. F. Lehmanns, 1964.

Kosin, Rüdiger. *The German Fighter since 1915.* London: Putnam, 1988.

Morzik, Fritz. *German Air Force Airlift Operations.* USAF Historical Studies No. 167. Maxwell, Ala.: Air University, 1961. Reprinted, New York: Arno Press, 1968.

Smith, J. R., and Antony L. Kay. *German Aircraft of the Second World War.* Charleston, S.C.: Nautical & Aviation Publishing, 1972.

Japanese Aircraft

Francillon, R. J. *Japanese Aircraft of the Pacific War.* London: Putnam, 1970.

Horikoshi, Jiro. *Eagles of Mitsubishi: The Story of the Zero Fighter.* Seattle: University of Washington Press, 1981.

Mikesh, Robert C., and Shorzoe Abe. *Japanese Aircraft 1910–1941.* Annapolis, Md.: Naval Institute Press, 1990.

Peattie, Mark R. *Sunburst: The Rise of Japanese Naval Air Power, 1909–1941.* Annapolis, Md.: Naval Institute Press, 2001.

Tagaya, Osamu. *Mitsubishi Type 1 Rikko 'Betty' Units of World War 2.* London: Osprey, 2001.

Russian/Soviet Aircraft

Anderson, Lennart. *Soviet Aircraft and Aviation: 1917–1941.* London: Brassey's, 1994.

Durkota, Alan, Thomas Darcey, and Victor Kulikov. *The Imperial Russian Air Service: Famous Pilots and Aircraft of World War I.* Mountain View, Calif.: Flying Machines Press, 1995.

Gunston, Bill. *Aircraft of the Soviet Union: The Encyclopedia of Soviet Aircraft since 1917.* London: Osprey, 1983.

———. *Tupolev Aircraft since 1922.* London: Brassey's, 1995.

Kerber, L. L. *Stalin's Aviation Gulag: A Memoir of Andrei Tupolev and the Purge Era.* Washington, D.C.: Smithsonian Institution Press, 1996.

U.S. Aircraft

Bowers, Peter M. *Boeing Aircraft since 1916.* London: Putnam, 1989.

———. *Curtiss Aircraft 1907–1947.* London: Putnam, 1979.

Boyne, Walter. *Boeing B-52: A Documentary History.* London: Jane's, 1981.

Craven, W. F., and J. L. Cate. *Men and Planes,* vol. VI in *The Army Air Forces in World War II.* Chicago: University of Chicago Press, 1955.

Crickmore, Paul F. *Lockheed SR-71: The Secret Missions Exposed.* London: Osprey, 1993.

Dorr, Robert F. *B-29 Superfortress Units of World War II.* Botley, Oxford: Osprey, 2002.

————. *F-86 Sabre: History of the Sabre and FJ Fury.* Osceola, Wisc.: Motorbooks, 1993.

Fails, William R. *Marines and Helicopters, 1962–1973.* Washington, D.C.: U.S. Marine Corps, 1978.

Francillon, René J. *Douglas A-3 Skywarrior.* Arlington, Tex.: Aerofax, 1987.

————. *Grumman Aircraft since 1929.* London: Putnam, 1989.

————. *Lockheed Aircraft since 1913.* London: Putnam, 1987.

————. *McDonnell Douglas Aircraft since 1920.* London: Putnam, 1979.

Futrell, Robert F. *The United States Air Force in Korea, 1950–1953.* New York: Duell, Sloan and Pearce, 1961.

Goodall, James. *SR-71 Blackbird.* Carrollton, Tex.: Squadron/ Signal Publications, 1995.

Hagedorn, Dan. *North American NA-16/AT-6/SNJ Texan.* North Branch, Minn.: Specialty Press, 1997.

Hennessy, Juliette A. *The United States Army Air Arm: April 1861 to April 1917.* Washington, D.C.: Office of Air Force History, 1985.

Knaack, Marcelle Size. *Post-World War II Bombers 1945–1973,* vol. II in *Encyclopedia of U.S. Air Force Aircraft and Missile Systems.* Washington, D.C.: Office of Air Force History, 1988.

————. *Post-World War II Fighters 1945–1973,* vol. 1 in *Encyclopedia of U.S. Air Force Aircraft and Missile Systems.* Washington, D.C.: Office of Air Force History, 1978.

Maurer, Maurer. *Aviation in the U.S. Army, 1919–1939.* Washington, D.C.: Office of Air Force History, 1985.

Mersky, Peter B. *U.S. Marine Corps Aviation: 1921 to the Present.* Annapolis, Md.: Nautical & Aviation Publishing, 1983.

Rausa, Rosario. *Skyraider: The Douglas A-1 "Flying Dump Truck."* Baltimore, Md.: Nautical & Aviation, 1982.

Styling, Mark. *Corsair Aces of World War 2.* London: Osprey, 1995.

Swanborough, Gordon, and Peter M. Bowers. *United States Military Aircraft since 1911.* Washington, D.C.: Smithsonian Institution Press, 1989.

————. *United States Naval Aircraft since 1911.* Annapolis, Md.: Naval Institute Press, 1976.

Tillman, Barrett. *Hellcat Aces of World War 2.* London: Osprey, 1996.

————. *Wildcat Aces of World War 2.* London: Osprey, 1995.

Wegg, John. *General Dynamics Aircraft and their Predecessors.* London: Putnam, 1990.

Miscellaneous

Brown, Eric M. *Duels in the Sky: World War II Naval Aircraft in Combat.* Annapolis, Md.:
　　Naval Institute Press, 1988.

――――. *Wings of the Navy: Flying Allied Carrier Aircraft of World War II.* London: Jane's,
　　1980.

Green, William. *Famous Bombers of the Second World War,* vol. 1 and vol. 2. Garden City,
　　N.Y.: Doubleday, 1967.

――――. *Famous Fighters of the Second World War,* vol. 1. Garden City, N.Y.: Doubleday,
　　1965; vol. 2, 1967.

Groves, Leslie R. *Now It Can be Told.* New York: Harper, 1962.

Hallion, Richard P. *Storm Over Iraq: Air Power and the Gulf War.* Washington, D.C.:
　　Smithsonian Institution Press, 1992.

Morrow, John H., Jr. *The Great War in the Air: Military Aviation from 1909 to 1921.*
　　Washington, D.C.: Smithsonian Institution Press, 1993.

Polmar, Norman. *Spyplane: U-2 History Declassified.* St. Paul, Minn.: MBI Publishing,
　　2001.

Polmar, Norman, and Floyd D. Kennedy. *Military Helicopters of the World: Military Rotary-
　　Wing Aircraft since 1917.* Annapolis, Md.: Naval Institute Press, 1981.

Roskill, S. W. Roskill. *White Ensign: The British Navy at War, 1939–1945.* Annapolis, Md.:
　　U.S. Naval Institute, 1960.

Taylor, John W. R. *Jane's All the World's Aircraft.* London: Jane's (various editions).

In addition, the authors made use of articles in the following journals:

Air Enthusiast (UK)

Air International (UK)

American Aviation Historical Society *Journal* (US)

Aviation Week & Space Technology (US)

Flight (UK)

Flying Review International (UK)

Military Parade (Russia)

Naval Aviation News (US)

The Hook (US)

About the Authors

Norman Polmar is an analyst, consultant, and historian in the naval, aviation, and intelligence fields. He has been a consultant to several members of Congress as well as to three secretaries of the navy and two chiefs of naval operations. He has also held the Ramsey Chair of aviation history at the National Air and Space Museum.

His almost 40 books include several on military aircraft, as well as several editions of *Ships and Aircraft of the U.S. Fleet*. He writes columns for *Proceedings* and *Naval History* magazines, both published by the US Naval Institute.

Dana Bell is an archivist for the National Air and Space Museum, where he evaluates, organizes, and prepares documents for use by researchers. Previously, from 1976 to 1981, he was a photo researcher at the US Air Force's Central Still Photo Depository.

Bell has researched and written numerous books and articles on aviation history. His study of US military aviation colors and markings has led to groundbreaking publications on the subject as well as lectures at a variety of venues, including the Air Force Academy and Air Force Museum.

This, his nineteenth book, is his first collaboration with Norman Polmar.